*A publication of the
Association of Governing Boards
of Universities and Colleges*

GOVERNING INDEPENDENT COLLEGES AND UNIVERSITIES

Richard T. Ingram
and Associates

Foreword by Clark Kerr

GOVERNING INDEPENDENT COLLEGES AND UNIVERSITIES

*A Handbook for Trustees,
Chief Executives, and
Other Campus Leaders*

Jossey-Bass Publishers · San Francisco

Substantial discounts on bulk quantities of Jossey-Bass books are available to corporations, professional associations, and other organizations. For details and discount information, contact the special sales department at Jossey-Bass Inc., Publishers. (415) 433-1740; Fax (415) 433-0499.

For sales outside the United States, contact Maxwell Macmillan International Publishing Group, 866 Third Avenue, New York, New York 10022.

Manufactured in the United States of America

 The paper used in this book is acid-free and meets the State of California requirements for recycled paper (50 percent recycled waste, including 10 percent postconsumer waste), which are the strictest guidelines for recycled paper currently in use in the United States.

Library of Congress Cataloging-in-Publication Data

Ingram, Richard T., date.
  Governing independent colleges and universities : a handbook for trustees, chief executives, and other campus leaders / Richard T. Ingram. — 1st ed.
    p.   cm. — (A joint publication in the Jossey-Bass higher and adult education series and the Jossey-Bass nonprofit sector series)
  Includes bibliographical references and index.
  ISBN 1-55542-567-4
  1. Private universities and colleges—United States—Administration—Handbooks, manuals, etc. 2. College trustees—United States—Handbooks, manuals, etc. 3. College presidents—United States—Handbooks, manuals, etc. 4. College administrators—United States—Handbooks, manuals, etc. I. Title II. Series: Jossey-Bass higher and adult education series. III. Series: Jossey-Bass nonprofit sector series.
LB2341.I532   1993
378.1′00973—dc20   93-19511
                                                                  CIP

FIRST EDITION
HB Printing   10 9 8 7 6 5 4 3 2 1   *Code 9361*

A joint publication
in
The Jossey-Bass
Higher and Adult Education Series
and
The Jossey-Bass
Nonprofit Sector Series

*This book is dedicated to the more than forty thousand
trustees and chief executives of independent higher education,
who are ultimately responsible for
the quality of the education
at some sixteen hundred of the nation's thirty-two hundred
nonprofit colleges and universities.*

Contents

    • A Gift of History • The Independent Sector of
    Higher Education • What Motivates People to Serve
    as Trustees? • What Is Likely to Distinguish This
    Decade from the Last? • The Ambiguities of College
    and University Government

Tables, Figures, and Exhibits

Tables

Figures

Exhibit

Foreword

The responsibilities of boards of trustees hold an increasingly important place in the mixed system of governance of American institutions of higher education. This is especially true today because campus leaders are finding that governance, the traditional internal process of making decisions through consultation and consensus building, is eroding. Traditional governance is in jeopardy for several reasons: more litigation against institutions, loss of public respect for the conduct of faculty and for intercollegiate athletics, concern about how tuition policy is set, the declining influence of presidents, more fractionalization on campus along tribal lines, and more disagreement over institutional missions. When the effectiveness of campus governance is in decline, as it now seems to be, trustees are held more closely to account, and their roles become more essential than in times of greater stability.

From the founding of Harvard College in 1636 until the Civil War, trustees generally ruled supreme, often with church support. Then came an era of strong presidents (the "giants"), as higher education institutions greatly expanded in numbers and in mission. Beginning about the time of World War I, faculties began a rise to power that lasted until the 1960s, when state governments began to strengthen their supervision and control. Also at that time, students, first through political action and then through their exercise of choice in the mass market of higher education, became a force to be recognized. The result has been very mixed forms of governance. Once again, however, the trustees are gaining in influence. How well will they handle their enhanced role?

There is no prototypical board of trustees, for boards vary in composition and function according to their often very different environments; but one marked line of differentiation is between boards of independent and of public institutions. Independent boards have greater ultimate responsibility, because public boards share theirs with the governmental authorities that appoint and supervise them. Independent boards, in contrast with public boards, also have at least seven other special characteristics:

- They are self-appointed; the selection of new members is of great importance to them.
- They are usually larger and are more likely to delegate considerable authority to an executive committee.
- Their members, approximately one-third of whom are alumni, generally start out with more knowledge of the institution and devotion to it than do members of public boards—thus, they need reorientation rather than orientation to the institution.
- Their members usually have personal friends on the faculty and thus have established the channels of communication that presidents may lack.
- They are unified by a concern to preserve the institution rather than to act as watchdogs for the external public.
- They are usually more interested in student affairs and in educational policy, as well as in fund raising and investments, than are their counterparts on public boards.
- They have more devotion to the institution's heritage than do members of public boards and thus are more concerned over what to preserve and how to do it.

Independent boards also operate in very different institutional contexts than do public boards. They have a single campus, rather than multiple campuses, to govern. These campuses are, on average, smaller—often one-quarter the size of public campuses.

They are less subject to governmental control and influence, although behind some boards stands a sponsoring church that insists on sharing governance. Thus, the environment for decision making is far more favorable for independent boards than for their public counterparts.

The trustees and presidents of independent colleges and universities have a special responsibility to preserve the diversity of institutions and to help ensure that this sector of higher education serves as a check and a balance on the costs and the quality of public institutions. The better the independent sector is, the better the public sector will be.

Given the unique characteristics of boards of independent higher education and the contexts within which they operate, it is entirely appropriate that a special resource exist for them. This handbook, and its companion volume on public boards, is well written and edited. The presentations, by authors with a deep knowledge and experience of their subject, cover all the essential issues. The best system of private higher education in the world now has the best handbook on trusteeship.

I wish two particular parts of this handbook could be put on a card and given to each new trustee: John Nason's list of responsibilities (Chapter Six) and Paul Ylvisaker's list of values to uphold (Chapter Thirteen).

The main theme of the volume is the importance of strategic planning—rightly so, given the long-run changes now confronting higher education and the society it serves. A word of caution is in order, however. While excellent general ideas abound here, each institution of higher education is in some way unique. Thus, trustees should not only read the broadly applicable advice that follows but also think how it can best be adapted to their particular institution. The authors have done their part. It is now up to the readers: What from this book responds to the needs of our institution and board and to our quest to do better?

Tom Ingram has shown splendid leadership in creating this handbook, which continues a series of publications on trusteeship undertaken nearly twenty years ago by him and Bob Gale, president emeritus of the Association of Governing Boards of Universities and Colleges (AGB), with John Nason's definitive *The Nature of Trust-*

eeship (1982, originally published under the title *The Future of Trusteeship*). Gale and Ingram and their colleagues at AGB have done a great deal to raise the expectations for and the performance of trusteeship.

Berkeley, California   Clark Kerr
August 1993   President Emeritus
                                                University of California

Preface

W. C. Fields was once asked to give his opinion about a novel he had read. His quip went something like this: "Well, I'd say, on the whole, it's a good book. The only trouble with it is—the covers are too far apart!" And so it may be with *Governing Independent Colleges and Universities*. Its length is testimony, however, to the complex responsibilities that boards and trustees face in coping with difficult issues in difficult times. The book is meant to serve as a resource—to be pulled off the shelf when needed for any number of purposes, including in-service education programs at regular board meetings or retreats.

The first edition was published in 1980 for trustees, chief executives, and other leaders in the public *and* private sectors. It is time for a revision, and for a volume that leaders in independent higher education can call their own, one dedicated to the fascinating world of independent trusteeship. Although the responsibilities of governing boards are fundamentally the same in public and private higher education, the environments within which public and private boards meet their public trust are very different. Thus, there is a clear need for two completely new books: this one and its companion volume for public college and university leaders.

Much can be said about the membership, organization, development, and performance of governing boards in private higher education. The volunteer trustees who serve this finite yet very diverse sector of higher education function in one of the most complex political, economic, and social environments ever created. Trustees have functioned very effectively in most colleges and universities, in large measure because they can be and are carefully selected. At some private institutions, however, "financial" problems are really governance and leadership problems. Trustees need all the help they can get in this tumultuous period of change.

Of the eighteen contributors to this volume, ten are current or former trustees and four are current or former chief executives. All the contributors are longtime students of trusteeship who share the following convictions about a unique, if imperfect, institution that has served higher education and the nation with distinction:

- Volunteer trusteeship is currently undergoing the most stringent test of its viability and competence since the 1960s and the period of student unrest caused by the Vietnam War.
- Boards, trustees, and chief executives must think and act more strategically than they have done or have had to do thus far.
- Boards and trustees will have to be much better informed about the academic programs, services, quality of teaching, and research programs of their institution. Inevitably, an extended period of very difficult decision making with their administrations and faculties lies ahead.
- Boards and their most influential members must be much more assertive and effective advocates both for higher education and for their institution.
- Boards and trustees must more resolutely pursue their commitment to periodic self-study and third-party assessment to help ensure the highest possible performance standards.

Overview of the Contents

Governing Independent Colleges and Universities is divided into three parts. Part One will help the reader understand the context within which trustees must function—the swirl of financial, demographic, social, legal, and planning issues that keeps trustees and everyone who works with them on their toes. A brief look at the emergence of private sector higher education and the origins of citizen trusteeship, a tradition largely misunderstood and underap preciated by the general public and political leaders, is offered in Chapter One. Chapter Two describes the diversity and characteris- tics of the private sector and some of the key trends affecting insti- tutional missions and purposes. Chapter Three covers the major global, national, and campus economic forces that are challenging conventional wisdom about revenues and costs. How boards can reduce exposure to personal and institutional liability is the subject of Chapter Four, which emphasizes the duties of loyalty and care; use of legal counsel; immunity and indemnification; and insurance. Chapter Five illustrates how trustees can think and act more stra- tegically in helping to shape the future of their institutions. The first five chapters are thus devoted to describing some of the many issues yet to be addressed in what will be an extended period of reassessment and change. Taken together, they describe a higher education system in transition.

Part Two is devoted to key responsibilities of governing boards. Following an overview in Chapter Six of the board's job description and some reminders of what is expected of individual trustees, the most visible of all board duties—selecting the chief executive—is discussed in all its nuances in Chapter Seven. Chapter Eight explains what has been learned about the tricky business of assessing the presidency, and in particular how boards should sup- port their incumbent. Chapter Nine addresses the fiduciary respon- sibilities of the board within the context of fund accounting and the interrelationship of revenue, expenditures, programs, endowment, and plant management; the chapter particularly emphasizes finan- cial reporting and the audit committee. Chapter Ten describes the characteristics of sound investment policies and practices, endow- ment management, and portfolio performance assessment. Chapter Eleven, based on the author's personal experience as a trustee and capital campaign chair and on the results of a comprehensive na- tional survey, offers practical advice on how the governing board and its members can ensure a solid fund-raising strategy.

Chapter Twelve reminds us of who our many campus and

external constituencies are, the care that should be taken in communicating with and relating to them, and the importance of both representing and protecting the integrity of the institution. The principles and values that should guide institutional leaders as they wrestle with increasingly complex political, social, and ethical issues are the subject of Chapter Thirteen. Academic tenure and the importance of trustees' understanding the policies and practices that govern the employment and performance of faculty are described in Chapter Fourteen. The current obsession with quality and the reasons trustees should be concerned with it are explored in Chapter Fifteen.

The ten chapters in Part Two thus help the reader cope with the inevitable ambiguities of academic trusteeship, by clarifying the distinction between board and executive responsibilities.

Part Three offers advice to those who recognize that *every* board can be better. Effective academic trusteeship is learned, not innate; education of trustees should begin with a substantive orientation and continue through in-service programs. Chapter Sixteen discusses the increasingly important processes of selecting new board members, orienting them to their trusteeship and to the institution, and developing the board through in-service education programs. Chapter Seventeen looks at the many elements that contribute to the effective organization of the board, as well as at the issues of board size, terms of office, officership, faculty and student trusteeship, and staffing. How to make meetings more productive and satisfying is discussed in Chapter Eighteen, and Chapter Nineteen clarifies for the chief executive and the board chair their mutual and distinctive responsibilities in leading the board. Chapter Twenty addresses periodic assessment of board performance and suggests several strategies for meeting that responsibility.

The resources at the end of the book reinforce the concepts and advice offered throughout. Resource A gives an illustrative statement of trustee responsibilities that can be adapted by institutions whose boards wish to clarify what is expected of incumbent and prospective members. Resource B comprises data from a recent national survey that allow comparison of several key board characteristics, policies, and practices with those of other independent college and university boards. Resource C sets forth performance standards in survey form for the governing boards of independent colleges and universities as an illustration of those the Association of Governing Boards of Universities and Colleges (AGB) makes available to other private (and public) institutions. Resource D offers an updated, illustrative set of board bylaw provisions, together with a discussion of related issues for consideration (also see Chapter Seventeen). Resource E provides a set of guidelines for trustees on avoiding conflict of interest; the guidelines emphasize prompt and full disclosure and the adoption of appropriate policies and procedures to deal with an increasingly important set of concerns. Finally, Resource F recommends the best of the available literature as further background for each chapter.

AGB is dedicated to helping trustees and chief executives make good decisions in these difficult times. It provides its members with the information and the tools to help them think and act strategically. As a continuing education resource, AGB seeks to strengthen board performance and board–chief executive relationships through its member programs, services, and publications.

Change comes more easily in adversity than in prosperity, but trustees and their chief executives will not have an easy time deciding what should and should not be changed. They are in the eye of a storm caused by significantly declining resources and the academy's diminished public standing, at least among state and federal public policy leaders. The buck ultimately stops in the boardroom, where trustees exercise their authority and responsibility—with equal measures of restraint and good judgment, it is hoped. Although the contributing authors express their own views on these and many other issues, views not necessarily shared by the AGB, this book confirms the AGB's conviction that college and university trusteeship must be better understood and nourished— first and foremost by those who would practice it responsibly—if it is to fulfill its promise to higher education and the nation.

Acknowledgments

Special thanks, first, to the contributing authors for their superb work. All of them were fun to work with over the long course of this project! And to my mentors—especially Bob Gale, Clark Kerr,

John W. Nason, John W. Pocock (1916–1992), and J. L. Zwingle (1906–1990)—I acknowledge their outstanding efforts to advance volunteer trusteeship, and offer them my heartfelt thanks for helping to shape my thinking about the issues confronting higher education and the country. These leaders have left their mark on the academic landscape.

To the Teachers Insurance Annuity Association (TIAA) and the College Retirement Equities Fund (CREF), and to my friend and colleague Peggy Heim, I express special thanks. TIAA-CREF made possible the national survey in Resource B and otherwise supported the research necessary to complete the book.

Finally, special thanks to the AGB board of directors for the opportunity it has given me to lead the association through its own transition. Its programs, services, and publications are needed more than ever. I also extend much gratitude to the AGB staff for their help along the way—most especially to Gretchen Wyman and Donna Fowler. Gretchen Wyman is the most patient and able person on the face of the earth, and Donna Fowler is one of the top editors and writers in the country. Their competence and commitment enabled me to complete this work. Thanks to all of you.

Washington, D.C.   Richard T. Ingram
August 1993

The Authors

Richard T. Ingram is president of the Association of Governing Boards of Universities and Colleges in Washington, D.C. Before joining the association in 1971, he held positions in the Department of Student Life at the University of Maryland, served as admissions and personnel officer of the U.S. Military Academy Preparatory School, taught high school, and served as adjunct faculty member at the University of Virginia and the University of Southern California.

Ingram was awarded his B.A. degree (1963) in social sciences education by Indiana University of Pennsylvania, his M.Ed. degree (1964) in secondary education by the University of Pittsburgh, and his Ed.D. degree (1969) by the University of Maryland. He has been a teacher, researcher, consultant, and writer in the fields of higher education trusteeship, administration, and planning for more than twenty years. He has led scores of workshops and retreats for boards of trustees and chief executives in both the public and private sectors of higher education.

A trustee of Connelly School in Potomac, Maryland, and former trustee of the University of Charleston in West Virginia, Ingram serves as secretary and treasurer of the board of directors of United Educators Insurance Risk Retention Group, and as advisory commissioner of the Education Commission of the States. He is a former member of the TIAA-CREF Advisory Council.

E. Grady Bogue is professor in the Department of Educational Leadership at the University of Tennessee and chancellor emeritus of Louisiana State University in Shreveport, where he served as chancellor for ten years. Bogue has written articles in journals such as the *Harvard Business Review, Educational Record,* the *Journal of Higher Education,* and *Phi Delta Kappan* and four books, the most recent of which is *The Evidence for Quality* (1992, with R. L. Saunders). He has been a consultant on planning, evaluation, quality assurance, and leadership to colleges and universities and to state-level planning agencies and corporations. He holds three degrees from Memphis State University: a B.S. degree (1957) in mathematics, an M.S. degree (1965) in education, and an Ed.D. degree (1968).

Richard P. Chait is professor of higher education and management and director of the National Center for Postsecondary Governance and Finance at the University of Maryland. Previously he was the Mandel Professor of Non-Profit Management at Case Western Reserve University, associate provost at Pennsylvania State University, and assistant professor at the Harvard Graduate School of Education. He earned both his B.A. degree (1966) from Rutgers University and his M.A. degree (1968) from the University of Wisconsin in American history, and his Ph.D. degree (1972) in educational administration, also from the University of Wisconsin. He is coauthor of *The Effective Board of Trustees* (1991) and a trustee of Goucher College.

Shirley S. Chater has been president of Texas Woman's University since 1986. She previously served as vice chancellor for academic affairs at the University of California, San Francisco, and has served as a senior associate with the Association of Governing Boards of Universities and Colleges, Presidential Search Consultation Service. She received her B.S. degree (1956) from the University of Pennsylvania, her M.S. degree (1960) from the University of California, San Francisco, and her Ph.D. degree (1964) from the University of California, Berkeley. She earned a certificate from the Senior Executive Program, Massachusetts Institute of Technology, Sloan School of Management, in 1982.

Jon W. Fuller is former president of the Consortium for the Advancement of Private Higher Education. He previously served for fifteen years as president of the Great Lakes Colleges Association. He is a trustee of Rollins College.

Robert L. Gale is president emeritus of the Association of Governing Boards of Universities and Colleges, where he served as president from 1974 to 1992. A trustee of Carleton College since 1970, Gale serves on the boards of the National Executive Service Corps, CARE, the Alliance of Independent Colleges of Art, and the National Center for Nonprofit Boards. He frequently speaks before national organizations, governing boards, and foundation boards. He has served as president of Gale Associates; director of public affairs for the Equal Employment Opportunity Commission; director of recruiting and of public affairs, U.S. Peace Corps; vice president of Carleton College; and editor-in-chief of Maco Magazine Corporation. He earned his B.A. degree (1948) in mathematics from Carleton College.

Katharine H. Hanson has served as a senior-level administrator in both the public and independent sectors of higher education. She has been a trustee at Stanford University and an officer of that board. Currently, she directs the Consortium on Financing Higher Education (COFHE) in Cambridge, Massachusetts. Hanson also serves as a consultant to senior officers in a number of colleges and universities in the United States and abroad. For several years, she has taught in the Harvard IEM and MDP programs as a guest lecturer on policy issues in higher education. She received her B.A. degree (1969) in economics from Stanford University and her M.B.A. degree (1971) from Boston University.

Sandra L. Johnson is manager in the National Higher Education/ Nonprofit Group at Coopers & Lybrand. This group coordinates the college, university, and nonprofit auditing, tax, and consulting practice for the firm's 102 offices in the United States.

Johnson edits Coopers & Lybrand's *Higher Education Management Newsletter* as well as the *Nonprofit Management Newsletter*. She also writes articles for higher education publications. Johnson coauthored *The Decaying American Campus, a Ticking Time Bomb* (1989, with S. C. Rush).

She has a B.S. degree (1974) in public communication from Boston University and an M.B.A degree (1986) from Simmons College. She is a certified public accountant in Massachusetts.

David M. Lascell is a partner in the law firm of Hallanbeck, Lascell & Pineo in Rochester, New York. He served as chair of the board of trustees of Wells College for more than ten years. Lascell has also been a director of the American Council on Education; trustee of Rochester Area Colleges, a consortium of public and private colleges in upstate New York; and a member of the board of directors of the Association of Governing Boards of Universities and Colleges from 1980 through 1991. He is a director of the Common Fund, chair of the board of the National Center for Nonprofit Boards, and a trustee of Mount Vernon College.

Sanford H. Levine is university counsel and vice chancellor for legal affairs of the State University of New York. He received both his A.B. degree (1959) in political science and his J.D. degree (1961) from Syracuse University. Active in the practice of higher education law for more than twenty years, he served as president of the National Association of College and University Attorneys in 1986–87.

Judith Block McLaughlin is educational chair for the Harvard Seminar for New Presidents, lecturer at the Harvard Graduate School of Education, and research associate in the Department of Sociology at Harvard University. She has published journal articles on presidential searches and higher education governance and is coauthor of *Choosing a College President* (1990, with D. Riesman) and *An Education of Value* (1985, with M. Lazerson and B. McPherson). She earned her A.B. degree (1970) in sociology from the University of North Carolina, Chapel Hill, and both her M.A.T. (1971) and Ed.D. (1983) degrees from Harvard University.

Joel W. Meyerson is director of AGB's Strategic Policy Institute. He is also co-director of the Stanford Forum for Higher Education Futures. Previously, he was partner and director of the higher education and nonprofit practice of Coopers & Lybrand. He was a faculty member at the Harvard Institute for Educational Management and serves on several advisory panels, including the Massachusetts Board of Regents task forces on capital maintenance and tuition policy. Meyerson is author or coauthor of many publications, including *Strategy and Finance in Higher Education* (1992), *Productivity and Higher Education* (1991), and *Strategic Analysis: Using Comparative Data to Understand Your Institution* (1990). He received his A.B. degree (1973) in history from Vassar College, his A.M. degree (1980) in American studies from Brown University, and his M.B.A. degree (1978) from Columbia University.

Louis R. Morrell is vice president for business and finance and treasurer of Rollins College. He earned his B.S. degree (1958) from Babson College and his M.B.A. degree (1968) from the University of Massachusetts. He has considerable experience in the investment of college and university endowments, having served on investment committees and provided senior staff support to them. He has written many articles, and made conference presentations, on endowment management.

John W. Nason serves as consultant to colleges, universities, and philanthropic foundations. A former president of both Swarthmore College and Carleton College, he has served on several college and foundation boards. He is the author of many books, including *Trustees and the Future of Foundations* (1977), *Presidential Search* (1979), and *The Nature of Trusteeship* (1982).

John W. Pocock, until his death in 1992, was chair emeritus of the College of Wooster in Ohio. He had served as senior vice president of Booz, Allen & Hamilton, as director and chair of the board of directors of the Association of Governing Boards of Universities and

Colleges (AGB), and as chair of the AGB/NACUBO (National Association of College and University Business Officers) steering committee on the financial responsibility of governing boards. Most recently, he had been editor and principle author of *Fund-Raising Leadership* (1989) for the AGB. He consulted with numerous colleges and universities in this country and in developing nations and wrote and spoke widely on governance issues in higher education.

Samuel Reid Spencer, Jr. is president emeritus of Davidson College, which he headed from 1968 to 1983 after eleven years as president of Mary Baldwin College. In 1990–91 he was interim president of Hollins College. He chairs the board of Union Theological Seminary, one of four institutions he has served as a trustee. He has also chaired the Board of Foreign Scholarships, to which he was appointed by President Carter. After graduating from Davidson College (1940) and serving five years in the U.S. Army, he earned his A.M. degree (1947) and Ph.D. degree (1951) in American history from Harvard University. The author of three books and numerous articles, he has been awarded seven honorary degrees.

Barbara E. Taylor is vice president for programs and research at the Association of Governing Boards of Universities and Colleges, where she directs a variety of workshops and seminars and designs and conducts research projects that explore board responsibilities and performance. She is the author of *Working Effectively with Trustees* (1987) and coauthor of *The Effective Board of Trustees* (1991), with R. P. Chait and T. P. Holland), and has written numerous articles, book chapters, and case studies about the governance and financing of higher education. Taylor is a trustee of Wittenberg University. She received her B.A. degree (1968) in English from the State University of New York, Potsdam; her M.S. degree (1969) in counseling from Miami University; and her D.Ed. degree (1982) from Pennsylvania State University.

Paul N. Ylvisaker was dean emeritus and Charles William Eliot Professor at the Harvard Graduate School of Education at the time of his death in early 1992. He had taught at Bethany Lutheran Junior College, Swarthmore College, Princeton University, the

University of Pennsylvania, and Yale University. He also served as New Jersey commissioner of community affairs, as chairman of the Task Force on Cities under President Johnson, and as member of a United Nations technical assistance mission to Japan. Ylvisaker was chair of the Association of Governing Board of Universities and Colleges Higher Education Issues Panel and senior consultant to the Council on Foundations.

GOVERNING INDEPENDENT COLLEGES AND UNIVERSITIES

PART ONE

Understanding
the Environment
of Independent
Higher Education

Members of private college and university governing boards are finding themselves in the midst of a maelstrom of conflicting values and ideologies that, in the end, only they can negotiate themselves and their colleges and universities through successfully. Trustee service is increasingly a high wire act in a complex and demanding society whose people expect flawless performance from all of its institutions.

Trustees and governing boards will need to reconsider nearly all conventional wisdom about independent higher education, including how it is and should be financed in a period of limited resources and how its essential mission must be protected in a litigious environment that is unparalleled in the world.

Part One is devoted to helping the reader understand the intricate environment within which the volunteer trustee and academic governing board function. Its five chapters highlight the roots, traditions, and ambiguities of academic trusteeship within the context of how the current decade is so markedly different from the last one. It elaborates how wonderfully diverse, resilient, and adaptable the independent sector of higher education is as it confronts new challenges in a changing and increasingly multicultural society.

1

In sum, this section describes a higher education system in transition, in which strategic thinking and acting by trustees and chief executives have never been more important to the system— and, therefore, to the nation.

CHAPTER 1

Exercising Stewardship in Times of Transition

Richard T. Ingram

Citizen trusteeship in American higher education has been variously described as a "gift of history" (Kerr and Gade, 1989, p. 17), "a barrier to rational progress" (Galbraith, 1967, p. 37), "the keeper of the social conscience" and "protector of the public interest" (Millett, 1962, p. 183), and as having done "more injury than Benedict Arnold" (Wayland in Rudolph, 1965, p. 172). For eons, college and university trusteeship has been criticized more often than it has been praised by academic, business, or government leaders.

But there can be no doubt that trusteeship is here to stay. It will not become the "harmless anachronism" predicted by Galbraith (1967). As imperfect as they are, governing boards have proven their value in the American version of participatory democracy, which is averse to monopoly of power and which provides systems of checks and balances. William F. Buckley once quipped that he "would sooner be governed by the first two thousand names in the Boston telephone directory than by the two thousand members of the faculty of Harvard University" (*AGB Notes*, 1971, p. 1). Higher education trusteeship is an extension of the American ethos and dates back to Harvard in 1636, although its roots are found in Western Europe some four centuries before.

3

The university was and continues to be one of the most complex organizations ever created by human beings; it has always been a major source of tension within the societies that support it, as well as their source of hope for the future. And citizen boards find themselves squarely in the middle of these tensions and hopes—between the academy and its many constituencies.

The continuing challenge for members of governing boards is to meet more effectively the purposes and expectations so ambiguously held for them by a demanding and troubled society. The thesis of this chapter, indeed of this book, is that the citizen board of trustees is our best hope for sustaining the one institution among precious few that has maintained a strong competitive edge. The citizen board is the one institution that has emerged as the best alternative to governmental or exclusive faculty control, but it needs to be much better understood and nourished than it is currently—by those who practice it (trustees themselves) and by those who criticize its shortcomings without offering a viable alternative.

One of the ironies of our time is that the general public, including many of the nation's elected political leaders and corporate executives, does not fully understand or appreciate what it is that trustees and governing boards do and do not—indeed should not—do. The existence of trustees and boards has contributed to spirited competition between and among institutions that has kept American higher education the envy of the world.

Some opinion makers do not seem to understand that the majority of volunteer trustees annually devote significant time to their responsibilities, but cannot and need not know their institution's or system's every nuance, nook, and cranny. Some critics are not aware of how different and fragile the academy's culture is compared with virtually all other types of organizations. Such misunderstanding ranges from being inconsequential to being harmful to the essential role that academic institutions have in a free society. This is not to suggest that faculties, administrators, or trustees are above criticism. Indeed, mistakes are made—some of them big ones. And the university *is* slow to respond to the needs of the society that supports it financially; it always has been, for many and complex reasons.

It should not surprise us that faculty, students, and alumni are equally mystified by what goes on in the boardroom. Trustees have the obligation to be clear about their responsibilities and the broader context for their stewardship: to help educate others, to correct misunderstandings, to interpret, and to help the community of scholars to know when and what changes are legitimate, indeed essential, to make.

Robert Ulich writes in his anthology of the ideas of the great thinkers on education that "we are fumbling around in education because we know so little about the future and do not bother to know enough about the past" (1959, p. v). This chapter offers a glimpse of trusteeship's past, present, and likely future as an important and evolving property of American higher education. This chapter makes the case that this decade requires competent trusteeship and that such trusteeship is even more important than it was in the past to higher education's and, therefore, the nation's future. Six persistent myths are addressed along the way.

A Gift of History

The concept and practice of lay citizen trusteeship have a long and distinguished history, one that precedes the discovery of the American continent by at least two centuries. Academic trusteeship originated in Western Europe, contrary to some beliefs.

Myth one: the origin of the lay governing board is found in the American corporation. This myth is apparent in a statement by the Assembly on University Goals and Governance (1971, p. 52): "For too long, colleges and universities have borrowed their governance models from business and public administration. Neither is appropriate for most functions of academic institutions." Actually, the roots of boards of lay trustees are not found in the corporation. They are found in the Protestant Reformation, especially in Calvinist institutions of higher education.

Kerr and Gade (1989) offer a brief and superbly written history that tracks boards as far back as the mid-fourteenth century in Italy and Germany, when student universities on the Bologna model "were placed under public control in response to perceived excesses against both the professoriate and the townspeople" (p. 17). John Calvin's Academy, founded in Geneva in 1559, was the first of the Reformation colleges to embody the theory of lay (nonclergy and nonacademic) control. Spain had social councils of prominent local citizens for each of its universities dating back to the twelfth century, which helped to ensure proper student discipline and use of public funds. Other countries of Western Europe followed suit and have their own fascinating stories.

In colonial America, the first governing board for Harvard was established in 1642. The Board of Overseers was made up of "leading men" from throughout the colony, but President Dunster persuaded the overseers to seek a charter from the colonial government to permit a second board internal to the college. The subsequent group, the President and Fellows of Harvard College, was intended to help overcome the overseers' problem of traveling great distances to attend meetings. Their relative youth and rapid turnover ensured, however, that the external overseers retained authority. Some local ministers were eventually added to the second board, thus bringing the concept of the lay board to Harvard and the colonies.

The College of William and Mary in Virginia was the second colonial college with two boards (1693) and Brown in Rhode Island became the third. The dual board model did not hold up, however, perhaps because of role conflict. Yale College (1701) served as a model for those that followed for quite some time: it had a single self-perpetuating board consisting originally of all clergy.

Until six of the original thirteen states chartered public universities, the notion of "public" and "private" as we know it today did not exist; the provincial college was established for public purposes and was thought of as a community institution. When the idea of the public university began to emerge after 1785, state charters first incorporated self-perpetuating boards of trustees that were often dominated by religious groups. Thus, they followed the "private" model of a single board and, eventually, gave way to appointed or elected boards without clergy representation.

The historical chapter by Kerr and Gade (1989, chap. 3) should be read by all trustees, as should an excellent chapter on the same subject in Cowley (1980, chap. 3). The concept and practice of citizen trusteeship in higher education preceded corporate America by many, many years. Indeed, the corporate board of directors was more likely influenced by the college and university experience rather than the other way around. There are undoubtedly lessons still to be learned and shared between the academy and the business community, but there is no evidence that the corporate sector ever dominated higher education in the powerful ways alleged by social critics such as Upton Sinclair and Thorstein Veblen.

The Independent Sector of Higher Education

Until about 1940, more students were enrolled in private colleges and universities than in public ones. The massive growth of the higher education enterprise following World War II was a public sector phenomenon in response to a national commitment to access. The tremendous growth in numbers and size of public, tax-supported colleges and universities brought with it a decline in the private sector's share of total enrollment from 50 percent in 1950 to about 20 percent in the 1980s.

Because there are many fewer boards in the public sector (some 55 percent of fourteen million students are on public campuses governed by "system" or multicampus boards) and because they are much smaller in size, the vast majority of the nation's trustees of higher education are found in the private sector—nearly forty thousand out of fifty thousand women and men. It is they who represent so clearly the spirit of philanthropy and volunteerism in our unique system of higher education, as their predecessors did. And it is they who carry the challenges and joys associated with ensuring the future of a healthy and viable, albeit currently belea-guered, independent sector. Their individual and collective respon-sibility to do so has become much more difficult in recent decades, for the many complex reasons elaborated in this book.

The breadth of missions among the sixteen hundred inde-pendent institutions is extraordinary: liberal arts colleges; seminar-ies; historically black colleges; church-related colleges (about eight hundred institutions); women's colleges; two-year colleges; research universities; Native American colleges; institutes of art, design, and music; Bible colleges; and schools of law, medicine, and business. Chapter Two provides a fuller picture of the diverse independent sector that enriches the social, cultural, and economic life of the nation with minimal help from state government. No other country in the world can claim such diversity; little wonder that other nations are exploring ways to develop private sectors to complement their systems of tax-supported higher education. At the heart of the enterprise are a multiplicity of citizen governing boards whose members share most of the same responsibilities as their public sector peers, except for that of finding their own successors.

Myth two: independent higher education serves primarily the socioeconomic elite and does not share the public sector's strong commitment to access and diversity. The 1986 median family income of students enrolled in independent colleges and universities was about $2,000 more than those in public institutions. Furthermore, recent studies conducted in some states show that the family incomes of students enrolled in flagship state universities are frequently higher than at comparable independent institutions. And, overall, private and public institutions enroll about the same proportions of minority students, with the exception of Hispanic students, who are disproportionately enrolled in the public community college (*Education Commission of the States Task Force on State Policy and Independent Higher Education,* 1990, p. 8).

One of the most significant reasons for the large increases in tuition in private colleges and universities through the 1980s was their commitment to institutionally funded student financial aid. Depending on the type of private institution, the percentage of undergraduate students receiving such aid varied between 47 and 63 percent nationally in recent years (for many individual institutions it is higher). Unless federal or state policies address what is widely accepted as a fundamental problem with the underfunding of student aid, the "tuition gap" between private and public higher education is likely to grow. In 1987–88, this gap averaged $5,300, which is an increase of 40 percent in constant dollars since 1975–76 (*Education Commission of the States Task Force on State Policy and Independent Higher Education,* 1990, p. 18).

Although the gap is beginning to decrease as the pressures to hold private tuition down and to contain costs mount, and as tuition rises in public institutions to make up for reduced state appropriations, the private and public sectors share a very real set of problems. Among them is the problem of sustaining commitments to access and diversity at a time of dramatic national demographic change. Furthermore, deferred maintenance has reached alarming proportions, the cost of sophisticated computer and laboratory equipment has skyrocketed, and the recent gains in making faculty salaries competitive are evaporating in both sectors.

Thus the pressures on trustees to give more of their own resources and to actively help raise more private dollars are very real indeed. The "capital campaign" has become a constant preoccupation in most institutions as the rest period between campaigns gets shorter and shorter. See Chapter Three for a fuller accounting of the economic changes that should concern trustees of private higher education.

The economic pressures on trustees in private higher education partly explain why the sector has not made better progress in bringing more minority trustees to its boards (see Resource B); but the sector can and should do better for moral and practical reasons. Prominent and influential minority leaders can be personally generous and bring access to private gift dollars, talent in needed areas of policy expertise in all fields, and advice on minority student recruitment and retention. While it is true that the most committed and generous trustees are often those who have some personal or familial tie to the institution, it is equally true that many trustees who have had no prior connection with the college or university quickly develop the necessary affection and commitment to be extremely effective. Those institutions that have made a commitment to increase the diversity of their boards have not found it to be easy, but it is possible and very beneficial.

Myth three: because the practice of trusteeship is more art than science and governing boards vary so much in their composition and structures, we have very little useful information about what characterizes effective governing boards. Actually, a number of useful studies in recent years have added to our understanding about what policies, practices, and strategies in board building work better than others. The Association of Governing Boards of Universities and Colleges (AGB) deserves much of the credit for stimulating the study of trusteeship in American higher education, but so do the chief executives and trustee leaders who have experimented and continue to experiment with different models. It is the kind of experimentation that can only happen or happen best in the private sector where such freedom is possible—first and foremost with regard to the selection of trustees and the organization of boards (made possible by larger numbers of members and the consequent division of labor).

This book reflects much of what has been learned about the practice of trusteeship, especially in the past decade or so. A few studies are more specific about what distinguishes effective from ineffective boards of private colleges and universities. Among them is a comparative study of twenty-two private institutions that are diverse in the selectivity of their student admissions criteria, which is discussed in *The Effective Board of Trustees* (Chait, Holland, and Taylor, 1991). The book elaborates on each of these qualities:

- The board understands and takes into account the culture and norms of the organization it governs.
- The board takes the necessary steps to ensure that trustees are well informed about the institution and the board's roles, responsibilities, and performance.
- The board nurtures the development of trustees *as a group*, attends to the board's *collective* welfare, and fosters a sense of cohesiveness.
- The board recognizes complexities and subtleties in the issues it faces and draws upon multiple perspectives to dissect complex problems and to prepare appropriate responses.
- The board accepts as one of its primary responsibilities the need to develop and maintain healthy relationships among key constituencies.
- The board helps envision and shape institutional direction and helps ensure a strategic approach to the organization's future.

Sprinkled throughout this work are other useful generalizations that tend to characterize effective boards. According to Chait, Holland, and Taylor, effective boards provide numerous opportunities for trustee education, engage in self-reflection and seek performance feedback, learn from mistakes, create a sense of inclusiveness among trustees, set goals for themselves, groom members for leadership, perceive subtlety and nuance, tolerate ambiguity, pursue in-

formation, encourage debate, respect the involvement of other constituents in decision making through consultation, minimize
conflict and avoid win-lose situations, think and act strategically,
anticipate problems and act accordingly, establish priorities and
work plans for the board and its committees, establish a "governance
information system," and focus attention on how the board spends
its time.

*Myth four: the large, highly selective, nationally and inter-
nationally prominent, or exceptionally well-endowed colleges and
universities are likely to have governing boards that serve as models
for the mainstream of independent higher education.* Just as colleges and universities should be cautious in adapting or adopting
governance concepts from the corporate boardroom, so should they
avoid assuming that large, highly selective, nationally and interna-
tionally prominent, or exceptionally well-endowed academic institutions are necessarily models to be emulated. Anecdotal information and some empirical data (Chait, Holland, and Taylor, 1991)
suggest otherwise.

For some of the nation's elite institutions, governance structures have been maintained that are inappropriate or unwieldy
(most traditions are difficult to change); the trustees have been con-
ditioned or continue to condition themselves to stay strictly on the
"business side" of their institutions (academic, programmatic, and
faculty-related policies are largely off-limits); and board development and trustee education initiatives are considered inappropriate
("Our trustees are very busy, discerning people who do not sit still
for workshops and retreats"). The link between annual budgets and
academic priorities and programs is often ignored. For some, giving
a handsome annual and capital campaign gift and exercising influence where it may be requested essentially define a good board
member. Especially given the effects of the current recession on all
institutions, the current "financial problems" of some of our leading institutions may really be governance problems.

There is little doubt that all independent institutions can
learn something useful from one another, as well as from corporations and public colleges and universities. But simple logic argues
that the converse is equally true; surely no sector or institution of
higher education holds a monopoly on wisdom.

What Motivates People to Serve as Trustees?

Why are people willing to serve on independent college and university boards in the midst of the continuing and new pressures brought by a persistent recession, dramatic shifts in the nation's demography, ever higher expectations to give and to help raise private support, and the very real prospects of having to devote even more of their time away from their occupations, businesses, and families? There are as many reasons as there are board members, but these are some of the best:

• *They were asked to serve.* People are flattered to be asked to serve on a board by someone they respect or admire, and they instinctively want to please that person by saying yes. The reality of the commitment comes later; rarely are trustees honestly told what serving on a board requires of them (although most would have accepted anyway).

• *They have a deep and abiding conviction that a college or university is more consequential to future generations than virtually any other institution.* People can make a difference and contribute something to an enterprise that will outlive them.

• *They want to give something back to society.* People attribute their personal success to the education they received and find tremendous satisfaction in working with others who share the same values. Particularly if the institution is their alma mater, "giving something back" takes on special importance.

• *They feel that board membership is a great honor and promises to be intellectually stimulating.* Interpreting a complex social institution to those who often misunderstand it, addressing current social issues with other thoughtful people, and conveying society's needs to the academic community are challenges that bring their own rewards. Higher education trusteeship is considered by most Americans to be the crown jewel of volunteerism because of the people and issues connected with the enterprise. For every five thousand citizens, only one is a current member of a board of trustees or regents in public or private higher education.

There are other good motivations, to be sure, but there are also some inappropriate and even dangerous motivations. Unfortunately there are trustees who mistakenly believe that they, as individuals, possess special authority and are entitled to certain prerogatives when, in fact, only *the board as a corporate body* has legal power. There are trustees who bring personal causes or agendas to boardrooms before they fully understand the university or their responsibilities. And conflict of interest issues are unfortunately not uncommon.

The best trustees are open-minded, understand the vital importance of helping to build consensus, and are willing to learn how to be effective team members. They hear as well as listen and help the board to ask the right questions at the right time. Trusteeship is hard work that requires tempered egos and a good measure of humility.

What Is Likely to Distinguish This Decade from the Last?

The mettle of trustees and boards in the independent sector will be tested through the remainder of this decade as never before—at least in recent history. The real value of governing boards as an alternative to direct governmental and faculty control will either be made more apparent to the general public, elected political leaders, and opinion makers, or a new round of severe criticism is in store that has not been seen since the 1960s, when students discovered trustees and removed their veil of anonymity.

Why is this likely? What are the crosscurrents that promise to make boardroom experiences even more challenging? Some of these crosscurrents are not new but are extensions of those experienced for the past several years and even earlier decades: shrinking resources coupled with rising public expectations for quality programs, more productivity, more obvious impact on economic development, more relevance to and help with pressing social problems, and ever better facilities. "Doing more with less" will be a central theme for quite some time; boards will need to provide more help to presidents and chancellors by taking more of the heat for unpopular decisions.

Myth five: the boardroom issues and practices of private higher education trusteeship will look very much the same as those of the past two decades. New pressures and developments are likely to be high on board agendas. Some of these are discussed below.

End to Sanctuary

Higher education will no longer receive favored status, although, among all institutions supported by modern society including medicine, it has earned and is likely to retain the respect and confidence of the majority of American citizens. But public confidence has been severely shaken. The flagship or research university—whether public or private—is under the microscope as never before. Its mistakes will produce adverse public opinion about all colleges and universities. Investigative reporting about academe is the new game in town. All institutions will be affected by the improprieties or faulty judgments of some, reminding trustees and chief executives of how interdependent higher education really is.

Calls for Relevance

Higher education cannot continue to give the impression that it is aloof from the urban and other ills of American society. It must demonstrate a willingness to contribute to the search for solutions to real and pressing social and economic problems. Many hundreds of colleges and universities have reached out to K-12 education in their communities to establish cooperative programs designed to strengthen curricula, teacher preparation and development, and programs that encourage minority youth to continue their education. The knowledge and research efforts of faculty and other institutional resources must be extended to other endeavors: to the administration of justice; problems of homelessness, crime, and drug abuse; and economic development. Governing boards can encourage faculty leadership in these directions by urging administrative and academic leaders to provide incentives.

From a traditional point of view, this may seem to be beyond higher education's mission and scope, which are teaching and research. But public service, the hallmark of the land grant university and the community college, should be renewed as a major commitment in independent institutions. It will not be easy. Entrepreneurial faculty have become accustomed to being paid for consulting on their own terms. The press of increasing teaching loads, expectations within disciplines for more and better research and publishing, and other duties expected by their departments and institutions often preclude new public service initiatives.

At the same time, however, trustees should be mindful that there are limits to the search for "relevance" in the academy. The university cannot be, indeed must not be, as relevant as the morning news lest its basic mission and purposes be compromised. Helping institutional officers and the faculty cope with the inevitable tension between the demands for change and the need for continuity is a critical governing board responsibility.

There has been much talk and some recent study on the subject of redefining "scholarship" across disciplines, but the incentives to improve teaching and the credibility of the undergraduate curriculum in the large and comprehensive university must come from the top. There is some new evidence that faculty are ready for changes in the traditional requirements that have ruled promotion and tenure decisions for so long and open to incentives that reward superb undergraduate teaching. Trustees and presidents should join with faculty to decide what is possible and desirable for everyone—especially the institution. Deciding which of the academy's traditions should prevail and which should change will not be easy. Trustees live in especially interesting times.

Acceptance of Fund-Raising Responsibility

All trustees surely accept their responsibility to ensure good fiscal management, to give generously to annual giving and capital campaigns, and—at least conceptually—to actively participate in fund raising. But there is new urgency in all of this if independent colleges and universities are to maintain their competitive edge. Overall, trustee giving and fund-raising records need to improve (see Chapter Eleven and Pocock, 1989b).

Time for Restructuring

Economists now tell us that the decade of the eighties was good to higher education, with a real growth rate of about 2 to 3 percent per year. They tell us that administrative rather than academic staffs grew significantly, especially the number of middle managers.

Comparing the organization charts from the late 1970s with those of the early 1990s is very revealing. We are told that new ways must be found to do more work, more creatively, and with fewer people and better use of technology. Thus, it is time for change—an opportunity that can come more easily in adversity than in prosperity.

Economic pundits tell us that a strong national economy will not return soon—at least not one that produces real and sustained growth in personal discretionary income and the tax revenues with which all of higher education is intimately linked. It is time to reconsider institutional missions, to do what we do best, to "right-size," to become more "productive" and efficient, and to "grow by substitution." Although there is considerable skepticism about whether higher education institutions will really look all that much different in five or ten more years, trustees must prepare to be active partners in the debates yet to come. Although the largest academic institutions will likely experience the most change, with considerable pain, all colleges and universities will undergo some change. It is time for a different strategic vision in the boardroom.

Need for Strategic Vision

Trustees are often criticized for their inability to think and act strategically. Their meeting agendas do not focus on long-term issues but on short-term managerial and governance issues. It is probably a fair criticism, one that is shared with presidents and chancellors who by and large shape board agendas and the information that supports them.

If trustees and governing boards are to be helpful in reshaping their institutions and management structures where necessary, they and their chief executives will need access to information and strategic options that are not available now. They need encouragement to think more strategically, and they need to be given the kind of useful data and analytical information that suggest viable courses of action. It is time for trustees, chief executives, and their staffs to consider what new data and information are needed.

Preparation for Diversity

Demographers tell us what we already know: a much more diverse population is not on its way—it is already here! Our colleagues in

Arizona, California, New Mexico, Texas, Florida, and New York understand the implications of providing access to diverse student populations in the "traditional" college or university. The mainstream of higher education has become more aware of what needs to be done; there is less rhetoric and more study. But frustration continues when it comes to action or to meeting self-imposed goals in minority faculty and staff hiring, minority student recruiting and retention programs, or diversifying board membership.

The complexions of student bodies will be changing dramatically over the remainder of this decade and well into the next. And so will teaching methods, campus cultures, and how academicians think about their work and their responsibilities to their institutions and society. In hundreds of communities blessed with a college or university, the "average" or typical student is no longer Caucasian and between the ages of eighteen and twenty-four. Therefore, we must do more than deal with stereotypes; we must change deep-seated attitudes about what an "American" is supposed to look and be like.

At least in the foreseeable future, some big problems loom. Precisely when the philosophy and practice of open student access is taking on new and urgent significance, the weakening economy is causing public institutions to cap enrollment or even to downsize. A weakened economy is no friend of access and diversity as tuitions and fees rise, institutional student aid is capped, and the federal contribution takes the form of more loans at the expense of grants. Many from the new pool of students are very reluctant to encumber themselves with loans; trustees should be concerned about the increasingly large numbers of students who graduate with the burden of significant debt.

The role of the board and the chief executive is as simple and clear as the issues are complex: Staff and faculty will not act on institutional priorities in this area unless there is consistent and persistent leadership at the top of the governance ladder.

Concern for the Presidency

The annual turnover rate of presidents in independent colleges and universities is about 13 percent, 1 percent less than their public sector peers. Between 1984–85 and 1991–92, the turnover rate varied between 11 and 14 percent annually with an average tenure of about seven years (*AGB Reports,* Nov./Dec. 1992, p. 2). Clearly, the days of typical fifteen- or twenty-year presidencies, prevalent only a few decades ago, are gone in higher education as they are in the other sectors of society.

Undoubtedly there are many reasons for shorter terms. There is need for further study, but many believe that the position has become extremely difficult and demanding because as the saying goes, a president's friends come and go and his or her detractors accumulate. One could easily conclude, on the other hand, that being president *of anything* is difficult and demanding these days! Academic presidents and chancellors are surely no more perfect than their boards, but the *only* place they can seek support that really makes a difference *is* from their boards.

A recent study of the presidency in different institutional settings and the complex factors that influence effectiveness of academic leaders lead Birnbaum (1992, p. 195) to estimate that "a quarter of college presidents will follow the path of the exemplary president; a quarter, that of failed president; and half, that of modal president." While he contends that our knowledge of organizational leadership is too limited to increase the proportion of exemplary presidents, there is no doubt that governing board performance has much to do with presidential performance, and vice versa.

This is a time to reassess how trustees stand up under pressure in full partnership with the president or chancellor. It is no time to allow chief executives to doubt whether their trustees and boards will stand behind them (better yet, in front of them) when the heat is turned up—often as a consequence of decisions that boards themselves ultimately made. All boards must be concerned about the integrity of the presidency. The job is difficult enough without the board being perceived as adding to the tension with which the president or chancellor must contend. How boards are viewed on this score will surely affect the public's perceptions of their (and their institution's) integrity and reputation, along with their ability to attract and keep strong executive leaders. Effective presidents and chancellors are needed now more than ever. And it is time to assess their performance on very different criteria and values than those based on the growth and expansion characteristic of earlier decades.

Proactive Public Policy

Many trustees and regents bring significant personal influence with elected public officials to their trusteeships, and some institutions use this resource selectively and to good advantage. Chief executives are usually very astute in such matters, especially when their own college or university is directly involved. The dependence on influential board members in this way is a simple extension of their advocacy role. But the prospects for more governmental regulation and inappropriate intrusion is likely to require a more proactive networking of trustees within the independent sector, within states, or even nationally.

Aside from possible initiatives at the state or federal level that may threaten both the essential autonomy of higher education institutions and systems, and academic freedom as it is broadly understood and accepted, much more may be at stake. There is the very real prospect, especially at the state level, for governors and legislators to propose harmful, even dangerous public policy in one form or another on almost any issue—for perfectly pure reasons from their own perspectives. This possibility has always been present, of course, but the *probability* seems higher than ever before. Will trustees and presidents be prepared to respond? Will presidents and chancellors really welcome more help from their boards and individual trustees than has been the case thus far?

A recent headline makes the point: "How Aggressively Should Colleges Lobby Governors and Legislators for Money in the Midst of Recession?" In the article, a former governor who is currently president of a private university says, "Many of the very people whom higher education should rely upon to press its cause are already on their boards of regents and trustees. Given the resources that are available to them in terms of the trustees, faculty members, alumni and others, the higher education community has never really unified. As a result, higher education is frequently the first thing cut and the last thing restored" ("How Aggressively Should Colleges . . . ," 1992, p. 23).

This is a delicate area for chief executives because they understandably worry about the wrong trustee inadvertently saying or doing the wrong thing at the wrong time with the wrong legislator or governor. And they are concerned that any serious trustee involvement in public policy at the state or federal level may inadvertently "politicize" their boards. Public policy at the federal level is considered by many presidents and chancellors to be their exclusive domain, one best coordinated by their associations in Washington, D.C.

At the same time, however, chief executives may not be the effective lobbyists they once were at either the state or federal levels. The end of sanctuary is very real, and presidents, chancellors, and their representatives, unfortunately for everyone, are increasingly seen by political leaders as protecting the status quo.

All of this needs more thought and study, of course, but we know at least two things in the meantime: First, some trustees can be very effective spokespersons on behalf of their institutions and for higher education as a whole, especially at the state level and perhaps at the federal level as well; second, great care must be taken to avoid conflict within and between sectors.

Chief executives and trustees should make clear their convictions that the nation needs strong systems of both public and private higher education; leaders from each sector should seize opportunities to support the other sector. Unfortunately, however, there are signs that in some states the two sectors may be confronting one another in the halls of government. Surely this can only result in a lose-lose situation if it continues. This is a time to hold on to one another and to take some risks by building new coalitions with trustees who can make the right difference.

The Ambiguities of College and University Government

Myth six: there is now a reasonably clear and generally accepted understanding of how policy decisions are made in the academic institution and the roles and responsibilities governing boards properly assume as part of the process. Ambiguity reins supreme in academic decision making with regard to where governing board authority begins and ends. Professor Burton Clark offers a helpful perspective: "Anyone who seriously and intensively probes the authority structure of his own college . . . and presents his observations for public consumption, is likely to make enemies and may have occasion to travel. . . . Academic authority is a peculiarly subtle and complex matter, a murky business that has caused highly intelligent men to veer away and throw up their hands" (Mason, 1972, p. 17).

Mason (1972) opines that the board is supreme and sovereign *in a legal sense only,* that in reality its primary and most legitimate functions are to represent the public interest and to ensure basic fiscal integrity. He goes on to conclude that the board's responsibilities are to remind the university that it is part of ordinary human society, to shield the university from dysfunctional public pressure, to tell the university what extremes of academic freedom cannot be tolerated, and to champion the university, especially when it is threatened by ignorance or ill will.

Mason also argues from the faculty perspective of the 1970s that boards do not own or manage the university, legal provisions in charters and enabling legislation notwithstanding. They should forget about any notion of approving educational programs (p. 29). He argues that the concepts of fiscal integrity and the public interest cause most of the ambiguities in academic trusteeship.

But how can trustees be expected to shield the university from dysfunctional public pressures and to ensure fiscal integrity when they are otherwise expected to stay at arm's length from its academic programs? How can trustees be expected to be champions in the midst of grave crises unless they are an integral part of institutional decision making with a real sense of institutional ownership? How can able citizens be asked to defend the institution, to "be there" when they are really needed, without their having a continuing and thorough knowledge of their institution or helping to determine what it is and does? We cannot have it both ways; thus the ambiguity and the need for balance.

Trustees and regents are and will be on the hot seat for many years to come, kept there by the law and a litigious society, by elected political leaders, by a demanding public that expects quality but at the lowest possible price, and by a society that expects its academic institutions to help with pressing social and economic problems. While board members must be respectful of the fact that they are a vitally important *part of* institutional governance and remember that real change within an academic institution comes from building consensus, trustees cannot afford to be either passive or merely symbolic.

The men and women who volunteer their time and resources to serve on governing boards reasonably expect them to be used well. Their ultimate commitment to their institutions, in good and bad times, will be in equal proportion to whether they are being taken seriously—by their administrations, especially their chief executives, and by their faculties. But trustees and boards should seek to stand neither up too close nor back too far; rather, they should constantly seek to find the balance between the exercise of authority and the exercise of restraint.

It is time to address these and the many other issues of our times within the context of finding better ways to communicate with everyone who has a stake in higher education, of building new coalitions and more trust to accomplish what must be done, and of avoiding the "we-they" syndrome so prevalent in contemporary society and in higher education. But how to let everyone in on the act and still get some action is perplexing; in the end, judgments must be made in the boardroom. The buck will always stop with the chief executive and the board.

There has never been a more exhilarating time to serve on the board of a college or university, and there has never been a time when citizen boards of the nation's most capable individuals were needed more than they are today—boards composed of men and women who have exceptionally high tolerances for ambiguity; genuine love of higher education and its role in a free society; the strength of deep convictions; and the values that will hold them, and higher education, in good stead in the face of what is yet to come.

CHAPTER 2

The Demography
of Independent
Higher Education

Jon W. Fuller

Most independent colleges and universities retain more focused institutional missions than do their public sector counterparts. The political process seems inevitably to work to widen the defined missions of public institutions, so that these institutions come to serve (and gain support from) a number of different constituencies and interests. Independent colleges and universities were almost all founded with much sharper definitions of what kind of education they were to provide for which groups of students. While independent institutions naturally change the definition of their mission over time, their institutional cultures and governing arrangements reinforce the importance of a distinctive mission. Boards of trustees play a crucial role in sustaining and, as appropriate, changing their individual college's or university's mission.

That clarity of purpose is an important element in attracting and retaining the support of students, faculty, trustees, and friends. It accounts for the opening each year of brand-new independent institutions, each intended by its founders to serve a particular set of students and to provide specific kinds of educational opportunities. It is the variety of institutional missions, each created and maintained by the board, faculty, and friends of individual colleges

23

and universities, that accounts for the most striking characteristic of the independent sector: its diversity.

Diversity in the Independent Sector

Most people think about higher education in terms of the two or three institutions that they have personal connections with and know best. Discussions about higher education often divide institutions into "public" and "independent" (or "private") categories. Those broad groupings hide the rich diversity of American higher education, particularly in the independent sector, because institutions differ widely in size, resources, type, and, most fundamentally, mission. Although there are some similarities shared by most American colleges and universities, public and independent alike—including an allegiance to the ideal of liberal arts education, the almost universal use of the course or credit hour to measure student progress, and even the striking architectural similarities of many campuses—the differences are important to understand.

Although we often talk about having a "system" of higher education, what we really have is a very decentralized product of hundreds of decisions by church and community groups, city councils, state legislatures, and others. There is some sense of system among the public institutions in some states, but the overall "system" is not the result of any overall grand plan. It is uniquely American in this regard.

Size

In general, independent colleges and universities are smaller than those in the public sector. More than twenty public universities have enrollments greater than any independent institution. Of the one hundred largest universities, only six are independent, and three of these are located in the Boston area.

The stereotype of the small college located in a small community is accurate for a significant part of the independent sector. There are hundreds of four-year private colleges with enrollments of under one thousand students, but fewer than three dozen public four-year colleges are that small.

Resources

Institutions within the independent sector also vary greatly in terms of their resources. Only a few have large endowments, highly selective admissions, and high tuition rates. The endowment dollars in higher education are highly concentrated in a few institutions. Fewer than fifty colleges and universities hold half of all endowment dollars—and 20 percent of the wealthiest institutions are public.

Most colleges and universities have endowments too small to provide much help in meeting their annual budgets. The vast majority of private colleges and universities are primarily dependent on tuition, their largest source of revenue. (See Chapter Three for a more complete discussion of this topic.) Trustees at institutions fortunate enough to have significant endowments should recognize how unusual that situation is.

Tuition

Press stories about tuition rates naturally focus on those institutions charging the most. But tuition levels in the private sector range from the level at Berea, which charges no tuition, to that at Bennington, which is regularly featured in press reports about high tuition rates. The average tuition rate for private colleges and universities in 1991-92 was $8,353, far lower than the general public impression. And because most independent colleges make available significant amounts of financial aid, the *net tuition* is even less (see Chapter Three).

Reputation

Reputation and prestige generally reflect an assumption that more is better. Various institutional rankings are of great interest to the public—and to trustees, administrators, and faculty members within higher education as well. But most rankings boil down to which places have the most of the things that are most easily measured: large endowments, high tuition rates, large enrollments, and high average SAT scores. Alexander Astin sums up the situation in

Achieving Educational Excellence: "The most prestigious institutions attract the best-prepared students from the most affluent and highly educated families, spend the most on their educational programs, pay their faculties the highest salaries, and charge the highest tuition and fees" (1985, pp. 10–11).

We are not very good at measuring differences that might be more useful and that could provide better assessments of how well each institution fulfills its own distinctive mission. The size of a library is of some importance, but the degree to which students use it is a better measure of what's happening educationally. How much students know when they enter college is important, but how much more they have learned when they graduate is more significant. Large endowments and high instructional budgets are generally good, but some measure of productivity and efficiency would also be informative.

Trustees need to go beyond simple comparisons of their institutions with lists of "peer institutions" and ask how their college or university performs in terms of its own mission, what difference it makes in the lives of its students, and how effectively it uses the resources it has available. Astin (1985, p. 16) says, "The major purpose of any institution of higher education is to develop the talents of its faculty and students to their maximum potential." There is no quick or easy way to measure how well any particular college or university is achieving that purpose, but this key judgment must be made—above all, by its trustees.

Institutional Types

Each institution is different, and those closest to it rightly prize its distinctiveness. But larger groupings are inevitably used by journalists and researchers to allow generalization and comparison. The most widely used groupings are the Carnegie classifications, developed by the Carnegie Foundation for the Advancement of Teaching (1987).

Because the Carnegie classifications are so widely used to group institutions for comparison, trustees need to be aware of how broad and therefore imprecise some of those categories are. National magazines use the categories in their annual rankings, researchers use them to develop charts of average costs or productivity, and institutional administrators regularly make comparisons of their own institution with some set of peer institutions. It is important to look carefully at the definitions in order to know when particular comparisons among institutions make sense and when they do not.

The Carnegie classes, first developed in the early 1970s, group institutions on the basis of their functions and to some extent their size. The main categories are

- Research universities
- Doctorate-granting colleges and universities
- Comprehensive colleges and universities
- Liberal arts colleges
- Two-year community, junior, and technical colleges
- Professional schools and other specialized institutions

Most of these categories are further subdivided, generally on the basis of size.

Independents constitute about 33 percent of the research universities, just under 50 percent of the doctorate-granting and comprehensive schools, and 95 percent of the liberal arts colleges. Only 25 percent of the two-year institutions are independent, but 90 percent of the professional and specialized institutions are (the largest grouping of the latter are schools of religion and theology).

A recent analysis of shifts among the institutional types by economist (and former college president) David Breneman (1990) caused him to raise the question, Are we losing our liberal arts colleges? He noted that a decreasing number of colleges focus their academic offerings primarily on the traditional arts and sciences as more colleges enroll most of their students in preprofessional courses, such as business or nursing. Other liberal arts colleges have added one or more graduate professional schools. Many of these colleges believe that the traditional liberal arts continue to be at the heart of their programs, and the more practical and professional courses are influenced by the institution's liberal arts tradition. Breneman observed that there have been significant changes in the courses students seek and that many colleges offer.

These changes point up the ambiguities of any general classification scheme. Does one classify an institution by counting the courses of various types in its catalogue or by looking at the less precise but probably more important issues of institutional tradition and mission? Trustees need to be cautious about the labels or categories applied to their college or university, and to look to the more important issues of how well the institutional mission has been defined and how well its programs carry out that mission.

Heritage and Mission

Independent colleges and universities, far more than their public counterparts, are shaped and influenced by their specific histories. They were generally founded with much more specific purposes and missions than were public institutions, and although those naturally change and evolve over time, institutional history still has an important influence. Although most formal college histories are not literary prizewinners, trustees should be informed about the history of their institutions.

Each institution comes to have a distinctive culture, shaped by its history and reflected in its academic program; social environment; and features such as its traditional ceremonies, favorite stories, and institutional heroes. The institutional culture sets limits on what any particular college or university might do and provides the menu of opportunities for its most distinctive and effective contributions to the larger society.

Religious identification and purpose is now uniquely the province of independent colleges and universities, although during much of the nineteenth century it was not uncommon for state colleges or universities to be effectively controlled by a particular denominational group (Rudolph, 1990). For some, religious identification remains a central and highly visible element of their mission and institutional purpose. There still are many colleges in which a majority of students and faculty are affiliated with a particular denomination; but for many more, religious origins are a part of their history, contributing to institutional tone and style rather than being a central factor in everyday campus life. Only a few independent institutions are entirely secular in their history and practice, however.

Almost all institutions have a strong regional focus. For some colleges and universities, there is perceived prestige in being identified as "national" institutions, that draw students from across the country and enjoy name recognition and visibility in distant communities. In fact, probably only the U.S. military academies are without some distinctive regional flavor. And for many institutions, regional identification is an important part of their culture and purpose. Some of the colleges located in Appalachia are probably the clearest examples of this: Berea and Warren Wilson are known as "Appalachian" institutions.

Many other institutions serve special populations: the historically black colleges and universities are a prominent example. More recently, colleges have been founded specifically to serve American Indian students, and many of them are controlled by specific tribes. Others have come to focus their service on Hispanic students, although most of these institutions were established to serve a more general population and have responded to the needs and opportunities presented by demographic changes in their regions.

Some independent colleges and universities have created significant programs specifically to serve adult students. Many women's colleges (and former women's colleges) have given special and particularly effective attention to the higher education needs of adult women. Many independent colleges, because their relatively small enrollments allow for special attention to individual students, have come to serve significant numbers of students with physical or learning disabilities. Some have given this deliberate emphasis, as in St. Andrews Presbyterian College's creation of a barrier-free campus in Laurinburg, North Carolina.

But size and location also present constraints for many independent institutions. Many were deliberately founded in small towns when those locations were favored for having fewer distractions and temptations. That puts many institutions at some distance from concentrations of adult students or minority populations, so they must continue to serve, at least for the most part, traditional-age students who are able to take up residence in the college's dormitories and pursue their studies full time. It is important for each institution to look carefully at its traditions, location, resources, and educational strengths as it decides which specific educational needs it should seek to meet.

Independent colleges and universities are shaped and to some degree constrained by their locations and their individual histories and institutional cultures. Those constraints are distinctive features of most independent institutions and also a source of stability and strength. At the same time, smaller size and independent governance allows them to respond more quickly and intentionally to needs and opportunities around them. That responsiveness is a distinctive characteristic of independent institutions.

The People of Independent Colleges and Universities

Let us now consider the characteristics of some of the groups who people universities—students, faculty, and trustees.

Students

Although colleges and universities provide other services to their communities and some carry a special responsibility for research, their primary emphasis is on teaching and the education of their students. While there is wide variation in their individual levels of success (and no agreement about how that success should be measured), most of the evidence suggests that independent institutions do a good job in the education of most of their students.

One indicator is in the surveys of student satisfaction. Students in independent institutions, and particularly in the smaller colleges, consistently report higher levels of satisfaction with the education they are receiving than do students in public institutions. These reports are confirmed by the higher levels of student retention at independent colleges and universities. Students of all ethnic backgrounds who enter independent institutions are more likely to complete their degrees than students entering public institutions (see Table 2.1).

Contrary to the general impression, students at independent colleges and universities do not come from wealthier families than those in the public sector. Data about the family incomes of students in the two sectors are not readily available, but those that are avail-

Table 2.1. Bachelor's Degree Completion Rates for the
High School Class of 1980, by Ethnic Group.

	Black	Hispanic	Asian American	White	All students
Private	31.4%	24.9%	58.0%	57.6%	54.2%
Public	25.9%	23.3%	44.7%	46.0%	42.7%

Source: Adapted from National Institute of Independent Colleges and Universities, 1992, p. 16. Used by permission.

able suggest that median family incomes are very similar between independent and public four-year colleges and universities. In a few states where more detailed data are available, the students at the public flagship research universities come from families with significantly higher incomes than the students in the independent colleges and universities of that state (National Institute of Independent Colleges and Universities, 1992, p. 12).

On various achievement measures, graduates from independent colleges and universities score consistently higher than do graduates of public institutions. Although independent institutions enroll only 21 percent of all students, their graduates account for more than 50 percent of the "leading executives"in the 1990 *Standard & Poor's Executive/College Survey.* Forty percent of all Ph.D.'s are awarded to graduates of independent colleges or universities, and other measures (winners of Rhodes scholarships or of distinguished graduate fellowships and prizes, for example) show a similar disproportionate degree of achievement for the graduates of independent institutions.

Faculty

Independent and public institutions hire faculty initially from the same graduate schools. Just over a third of all new doctorates are awarded each year by independent universities, the remainder by public universities.

Most faculty members spend all of their careers at a single type of institution. It is unusual for a faculty member at midcareer to move from one type of institution to another. Indeed, it is unusual for a faculty member at midcareer to move at all; most faculty members receive tenure at a college or university and then spend the rest of their careers there.

Most surveys of faculty find those teaching at independent institutions satisfied with their careers and proclaiming strong loyalty to their institution. Independent colleges and universities are generally smaller than their public counterparts, which allows them to be less bureaucratic in their procedures and gives individual faculty members a greater sense of control over their professional lives. Independent institutions are also more likely to have and hold a clearly defined mission, and that clarity of focus also enhances the morale of faculty and other institutional staff.

Higher education may be approaching a time when there will be a shortage of new faculty. This almost certainly will be the case in some fields; in a few fields, the shortage is already with us (Bowen and Sosa, 1989). One factor that partly accounts for the depressed supply of new doctorates is the long lead time between a student's decision to seek a Ph.D. and a likely faculty career and the time he or she is ready to begin that career. In many fields, the time from baccalaureate to doctorate is a decade or even more.

In the 1980s, when today's graduate students were making their career choices, there was a general oversupply of new faculty. Undergraduates in those years could see that young faculty members were finding it very difficult to find a permanent position—in some cases, any position. The popular press carried sensational stories about Ph.D.'s driving taxis or in other lines of work that would likely make alert undergraduates think twice about starting graduate school and putting themselves on a similar course. As a result, the number of American students pursuing graduate study dropped in most fields.

Every projection of faculty retirements shows an increasing number through the 1990s. Most of these retiring faculty members entered the profession in the early 1960s, when American higher education was growing rapidly, there was a high demand for new faculty, and many government and private programs encouraged students to choose the profession by supporting them during their graduate study. In the late 1990s, when we can expect increasing numbers of retirements among faculty, the numbers of traditional-age (eighteen- to twenty-two-year-old) college students will once again be increasing, creating a demand for additional faculty.

All this depends on a series of individual faculty decisions, of course, and projections tell us only what *might* happen if current trends continue. For example, despite the lifting of a mandatory retirement age, faculty members have actually been retiring earlier, not later. That trend may change, and institutions may choose to offer incentives to make it change by making teaching, perhaps on a less than full-time basis, more attractive for older faculty members. Some new faculty members may be recruited by giving individuals now in other professions incentives to change their careers. For example, in the sciences, where some of the greatest faculty shortages are forecast, a large majority of Ph.D.'s have followed careers in industry or government, not in higher education.

It is clear, however, that colleges and universities will find recruiting the new faculty they need from among the ranks of each year's new Ph.D.'s increasingly difficult. The specific shortages will differ by field and for each institution, depending on the specific pattern of faculty retirements ahead. For trustees, there should be two concerns: first, it may be more difficult for their institution to sustain academic quality, which primarily reflects the quality of an institution's faculty; and second, there will be pressures to increase faculty compensation, already a large component of any institutional budget.

The familiar pattern has been to hire new faculty for about half the salary of the retiring faculty member being replaced. Greater competition for new faculty will inevitably drive up entry-level salaries and, eventually, all faculty salaries. Turning to other sources, such as individuals making midcareer shifts from business or government, will also mean comparatively higher salaries for those new faculty members. The specific analysis and plans to deal with future faculty recruitment for each institution must be made by that faculty and administration; trustees have the responsibility to be sure appropriate projections and plans have been set in place.

Trustees

Trustees have a vital and distinctive role in independent colleges and universities. While there are significantly more students and more faculty associated with public institutions, there are far more trustees in the independent sector (about forty thousand of the nearly fifty thousand trustees nationally). This reflects the much larger average size of boards at independent institutions, about thirty members, and the fact that many public institutions are part of multicampus systems that have single governing boards with an average of fourteen members.

Although independent college and university boards are gradually coming to reflect more closely the diversity of contemporary American society, the trustees at independent institutions are still predominantly white, male, and over the age of fifty (see Resource B). As changing demographic reality makes it more important for colleges and universities to attract increasing numbers of minority students and faculty, the composition of boards must also change to better reflect that reality. As each institution's efforts toward diversity are increasingly central to its future vitality, having the experience and perspectives of racial and ethnic minorities and women represented at the board table will be more and more important.

Strengths and Vulnerabilities of the Independent Sector

Independent colleges and universities bring unique strengths to the nation's higher education system. But they also have some unique vulnerabilities.

Institutional Openings and Closings

Independence inevitably carries a greater sense of vulnerability. Each independent college or university must survive on its own resources. While many of today's strongest independent colleges and universities were founded in the nineteenth century (or earlier), a high percentage of the institutions founded during the nineteenth century did not survive into the twentieth. The possibility of having to close or to merge with another institution is real for all but the most well-endowed independent colleges and universities.

Over the past two generations, each year has seen a few independent institutions close or lose their identity through a merger.

But during that same time, each year has seen the opening of a *larger* number of *new* institutions. The more rapid, and therefore more dramatic, growth of the public sector has overshadowed these important facts about independent colleges and universities: the past four decades have been a time of steady growth in the total number of students enrolled, in the numbers of degrees awarded, and in the total number of independent colleges and universities.

Demography

One of the most accurate projections any social scientist can make is the size and composition of the traditional college-age cohort over the next eighteen years. Projecting future college *enrollments,* however, is more difficult. The deceptively good news is that the recent annual declines in the traditional college-age cohort will soon end and the numbers of eighteen-year-olds will increase every year through the late 1990s and the first decade of the twenty-first century. Much of that increase will come from groups, primarily African Americans and Hispanics, who have not been as likely to enroll in higher education and are more likely to choose public rather than independent institutions, particularly two-year public colleges. Further, it now seems likely that fewer high school graduates will come from families able to pay most independent college or university tuitions without significant amounts of financial aid, and more students will be from families who will find it difficult to pay public institution tuitions without at least some financial aid.

Changing demographics are placing pressures on trustees and public policy leaders who recognize the need for higher education, both public and private, to be accessible to all students who qualify for admission. In both sectors, students and their families have been paying an increasing share of the cost of education. Changes in the ways of paying for higher education almost certainly will be incremental. Some form of income-contingent repayment of loans seems likely to play a more important role, as does some form of payment or credit for public service, perhaps a new version of the GI bill that played such an important part in the expansion of higher education following World War II. The new socioeconomic composition of the college-age population makes it likely that such changes will have to be more comprehensive than in recent years.

One other consequence of changing population patterns that presents special challenges to independent colleges and universities is the general geographic shift of population within the United States. The more rapid population growth in the West and the South, and the slower growth (and in a few cases actual decline) in the Midwest and Northeast, means that potential students are moving away from the states where the largest numbers of independent colleges and universities are located. Some independent colleges and universities may find it harder to fill their classrooms.

Reputation and Measures of Productivity

In the important fields of science, independent institutions have been particularly productive. Faculty at the independent research universities consistently win distinguished prizes in science and receive significant amounts of competitive grant support from federal agencies and private foundations. Higher percentages of the students in independent institutions earn baccalaureate degrees (Carrier and Davis-Van Atta, 1986; Project Kaleidoscope, 1992). Some of those differences, of course, are accounted for by different institutional missions, but the independents' edge seems to hold even when one compares only institutions having similar missions and institutional reputations.

Independent institutions also seem to retain an edge in producing leaders in business and public life, although that is less pronounced than it was a generation ago. Independent institutions seem to retain a clear lead in that central academic matter of Ph.D. productivity. Larger percentages of the graduates of independent colleges and universities go on to earn Ph.D.'s, and more than a third of all Ph.D.'s are awarded by independent universities.

Challenges and Resources for Independent Institutions

The distinctive strengths of independent colleges and universities include their distinguished heritage and their continuing reputation for leadership and quality, combined with the autonomy and flexibility that goes with their independence. These institutions and the trustees who bear responsibility for them are faced with the important question, How well will they use those advantages in facing the significant challenges to all higher education institutions in the years ahead?

Colleges and universities should and do change in response to new problems and new opportunities. The key to making sure these changes are positive is to retain a clear definition of the institution's mission and to measure proposed changes against that mission.

As institutions inevitably come under increasing financial pressures, there will be temptations to follow short-term market advantages in the recruitment of students and in efforts to attract donors. But over the long run, those colleges and universities that sustain a clear and demonstrable commitment to their institutional missions will be the ones that survive and prosper.

Students and their families want a clear reason to choose a particular college. The reasons are sometimes price or convenience, but surveys suggest that the quality of the academic program ranks first for most students. An institution with a clearly defined mission, to which its academic programs obviously relate, will have a long-term advantage over others whose focus and mission are less clear.

Donors also need a clear reason to give to a particular institution. There is almost always a personal connection: they or someone they care about received an education at the institution and the value of that education commands their loyalty and support. A clearly stated mission, which is changed only gradually and for good reason, provides a focus for donor support as well.

Finally, for faculty, administrators, and ultimately trustees, a focus on institutional mission as the reference point for all major decisions provides coherence and confidence, which are vital advantages for institutions facing significant challenges and seeking to treat those challenges as opportunities for continued service and support.

CHAPTER 3

The Economics
of Independent
Higher Education

Katharine H. Hanson

The economics of higher education is a subject that is always appearing in some guise or another on the agenda of boards of trustees. It is not, however, a topic often discussed directly; instead, it is the background for topics such as the approval of the annual operating budget, decisions to be made about building and borrowing, or the setting of next year's tuition and fees and financial aid policies. It also underlies topics such as enrollment planning, long-range planning, investments, and the next fund-raising campaign.

It is not an easy subject, especially for new trustees, because the "business" of higher education is a complex mix of services and products for private and public purposes. Students, for example, are not only the major consumers but they are also the principal "products" of their college or university. Furthermore, the language used to describe the financing of colleges and universities is distinctive, the accounting systems are different, and many goals and values of the institution are not easily described or even measured by the economic terms so familiar in other sectors.

While independent and public institutions operate in a common economic environment, they relate to this environment in different ways and there are major differences in their internal economies. This chapter will address the economics of the independent sector.

It is intended to give trustees a sense of what they need to know to make informed decisions on some of the most difficult and basic issues that regularly appear on their agendas. We begin with a discussion of the broad external economic context and some of the key factors that are important to monitor in an ever-changing, ever more complex climate. Then we turn to a discussion about the factors that are most important to the internal economy of a campus. Finally, we suggest some questions that need to be asked by trustees on a regular basis.

Trustees are not expected to become experts on the economics of higher education or the technicalities of how private higher education is financed. But they do need to understand the basic elements that influence and, in some cases, constrain the operation of an academic institution. Trustees need to remember that while each institution has its own special history and its own local climate, many economic characteristics and issues are shared by peer institutions. Trustees should realize also that their principal challenge is to select and appoint good managers who can make and implement decisions within the policy guidelines set by the board. The institution and the governing board will benefit more from senior administrators who can make good decisions and provide the board with the information necessary to evaluate decisions in relation to institutional policy than from a room full of "expert" trustees who are inclined to micromanagement.

The Big Picture

For much of the history of higher education in this country, colleges and universities, particularly those in the independent sector, have paid scant attention to the larger economy. This was partly because they were not very vulnerable to the elements that drive changes in the national economy and partly because colleges perceive themselves as being somewhat immune from business and social commerce. This attitude changed radically in the late 1970s with the realization that colleges and universities are indeed vulnerable on many economic fronts and that their capacities to control their financial health had become more tenuous. Economist and Federal Reserve Board member Larry Lindsey (1990) has observed that higher education's metaphor has been transformed from the ivory tower to a major crossroads of modern society. Its capacity to generate revenues as well as control expenditures is increasingly subject to economic events that are national and, in the 1990s, even global in scope.

We can think about the economic forces that drive colleges and universities from two perspectives: external and internal. The external forces include some that are demand driven, such as the competition with other institutions for students, faculty, and prestige. Other broader external forces are imposed by laws and regulations, the need to respond to external critics, sources of support (for example, benefactors), and the responsibility to provide leadership and services to the community. Many external forces are easily recognized and often blamed (or credited) as the reasons for price increases or increased expenditures.

The internal forces are often overlooked because it is harder to recognize the economic impact of operating systems and decision processes on the costs of the enterprise. Universities, unlike many businesses, have not traditionally assigned their highest values to efficiency or reducing waste and redundancy. Instead, they have focused on high-quality or the most intellectually exciting or interesting work, at whatever cost. Furthermore, most higher education institutions have a curious (and usually inefficient) blend of a central bureaucracy and a tradition of decentralized decision making and responsibility. Only recently has this tension been recognized by some leading independent institutions as a major problem that needs to be addressed if their efforts to introduce quality management programs and achieve stronger control over their economic destinies are to succeed.

The Industry of Higher Education

Higher education is a much bigger industry than most people realize. In 1991, higher education served more than 14 million students, employed more than 2.6 million people, and operated with revenues exceeding $150 billion. According to economist Carol Frances (1990), the industry is twice the size of the American aerospace industry and almost three times the size of the auto industry.

Spending by higher education accounts for about 2.9 percent of the U.S. gross national product (GNP). Its percentage of the GNP has increased substantially in the past thirty years; it was only 1.4 percent in 1960. The industry includes some 3,500 accredited colleges and universities.

There is an even larger industry, called "postsecondary education," which includes not only the traditional colleges and universities but another 11,500 institutions that provide some form of educational services or postsecondary/vocational training. The latter include the majority of the proprietary or for-profit schools, and they wield substantial local economic and political clout. In addition, there are employee educational services offered by many large corporations. Though often not visible, there is real and growing competition between corporate educational programs and traditional institutions. There are also increasing opportunities for collaboration between colleges and industry; however, this chapter focuses only on accredited and tax-exempt institutions.

In terms of the *number* of institutions, the percentage of independent institutions (49 percent) is greater than the percentage of public institutions (45 percent); the proprietary sector makes up the remainder. But, when compared in terms of *student enrollments,* the public sector dominates the market, with independent four-year schools accounting for less than 20 percent. The public sector has increased its share of the market steadily over the past two decades.

The Financing of Higher Education

The financing of higher education has several aspects. In general, the three principal sources that cover the costs of instruction are public funds, tuition payments, and philanthropy. According to Martin Kramer (1985, p. 58), taken together these sources account for more than 70 percent of instructional costs and about half of the total national costs of putting students through college. This is critical to understanding the national debate about the future funding of higher education.

If we look more closely at the two major sectors of higher education, we see that revenue patterns for public institutions are

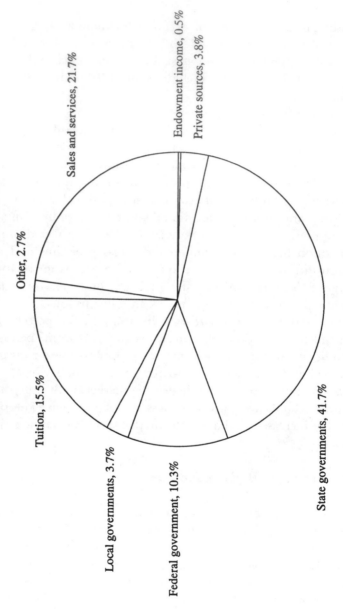

Figure 3.1. Sources of Current-Fund Revenue for Public and Private Institutions of Higher Education, 1989–90.

Endowment income, 0.5%

Private sources, 3.8%

Sales and services, 21.7%

Other, 2.7%

Tuition, 15.5%

Local governments, 3.7%

Federal government, 10.3%

State governments, 41.7%

Total revenues for public institutions = $88.9 billion

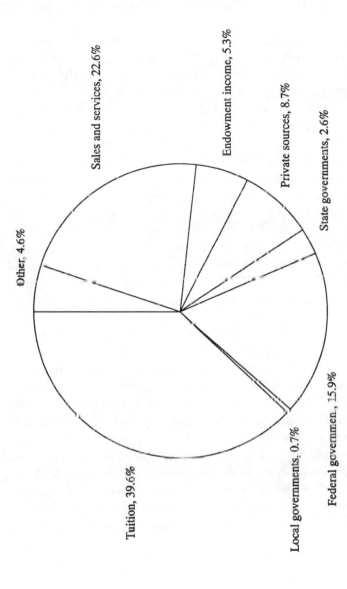

Sales and services, 22.6%

Endowment income, 5.3%

Private sources, 8.7%

State governments, 2.6%

Other, 4.6%

Tuition, 39.6%

Local governments, 0.7%

Federal government, 15.9%

Total revenues for private institutions = $50.7 billion

Source: U.S. Department of Education 1990.

quite different from those of the independent sector. The following figures make it easier to understand how much more the independent colleges and universities are directly dependent on the market, and thus on public response to tuition and fees, than their state-supported public counterparts. Figure 3.1 shows the dramatic difference in sources of revenue for the two sectors. Independent institutions' greater dependence on tuition income means that changes in demand (enrollment) have greater and more immediate financial effects on the institutions. Their greater dependence on private gifts and endowment income means that changes in tax laws that encourage (or discourage) giving are of vital interest to the independent sector.

Within the independent sector, there is substantial variation in the degree of tuition dependence. Generally, the least well-endowed institutions are the most tuition dependent, often for more than 75 percent of their revenue, while those with the largest endowments obtain less than 50 percent of their revenues from tuition and fees. There is another private sector variation worth noting: the typical research university depends on federal grants and contracts for more than 10 percent of its revenue, while for the baccalaureate colleges this source is usually less than 5 percent.

Another aspect of the economics of higher education is the relationship between tuition charges and current-fund expenditures per full-time student. Figure 3.2 shows these data over time and clearly illustrates the considerable differences in the patterns and history of the two sectors. Although the expenditure lines in both sectors are similar, the difference in the importance of tuition revenues in meeting those expenditures is shown by the much more parallel movement of the private sector lines. Figure 3.2 also helps to illustrate another point of concern, the private sector's increasing dependence on tuition in the late 1980s. When federal and local support resources stagnate or decline, tuition charges must go up faster than expenditures to make up the difference. This results in an even wider public-private price differential.

In view of the relatively recent increase in public awareness and criticism of the costs of higher education, particularly in the independent sector, trustees should know something about the long-term trends. The national consumer price index (CPI), often

**Figure 3.2. Indices of Average Undergraduate Tuition Charges
and of Current-Fund Expenditures per Full-Time Equivalent Student,
Academic Years Ending 1971 to 1988.**

Public Institutions

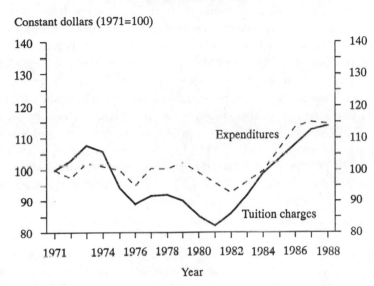

Private institutions

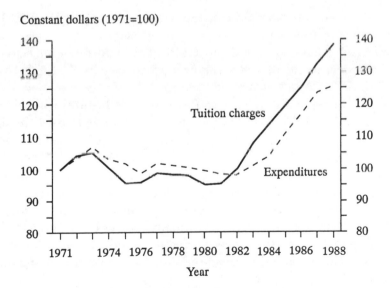

Source: Alsalam, 1990a, 1990b.

used as a standard against which to measure the reasonableness of price increases, is derived from a "market basket" of typical goods and services purchased by individuals. However, it is not a very appropriate standard for higher education because the typical market basket for colleges and universities is quite different from that of individuals. The largest portion of higher education's annual expenses are related to labor costs (typically about 70 percent of the operating budget), which tend to increase faster than the CPI. Colleges and universities also face unusual costs that run in excess of the CPI, such as the maintenance of a library and the cost of acquisitions and the cost of specialized research equipment and supplies. These differences have been recognized by economists, and a specialized index that reflects the market basket for colleges, called the higher education price index (HEPI), has been constructed to account for the differences. This index lagged behind the CPI for much of the 1970s, largely because salary and wage increases were restrained in higher education, and ran ahead of it in the 1980s. Although the HEPI is a better indicator for monitoring the growth of institutional expenditures, the standard economic indicators bear watching in order to monitor the relative affordability of tuition and fees. The HEPI index is annually updated and published in the early fall.

When you judge an institution's cost growth by the HEPI, you must realize that to experience *real* growth, most colleges and universities have to exceed the HEPI. The hard question before trustees and presidents today is how much growth can be funded by substitutions rather than by additions.

The relationship between the increase in institutional prices and families' ability to pay is a matter of ongoing public debate. In the 1980s, the growth in the cost of attending an independent institution rose faster than family income, making private higher education less affordable for the average family. Median family income and personal disposable income are two common economic measures that are tracked in relation to the increase in institutional charges. While the popular press usually focuses on the growth of announced tuition (the "sticker price"), the more meaningful economic comparisons are between the ability-to-pay measures and the net tuition price.

Another important long-term economic pattern to watch is the relationship between the general condition of the national economy and enrollment demand. Common wisdom says that the demand for education *rises* as the state of the economy declines and that, in uncertain economic times, people seek security in the highest quality education they can obtain. Economists who track college enrollments have shown that college enrollments have consistently followed this cycle since 1945 (Frances, 1990). Many graduate education programs are even more sensitive to this phenomenon than are undergraduate programs.

Public funds and philanthropy have been and will continue to be important sources of income (see Figure 3.3). The Council for Aid to Education (CFAE) tracks trends in voluntary support, and according to CFAE data, voluntary support has a reassuring track

Figure 3.3. Trends in Voluntary Support of Higher Education.

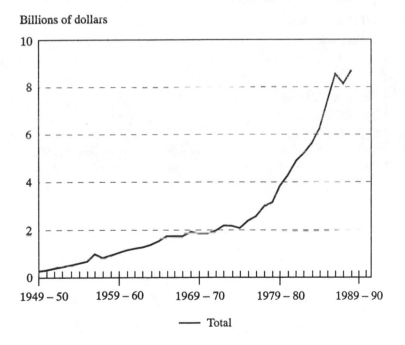

Billions of dollars

Source: Council for Aid to Education, 1990.

record, with a steady increase from 1949 to the present (Council for Aid to Education, 1991). Most experts believe that philanthropy will become an even more important resource for independent institutions than it is today.

As we saw in Figure 3.1, public funds come to the independent sector from two main sources, the federal government and, in some states, state support to financial aid programs. Although public funds have grown over the past thirty years, the rate of real growth in recent years has more often been zero or negative. Figure 3.4 compares federal budget allocations for two national priorities, education/training and defense. The public and proprietary sectors have been the principal beneficiaries of the growth in funding for education, particularly as federal aid programs have been broadened to include less than half-time students and extended to proprietary school students.

Figure 3.4. Federal Budget Allocations for National Priorities.

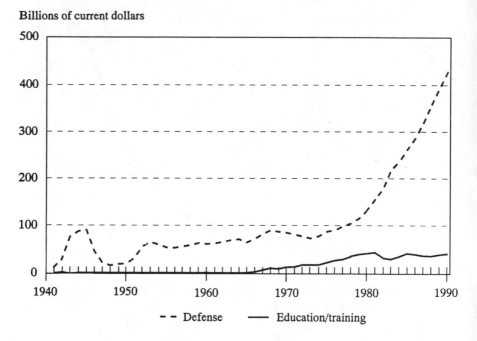

Source: Hanson and Meyerson, 1990. Reprinted by permission.

The International Economic Factors

In addition to thinking about the broad national economic context, trustees should recognize that there are international economic factors that may be important to their institutions. We will briefly discuss two such factors: the strength of the U.S. dollar and the demand for American education from abroad. There are several ways in which strength of the U.S. dollar and the attractiveness of the U.S. economy to foreign investors influence American colleges and universities. One influence is on our capital markets, on which many independent colleges and universities depend for their capacity to borrow or to sell bond issues to support their building and plant renovation needs. A change in the Japanese banking structure can result directly in a higher cost of capital to American colleges and universities. The strength of the U.S. dollar also influences the relative affordability of American colleges for foreign students. Since foreign students have little or no access to our financial aid programs, they are quite conscious that the relative cost of education is much less when the U.S. dollar is low. Foreign students have had a significant role in evening out enrollments in the United States, especially in our graduate schools in recent years.

The demand for education from abroad is also an important factor because it may directly affect American colleges on at least two fronts. First, the market for the highest quality faculty is increasingly international. Not only are there international "superstars" who are heavily recruited, but far more important to most colleges is the fact that large numbers of our recent Ph.D. graduates are not U.S. natives. While they may choose to work and teach in the United States in large numbers, a worldwide increase in demand for education will draw them out of the United States at a time when domestic faculty shortages are predicted. We already can see the increased foreign demand for faculty in the renewal of higher education systems in Eastern Europe, and the coming together of the Western European Common Market countries may have a similar effect.

As the world economy becomes more interdependent, trustees need to be aware of international economic trends because they will present both new planning challenges and new opportunities for growth and outreach for American institutions.

Regional and Local Economic Conditions

Although the national economic environment is important, local and regional economies often have a decisive, immediate impact on independent institutions. Trustees need to know if the points of reference for their institution are local, regional, or national. While it may sound obvious, this factor is often overlooked when considering economic data and the decisions based on them.

The state of the local economy will frame many of the economic decisions of the institution. With the exception of faculty salaries, which are often framed by broader markets, the campus salary structure, the cost of basic supplies and services, and the building cost per square foot are examples of issues that must be assessed within the context of the local or regional economy. For most institutions, the application and enrollment decisions of their students are made within a regional economic context, and therefore good enrollment planning and marketing respond first to that environment. Trustees need to know when their local or regional economic indicators differ from national trends, and they need to know how their institution has fared in response to past cycles of local and regional economic change.

The Economy of the Campus

The microeconomies of colleges and universities at the campus level are nearly as diverse as the variety of institutions in the independent sector. Trustees have an obligation to learn enough about their campus to make judgments about the administration's recommendations for annual operating budgets, tuition levels, and financial aid policies; the development and funding of capital budgets; the policy (not day-to-day) management of their institution's endowment (see Chapter Ten); and recommendations for institutional fund-raising campaigns. One of the first managerial duties of a college or university is to provide its new trustees with the basic information needed to know the institution. A well-briefed trustee will know what business the college is in. What is the mission of this college or university? might be a trustee's first question. Other questions include: Who are the primary populations served? Is research a major activity? Is continuing or adult education an important focus? The economy of the institution will be the joint result of its history and the answer of the current administration to that basic question, What is the business of this place? This question is one that gets regularly revisited in long-range planning but is not otherwise considered as often as it should be.

Expenditure and Revenue Patterns

While no institution of higher education considers itself (or is) typical, there are broadly similar patterns of major expenses and revenues across types of institutions within the independent sector.

Nordhaus (1990) found that the most critical and volatile revenue source for research universities is not tuition or endowments, but income from the federal government. Thus, large universities are more vulnerable to the vagaries of the national economic and political climate than are small colleges. The latter are most subject to the local economic environment and their internal economies.

A recent study of the latest available federal government data by Schapiro, McPherson, and O'Malley (1990) examined expenditure patterns from more than 990 independent institutions. The work compared expenditures for instruction with other major categories of expenses and examined the different patterns of private research universities and four-year colleges. Figure 3.5 shows that there are distinctly different patterns for these types of institutions. "E and G expenditures" refer to the expenses that are related to "education" and the "general" operation of the college. These are usually considered with the exclusion of the cost of financial aid (net of aid) and are divided for analysis into five general subcategories of expenditure. E&G does not include capital expenditures.

It is not possible to describe here the many differences between the campus economies of research universities, comprehensive universities, four-year liberal arts colleges, and two-year colleges. It should be noted that the economics of a medical campus

Figure 3.5. Typical Education and General Expenditure Patterns (Net of Aid) for Independent Colleges and Universities.

College

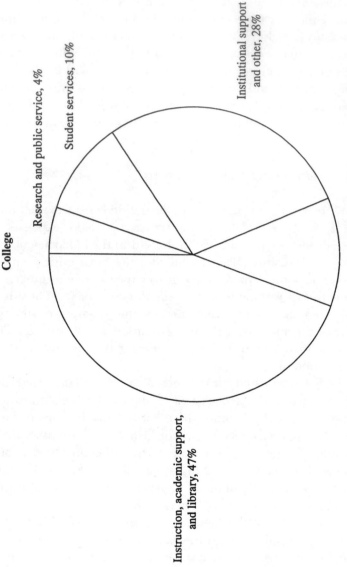

Research and public service, 4%

Student services, 10%

Institutional support and other, 28%

Operations and management, 11%

Instruction, academic support, and library, 47%

University

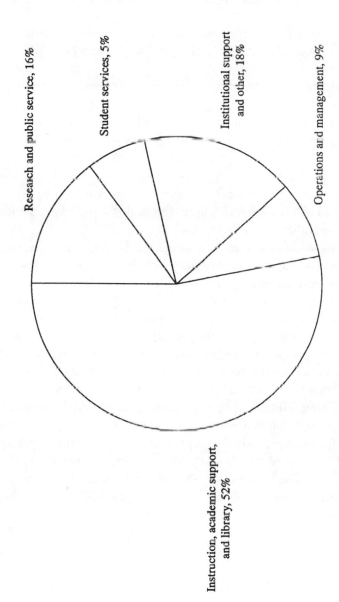

Research and public service, 16%

Student services, 5%

Institutional support
and other, 18%

Operations and management, 9%

Instruction, academic support,
and library, 52%

Source: Integrated Postsecondary Education Data System (IPEDS) 1986. Drawn from Schapiro, McPherson, and O'Malley (1990).

are probably more complex than any of the above and usually require some special expertise on the part of the trustees.

Economic Behavior Patterns

Independent college trustees need to understand something about the economic forces that operate within their institution. They need to have a sense of what major factors will constrain and influence their decisions about such topics as tuition and financial aid policy, and they need to understand the campus economic environment as a background for decisions about the endowment, the operating budget, and other major expenditures.

As indicated at the beginning of this chapter, many of the economic terms and concepts common to business and industry do not translate comfortably to higher education. Traditional measures for discussion and analysis are confounded and resist measurement. For example, the concept of productivity in higher education is difficult enough to describe, let alone measure. Productivity, which is normally measured in terms of the cost of producing a unit of a product or service, becomes a very complex problem. Colleges and universities "produce" instruction, student services (housing, athletics, counseling, and so on), research, and public services. Yet campus accounting systems usually relate costs to items of expenditures (for example, salaries, supplies, and equipment), not to the units of "products" (such as courses taught, degrees awarded, or research completed); therefore, the information needed to measure productivity is not readily available. A more difficult issue, however, is the interrelationship among higher education products—for example, instruction and faculty research and scholarship—and the resources that produce them; this is known as the joint product problem.

Nevertheless, trustees will have to make decisions that relate to the three factors we know are related to institutional productivity: the inputs (students, faculty, equipment, and so on), the output or products (degrees awarded, new knowledge, services to the public, and so on), and the important but elusive factor of quality. Institutional productivity is a major challenge that is being studied with growing intensity, and a body of research is emerging that may yet enable us to measure and assess productivity on a campus.

There are some theories that will help trustees understand the economic behavior of their campus. In his classic study, *The Costs of Higher Education*, Howard Bowen (1980) examined the factors that determine the economic behavior of a campus and he developed a theory of revenue and cost that is widely accepted as a description of the behavior of the past two decades. He summarized his model into "Bowen's laws." They are:

1. The dominant goals of institutions are educational excellence, prestige, and influence.
2. In quest of excellence, prestige, and influence, there is virtually no limit to the amount of money an institution could spend for seemingly fruitful ends.
3. Each institution raises all the money it can.
4. Each institution spends all the money it raises.
5. The cumulative effect of the preceding four laws is the movement toward ever-increasing expenditures.

Needless to say, while these "laws" ring true to many trustees (and parents who pay tuition), they are likely to be a source of great discomfort in the 1990s for both administrators and trustees. As a result, there are renewed attempts to change institutional behavior to include more emphasis on savings (building and preserving the endowment), cost containment (creating new incentives for more restraint on the expenditure side), and reduced reliance on the capacity to generate new revenues by traditional means (such as increasing tuition and fees).

Another economist, William Baumol (1983), formulated a theory that further explains the seemingly intractable problem of ever-increasing costs. He pointed out that two critical characteristics of the campus are the very labor-intensive production processes and the failure to exploit technological progress to change the way basic services are delivered. In most industries, new technology brings innovation and efficiency, but not on the campus. The advance of technology has resulted in better quality and expanded services on campus (and often, even greater operating costs), but it has not

changed the basic structure of teaching. Baumol describes this as
"the cost disease," when real expenditures rise over time but
productivity does not. The result is that the campus has to increase
income just to maintain a steady level of operations.

A third explanation of the difficulty of changing the economic behavior of the campus is related to the organization's basic
form. Economic researchers have observed that understanding the
way that the typical campus is organized is key to understanding its
economic behavior. Faculty and administrators do not have incentives to be as efficient as they could be. Henry Levin (1989) and
others have observed that campus resources are used for two ends:
to achieve *institutional* goals and the more *personal* professional
development and special interests of the faculty and administrators.
William Massey (1991) characterized this phenomenon as output
creep. He has postulated that faculty or administrators pursue their
own objectives when they add new campus goals or create new
products other than instruction. The result is an increase in output,
but this output does not meet basic institutional objectives, and it
drives up costs, especially the cost of an undergraduate degree. In
other words, a campus organization in which faculty have great
autonomy to pursue their own goals is part of the problem when
efforts are made to increase productivity or cut costs.

One of the basic responsibilities of trustees is to protect the
long-term interests of the institution. This delicate balancing act
between meeting the current operating demands and preserving options for future generations often requires tough decisions on the
part of the board. To make decisions, trustees must be informed
about the basic financial condition of the institution as well as have
an understanding of the internal and external economic factors that
shape the course of the future.

Trustees should routinely ask for information about the future impact of the current year's decisions. For example, trustees
should know if the institution is maintaining the real value of its
capital assets and the value of its endowment per student. They
should know about key economic relationships, such as the link
between an increase in tuition and fees and their institution's financial aid budget. The remainder of this chapter is devoted to a discussion of some of these important relationships.

Key Economic Relationships

The annual approval of tuition and fees is one of the trustee decisions most fraught with anguish. It is almost always a hard decision made after months of background preparation and the weighing of mostly unpleasant alternatives. It is both an economic and a political decision. The tuition decision is an example of an institutional decision that requires analysis of both the external economic environment and the internal economy of the campus.

As was shown earlier in this chapter, tuition and fees are a major source of revenue to independent colleges and universities, and the principal one that is under institutional control. Tuition and fees are the price the institution sets for instruction and student services; yet the price never fully reflects the costs of providing these services. To understand this discrepancy better, trustees should compare the E&G expenditures per full-time-equivalency (FTE) student with both the gross and net tuition revenues per student. The net tuition comparison is important because it brings financial aid into the economic picture. Net tuition is the gross amount of tuition revenue less the institution-based financial aid. As noted before, financial aid is a major expense item for most institutions, and financial aid policy and tuition decisions are closely linked at several points. Trustees should know how much financial aid is funded by the institution and how much by extrainstitutional sources, and they should know how these figures compare with the past several years. Trend data can be very revealing on this subject.

A definitional aside is in order here. There are really three major components of what independent colleges call tuition and fees. First is the tuition, which is the basic charge for instructional costs, often expressed in terms of credit hours. The tuition charges generally do not reflect the full cost of providing these services. Second, there are required fees for services such as health care, athletics, and student activities. These are usually linked to the real cost of providing such services; for example, in most colleges, room and board services are set up as self-supporting auxiliary services. Finally, there are optional fees that students choose to incur to participate in some specialized activity, such as music lessons. These fees usually reflect the cost of providing the service. It is obvious, but not often debated, that most independent institutions price their services at the same rate for all undergraduates without regard to the real variations in the costs to deliver them. For example, the tuition costs per credit for a small advanced course in physics and a large lecture in freshman economics are the same. There are different tuition rates set for graduate programs and for professional schools, but they, too, are heavily subsidized by other sources of revenue.

Although the public and media most often react to the stated tuition (the so-called sticker price), the large majority of students are likely to be receiving some form of financial aid. In most independent institutions, unrestricted income, which is mainly derived from tuition revenues, is a major source of financial aid. Thus, the grant aid provided from institutional revenue is, in effect, a discount against tuition.

Two key indicators for trustees to monitor are the rate of growth in the aid budget that is funded by unrestricted dollars and the total percentage of the unrestricted budget that funds the financial aid program. When the aid comes from the institution's own operating budget, trustees are voting for a further financial aid obligation when they adopt a new tuition level. Some institutions adhere to a policy of meeting full need, with the difference between an institution's "sticker price" and a family's capacity to pay calculated by a standardized aid analysis formula, perhaps with some institutional adjustments. In these institutions, the trustees' tuition decision is an especially difficult one because the goal of greater unrestricted revenues must take account of the commitment to spend some of those same revenues on an increased aid budget (assuming the mix of students and the level of funds available from other sources remain constant). For institutions with fewer resources for financial aid and those that cannot meet full need, the tuition decision will directly test the market demand for the institution.

Key Questions Trustees Should Ask

Trustees exercise their responsibilities largely by asking timely questions of themselves and their academic leaders. The following twelve key questions stem from the preceding pages of this chapter:

1. Do long-range planning, operating, and capital budget-planning documents include discussions of the external economic environment and the key factors that may affect the institution?

2. What major elements of the institution's expense or revenue categories are vulnerable to international, national, regional, or local economic conditions? Which indicators are monitored regularly and which are incorporated into the institution's planning assumptions?

3. How do the growth rates and trend lines of major categories of expenditures compare to local, regional, or national levels? Compare to the HEPI or a group of peer institutions?

4. What are the growth rates and trends for the major categories of the institution's revenues? What key indicators, ratios, and relationships between expenditures and revenues are being tracked? Are these revenue data the most informative and helpful?

5. What happened the last time there was a major change in the economic indicators? How did it affect student applications? Students' ability to pay? Labor costs? Cost of capital? The flow of gifts and grants? Endowment earnings?

6. How is the institution organized in terms of making the decisions that drive the major categories of expenditures?

7. What is the real operating condition of the institution? Are the real values of the physical plant and the endowment being maintained? Are we maintaining the value of our human resources?

8. What is the level of institutional debt? Is there a policy governing the growth and uses of debt?

9. If the institution is growing or shrinking in the size of its student body, how do the academic programs where change is greatest affect the central goals of the institution?

10. Is there any danger of the train running ahead of schedule? In other words, are the economic and financial decisions made this year, for this cohort of students, faculty, and staff, going to be at the expense of future generations?

11. Do the various constituencies on campus—especially the ad-

ministration and the faculty—view the economic condition
and challenges of the institution in similar terms?

12. What aspects of the political climate and trends at the local,
state, and national levels have financial implications for the
institution? How is the institution taking them into account?

Comprehending the economics of private higher education
is a learning process that will last as long as a trustee serves on the
board. It is getting to be more and more complex, but the good news
is that we are also developing better tools of analysis and bringing
more professional managers into higher education. The role of the
independent college or university trustee is not to manage, not to
plan, and not to represent a special constituency, but to authorize,
review, and evaluate these processes with the whole institution's
welfare and future at the center of concern. To do this, the effective
trustee must keep an eye on the horizon, listen closely, ask the hard
questions, and support effective administrators.

CHAPTER 4

Coping with
a Litigious
Environment

David M. Lascell
Sanford H. Levine

We live in a litigious society. Colleges and universities are involved in litigation over a wide range of matters. Trustees in both the public and private sectors of higher education have a responsibility to reduce their personal and institutional vulnerability to suits through enlightened policies and practices. To meet this responsibility, trustees must understand the nature of institutional and personal liability and their fiduciary duties of loyalty and care to their institution.

The Present Environment

Trustees should know the major sources of lawsuits against the academy and ask themselves whether they should insist on much greater use of alternative dispute resolution techniques and expertise, such as mediation and arbitration. And insisting that their college or university take measures to reduce its exposure and risk is especially important.

Note: We gratefully acknowledge the assistance of Michael J. Cooney of Nixon, Hargrave, Devans and Doyle in Rochester, New York, in the preparation of this chapter.

Growth of Litigation

Higher education's increased exposure to legal liability should not come as a surprise. There is a perception, supported by the increase in the number of lawsuits filed and in the number and size of awards made, that society as a whole, particularly since the 1960s, has become more litigious (Helms, 1987). Furthermore, educational institutions appear to be less insulated from these developments than in the past, in part because of the major increase in federal regulation of activities in institutions that receive any federal funds. Disaffected constituents (particularly faculty and students) and outside entities are no longer hesitant to bring their claims into the courtroom (Zirkel, 1989; Helms, 1990). Legal challenges, once rare in connection with colleges and universities, now play a prominent role in the business of higher education (Kaplin, 1985b).

Educational institutions have activities and interests broad enough to expose them to an enormous array of legal claims, ranging from employment termination and discrimination to consumer fair practice and trade complaints to environmental liability and First Amendment charges. As corporate entities with a distinct educational mission, colleges and universities provide fertile ground for controversy.

Colleges and universities face many of the same problems that confront any business enterprise. For example, institutions must respond to routine claims of negligence and contract liability. Breach of contract claims that involve construction, employment, and services, to name a few, continue to arise, as do negligence actions. If the institution operates a teaching hospital, medical malpractice claims are another major source of litigation.

In contrast to the for-profit corporation, the academy faces some unique exposure. For example, faculty tenure matters continue to provoke a considerable number of lawsuits. These suits often involve claims of discrimination under federal or state law or deprivation of a constitutional right. Similarly, the number of suits about academic and disciplinary actions that involve students continues to grow as students contest institutional decisions (mainly on constitutional and contract grounds) in the hope of securing judicial reversal of those decisions.

In 1990, for example, the United Educators Insurance Risk Retention Group, a major liability insurer of private and public institutions, found that more than 70 percent of its claims were employment related, and one quarter of these alleged some form of prohibited discrimination (McMullan, 1991). Almost 60 percent of the claims made for general institutional liability allege serious bodily injury. United Educators has also found that, despite the concerns of the commercial market, there was a low rate of university claims arising from child-care facilities, campus security, host liquor liability, and product liability.

New issues, however, continue to emerge in the law of higher education, reflecting "a dynamism and ferment that show no signs of abating" (Dutile, 1990, p. 151). Several significant problems for colleges and universities in the 1990s have already arisen. Has higher education entered an extended period of austerity, which will in turn sharpen the issues of faculty and student "rights" in the event of program and campus closures? How will institutions adapt to a rapid increase in ethnic diversity on campuses? Can the regulation of offensive conduct be balanced with constitutional free speech protection? Will institutions improve their self-regulation of scientific integrity in research programs? Will higher education continue to be subject to new and expanded governmental oversight and regulation? Do antitrust laws extend to all cooperative and collegial efforts among competing colleges and universities? Will courts become more assertive in settling intrainstitutional controversies, setting aside traditional judicial deference to the expertise of the academy? Should institutions utilize alternatives to judicial litigation, such as mediation and arbitration, to promote early resolution of disputes?

Reduction of the Exposure

The increased litigiousness of society must not deter trustees from carrying out the educational missions of their institutions. Although eliminating the threat of legal challenge (or indeed stopping a lawsuit), may be virtually impossible, trustees can take steps that will reduce the institution's exposure to liability. Trustees should critically and periodically examine all major policies and procedures to ensure that they are consistent with legal requirements and to see that they are not applied arbitrarily or capriciously. This examination is an integral part of trustee responsibility for fundamental institutional decision making and policy setting.

Legal Role of the Trustee

The college or university trustee's experience with our litigious society is in many ways unique. Consider, for example, the different ways in which a trustee may become involved in litigation (Kurtz, 1988). Most often, trustees will be sued in their representative capacity as trustees for the actions or omissions of the institution, although such actions rarely directly arise from the activities of the board. Today's trustee may be held to answer for a policy put in place decades before the trustee was seated on the board or for an action committed by an employee of whom the trustee has no personal knowledge.

On a very few occasions, trustees have been sued individually, which put their personal assets, as well as their reputations and those of their institutions, in jeopardy (Porth, 1975; Peat, Marwick, Main & Company, 1987). The trustee's personal resources may attract an action, or perhaps the plaintiff wishes to place pressure on the board and get the attention of the trustees as well as the larger community by naming the trustees in a lawsuit. Virtually any claim can become a harrowing experience that takes a significant toll on all parties, even if the institution or its trustees are satisfied with the outcome (LaNoue and Lee, 1987). Happily, and to the best of our knowledge, however, no college or university trustee has had personal assets attached in final settlement of a claim. But it could happen and it is this threat, however remote, that calls for individual and collective diligence by board members.

The fiduciary duties and obligations of the trustee encompass the entire institution, not just a part of it. Only the board and chief executive are in a position to take such an institutionwide perspective, which is why in the final analysis, they are held legally responsible for the institution (Hadden and Blaire, 1987). Yet there may be many circumstances that require the trustee to choose between various interests within the institution. The trustee's job becomes especially difficult in circumstances that involve competing special-interest groups, whether these groups are students, faculty, administrators, or groups external to the university, including alumni. Even in determining the proper extent of trustee indemnification or insurance, the trustee is faced with the conflict, at least conceptually, between his or her personal interests and those of the institution. The knowledgeable trustee recognizes this sometimes unenviable position and prepares to meet those conflicts and ambiguities before a crisis occurs.

Even when trustees are not personally named in litigation, they still have a responsibility to the institution to minimize legal liability. In most cases, this also means addressing potential areas of liability before they exist. Trustees are always concerned with legal questions; the only issue here is at what point trustees should become involved in resolving the questions. The same tools that serve trustees so well with regard to making other decisions that affect the institution (using committees and experts and creating well-developed policies, for example) should be used when trustees approach legal questions. The most important requirement of trustees is to be aware and informed of the possible legal ramifications of the institution's practices and policies.

Duty of Loyalty to the Institution

Historically, there has been a move away from viewing the college or university trustee's responsibilities in a limited, strictly defined manner toward seeing the trustee's role as more like that of a corporate director. However, the duty of loyalty remains absolute in many cases: trustees must place the interests of the college or university they serve first and foremost. This sometimes places the trustee in a difficult position with respect to demands from faculty, students, alumni, the community, and outside business interests. Divining where the best interests of the institution end and those of these constituents begin is not easy.

The most obvious occasion on which the trustee must avoid breaching the duty of loyalty is with respect to transactions that involve the trustee personally. Financial dealings that may directly benefit trustees through compensation, other perquisites, or profit provide clear situations in which a trustee may be held *personally* liable.

Prohibited conflicts may also involve "indirect dealing." To avoiding direct or indirect conflicts, trustees must be alert to personal situations that may cause conflicts and to how these conflicts may affect the college or university.

The trustee may fulfill the duty of loyalty if he or she avoids or mitigates situations in which there is a direct or indirect conflict between the interests of the institution and those of the trustee. Identifying potential conflict situations is a large part of this responsibility. The options then open to the board of trustees are often quite limited, sometimes by the state's nonprofit or corporate law. The duty of loyalty might be best described as "doing no wrong."

The first step is to recognize that a conflict may exist. Some trustees are quite aware of the potential of a conflict, while others may need to be helped to see it. Trustees' relationships with family members and other nonprofit and profit-making institutions for which they are a trustee, director, manager, officer, partner, shareholder, or key employee *must* be disclosed at the onset. Then the relationships must be regularly reexamined to assure that a change in circumstances will not disadvantage the institution. Distilled to its most useful form, the standard is not whether the trustee is receiving a benefit, but whether the institution's interests are or could be adversely affected by a conflict or the *perception* that a conflict exists.

Although there is no absolute bar to financial dealings between the trustee or officer and his or her institution, such dealings are often subject to the principle of "closest scrutiny." State laws that govern nonprofit institutions commonly provide for those instances in which the personal interests of the trustee *may* come into conflict with those of the institution. These often necessitate full disclosure of the possible conflict or a vote by disinterested trustees, or both. Almost all the state laws prevent payment for work as a trustee or director of nonprofit institution. In some situations, such as those in which a trustee's business interests are involved, an absolute prohibition on possible self-dealing transactions may also be advisable. All trustees must be aware of any state law provisions that govern such a situation and should educate themselves *before* the need becomes pressing, or before they accept appointment or election to the board.

Further, the institution should have its own policy with regard to conflicts of interest, not only at the board level but throughout the organization. Such policies may be modified to address specifically the conflicts different groups at the institution may encounter. Admissions personnel, purchasing agents, and faculty may all face different situations, and the institutional policy should be broad and yet detailed enough to speak to each.

Duty of Care

The standard of care for a college or university trustee is a matter of state law. Statutory standards range from those of reasonableness to gross negligence. Willful or wanton misconduct or illegal acts are, without exception, violations of the standard of care. The standard of care has a dual function; it defines both the trustee's personal liability and the institution's liability for suits brought against it. If trustees meet their duties with respect to the standard of care, then both they and the institution are free from liability.

The standard against which conduct is measured is the same as the "business judgment rule" in for-profit corporations. Trustees coming from the corporate environment will be familiar with this rule. The rule essentially states that neither a court nor any person shall sit in judgment of a board's action in the absence of bad faith or a conflict situation. The burden is on the person questioning the board's actions to show why the board's judgment should not be respected. The rule arises out of the expectation that corporate directors (or university trustees) are better equipped to evaluate institutional matters than are outsiders.

Following the corporate business judgment rule will not necessarily prevent liability in actions brought against the institution by members of the public at large. Even when the board properly exercises business judgment, the institution may be liable for actions that affect the public, regardless of whether procedural requirements were satisfied. For example, adopting a campus public safety plan may be good business judgment, but a person assaulted may still succeed in bringing an action against the institution.

Identifying and solving challenges that arise from the trustee's duty of care is difficult. Quite simply, the duty of care will apply to many more matters than will the duty of loyalty. The statutory schemes envision, and case law makes quite clear, that the duty of care is met through *active* participation in the affairs of the institution. The trustee who expects to satisfy the standard of care by "doing no wrong" will be gravely disappointed, the duty of care requires that all trustees do what is right.

Fulfilling the duty of care is not impossible, however. By acting in a responsible, prudent manner, trustees can adequately counter any future challenge to the sufficiency of their actions. Diligently attending meetings, including committee meetings; reading and reviewing reports; and actively participating in the conduct of board affairs by inquiring into matters at issue largely meet the requisite standard.

Sometimes, of course, the trustee must rely upon the opinion of others whose expertise uniquely qualifies them to respond to a particular inquiry. Trustees rely on board committees to fulfill specified functions, such as finance or fund raising. The board regularly relies upon reports from institutional officers in matters such as admissions, finances, risk management, physical plant, and campus safety. The opinions of outside authorities are also helpful. In meeting the challenges of today's litigious society, reliance upon legal counsel, both before and during any actual litigation, is an opportunity for the board to use expert advice in tackling difficult problems. A good board learns from its mistakes or those of others and does not repeat them.

Though such advice may certainly be useful in assisting the board to achieve its objectives, questions still arise about the extent to which a board can rely upon the advice of outside experts without making a direct inquiry of its own. The standard that permits such reliance varies under different state laws, from no specific provision on the point to an approved reliance upon financial statements (as in New York) to a broad safe harbor with regard to expert opinions (as in California). Trustees should be aware of the standard that applies in their state. Also, it is important that the decision to delegate encompasses the same considerations of prudence and care that the board's decisions do generally. The choice of what matters to delegate and to whom should be made with the same measured, thoughtful consideration as are all decisions of the board.

Setting Good Policies

Ensuring the soundness of the policies and practices in place requires ongoing review of their adequacy, appropriateness, practicality, and fairness. The board may need to serve as a court of appeal under certain very limited circumstances.

Importance of Continuing Review

Although a governing board can substantially minimize the incidence and impact of adverse litigation by properly crafting, implementing, and reviewing policies and procedures, this process must be a continuing one (Marks, 1987).

The ultimate responsibility for the activities of the institution rests in the board, and the bylaws of the board form the nucleus for all other institutional policies. Although the bylaws may allow the board to delegate authority to committees, officers, administrators, faculty, and others, the board may never abdicate institutional responsibility. As the working document for the conduct of board affairs, the bylaws should reflect contemporary policy and practice, consonant with the requirements of state law (Moots, 1991). Good institutions review their bylaws regularly and good board members are familiar with their contents.

Faculty matters, for example, present an increasing challenge to college and university trustees, especially with regard to employment discrimination charges involving race, sex, age, and disability. Such allegations not only involve great legal and administrative expense, but also come at great cost to the institution's reputation and ongoing relationship with faculty or other employees. One of the most reliable ways to avoid such allegations is through the maintenance of a thorough faculty and employee handbook that clearly addresses all policy matters with regard to faculty, including tenure, promotion, salary, sabbatical, retirement, and so on. In unionized institutions, these policies may also be subject to the requirements of collective bargaining under federal or state law.

Such policies require a great deal of thought. In the faculty context, for example, dismissal or termination is commonly preceded by the opportunity for a hearing or "due process." The exact parameters of this hearing should be set forth, including the notice to the faculty member about the hearing, the faculty member's access to evidence, the ability to open the hearing at the faculty member's request, and the protection afforded the faculty member in order to avoid unwanted publicity. It is also imperative that the faculty member's right to representation be explicitly set forth, including whether that right includes active representation by a practicing attorney. By setting these ground rules, the administrator lessens the possibility that the decision reached will be unfair and therefore successfully challenged.

Three guides to institutional policy making should always be considered:

1. Policies should be put in place only after the board has considered the different options and risks attending each one.
2. Policies must be monitored to assess change in risks and ability to address these changes.
3. Policies may actually place the institution at a disadvantage if the administrator is not willing to or capable of applying them correctly and evenhandedly. The board must consider their practical application.

Board as Court of Appeal

A college or university board will sometimes act as a court of appeal with regard to conflicts within the institution. While the role of arbiter is seldom a desirable one, especially when the trustees' judgments may later be subject to court scrutiny, this is a necessary but rare function. The object is to define clearly those situations and conditions under which the board will be required to arbitrate conflicts and to create guidelines that define the board's exact role. In this role, the board should normally be confined to satisfying itself that established policies and rules of procedure were followed.

Arbitration arises most often with the sensitive relationships among the chief executive of the institution, his or her staff, and the faculty. Generally, however, appeal processes, including those involving tenure disputes, should be confined within administrative or academic departments.

There has been a perceptible rise in the number of lawsuits concerning faculty grievances, which may result in an appeal to the board if the president or other administrative body cannot deal with the complaint effectively. Established procedures are especially important here to ensure that only those matters the board has already decided it will consider come before it. A periodic legal review of the faculty handbook is also suggested.

Comparison of Public and Private Institutions

Although the fundamental concerns of the trustees, to identify risks and minimize the institution's exposure to them, are the same whether the institution is public or private, there are some significant differences that depend on the institution's type. Constitutional claims, for example, may not be pressed against private institutions without some finding of state action.

Conversely, public institutions may enjoy immunity through the Eleventh Amendment to the Constitution, which prevents private citizens from filing suit in federal court against state governments. State-run educational institutions are therefore immune from some kinds of suits in federal court.

State laws may also provide immunity to the state and its constituent institutions. The rationale is that the educational institution is an extension of state government, so unless immunity is waived, the college or university will be immune from certain types of suits.

However, state sovereign immunity is riddled with exceptions as a result of judicial decisions and legislative action. The activities in which the institution is involved may also be proprietary or private in nature, so that, under state law, the institution is afforded no more protection than a private institution.

State-run educational institutions also have a responsibility under the Fourteenth Amendment to the Constitution to protect the rights of citizens. Private institutions do not share this responsibility unless they are acting as agents of the state or involved in "state action." A common statutory basis for actions against private colleges and universities is the civil rights provisions in section 1983 of title 42 of the U.S. Code, which applies to activities "under color of state law." Although the plaintiff must demonstrate the governmental involvement in the challenged activity, the courts have not set forth any precise norms on which the private institution trustee may rely.

Particularly unsettling is the development that by accepting government funding, a private institution may become a state instrumentality, and thus be subject to the Fourteenth Amendment or perhaps other regulation. Recent legislation, such as the Drug-Free Schools and Communities Act, is specifically written with the intent of tying compliance to the receipt of any federal funds. The reach of federal regulation even into private institutions has become pervasive, and institutions must be alert to this new legal landscape.

Immunity, Indemnification, and Insurance

The changing concept of charitable immunity, the applicability of indemnification, and the importance of adequate liability insurance are subjects for trustee concern.

Charitable Immunity

In the past, many states insulated educational institutions from lawsuits, providing immunity on account of their charitable activities. This once venerable doctrine has been all but abolished in most states. Even where it is still in force, recent cases demonstrate that the doctrine is viewed unfavorably.

The trend has been just the opposite for charitable immunity of trustees in their personal capacity. Recognizing that charitable organizations have been increasingly subject to suit, and that worthy individuals might not be willing to serve as directors or officers if their personal assets were exposed, many states have enacted some form of statutory immunity for those serving nonprofit organizations, including colleges and universities. Many states have passed "volunteer protection" laws with varying degrees of immunity.

Delaware, for example, allows a corporation to eliminate or limit the personal liability of its directors for duty of care violations by adding a provision to this effect to the corporate charter. The statutory protection covers only actions by the institution. Not surprisingly, transgressions against the duty of loyalty (improper benefit), intentional misconduct, or knowing violations of the law are not covered.

Other states, such as Tennessee and Arizona, have simply provided that trustees are immune from suit. Such protection does not apply, however, in cases of intentional or sometimes grossly negligent conduct. Some states, such as Virginia, allow a corporation to limit the personal liability of trustees to the amount of their compensation. Texas limits a trustee's liability to prescribed monetary limits if, among other things, the organization has liability insurance that covers the remaining exposure. Because the protection provided by these statutes is different in each state, trustees are urged to consult their institution's state law for changes that may affect them.

Indemnification

Indemnification is an agreement by the institution to prepay or reimburse expenses incurred by an officer or director in defense of an action. This may include not only the costs of defense, but amounts in settlement, fines, or penalties as well. Most state laws permit an institution to indemnify its trustees and officers when they are acting to further the institution's purposes. These laws are often very specific as to what costs will be covered by the corporation and under what circumstances. As a general rule, willful, wanton, or illegal misconduct is not covered.

In some states, indemnification is mandatory in certain situations. For example, in California and Delaware, it is mandatory when the director or trustee is successful in refuting the merits of a claim. In those instances, if the institution refuses to indemnify, a trustee may bring a court action, demanding that the institution indemnify him or her. In other states, indemnification is permissive, depending upon the provisions in the organization's certificate, charter, or bylaws. Trustees should ask their institutions the following questions about indemnification policies:

- Does indemnification cover derivative suits on behalf of the entity; that is, those by the corporation or another acting in its stead, such as the state attorney general? Third-party actions by an outsider? Is the legal standard the same in both cases?
- Does indemnification cover the cost of any judgment, attorneys' fees, or settlements with or without court approval?
- Is a board finding as to the propriety of an action required before the organization can indemnify a trustee?
- Is advancement of legal costs covered, and on what terms?

The answers to each of these questions should be clear to trustees so that they know precisely what is covered and when.

Insurance

Insurance is used to spread risk, to reduce costs to an acceptable level, and to provide funds for payment of losses. In the case of trustees personally, liability insurance provides a vehicle for indemnification (United Way of America, 1988; Tremper and Babcock, 1990).

Insurance carriers classify risks in discrete categories, which are not necessarily the same ones that the trustee or the institution would use. Finding coverage for all the institution's insurance needs in one policy is not common. As a result, the institution must piece together different policies, with the possibility of gaps or needless overlaps in coverage (Singsen, 1988). Today, an increasing number of institutions use a combination of commercial insurance policies and self-insurance to meet their needs. Self-insurance has been most frequently used for workers' compensation and as a "deductible," or a self-insured retention (SIR), in a general liability policy.

Reading the insurance policies is an important first step toward identifying where the institution is needlessly exposed, but most policies, with their numerous riders and addenda, are not written with ease of reading in mind. Access to an insurance broker, an attorney skilled in insurance matters, or an insurance adviser is invaluable in sorting through the coverage (Stone and North, 1989). Keep in mind, though, that the board should seek an adviser other than the broker who sells the policy.

Delivery of Legal Services

Governing boards have the responsibility to ensure that their institutions have adequate legal counsel. They also have responsibility for seeing that it is used effectively and that its effectiveness is assessed periodically.

Assessing the Need for Counsel

In a litigious environment, the question of whether to retain or employ counsel is rhetorical. All colleges and universities, whether public or private, secular or religious, large or small, need legal advice or representation. Before trustees choose a lawyer or law firm for a particular service or on general retainer, they must first recognize the potential functions counsel can perform and then clarify expectations appropriate to their particular institution and needs.

Although many possible roles, from advisor to litigator, have been identified for legal counsel (Daane, 1985), most institutions expect counsel to:

- Advise trustees of the laws and regulations applicable to their institution
- Apprise trustees of new legal developments and their impact
- Defend the institution in litigation and initiate actions, when appropriate
- Negotiate agreements on behalf of institutional interests
- Prepare and review college and university documents
- Review policies and procedures that relate to faculty, staff, and students

Meeting the Need for Counsel

Private colleges and universities have two basic options when seeking legal advice or representation. These are in-house counsel or outside counsel. When deciding on the type of representation needed, trustees must consider these questions: Will counsel be retained solely for litigation purposes? Will counsel be needed on a daily basis, or will there be an intermittent need for services? Is a specialty required? What level of funding is available for legal assistance? How many lawyers are needed? Trustees should assess the relative advantages and limitations of each option.

In-House Counsel. In most cases, full-time attorneys are desirable as university counsel or general counsel, and this is generally the most appropriate choice for larger private or public institutions. The number of full-time in-house legal counsel has more than doubled since the early 1970s (National Association of College and University Attorneys, 1984). These attorneys are immediately available to provide regular assistance to trustees and administrators in the management of university business. Performing much the same function as corporate counsel in the business community, in-house attorneys are not only able to aid colleges or universities when legal controversies materialize, but also can assist in adapting institutional policies and procedures to avoid lawsuits. The benefits of university counsel include:

- Immediate availability for consultation
- Sensitivity to the collegial nature of the institution
- Knowledge of higher education law and an understanding of the educational mission of the college or university
- Generally lower costs than attorneys who bill by the hour
- Familiarity with members of the college or university community and greater knowledge of current institutional concerns
- Practice of the principles of "preventive law" that can help to reduce exposure to lawsuits in the short and long haul

On the other hand, in-house attorneys may lack certain highly specialized knowledge and skills (National Association of College and University Business Officers, 1982) in fields such as patents or taxation. Some institutions separately employ counsel in these fields, just as they employ "risk managers" who may or may not be legal counsel.

Outside Counsel. This option may be better suited to smaller institutions or those without frequent need for legal services. A private law firm may provide legal guidance as the need arises and thus be more economical. There are advantages in this, such as:

- Specialists can be selected to handle precise needs.
- Attorneys will have experience with local court practices.
- Access to expertise and legal networking can be obtained.

On the other hand, the services of outside counsel may become expensive because fees are billed at hourly rates. Furthermore, the institution will be one of many clients and may not receive immediate attention. With only intermittent contact with the institution, outside counsel also may not have the opportunity to practice preventive law.

Is there a happy medium? Instead of retaining either in-house counsel or outside counsel exclusively, trustees may wish to combine both types of legal assistance. For instance, they may find that using in-house counsel for institutional matters and outside counsel for litigation and other special issues can be the most effective form of representation.

It deserves saying that trustees who are practicing attorneys and law faculty have often in the past provided legal services as an adjunct to their other responsibilities, with or without compensation. There are major disadvantages in continuing this practice. Aside from doubts about the adequacy of service, there is usually a conflict of interest per se in such practices. It is important for trustees to maintain independence of judgment to be effective, and any attempt to serve as both attorney and trustee severely compromises this independence. Although opinion may vary on this subject, as a general matter the practice is to be discouraged.

Role and Use of Counsel

Who should be considered the actual client? After all, within a college or university a number of possibilities exist: the institution as a whole, the governing board, the administration, the faculty, the student body, the alumni, and others. *Trustees and administrators must recognize that counsel's primary loyalty is to the college or university itself.*

Because counsel works chiefly with trustees and administrators, however, these constituents generally perceive themselves as the clients. As a consequence, legal counsel in some cases may be placed in awkward or inappropriate situations that pose an ethical problem or conflict of interest. In these situations, separate counsel may be required.

In the case of a board's consideration of whether to terminate or dismiss the institution's chief executive, by contrast, the governing board would be the client. In such a case, indeed most cases, the board *is* the institution in a legal sense.

Should counsel play a policy-making role? Some trustees believe that an attorney should ordinarily assume a passive role in the decision-making process; that is, counsel should be called upon only to facilitate, explain, or defend policies promulgated by the board. Confining counsel solely to this reactive role, however, may be too rigid.

Trustees should consider using counsel in a preventive capacity (Weeks, 1980). If attorneys are consulted early in the decision-making process, they will be able to advise trustees about any potential exposure to legal challenge. In this manner, counsel can assist the administration and board in achieving an intended policy's objective within legally appropriate options. If counsel is used in this way, however, there is a fine line between having counsel *apprise* the administration and board of legal ramifications and having counsel *make* policy. It is not the function of counsel to choose alternatives or decide policies. These prerogatives must remain with the board and chief executive.

Evaluation of Legal Counsel

How do trustees evaluate their attorneys? Trustees employ specific criteria in evaluating other aspects of institutional policies and practices, and legal counsel should not be immune. As with all methods of evaluation, the parameters should be clear, concise, and communicated to those who will be evaluated.

The grounds on which counsel is judged will, of course, be quite specific to the relationship between the attorneys and the institution. No list can be exhaustive, but some matters that the board may wish to consider include:

• *What does the institution need?* The choice whether or not and how to involve legal counsel, whatever the form, belongs to the board. A needs assessment, often in conjunction with counsel, is the first step to any evaluation.

• *Has counsel achieved the board's objectives? If not, why?* The outcome of a particular case cannot be guaranteed, but the trustees should expect thorough preparation and effective advocacy. For example: Is counsel prompt in responding to inquiries from the trustees or administration? Is counsel responsive to these inquiries? Does counsel present the institution with an evaluation of alternatives?

• *Has counsel achieved the board's objectives within established time and budgetary constraints?* Counsel should have clear guidelines as to these and other limitations. Legal costs, like other institutional costs, should be monitored.

• *What is the relationship of counsel to the institution?* The board's expectations will be quite different depending on the task at hand and who is called to address it. In general, in-house or outside counsel are expected to keep the interests of the institution foremost in mind, alerting the trustees and administrators to possible changes in the law, and taking a long-term view of the legal solutions available. Counsel hired to address specific issues, such as development and fund raising, on the other hand, would be expected to achieve more limited goals.

College and university trustees in both the public and private sectors of higher education must recognize that we live in a litigious society and that now more than ever legal issues affect the activities of educational institutions. As the guardians of the institution with the ultimate responsibility for its well-being, the board and each of the trustees individually must educate themselves about these legal issues and how to deal with the issues. The board should have a basic understanding of legal liability and the legal standards that apply to the board's operation. The board should also be confident in its ability to use legal counsel to address legal concerns, ideally before they become problems. Effective policies and good administrative practices can go far to minimize legal liability and allow the institution to achieve its goals.

CHAPTER 5

Planning for
Strategic
Decision Making

Joel W. Meyerson
Sandra L. Johnson

Strategic planning is the process of continuous adaptation to a changing environment. It involves periods of analysis, creativity, negotiation, and implementation. Although the process may vary—and in fact should be tailored to the needs of each institution—its ultimate goal is effective action.

There are many approaches to strategic planning. Our objective is to present a multiple-perspective model that borrows significantly from the literature on planning in the higher education, nonprofit, and corporate sectors. Although strategic planning by business organizations falls in and out of favor, it is critical to the future health of the academic enterprise because there are few commonly accepted performance measures set by the market. Instead, trustees and executives must rely on self-analysis, noting the satisfaction of key constituents within the institution and the institution's financial stability and public image.

Key Issues That Decision Makers Face

Strategic thinking has never been more important to the future success of our nation's colleges and universities. These institutions face significant management and academic challenges that will require making difficult resource allocation decisions. Financing operating and capital needs is likely to be one of the most challenging management issues. Revenue constraints will include:

- Changing demographic profiles and increasing demands on institutionally funded student financial aid programs
- Moderating tuition after a decade of annual increases that exceeded inflation
- Weakening financial support from federal and state governments
- Uncertain and increasingly volatile charitable giving and investment returns

To compensate for these constraints, institutions will have to control costs for utilities, equipment, and supplies for research and operating facilities, among other capital items. Salaries and benefits also will be a major challenge in the 1990s, especially given predicted faculty shortages in many disciplines and the size of the staff needed to administer institutions of higher learning. Another concern will be managing aging facilities and finding ways to fund their renewal and replacement.

Academic issues also are likely to assume greater strategic importance in the 1990s. These issues include serving a diverse student body, improving academic productivity, encouraging more students to pursue doctoral degrees to ensure an adequate supply of qualified faculty, renewing the institution's commitment to teaching, and continuing to enhance the curriculum so that students are prepared for life in the twenty-first century.

Given the significance of these management and academic issues, strategy formation will be an increasingly important tool on America's campuses. One of its objectives is to focus an institution's resources on the areas in which the institution has the greatest comparative advantage instead of diffusing them broadly. In this way, quality can be maintained or even improved while costs are reduced.

Role of Trustees in Strategic Decision Making

Making strategic decisions about the future direction of an institution is one of the trustees' key roles. Strategy promotes an institution's goals and objectives. It requires knowledge about the current environment as well as a vision for the future. Trustees can provide a perspective often unavailable elsewhere in the institution.

Trustees may be more objective about an institution's internal strengths and weaknesses and have a wide exposure to the external environment. Such a vantage point enables them to help management establish a clear mission and then evaluate its accomplishment. Trustees are personally dedicated to the long-term health of the institution, a commitment backed by significant expenditures of time and expertise. Their long-term outlook and objectivity and the administration's working knowledge of higher education make a valuable combination.

The active participation of the trustees is crucial in the strategic process. However, the most successful outcome is likely to result from an informed partnership of the board, key administrators, and faculty. One group cannot form a strategic vision and inspire the institution to realize it without the active cooperation of the others.

The Planning Process

Among theorists and practitioners alike, there is considerable disagreement over the best approach for developing and implementing strategy. Some favor a formal process that relies on analytical tools and methodologies. Others favor a behavioral approach that takes organizational politics into account and makes use of negotiation. Debate also centers on whether strategy should be a deliberate, active management process or a learned experience that emerges from past actions.

Planning groups may want to tailor the twelve-step process that follows to their own institutions, or they may want to choose an altogether different method from among those in the literature on strategic planning. According to Henry Mintzberg, "Effective strategies show up in the strangest places and develop through the most unexpected means. There is no one best way to make strategy" (1987, p. 70).

1. *Initiate and plan the project.* The first step is to form a planning group composed of board members, administrators, and

faculty. Their task is to prepare a detailed work plan, assign responsibilities, and establish a timetable for the project.

2. *Develop a preliminary mission statement.* An institution's mission is its purpose. Developing a mission statement is the starting point as well as the product of the strategic planning process. According to John Carver, "The most important work of any governing board is to create and re-create the reason for organizational existence. . . . It is a perpetual obligation, deserving of the majority of board time and energy" (1990, p. 56).

Defining the mission of an institution of higher learning may appear deceptively obvious: colleges and universities educate students, perform public service, and may also conduct research. However, preparing a good mission statement requires extensive discussion and analysis of the institution's values and traditions, unique characteristics, geographical market, relationships with and obligations to stakeholders, and relative emphasis on teaching, research, and service.

3. *Develop preliminary plans for academic and administrative units.* Planning groups from each major administrative and academic unit (for example, admissions, accounting, chemistry departments, engineering schools, and so on) should be formed to frame strategies and identify resource requirements for each area based on the institution's preliminary mission statement. The preliminary plans may include the purpose, goals, priorities, and current market position of each unit.

4. *Assess the external environment.* Political, economic, social, and technological trends—or PESTs—increasingly affect the competitive position and financial health of America's colleges and universities. Given the diverse backgrounds of trustees and their broad exposure to the external market, their talents can be used very effectively to monitor environmental changes and interpret data in the following four areas:

Political: state and federal support for research, education, and financial aid

Economic: inflation, family incomes, local and national economy

Social: public values, local and national demographics, supply of faculty, immigration and migration trends

Technological: information technology, telecommunications, improvements in machinery and equipment, innovations in physical plant operations, and toxic waste pollution control.

Planning groups should not overlook the increasing globalization of the world's economies when they consider political, economic, social, and technological trends. The following global influences affect higher education: foreign students, foreign-trained faculty, international study programs, overseas research partners, and foreign investment opportunities.

Planners may also want to consider the higher education "industry" as part of their assessment of the external environment. According to Michael Porter, "Competitive strategy is the search for a competitive position in an industry, the fundamental arena in which competition occurs" (1985, p. 1). He describes the following five forces that shape an industry, and we have added some considerations for colleges and universities:

- *Intensity of rivalry among competitors.* Colleges and universities operate in a highly competitive market.
- *Threat of new entrants.* Higher education is a mature "industry"; it may be more difficult to establish new institutions than it was several decades ago.
- *Threat of substitutes.* Public institutions could be substitutes for private colleges and universities. Foreign institutions of higher learning may be substitutes for U.S. colleges and universities.
- *Bargaining power of buyers.* Determinants include the price sensitivity of consumers (usually students and their families) given perceived differences in quality between institutions.
- *Bargaining power of suppliers.* Determinants include the concentration of suppliers, including faculty. Faculty members— especially "superstars" and those in the hard-to-hire fields— may be able to command a premium given the inadequate supply.

Within the external environment, colleges and universities may choose to pursue one of the three strategies that Porter (1985) has described. The first strategy is *price leadership*. Public institutions can offer lower tuition prices than private universities and often compete on this basis. Private institutions may function as price leaders within their peer group.

Organizations that compete by offering unique products or services follow the *differentiation* strategy. Although these organizations cannot ignore price, they may charge a premium because of the perceived uniqueness of their service, marketing, means of delivery, or other factors. Many institutions of higher learning pursue this strategy, either for the entire institution or for particular academic programs. For example, an institution that has a leading economics program, a renowned biology department, or an eminent law school is pursuing a differentiation strategy.

In the *focus* strategy, organizations select a segment of the market and tailor their products or services to fit that niche exclusively. Schools with strong religious affiliations or those that historically serve a black student body are following a focus strategy.

5. *Assess the internal environment.* Every organization has areas of excellence and mediocrity. The objective of an institutional assessment is to identify both strengths (the core competencies of the institution) to build upon and weaknesses to minimize. Appropriate areas for investigation will vary from institution to institution, but may include internal assessments and comparative analyses of the following (Taylor, Meyerson, Morrell, and Park, 1991):

> *Student body:* applications, acceptances, selectivity, matriculation, retention rates, diversity, geographical representation, alumni profile
>
> *Faculty and administration:* composition, growth, diversity, tenure, salaries and benefits, morale, ratio of faculty and staff to students
>
> *Academic programs:* expenditures, quality of faculty, library holdings, computing resources, facilities and equipment, demand, comparative advantage, scope of offerings
>
> *Research:* funding sources; quality of researchers, facilities, and equipment

Facilities: operating expenditures, deferred maintenance, planned construction, constraints of building usages

Tuition and fees: annual increases, internal and external financial aid

Other unrestricted resources: levels of past giving, size and number of gifts, sources of contributions, planned capital campaigns, level of endowment income, investment mix and return, size of endowment and quasi endowment

Results of operations: performance results, sources of revenue, cash-flow requirements, expenditures by category, overall financial flexibility

Satisfying "customers" or "stakeholders" is becoming increasingly important as more colleges and universities institute cost-containment and productivity programs. Many of these programs also focus on improving quality as it is perceived by an institution's stakeholders. A *stakeholder* is any person or group that competes for an institution's attention, services, and resources, or is affected by its output (Bryson, 1989). An independent institution's stakeholders may include students, alumni, faculty, staff, unions, trustees, grantors, suppliers, lenders, religious groups, and other institutions of higher learning.

Different stakeholders often judge an organization's performance using very different criteria. For example, students may be interested in small classes, the quality of campus life, the cost of their education, and the marketability of their degree. On the other hand, faculty may want capable assistants, adequate compensation, and sufficient time for research. An important part of the stakeholder analysis is determining how well the institution is performing according to the criteria of its various stakeholders. This analysis may reveal valuable information about an institution's internal strengths and weaknesses.

One model that the planning group may want to use to evaluate academic programs is the grid that was originally devised by the Boston Consulting Group and then adapted for higher education by George Keller (1983). Keller's model includes four categories:

- *Stars:* high quality and high student demand
- *Cows:* high quality and low student demand
- *Question marks:* low quality and high student demand
- *Dogs:* low quality and low student demand

Institutions may choose to nourish their "stars," phase out their "dogs," retain their "cows," and improve the quality of their "question marks." One limitation of this model is that quality and demand are very subjective and difficult to measure.

6. *Develop a vision of success for the institution.* A vision of success describes what an institution would look like if it were to achieve its full potential. The vision statement should be challenging and inspire employees to work towards a common goal. Most importantly, it should be communicated throughout the organization.

Sometimes called strategic intent, a vision is common to many successful organizations. According to Hamel and Prahalad (1989, p. 67), "Strategic intent implies a sizable stretch for an organization. Current capabilities and resources will not suffice. This forces the organization to be inventive, to make the most of limited resources. Whereas the traditional view of strategy focuses on the degree of fit between existing resources and current opportunities, strategic intent creates an extreme misfit between resources and ambitions. Top management then challenges the organization to close the gap by systematically building new advantages."

The planning group may want to consider the following questions to help determine its vision of success for the institution: "What special role do we play in America's higher education network? . . . What comparative advantages do we have over approximately similar places? . . . What academic fields and college services will be most needed by the country and our region in the next decade? With our traditions, endowment, location, and collection of faculty and administrators . . . what should our college aspire to be 10 years from now?" (Keller, 1983, p. 121).

7. *Review preliminary plans for academic and administrative units.* The planning groups from each major academic and administrative unit should reconvene to review their preliminary plans based on the analysis of the internal and external environment as well as on the vision of success identified in step six.

8. *Identify strategic alternatives and determine the institution's strategic plan.* Strategic alternatives, or challenges about which planners must make fundamental choices, often emerge from a review of the internal and external environments. This analysis may reveal potential changes in the market or the possibility of some event that will present threats or opportunities and affect an institution's ability to achieve its mission.

One good approach to identifying strategic alternatives is for the planning group to hold a brainstorming session. The most important ground rule for this session is that participants should be encouraged to suggest all ideas that come to mind without analyzing them, no matter how improbable some of them may seem. A facilitator who leads the discussion and writes down all of the ideas that emerge can be particularly useful.

The planning group may then want to narrow down the list of ideas to ten to twenty-five, if possible, reaching general consensus about which ideas should be included. Next, the costs and benefits of implementing each alternative should be weighed. This analysis will help to focus the planning group on the most important ideas. Few institutions have enough resources to fully support all deserving activities, so it is best to concentrate resources in the areas deemed to be most strategically important to the institution.

After this analysis, the list of strategic alternatives should be reviewed once more to cut it from ten to twenty-five ideas to a more manageable number. The final list of strategic alternatives will form the basis of the institution's strategic plan. The planning group also may want to revisit the institution's preliminary mission statement, which may need to be revised to reflect the new strategic plan.

Identifying strategic alternatives and formulating the institution's strategic plan can be difficult as well as exciting. Doing so involves conflicts about what should be done, how it should be done, and who will do it. Open discussion, negotiation skills, and strong leadership are critical to the success of the process.

9. *Operationalize the strategic plan.* The next step is to develop action plans that link the institution's strategic plan with the institution's budget. Implementing the strategic plan may require that the institution restructure its organization or renovate its facil-

ities, for example. Budget cuts in some areas may be necessary to free up funds for new initiatives. The importance of linking the budget and the strategic plan should not be underestimated. Academic, administrative, and trustee leaders may have carefully crafted a strategic plan, but the allocation of resources determines the course that is taken.

10. *Develop detailed implementation plans for each academic and administrative unit.* The next step is to develop action plans and measurable goals for the institution as a whole as well as for individual schools, academic departments, and administrative functions. Competencies in academic programs as well as in finance, technology, student support, admissions, development, and so forth contribute to an institution's success.

11. *Introduce the strategic plan and build consensus.* The planning group may want to hold sessions with key constituents to present the plan to the university community. Strategic planning will not work unless its goals are widely communicated and accepted by trustees, administrators, and faculty. According to George Keller, "Politically most of the key people need to be on board the strategy train when it leaves the station" (1983, p. 149). As a result, the planning group should communicate—and build commitment to—the themes of the strategic plan at critical points in their development. Frequent, informal discussions between key campus leaders may be more effective than formal planning meetings and documents (Schmidtlein and Milton, 1988–89).

12. *Review the planning process and monitor performance.* The planning group should develop measurable goals—that is, benchmarks—for all major areas, including financial position, campus facilities, curriculum, faculty and staff salaries and benefits, student life, enrollment, and so forth. Although quantitative measures may be harder to develop than in the for-profit world, "performance is the ultimate test of any institution" (Drucker, 1990, p. 139).

Trustees should regularly monitor the institution's performance against the established benchmarks and also ask the following question: Is this action plan and allocation of resources helping us achieve our long-term goals? Planning is an ongoing process that does not stop with the development of a single strategic plan;

rather, the plan needs to be retooled as new strengths and weaknesses as well as threats and opportunities present themselves.

Impediments to Planning

Higher education is not an easy environment in which to implement strategic planning successfully. Departments operate autonomously, different campuses may have very different needs and characters, decision making is often very political, and institutions are loosely organized and resistant to change. Many colleges and universities have tried strategic planning but not all of these efforts have been successful. For example, one study of planning in higher education indicated that few participants could describe specific benefits that resulted from their planning processes. Many institutions did not have good data on external trends or internal capabilities. Faculty members thought they were ineffectively involved, while administrators thought that faculty members were only interested in protecting their own interests. Planning documents provided limited operational guidance (Schmidtlein and Milton, 1988–89).

One authority on strategic planning and management studied two hundred companies and identified the following major mistakes to avoid (Koteen, 1989). Although this list was developed for corporations, it could apply to colleges and universities as well.

1. Assuming that planning can be delegated to a planner
2. Focusing on current problems to the exclusion of long-range plans
3. Developing goals that are not suitable for formulating long-range plans
4. Failing to involve major line personnel in the planning process
5. Failing to use strategic plans as standards for evaluating performance
6. Fostering an internal environment resistant to planning
7. Failing to integrate planning with the management process
8. Emphasizing formality rather than simplicity, flexibility, and creativity

9. Failing to review long-range plans with departmental and divisional heads
10. Rejecting the planning process through intuitive top-management decisions that conflict with the formal plan

Strategic planning is not a panacea. Answers to difficult problems do not always arise, and solutions—when they can be found—are never perfect. Sometimes big payoffs do occur; more often, however, strategic planning may help an organization avoid major mistakes or make incremental changes that are beneficial over the long-term.

Critical Success Factors

At least three factors are critical to the success of strategic decision making in the academic community: consensus, leadership, and managing the process of change. Effectively used, these factors will help institutions successfully overcome the impediments described above.

Faculty, trustees, and administrators share power on college campuses. "We need to think of the management of schools . . . as a partnership between the board and the professional staff. I use a side-by-side organizational chart, with the board of trustees in one column and the faculty in another column, and the president's office and various members of the administrative team in between. All three are centers of power, and centers of authority" (Drucker, 1990, p. 171).

The most successful approach to strategic decision making may be a blend of centralized and decentralized planning and leadership. Trustees are often in the best position to identify and address changes in the external environment. Trustees and senior managers will need to work together to identify institutionwide issues, allocate resources according to strategic priorities, initiate broad changes, or make decisions about eliminating or expanding academic or administrative programs. Faculty members also have a vision for the school, and they are most knowledgeable about developments in their fields and closest to students. They are in the best position to develop departmental plans, budgets, and curriculum changes.

Leadership is a critical success factor in any strategic planning process. A champion can provide the energy, momentum, and commitment necessary to carry the process through. Leadership is particularly critical if the institution must change to achieve its goals or if its external environment is unstable. Often this leadership can come from the board. Managing change is the subject of much thought, discussion, and writing because most organizations and individuals resist change. "A fundamental dilemma of strategy making is the need to reconcile the forces for stability and for change—to focus efforts and gain operating efficiencies on the one hand, yet adapt and maintain currency with a changing external environment on the other" (Mintzberg, 1987, p. 71).

If the institution must change to succeed, the seven-S framework can help trustees conceptualize the process. This framework consists of three technical or "hard" S's—strategy, structure, and systems—and four behavioral or "soft" S's—skills, staff, style of management, and shared values. Leaders must involve all seven S's to produce constructive change in an organization (Koteen, 1989).

One of the benefits of a clearly defined and communicated strategic plan is that it can inspire internal and external constituents to achieve common goals. Public disillusionment with higher education set in during the 1980s, and leaders will need to work hard to win support during the 1990s. Creating a strategic vision for the future as well as action plans to implement it, and communicating the plans widely, can help foster support for an institution.

Trustees can play a critical leadership role in strategic decision making by setting the tone and direction of the institution's plan. Quality is the watchword here as in other areas of institutional management. "For in the long run, as surely as excellence ends with clients, patients, students, or other customers, it begins with governance" (Carver, 1990, p. 211).

PART TWO

Fulfilling
Board Functions

Serving on a board of trustees of an independent college or university is one of the most revered of all volunteer initiatives in American society. Unfortunately, however, most citizens probably accept this calling without fully knowing what is expected of them or how difficult and challenging it will prove to be. Conscientious trusteeship is stimulating and enormously rewarding, but it requires a deep and abiding commitment and a willingness to learn how to exercise trusteeship effectively.

The ten chapters in Part Two are devoted to most of the key governing board responsibilities. Each chapter explores the boundaries of governing board and chief executive responsibilities—where the responsibilities are shared and where they should be distinguished from one another. The line between the board's role in "deciding" policy and the administration's role in "implementing" policy is often fuzzy and must be negotiated and renegotiated over time; these chapters provide helpful guideposts.

One of the most difficult concepts to grasp, especially for new trustees and regents, is that of "shared governance," a concept unique to academic trusteeship. Defining when and how the myriad of internal and external constituencies can and should be consulted on what issues surely constitutes one of the board's most challenging responsibilities, if effective leadership and a clear sense of institutional direction are to prevail. This is a particularly perplexing task in a period of declining resources. Several chapters in this section address these particular matters, but the net contribution of all of the chapters is their focus on how the inevitable ambiguities of academic governance can be reduced to reasonable clarity.

CHAPTER 6

Responsibilities of
the Governing Board

John W. Nason

If higher education is as essential to the health of the country as most citizens believe, and if governing boards constitute "the keystone in the governance structure of higher education" (Carnegie Foundation for the Advancement of Teaching, 1982, p. 72) as most students of the subject hold, then trustees embrace crucial responsibilities. The trustee role is complex and difficult, time consuming and rewarding. Four aspects of trusteeship need to always be kept in mind.

First is the tension—that sometimes bursts into conflict—between the legal structure in which the board as "owner" has final authority and the operating pattern in which authority is widely shared with faculty; administrators; sometimes with students; and in some church-related institutions, with denominational leaders. Shared governance defies conventional notions of organizational hierarchy. It fluctuates with the cultural temper of the times. It varies with the type of educational institution. But it is a fact of academic life, and trustees have an important role in making it work.

Second, trustees hold assets of the institution *in trust*. They are fiduciaries whose responsibility is to maximize the mandated benefits to the beneficiaries. Those beneficiaries include not only the current student body, but also future generations of students, the faculty and staff employed by the institution, and the society that supports the institution. Both private and public colleges and universities are chartered by the state and granted tax exemption on the premise that they serve the public good. This means that trustees need to look beyond the self-interest of the individual college or university to consider what is good for higher education as a whole and for society at large.

Third, in an earlier and simpler era, trustees were able to manage as well as govern their colleges and universities. That is no longer desirable or possible, and the sporadic efforts of misguided trustees to interfere with management usually end up creating more and worse problems. In carrying out their fiduciary responsibilities, trustees must keep their eyes on the long-term objectives and on management's success in reaching the objectives. There is no clear line between policy and management. Each board and administration must negotiate the "gray areas" where policy and management infringe on one another. Thoughtful and experienced trustees, however, recognize the difference and stay on the policy side of the line.

Finally, it is important to recognize the distinction between the governing board and the individual trustees that it comprises. The board governs the institution; individual trustees do not. The board hires, supports, and, if necessary, fires the president. The board approves the athletic policy. The board, usually through delegated authority, appoints the faculty. Individual trustees have no authority to do any of these things. At the end of this chapter, I shall discuss the responsibilities of individual trustees, but first let us examine the responsibilities of governing boards as such.

Appointing the President

Because the president is the central and normally the most powerful figure in a college or university, the selection of the president is the most important single decision for any board. During the selection process, divergent views on the nature and goals of the institution are strongly expressed. Internal conflicts, whether open or suppressed during the previous regime, get played out. In choosing the president, the board is taking a long-term gamble on the direction and future of the college or university. The board needs to know where it wants to go, and it needs help with this decision.

An analysis of institutional needs and future goals should be the cooperative work of faculty, staff, students, alumni, and trustees, and it should precede the process of search and selection. Various constituencies will want a voice in the selection. Often these groups agree on the kind of leadership they want, but different points of view may result in different preferences. Faculty may want a scholar who understands teaching and research, students want someone sympathetic to their youth culture, and alumni opt for a fund raiser who is good at public relations and an advocate of the extracurricular activities that loom so large in their memories. All these groups need to be consulted, and representatives of all or some of them may serve on the search and selection committee.

The president who is chosen may or may not be hail-fellow-well-met to students and alumni, colleague to the faculty, and team operator to the administrative staff, but he or she is not directly responsible to any of them. The president is the appointed agent of the governing board and directly responsible to it. The final selection of the new president is as difficult as it is important. It needs to be done with great care. Chapter Seven, written by a knowledgeable and sensitive student of the academic scene, explores the presidential selection process.

Supporting the President

Academic communities have sometimes been likened to organized anarchies. The president is buffeted by conflicting expectations and demands, and the job is exciting, demanding, occasionally rewarding, but all too often frustrating. In 1982, the Association of Governing Boards appointed a Commission on Strengthening Presidential Leadership, the findings and recommendations of which are found in two useful volumes, *Presidents Make a Difference* (Commission on Strengthening Presidential Leadership, 1984) and *The Many Lives of Academic Presidents* (Kerr and Gade, 1986).

The authors paint a disturbing picture: not only a short average tenure of seven years, but also a significant percentage of discouraged and unhappy presidents. All presidents need the support of their boards.

A wise board chair can save a president from serious mistakes and even catastrophe by giving thoughtful and sensitive advice. It may be a matter of rearranging the president's priorities. It may be recognizing that no president is equally good in all areas of operation and insisting that the total administrative structure be reorganized or buttressed.

Supporting the president includes being concerned about his or her physical and emotional well-being. The volume of demands on the president's time often precludes, or can seem to the president to preclude, time for relaxation. The board, and particularly the chair, should watch for signs of exhaustion, insist on adequate holidays, and make certain that the president has enough staff support to ease the burdens of office. The board's concern should also extend to the president's spouse and to the domestic arrangements for the president's family. Kauffman puts it bluntly: "Given the substantial investment a governing board makes in finding a president, it is simply good management for the board to conserve this important resource. Leadership is a scarce and precious asset that should not be taken for granted" (1974, p. 61).

Monitoring the President

College and university presidents are public figures. In all institutions, the president makes decisions and takes actions that affect the lives of faculty, students, and staff and that influence the response of parents, alumni, donors, and friends of the institution. Like it or not, the president's performance is judged, day in and day out, by those with whom he or she comes in contact. The closer boards are to their colleges, the more opportunity members will have to see presidents in action and assess their performance.

Assessment of the president is clearly essential. The president is the board's agent, responsible for carrying out board-approved policies and managing the institution with due regard for the best interests of all concerned. Are the policies of the board being honored? Does the president have vision? Is the administration efficient? Because people tend to judge institutions by their presidents, is the president a satisfactory symbol? Without assessment, it is impossible to provide the support discussed in the preceding section—so without assessment, the board evades a major responsibility.

How will trustees find out how the president is doing? That is the subject of Chapter Eight, but a few generalizations are relevant here. As colleges and universities have grown larger and more complex, the trend has been from informal monitoring to more formal assessment of the president. This is probably inevitable, but it is dangerous. If ineptly done, it can exacerbate the difficulties inherent in the president's position. Term appointments seem to be the current pattern, and they encourage more "official" reviews of the president. Whether it is formal or informal, monitoring the president needs to be done with great delicacy, and the results, unless they lead to termination, should remain with the president and the board.

Considering that the board's expectations constitute the criteria by which the president will be judged, it is surprising how often the board fails to communicate its expectations to the president. Trustees may think that they make clear to presidents-elect what is expected of them, but the presidents report that too often they are left in the dark (Neff and Leondar, 1992). One of the arguments for term appointments is that they give the board and president the opportunity to review the situation and to decide whether circumstances have so changed that different arrangements should be made.

Insisting on a Clear Institutional Mission

Every college and university was created to serve one or more specific purposes; to provide an educated ministry, to prepare citizens who could cope with the problems and prospects of a democratic society, to train young people in the arts and skills necessary for an honest living, to safeguard the true faith, to train schoolteachers, or—simply stated but not so simply achieved—to acquaint young people with their cultural traditions. Over the years and under the pressure of changing conditions, these original purposes have frequently been modified. Local institutions have become regional or national. Church-related colleges have sought to escape the dominance of their denominations and the limitation in clientele. Normal schools have become full-fledged institutions of arts and sciences. Colleges primarily concerned with teaching aspire to become research universities. Sometimes these changes are triggered by new social needs and sometimes by the urge to improve the institution's position in the academic pecking order.

There has been both loss and gain in the churning shifts in institutional purpose. The drive for upward mobility has raised the level of postsecondary education in America. The zeal that spawned so many small denominational colleges in the nineteenth century was often accompanied by limited vision and woefully inadequate resources. The struggling institutions had to enlarge their scope to survive. The result was an unintended process of homogenization, as some institutions sloughed off what made them distinct while others added new programs and services in the struggle for students and funds.

Someone—namely, the board of trustees—needs to ask: What is the mission of our college or university? What makes it distinct from other institutions? What difference would it make—and to whom—if it ceased to exist? Does it serve a special clientele? Does it fill a real gap and meet real needs? "The first thing an institution needs to do to start on a conspicuously higher course," writes Greenleaf (1974, p. 25), "is to state clearly where it wants to go, whom it wants to serve, and how it expects those served directly, as well as society at large, to benefit from the service."

Faculty, deans, and presidents—the professionals of the academic world—must carry the main burden of articulating a mission statement. For the most part, however, faculty are too preoccupied with their particular disciplines to be much concerned with the broader aspects of educational purpose, and presidents and deans are likely to be so overwhelmed with the immediate problems of running an institution that they tend to postpone what they recognize to be the larger and more important issues in favor of dealing with the less significant but more urgent ones. This is where trustees play an essential role. They cannot write the mission statement, and they should not try. But they can insist that the statement be written in such a way as to meet their approval. Once agreement has been reached, the statement should be made public. Until it is changed, it should be the lighthouse by which all decisions are guided.

Insisting on Long-Range Planning

Long-range plans are the strategies for achieving the institution's mission. The board's responsibility is to insist that the administration prepare such plans and participate in their final form.

A wise and experienced trustee of the University of North Carolina, William Dees, visited the University of Illinois in the early 1970s with a group from his board. David Henry (then president of the University of Illinois) had some advice for the North Carolina delegation along this line: do not worry about governing the university—you will govern it somehow and do it pretty well— worry about planning. Most boards of trustees, he suggested, particularly the big ones with overwhelming responsibilities, never get around to planning. They are absorbed by immediate issues and neglect the really important job of determining where the university should go and how it should get there.

Strategic planning is described in detail in Chapter Five. Here, suggestions for a few areas of investigation and how to proceed will suffice. Board members should ask a series of pertinent questions about the institution's future and insist on well-supported answers. For example, where does the president think the institution should be ten years down the road, and how does he or she plan to get there? How does the college or university compare with other institutions of the same type or in the same class? What needs to be changed to improve its standing? Over the next decade, where will the students come from to fit whatever size is foreseen? What new departments, schools, or divisions will enhance the institution's contribution to society? What programs or activities should be modified or eliminated? What additional physical facilities should be in place ten years hence? What will the budget look like? How will it be met? What changes will be needed in the ratio of sources of income among student fees, endowment income, gifts, and government grants?

The board will need to set aside time to deal with such questions. Charles Nelson (1979) offers four valuable suggestions. First, put the big policy questions near the top of the agenda so that they can be debated while members are fresh. Second, at least once a year, include on the agenda a major problem that sooner or later will demand a board decision. Discussion without the need for immediate decision will prepare the way for wise treatment when a decision must be made. Third, when the time comes for a major policy decision, the board should have before it not only the president's recommendation with supporting arguments but also alternative recommendations with the arguments for them. This allows the trustees to make decisions with full knowledge of the options. Fourth, every agenda item should face "the harsh test of relevance." Each item included must need board attention, and the amount of board attention should be determined by the relative importance of the item.

Reviewing the Educational Program

Teaching and research are the raison d'être of private higher education. In church-related colleges, teaching often includes the preservation and propagation of doctrines and behavior that are favored by the supporting church. Research is an elastic term for all kinds of intellectual activities. If trustees are ultimately responsible for the well-being and performance of their institutions, then they are responsible for the educational program.

It was not always so. In the eighteenth and nineteenth centuries, the founders of colleges and universities knew what they wanted, but gradually they delegated authority for academic affairs to presidents who in this century have largely yielded control of strictly academic affairs to the faculty. Conventional practice, at least until recently, has assigned responsibility for fiscal affairs and physical plant to the trustees, while reserving responsibility for the academic program to the president and faculty.

This practice makes no sense. How can trustees make intelligent decisions about physical facilities without knowing the changes occurring in the academic program and the pressures generated by those changes, a changing student body, and the institution's competition? How can they make intelligent decisions about the budget without knowing which academic programs are being expanded and which curtailed, how the teaching load has changed, how important the new student or faculty support activities are? In the final analysis, the group that sets the budget shapes the program.

Quite apart from financial control, if the trustees must approve the institution's ultimate goals and strategic plans, they must approve the educational program as part of those long-term objectives. What should be the ratio, for example, between teaching and research? Who is to decide whether a school of business administration or a department of classical archeology should be developed, or if classics and anthropology should be phased out? Should the college concentrate on bright students with high SAT scores or open its doors to students of lesser academic ability? What should be the principles and procedures for granting tenure? The trustees' role with respect to these and many other important academic issues is outlined in Chapter Twelve and examined in detail in *Trustee Responsibility for Academic Affairs* (Chait, Mortimer, Taylor, and Wood, 1985).

Two cautions should be noted with regard to the board's responsibility for educational programs. First, although the board has final authority, it should listen very carefully to the recommendations of the president. Presidents are presumably selected for their competence as professional educators. They are not infallible, but most know more about education in general and their institution in particular than does the average trustee. Their recommendations should be supported, but only after thorough board scrutiny.

Second, trustees should not meddle with the curriculum. The courses to be taught and their content are the responsibility of the faculty. Trustees may decide for or against a department of music. Having decided for it, they should leave the decisions on what should be taught to the faculty.

Ensuring Good Management

Good management, as we have seen, involves concern for both long-term goals and the programs designed to achieve those goals. Because education is a labor-intensive activity, good management necessitates carefully considered ground rules for the appointment and promotion of faculty and staff. It requires good procedures for recruiting, admitting, and disciplining students. At its heart is good administrative organization. The details are a waste of the board's time, but the board needs to make sure that the organization is efficient and the rights and privileges of all concerned are clearly stated and protected.

Because the trustees hold the institution in trust, they have always felt a special responsibility for its financial health. In the long run, income must equal expenditure if the institution is to survive. Short-term deficits are sometimes preferable to the long-term damage done by sudden, drastic curtailments in personnel and programs. Bank loans or the use of capital funds, such as the endowment, may bridge a temporary crisis. Sooner or later, however, a day of reckoning must come. Many faculty and some presidents who are sensitive to the hardships created by cutbacks are willing to let deficits continue either in the hope that some miracle will happen (a $5 million bequest!) or with the conviction that the needs of the present outweigh those of future generations. The trustees must then decide the relative claims of the present and the future.

When the budget is out of balance, income must be increased or expenses reduced. Retrenchment is never easy and never popular. One of the perennial problems of higher education is the pressure to add new programs and the reluctance to give up old ones. Presidents are often caught in merciless crossfire. They know that retrenchment is necessary. They spend many hours making all areas of the institution, academic and administrative, more efficient. Sooner or later, they arrive at the tough conclusion that cutting a little here and a little there will work only in the short run and that major surgery is the only real solution.

Some faculty and students will always argue that the administration itself is overstaffed and inefficient and that there is really no need for its insensitive and philistine program of curtailment. Other faculty, more realistic about the institution's plight, will agree that amputation is probably necessary, but not in their fields or departments. Here the trustees must come to the support of the president by strengthening his or her hand, perhaps meeting with the most vocal dissidents, and in the end accepting public responsibility for insisting that expenditures be reduced to match income.

The other and more attractive path is that of increasing income. Tuition and other charges to students may be raised, although the current public outcry against tuition increases suggests that we may be coming to the end of this device. Income from the endowment, the management of which is a trustee responsibility, may be increased, but this is an area where trustees need to keep in mind the claims of future generations. Fund-raising campaigns, which virtually every private educational institution runs, may be enlarged, and here the board must clearly take the lead. No trustees of private colleges or universities should consider themselves immune from fund raising. Private institutions cannot survive without donated funds, and every trustee should be prepared to give and solicit money. For some, the gift will have to be small, but it can still set an example for others. For some, access to people with money will be limited, but no trustee is completely exempt. Chapter Eleven outlines trustee fund-raising duties.

Most colleges and universities now have substantial investments in buildings and grounds, and the proper care of these physical assets has always been a continuing concern of the trustees. The business experience of individual trustees has helped many administrations with problems of construction and maintenance. The vision and enthusiasm of trustees have led to some of our most beautiful campuses. In periods of financial stringency, it is tempting to skimp on maintenance to provide better support of the "human element," but in the long run, this may prove very costly. The board has the responsibility to see the whole picture and safeguard the institution's resources. Chapter Nine is a thorough discussion of this critical trustee responsibility.

Preserving Institutional Independence

Since early colonial days, higher education in America has fiercely maintained its freedom from outside interference. The famous 1819 Supreme Court decision in the Dartmouth case confirmed the independence of private colleges from state control. In another case,

150 years later, the Court affirmed "the four essential freedoms of a university: to determine for itself on academic grounds who may teach, what may be taught, how it shall be taught, and who may be admitted to study" (Carnegie Foundation for the Advancement of Teaching, 1982, p. 4).

Independence, however, is not absolute. "Autonomy, in the sense of full self-governance," wrote the members of the Carnegie Commission on Higher Education (1973, p. 17), "does not now exist for American higher education, nor has it existed for a very long time—if ever. Autonomy is limited by the law, by the necessary influences and controls that go along with financial support, and by public policy in areas of substantial public concern. Autonomy in these areas is neither possible nor generally desirable."

Colleges and universities are a special kind of organization, so important to the health of society that outside groups are constantly trying to exploit them and so vulnerable that only watchful and determined boards can protect them. One of the great contributions of the modern college or university that is not always understood and appreciated is its role as a critic of society. It can perform this role only as long as it is protected from those who would silence its criticisms or twist them to serve some ulterior end. This is why academic freedom is so important, why boards of trustees must not permit outside groups or extremists within (such as the radical left during the turbulence of the 1960s and early 1970s) to muzzle the voices that express unpopular opinions.

There are many outside pressures seeking to influence what is taught or to change institutional polices. Donors will sometimes try to attach unacceptable conditions to their gifts. Alumni will sometimes seek to change a college's or university's athletic policy. Influential people will attempt to get special consideration for their friends' children. Business interests may bring pressure to stop research in areas where they fear the results might be detrimental. Both state and federal governments may attach to their support conditions that are an improper invasion of institutional autonomy. In academic governance, as in democratic government, the price of freedom is eternal vigilance.

Relating Campus and Community

The preceding section describes the role of trustees as a buffer between the institution and the surrounding community. Student misbehavior, the appointment of a radical professor, an invitation extended to a controversial speaker, or a losing football team can all invite public attacks. The college officials' defense tends to be discounted as self-serving. This is the time for trustees to speak up in defense of the institution and set the record straight. When they become trustees, people publicly identify themselves with the institution. This identification is important to the college or university, especially if the trustee is someone widely respected in the community. Being above the fray, at least when it originated, trustees are in a stronger position than anyone else to scotch rumors. They can explain what lies behind some controversial policy and note that it has the full approval of the board. They are, or should be, ardent advocates of the institution, equipped to sing its praises whenever possible and ready to do battle on its behalf in times of need.

Sometimes trustees may have to defend a policy with which they do not agree. Trustees may argue as much as they like at board meetings and in private conferences with the president and staff. Indeed, they will not be doing their job if they do not raise questions, challenge decisions, debate policies. But in public they must stand united with the administration. If trustees see the issue as one of principle or if their convictions do not allow them to accept the majority decision, they should resign. Short of that, trustees must maintain a solid front.

Governing boards serve as bridges as well as buffers, not only interpreting the campus to the community but also interpreting the expectations, needs, and changes in society to those whose lives are largely bound up in the academic community. Society is always changing, but established institutions tend to resist change. In part, this resistance is the result of inertia; it is always easier to continue doing what one is accustomed to doing than it is to venture into new fields or try new methods. Inertia is also, however, the result of the self-centeredness of most colleges and universities. Living and working together tends to isolate the members of the academic community. The community can shut itself off from the outside world or disparage the outside world for living by different (and inferior) values.

Therefore, forces producing long-term changes or trends in the outside world often go unnoticed or, if not unnoticed, disregarded. The famous 1954 Supreme Court decision *Brown* v. *Topeka Board of Education* foreshadowed many changes, but outside pressure during the 1960s was necessary to change admission practices and goals. Higher education has not yet made its peace with the implications of a primarily service-oriented postindustrial society. The competition among colleges and universities for students, faculty, public grants, and private gifts is steadily growing. Is that competition in the public interest? "In practice, few private college trustees think of themselves as performing a civic act, although governing boards were originally, as they still are, accountable to the state which charters them" (Wood, 1985, p. 146). Trustees have a responsibility to help keep their institutions relevant. They also have a responsibility for the health and progress of American higher education as a whole.

Serving as a Court of Appeal

At one time, student discipline and faculty appointments and terminations were settled by faculty, deans, and the president. Before World War II, to have an internal dispute be brought to the board for adjudication was rare, and recourse to the courts was almost unheard of. Since then (see Chapter Four for details), both boards and courts have become increasingly involved in the conflicts that arise from our preoccupation with civil rights. Faculty claim discrimination or improper procedure if they are not promoted, given tenure, or reappointed. Students or their parents challenge the right of the faculty and/or administration to expel students or impose other penalties for disciplinary or academic reasons.

Boards of trustees should insist that there be clearly established and publicized codes governing faculty status and student behavior, and these codes should include provisions of due process. Beyond this, there is little that trustees can do but insist that agreed-upon procedures be followed and accept jurisdiction if settlement fails at an earlier stage. The assumption is that, given orderly and fair procedures and intelligent administration, most cases will be resolved before reaching the board. But when one does come before the board, the trustees must decide on the merits of the case. The president and deans may not always be right, and if they are not, the board must be prepared to rule against them. If this happens very often, however, it may indicate that the time has come to look for a new president.

Assessing Board Performance

As we have seen, trustees play a central role in governing the institution and in determining its mission, goals, plans, and programs. They have a responsibility to evaluate the performance of the president, assess the adequacy of the administration as a whole, monitor the institution's progress toward agreed-upon goals, and assess their own contribution and performance. Indeed, the assessment of the president can be more gracefully conducted if it is made part of a review of the governance of the entire institution, the trustees included. Miriam Wood's perceptive analysis (1985) of the role of the board in ten private colleges leaves the reader with the uncomfortable feeling that boards are often more hindrance than help. If so, correction is in order.

Trustees ought to be asking themselves, What are our major responsibilities as trustees? Periodically, they ought to be asking related and frequently avoided questions: How well are we fulfilling our responsibilities? Are we doing things we ought not to do? Are we failing to do things we ought to be doing? Do we have the best possible board for this college or university? How can we bring about a change for the better? Are we spending our time and thought on the right questions? Are our operations (agenda, meetings, and committee structure) clearly designed to maximize our contribution to governance? Do we get the right information in the right amount at the right time? Wood concludes that "a significant and altogether unintended influence of the governing board has been to diminish the office of the presidency" (1985, p. 139). The board must ask, Is that true of our operations? Part Three of this book explores these issues in more detail.

There are various ways of going about this self-assessment. The chair can take the initiative for setting aside some part of one or more regularly scheduled meetings for this kind of review, or the chair can call a special meeting devoted entirely to the board's self-examination. The board can make use of the self-study materials prepared by the Association of Governing Boards in conjunction with or independent of the Board Mentor Program (see Resource C). A special board committee can be appointed to oversee self-assessment. Many institutions have found an outside consultant very helpful. Chapter Twenty outlines the possibilities in more detail. Socrates' famous dictum, "The unexamined life is not worth living," applies to governing boards as well as to individuals.

Responsibilities of Trustees as Individuals

Trusteeship is not a sinecure. It is quite widely and properly viewed as an honor, but to treat it only as such is to dishonor it. Trustees must work at their job. They must be prepared to devote significant time to serving their institutions. They must arrange their schedules to be able to attend meetings. They must do their homework. They should serve on committees. Above all, they must educate themselves (preferably with the help of the administration) about their particular college or university—its history, place in the educational scene, strengths, and problems—and about the state and problems of higher education in general. This education involves study not only of documents that relate to the institution but of the *Chronicle of Higher Education,* one or more educational journals, and an occasional book on the problems or prospects of education. The astute trustee will turn to the president for advice in this area.

Trustees should be prepared to back their interest with financial support. Private colleges and universities always need funds. They are always asking alumni, friends, businesses, and foundations for support. Trustees must take the lead in this appeal. Before asking others for contributions, they must demonstrate the urgency of the request by making their own gifts. As noted earlier, even if the gift has to be small, it is symbolic; in a different way, so is the contribution of the wealthy trustee. Donors will be influenced in their own giving by the leadership or lack of leadership of the trustees. In almost all campaigns, the personal contributions by members of the board will determine the size and success of the venture.

Trustees must be careful to avoid any behavior in which self-interest outweighs the good of the institution. An obvious example would be a case of conflict of interest, such as those examined in Resource E. But there are subtler instances in which an individual trustee promotes his or her private concerns (to reduce or increase minority enrollment; to get a relative or a favorite appointed to the staff or faculty; to fire the president, a dean, or a faculty member whom the trustee dislikes) by indirect methods. Any or all of these issues may be legitimate topics for discussion if they are out in the open. Politicking, however, leads to trouble, as does grandstanding; that is, when an individual trustee tries to speak for the institution or separate his or her position from that adopted by the board. Only the chair, the president, or designated members should speak for the board. Public statements by individual board members on current issues or policies still under consideration create confusion and exacerbate controversy.

What is needed above all from the individual trustee is commitment—commitment to the institution and commitment to the whole structure of higher education in America. Given genuine and whole-hearted commitment, the rest falls into place. The responsibilities of governing boards discussed in this chapter are demanding. The selection, protection, and assessment of the president; the insistence on long-term goals and strategic plans; the overview of educational programs; the preservation of institutional autonomy; communication between campus and community—all these involve time, energy, intelligence, and commitment. They also provide the enduring satisfaction that comes from knowing that one is a constructive part of a great educational enterprise.

CHAPTER 7

Selecting the
Chief Executive

Judith Block McLaughlin

Each year, trustees at three to four hundred colleges and universities select a new chief executive for their institutions. This decision is generally regarded as the single most important responsibility of a governing board. It is also probably the most visible manifestation of the board's leadership. With justification or not, boards of trustees are judged by the performance of the president they appoint.

But a search process succeeds or fails not only because of who is chosen at its conclusion. The search process itself is the object of great scrutiny by campus constituents. Unlike in the corporate world, where the choice of a chief executive is understood to be the sole responsibility of the board, often in close consultation with the outgoing executive, many constituencies within higher education believe they should be actively involved in the search for the new president. Long gone are the days when a college or university board of trustees could announce in a single breath the resignation of one president and the appointment of another. Today, constituents on most campuses expect that they will be informed about, if not directly participate in, the search for a new president. If a board fails to recognize this desire for participation, campus constituents may consider the search process illegitimate.

Thus, the question of how to conduct a presidential search is complicated. Not only must a governing board attempt to find the individual best suited for the institution at that particular point in its history but it must also do so in a manner viewed as legitimate by the members of the academic community. Even highly competent leaders will find it difficult, if not impossible, to succeed if the process by which they were selected has engendered distrust or dissension among constituent groups.

The successful presidential search, then, is one that identifies effective leadership for the college or university and does so in a manner that makes possible a successful entrée for the new chief executive. The successful search has one additional dimension. No other event in the life of an institution affords the same opportunity for institutional learning as does the search for a president. In the best cases, the search—and, indeed, the entire period of transition—offers the governing board and institutional constituents the chance to assess the institution's past, present, and future; listen to people inside and outside the institution; and gather different pieces of information about the institution and diverse perspectives on it. The successful presidential search, then, is also a process that heightens understanding of the institution by the board, the campus, and the new president.

This chapter will consider these three objectives of the successful search: selection of effective leadership, creation of a legitimate search process, and advancement of institutional learning. Although all three objectives are important, the search is complicated because the actions most appropriate for the attainment of one of these objectives, in many instances, are incompatible with those leading to the realization of another. Decisions that increase the likelihood of attracting the most qualified candidates, for example, may be antithetical to those that enhance that very candidate's legitimacy. This chapter discusses these dilemmas, looking especially at six phases of the search: the composition of the search committee, the definition of qualifications for the new president, the process of searching and courting, the policies and practices concerning confidentiality and disclosure, the decision about whether to use a search consultant, and the final stages of the search.

Composition of the Search Committee

Typically, the first issue that boards must confront during the search for a new president is who will be doing the searching. Many search processes become politicized and factionalized at their very outset over questions of committee structure and membership. Should one committee, two, or more be involved with the search and selection process? If more than one committee is involved, which committee will do what, and which will have the "real" power? Which constituencies will be represented and in what numbers?

The most common forms of committee structure are the single search and selection committee and the two-tiered process. Occasionally, multiple advisory committees will be employed, all reporting to a single search and selection committee. In the two-tiered process, the top tier generally consists of a selection committee chosen from the board of trustees or board of regents, while the second tier is a campus-based advisory committee that includes many campus constituents: faculty members, administrators, students, alumni, members of the local community, and so forth. The advisory committee is typically responsible for developing a large pool of candidates and then screening the long list to a smaller group who will be given further consideration. Sometimes, the advisory committee will also be responsible for interviewing candidates and forwarding an evaluation of them to the selection committee. In all cases, the selection committee retains the responsibility for the final selection.

The two-tiered model allows a large number of constituents to participate in the search process, which enhances support for the search. However, the two (or more) committees may prefer different candidates, a situation that will force a showdown at the last stages of the search process. Or the search can turn into a power struggle between the two committees. The advisory committee may be reluctant to relinquish the most exciting and significant part of the process—the actual selection of the president—to the selection committee. Advisory committees have been accused of "stacking the deck" so that the outcome is predetermined. Or the selection committee may be accused of already having made a decision, rendering the work of the advisory committee merely pro forma. At its best, the two-tiered structure permits campus constituents to participate in the search while preserving for the board the ultimate choice of the new chief executive.

The most popular committee structure is the single committee, which is charged by the board with all aspects of the search process, including the recommendation of a candidate or a slate of candidates for the board's final selection. At issue in the creation of this committee is what constituents should be represented on the committee. The tension between committee legitimacy and committee effectiveness is often evident. Many institutions establish large, broad-based search committees that include every conceivable constituency so that no important group will feel left out. On almost all campuses, faculty members are considered essential members of a presidential search committee. The concept of shared governance is widely accepted; to proceed through a search for a president without having faculty members on the search committee would render the outcome unacceptable at most institutions.

There is far less agreement on the question of which other constituents should be included on the committee. At some institutions, students are automatically included in the committee, but not at others. Some boards believe strongly that administrators should not be included on the search committee because they are, in effect, hiring their own boss. At other colleges and universities, administrators are a natural choice for the search committee. In some unionized institutions, a distinction is made between senior administrators, such as deans or directors, and other members of the professional staff, and this delineation carries over to the search committee. If someone from one group is included on the committee, someone from the other group must also be chosen. Nonprofessional staff members (for example, clerical, maintenance, and cafeteria workers) are occasionally appointed to the search committee, as well as individuals from off campus, such as alumni and local community leaders.

Given the number of groups that believe themselves to be important stakeholders in institutions of higher education, it is not surprising to find that many presidential search committees are large. But large committees, formed for representativeness, often hamper the effectiveness of the search process. With many people on the committee, there are multiple schedules to take into account in planning meetings, making full attendance at all committee sessions unlikely. In a small committee, all members are more likely to be present at all sessions to share in discussions and decisions. As search committee members work together to take stock of what leadership is most needed for their institution and what individual best exemplifies this leadership, all participants gain a greater appreciation of the complexities of issues and develop a deeper understanding of the institution.

If small committees are more desirable than large ones in terms of effectiveness and institutional learning, how can they be so constituted as to be considered legitimate by campus constituents? Individual institutional differences need to be taken into account. Each college or university must determine what is the appropriate committee structure and membership for its particular circumstances, keeping in mind that the committee must be deemed legitimate by the campus but must also be able to identify the best possible leadership for the institution. Committee members should bring to the search process multiple perspectives on the institution so that they can educate each other about the issues and circumstances facing new leadership. They should possess good judgment of people and be able to represent the institution well to prospective candidates. And they should be highly respected by their peers, so that their trustworthiness is above question.

Definition of Qualifications

The first order of business of most search committees is setting forth the list of qualifications for the job of president. In many searches, committee members are eager to get past what they see as a perfunctory task and get on with the more exciting work of evaluating people. They quickly draft a statement that tells prospective candidates and nominators little about what sort of person the institution is seeking, often because they have not thought hard themselves about what type of leader is needed.

When taken seriously, however, the process of defining the leadership needs of the institution not only produces a document that is informative for those who read it but also offers members of the search committee an opportunity to develop a better understanding of how others inside and outside view the institution—its strengths, weaknesses, issues, and opportunities. What at the college or university matters most to various individuals and groups? What are the diverse perceptions of the needs to which a new president must respond? How will the new president fit into the order of things, not only in the line of presidential succession but also in the array of problems and personalities currently at the institution? In what ways will the president serve as the symbol for the institution, and what are the important institutional symbols and myths that the president must recognize if he or she is going to be successful?

The answers to such questions are best discovered through extensive interviews with campus constituents by members of the search committee. This solicitation of diverse opinions enhances the committee's appreciation of the job facing a new president and helps it to define more clearly who is best suited for the job. It also increases the committee's interaction with campus constituents, thereby expanding the boundaries of communication and providing opportunities for many more people than can possibly join the search committee to have important input in the early stages of the search.

For the members of the search committee, the task of filtering through the diverse opinions and divergent agendas of institutional constituents is an opportunity to discover each other's interests, to go beyond initial preconceptions (for example, that trustees will want someone with extensive management experience, while faculty members will see scholarship as the top priority), and to negotiate differences and appreciate commonalities. Defining the qualities needed in a president is the first step in the committee's development of a mutual understanding of the institution and the profile of the person best suited to fill the post of president.

Process of Searching and Courting

Obviously, a search committee cannot select someone to be president who is not in their candidate pool. Nevertheless, many committees act more as selection committees than search committees. They spend far more of their time culling through the pages of applications and nominations that come to them as the result of advertisements than they do in active pursuit of people they might persuade to become candidates. In part, they do so because many members of search committees are not sure how to go about the work of searching.

The increasing use of consultants in the search process, discussed later in this chapter, is partially motivated by the hope that the consultant will expand the pool of applicants. Often, the process of courting is not done well because many committees prefer eager candidates; they want to be wanted. Indeed, candidates who campaign for the job can make members of the search committee feel good about their institution and about themselves for being connected with it. Whether candidates who most want the presidency, especially in the early stages of the search, are the most attractive people for the position remains an open question.

Occasionally, very strong candidates are actively job hunting, but usually the very best people are already well placed in jobs where they have considerable responsibility, are greatly respected, and are performing exceedingly well. Many such people will not have given much thought to leaving. Even those who may feel that a change of scenery or responsibility would be challenging are unlikely to have much time to pursue other options. Hence, the task of the search committee is to identify such individuals, talk with them about the presidency, encourage them to provide the search committee with preliminary information about themselves (for example, a curriculum vitae and papers presented at conferences), and studiously avoid forcing them to make a premature decision about their interest in becoming a candidate. The search committee should keep the conversation going to allow the prospective candidate and the committee to get to know each other better. During this period of discovery, both parties to the conversation act as buyer and seller; both are choosing and being chosen.

Policies of Confidentiality and Disclosure

Nowhere are the divergences between effectiveness and legitimacy more clearly evident than in the search committee's decisions about confidentiality and disclosure. Without exception, handbooks and consultants strongly urge that a policy of confidentiality be followed during the search process, that is, that the names of all candidates and all discussions about them remain the privileged information of the search committee. Confidentiality is considered important to attract and maintain a strong pool of candidates.

Many prospective candidates will not participate in a search unless they are assured of confidentiality because they do not want to jeopardize their effectiveness in their current positions. If they are seen by others as likely to leave, their ability to provide leadership in ongoing efforts may be seriously diminished. They are seen as lame-duck administrators, even if they (or a search committee) reach the decision not to continue in the search process. The higher placed the person, the likelier it is that he or she will suffer ill consequences from disclosure, and hence the less willing the person is to become a candidate in searches where disclosure is likely.

Additionally, prospective candidates often do not want it known that they are talking with members of a search committee because they are not at all certain they want to have their names considered for that presidency. Nothing curtails the process of mutual exploration faster than the disclosure of candidates' names! Premature disclosure of candidates' names also scares away candidates who do not want to harm their chances in future searches. They realize that their not having been selected president at one institution may be misread by others as a failure, as somehow indicating that they are not presidential material. Actually, many individuals who become presidents (and succeed admirably in the job) have been unsuccessful candidates at many institutions before they find a place that is a good match for their interests and talents. Attractive candidates realize that they have many options, and if they do not pursue one presidential possibility, another will come along.

In addition to limiting the pool of candidates, disclosure can negatively affect the search in other ways. It can lead to increased politicization of the search process. When candidates' names become public knowledge, search committee members often find themselves the objects of lobbying by supporters and detractors of the candidates. Candidates with strong political bases of support may proceed further in a search process than their qualifications would warrant because of the pressure brought to bear by important supporters of the candidate. Also, disclosure of candidates' names, committee deliberations, or ranking of candidates makes members of the search committee reluctant to talk candidly in committee meetings. Many opportunities for learning about the institution as well as for hearing others' honest assessments of prospective presidents are thus lost. The search committee that does not provide the conditions for a frank discussion of institutional needs and candidate qualifications is making its final decision on less than complete information.

The arguments in favor of confidentiality are persuasive, but the pressures for disclosure are also strong. Typically, people are curious about whom the search committee is considering, and many constituents believe they have a right to know this information. In public higher education, this "right to know" is often championed by representatives of the media in their efforts to bring presidential searches under the stipulations of open meeting and open records laws.

All states presently have open meeting and open records legislation (also known as sunshine laws) on their books, but the extent to which this legislation is applied to higher education searches varies greatly. In Florida, all aspects of the search must be made public, including the names of all candidates (both those who apply and those who are nominated by others), all letters of recommendation, all interviews, and all discussions and votes of the search committee. At the opposite end of the spectrum are searches at universities in Pennsylvania and Michigan, where all aspects of the search are conducted in executive session and no names of candidates are made public other than those of the new president. In these cases, state laws allow personnel evaluations to be conducted confidentially, and searches are considered to be personnel proceedings. The individual's right to privacy is considered alongside of the public's right to know.

At the outset of the search process, the trustees or regents, usually in consultation with board staff members, must determine their state's policy regarding confidentiality and disclosure and then decide accordingly the practices they will follow. Will the names of candidates and the discussions of committee members be shared beyond the membership of the search committee, and if so, with whom and with what likely consequences? If the committee decides to maintain confidentiality, how will it enforce this decision? What measures will be taken to prevent leaks? Many sincere pledges of confidentiality by search committees have been undermined by unanticipated disclosures, the result of successful sleuthing by investigative reporters or the consequence of carelessness or oversight.

Most search committees adopt a policy of confidentiality for most aspects of the search process. The difficulty arises in the last stages of the search as the committee confronts the issue of campus visits. Should the policy of confidentiality be waived so that campus constituents can meet a small group of finalists for the presidency? Or should confidentiality be maintained throughout the search? What is potentially gained and lost by involving more people in the final stages of the search?

The most obvious advantage of campus visits is the involvement of constituents and the legitimation of the search. Campus visits have become a tradition on some campuses, and their elimination might cause an outcry of protest from the campus. Faculty members, students, and administrators want to "see the merchandise," to participate, even if only minimally, in "comparative shopping." Campus visits also allow candidates to see the campus through eyes of others not on the search committee. Some candidates have become completely sold on an institution after the campus visit. Others have learned, during the many interview sessions of the campus visit, about institutional problems that made the presidency of that institution no longer appealing.

In some searches, the search committee is eager to elicit the reactions of campus constituents to finalists and welcomes input that will enable it to make its final decision. In other searches, however, the search committee has a clear preference for one candidate and holds campus visits only because they are expected. In such instances, the candidates and the campus are treated unfairly—the candidates, because some of them are risking the liabilities of disclosure when their chances to be chosen are negligible (but, of course, they are not told this, or they would not participate in the campus visit) and campus constituents, because they are led to believe their impressions will be taken into account when the visits are merely pro forma. Moreover, if campus constituents reach a different conclusion than the search committee on the basis of first impressions and limited information, the board of trustees—and, ultimately, the new president—is placed in a most difficult position.

The decision to hold campus visits may result in the loss of prospective candidates for the presidency. Many highly placed individuals, notably those who are presidents elsewhere, will not participate in a campus visit because of the publicity this brings their candidacy. For the reasons mentioned earlier, they do not want to jeopardize their effectiveness in their current position—or even their position itself. Boards have been known to fire presidents for looking at different positions, once this action becomes publicly known.

Aware of both the advantages and disadvantages of campus visits, some boards of trustees have decided in recent years to bring only the search committee's top choice to the campus for open meetings with faculty members, students, administrators, and staff members. The individual is presented as the candidate about whom the search committee is enthusiastic, although no binding decision has been made by the institution or the candidate. If the campus reaction is negative or if the candidate concludes after visiting the campus that the presidency is no longer attractive, the search committee can invite another finalist to the campus. Other search committees have decided to bring two or three finalists to the institution for meetings limited only to a small number of people beyond the membership of the search committee. These people are asked to take a pledge of confidentiality that they will not reveal the names of the finalists.

Whether to Use a Search Consultant

Ten years ago, search consultants were almost unheard of in many sectors of U.S. higher education. Today, an estimated 60 percent of presidential searches employ an outside consultant. This extraordinary increase in the use of consultants is due, in large measure, to the fact that searches have become such complicated affairs in recent years, for the reasons already discussed.

Search consultants can provide a board or search committee

with help in many areas, including deciding how to structure and manage the search process, defining qualifications for the presidency, identifying prospective nominators and candidates, interviewing candidates, conducting background investigations of finalists, and serving as an intermediary in negotiations with the top choice for president. The best search consultants are experienced navigators of the search process and are sensitive to the particular nuances and situation of each institution. They do not use a "cookie cutter" approach to the search process but rather appreciate the special needs and interests of each search committee and board with whom they work.

As soon as the *Chronicle of Higher Education* announces a search for a president or even before that, when word gets out on the grapevine that a president is stepping down, many consulting firms will write to express interest in assisting in the search process. The board of trustees or search committee then has a chance to look at these letters and accompanying brochures and decide whether to ask two, three, or sometimes more of the consultants to make presentations in person. Typically, members of the board or search committee will also contact people they know on other campuses who have held a presidential search recently to ask them about their experience with a consultant and whom they would recommend (or reject). If the search committee chooses a consultant on the basis of interviews, this process might be thought of as a trial run for the main task of choosing among finalists for the presidency.

What are some of the considerations on which the choice of a consultant should rest? Consultants differ enormously in terms of how much of the burden they carry and how long they carry it. Some consultants will spend a great deal of time in the early stages of the search, getting the process under way and helping the committee to determine what is required in a new president, and then will curtail their involvement, seeing their role primarily as advisers to the process. They do not attend search committee meetings and may not sit in on interviews with candidates. In contrast, other consultants will practically manage the entire process—screening resumes (either on their own or concurrently with screening by the search committee), interviewing candidates individually and providing the search committee with synopses of these sessions, conducting extensive background investigations, and so forth. A search committee should decide what sort of assistance it desires and make certain that the search consultant is prepared to offer this before reaching any agreement to proceed.

Search consultants differ, too, on their familiarity with higher education. Lack of experience with a college or university presidential search should not, per se, rule out a consultant. Several consultants have won high praise from the first committee they assisted. These consultants saw themselves almost as anthropologists: their first job was to size up the culture of the institution, to understand it from many different perspectives, before proceeding with the search. But the willingness of the consultant to put in the extra time to learn about the world of academe and to identify important resource people within it must be thoroughly examined by a search committee.

Ultimately, the quality of the work of the search consultant depends on the quality of the consultant's mind, that is, his or her judgment about people, perceptiveness and thoroughness. Additionally, the chemistry between search committee members (and especially the committee chair) and the consultant should be good for the relationship to work well during the search. As with candidates for the presidency, search firms (and particularly the individual consultant who will serve as adviser to the search) should be investigated thoroughly by a search committee.

Two caveats about the use of a search consultant deserve mention. First, a consultant's work should supplement, not replace, the work of a search committee and board of trustees. For institutional learning to occur, the committee and board must fully participate in the selection of the president, not delegate major chunks of the process to the consultant. But, second, the expertise of the consultant should be fully utilized. In many searches, the consultant pulls back or withdraws altogether at the time of negotiation with the candidate of choice. However, it is precisely at this time that the consultant can play a crucial role as go-between, a role that allows both presidential finalist and board of trustees to express their concerns openly and thereby to work out in considerable detail and to both parties' satisfaction the arrangements of the appointment.

Final Stages

Although search committee members are likely to heave a well-deserved sigh of relief when the selection of the new president is completed, their work should not be seen as fully done until they have evaluated the search process and drafted a summary of their findings, including the procedures they followed and their assessment of these procedures. The learning that has occurred during the search process should not be lost when the search committee disbands. Some committees will want to prepare two reports: a confidential report to the chairman of the board that documents the details of the search (to be retained as part of the archives of the institution) and a second report to the new president and the institutional community that describes what the search committee discovered about the institution through the search for new leadership.

The end of the search process is also a time for the board to consider the approach to be taken in the next presidential search. This search, it is hoped, will not occur for a long time, so specific requirements for search committee membership, search policies, and so forth should probably not be spelled out. But the board may want to establish a leadership transition committee that has responsibility for guiding the new president through his or her first year in office, serving as a sounding board for the president, and considering policies and procedures for future searches when these become necessary.

Participation in a presidential search process is a tremendously exhilarating and rewarding experience for the trustees involved. Search committee members are the most knowledgeable about their institution and, at least for some time, the most helpful to the new president and to the board in the transition to new leadership.

CHAPTER 8

Supporting
the President
and Assessing
the Presidency

Shirley S. Chater

The conclusion of the search process and the announcement of the appointment of the new president may be the happiest moments for the board of trustees. The beginning of the presidency and the celebration of the inauguration may be the highlights of the president's term of office. Sometime in between these events, the board and the president should prepare a statement of objectives and a list of criteria against which the board and the president will assess their working relationship over time.

The presidency is a lonely job. Typically, board members come to the campus only for board meetings and special events, but the president is on the scene twenty-four hours a day. The board's relationship is primarily with the president; the president's relationships are with the board and numerous other constituencies that sometimes pull in opposite directions. The annual turnover rate of presidents in independent colleges and universities from 1982 to 1985 was 11.6 percent, with presidents serving an average of seven years (Kerr and Gade, 1989, p. 86). In searching for the answer to why presidents quit, Alton (1982) noted that the relationship with the governing board was near the top of the list. Having spent time, energy, and money searching for the right president, the board will want to nurture its choice and make sure that he or she receives support and encouragement, gestures that will contribute to a long and effective tenure for its newly selected chief executive officer.

Board support to the president is maximized in those instances where both the board and the president understand the unique partnership that exists between them. The board is both legally and actually the dominant partner, as Houle (1989) points out. But he adds that "the exercise of power over its executive by a board should be considered a last resort, a signal that something has gone very much awry" (p. 87). The board-executive relationship is one of dual authority, carried out by a corporate board acting on the basis of group consensus and an individual executive acting with personal authority. Houle offers other ways that the respective roles of the board and the executive complement each other: the board as a corporate entity is continuous, the president, temporary; the board serves part time, the president serves full time; the board has ultimate responsibility for the institution, whereas the president serves at the pleasure of the board and has more immediate responsibilities.

Barbara Taylor (1987), drawing on the work of Kramer (1965), calls attention to the "exchange relationship" between board and president. The authority of the president, based on expertise, is exchanged for the formal legal authority of the board. The president receives support from the board, while the trustees receive recognition and prestige from their service to the institution. Through this exchange process, values are clarified and shared. Personal biases are usually put aside for the benefit of the campus community. The relationship between board and president is an intimate one, characterized by mutual care and trust.

Thus, supporting the president is an acknowledgment of the interdependence between board and president, and an acceptance of the exchange relationship that exists between the two. Like all successful relationships, this one also depends upon open and frequent communication. The board expects the president to orient and educate them about board responsibilities, to inform them about issues and challenges, to infuse them with enthusiasm and energy. The president looks to the board for advice, suggestions, ideas, plans, and approval for governance matters and hopes that the board will sustain and maintain, advocate and champion, uphold and encourage the leader of the institution.

Assessment as Support

Whether the assessment of the president is formal or informal, yearly or occasional, written or oral, it ultimately provides an opportunity for board members and the president to sit together to share views, exchange ideas, identify areas of strength, correct areas of weakness, and plan for the future. An assessment forces communication, and if fruitful and frequent communication between president and board existed prior to the assessment, few surprises will emerge during the scheduled conference. Planned assessments provide opportunity for positive feedback, suggested changes in emphasis or style, and reinforcement of vision and goals. The board and the president can mutually support each other only if goals are clear, strategies are planned, and authority is shared. A presidential assessment should be viewed as a way to strengthen the governance of a college or university, an opportunity to examine the relationship between president and board along with the leadership required from each. Occasionally, assessments are conducted to pave the way for the president's graceful exit following a campus crisis. In my opinion, this is not the time for a presidential assessment.

More appropriately, a troubled campus would benefit from an institutional needs assessment, where a committee of the board, the president, and an outside consultant would assess broadly the functioning of various campus constituencies and the relationships among them. Colleges and universities operate with principles of shared governance; administrators, faculty, staff, and students may not all share the same view of the college or agree about how to achieve that vision. An institutional needs assessment can be an effective way to outline priorities and leadership requirements. The assessment could lead to the recognition that a new style of leadership is required to achieve new goals, but more important, it identifies multiple challenges and the roles each constituency must play to create a comfortable campus climate.

Many in higher education believe the evidence is not conclusive on the extent to which presidential assessments strengthen the role of the president. Nason (1984) presents the most comprehensive guide to periodic review of the chief executive, together with arguments for and against specific methodologies and procedures. Nason (1980), Munitz (1980), and Kauffman (1978) argue for systematic evaluation because it is a board's responsibility to monitor the president and because assessment improves the leadership of an institution.

Others, such as Fisher and Quehl (1984), argue strongly that formal assessment creates rather than solves problems and diminishes the role of the presidency. The report of the Commission on Strengthening Presidential Leadership, directed by Clark Kerr, notes that "formal reviews have more often done harm than good" but that "reviews of presidents should be carried out informally and annually" (Kerr, 1984, p. 57). To be sure that presidential assessments empower the president, Fisher (1986), Ness (1986), and Shaw (1985) offer helpful procedural suggestions, such as self-evaluation by presidents and clear criteria for evaluations.

Most authors agree that each presidential assessment is situational; that is, the evaluation takes place within the overall context of the institution, including the present situation and events of the immediate past. Because the context is ever changing, the president may have had no chance of achieving the objectives set forth during his or her first year if a major crisis intervened and the priorities were shifted. The specific assessment methods used to evaluate the president will depend upon the institution and the people involved. No one perfect model exists for all institutions.

The Nature of Assessment

The debate about presidential assessment focuses not on whether an assessment should be conducted but on how it should be done. Two concerns are most often discussed: whether assessments should be informal or formal and whether to use a measurement instrument or an informal means of gathering data. On one end of the continuum is the informal assessment, in which the chair and/or a committee of the board quietly and confidentially share informally collected information with the president. At the other end of the spectrum is the formal, often public, review that uses interviews, questionnaires, or survey instruments to collect data systematically from large numbers of people who represent many campus constituencies.

To understand fully one difference between informal and formal assessment, it helps to differentiate between assessment (and evaluation) and measurement. Assessments and evaluations are value judgments. They are based on perceptions; that is, how one chooses to interpret both style and substance. We try to be objective, but evaluation involves more interpretation than we wish to admit. In the case of assessing a goal such as improving interpersonal relationships, we judge effectiveness or ineffectiveness based on our perceptions, which are unavoidably colored by who we are and how we see our world. Presidential leadership includes many intangible interpersonal skills that cannot be quantitatively measured.

Measurement, on the other hand, can be quite objective. We establish a measure, often in the form of criteria, and we count the results. For example, a university might set a goal to increase the percentage of minority students enrolled. The measure of the percentage increase from one year to the next is quantifiable and objective. Trends in extramural funding, alumni membership, or the number of grants and contracts can be similarly measured.

We should remember that presidential assessments will contain both objective and subjective evidence, even though we strive to make the assessment process as unbiased as possible. Objective measures of quantifiable achievements alone are insufficient because the intangible characteristics of leadership are often more important than the quantifiable ones. Presidents are being evaluated literally daily by faculty, staff, and students, and if board members visit the campus and have interactions with these constituencies, they hear how the president is viewed.

Trustees form perceptions that suggest that a president's leadership is positive or not, as the case may be. Informal evaluation seldom involves deliberate attempts to systematically collect information and almost never involves the use of consultants. Informal evaluation may be annual and tied to salary increases, or it may be set at two- to five-year intervals. It usually takes place quietly and confidentially between the board (or a committee of the board) and the president. A list of agreed-upon criteria and a self-evaluation by the president provide the data for the informal review.

Formal evaluations are more complex, involve more people, and typically take place every five to seven years. The evaluation tends to be public and focuses on the entire governance structure of the university, including the board. Data are often collected through questionnaires constructed by a committee of the board that is frequently assisted by an outside consultant. In addition, members of the board, by themselves or in cooperation with a consultant, may conduct personal interviews with faculty, staff, students, alumni, and community members.

According to presidents with whom I have spoken, the more formal the assessment, the less effective it is because the procedure threatens to undermine the authority and status of the office of the president and generates negative consequences. First, the public announcement that an assessment will be conducted frequently turns the assessment into a personality contest in which style and personal characteristics overshadow substantive criteria of competence. Second, a formal assessment complete with measurement instruments such as questionnaires or rating scales invites pass-fail judgments. Pass-fail judgments make it difficult for the board to focus on strengths of the presidency and suggestions for future goals and the means to achieve them. A president who receives a low score loses the power of the position as well as the personal power that comes from expertise and experience. The climate created by this assessment process is hardly conducive to building the self-confidence and courage necessary for new challenges and expanded visions. Nevertheless, there may be situations in independent colleges that call for a thorough public assessment that focuses attention not only on the president but also on the entire governance structure of the institution, the institution's mission, and its objectives. A crisis may call for the institutional needs assessment described earlier.

Nason (1984) recommends an informal procedure at regular intervals, an approach that is especially workable for independent colleges where a high degree of mutual trust and support has developed between the president and the board. Obviously, open and frequent communication, both written and oral, must have evolved so that the president and the board can exchange information candidly. Independent colleges appear to be ideal for this type of assessment, according to Nason, because their boards tend to be self-perpetuating and the values of incoming board members are generally similar to those held by present members. Also, independent colleges and universities function in less public and less political arenas than do public ones, despite the fact that accountability for all colleges and universities is increasingly demanded by various constituencies.

The Assessment Process

I believe that presidential assessment, like presidential selection and appointment, is a major responsibility of the board of trustees and that it should be done regularly, seriously, and sensitively. Nason (1984) adds three other purposes of presidential evaluation: to strengthen the president's position and improve performance, to review and improve the governance of the institution, and to review and reset institutional goals.

How can the assessment strengthen the president's position and improve performance? Unfortunately, compliments and words of praise to the president from trustees for deeds well done are rare. An assessment provides an opportunity for positive feedback for those objectives achieved. Knowing that the board supports particular achievements encourages the president and the administrative team toward greater creativity and challenges. Assessment that includes suggestions from the board about improvement in one area of management or leadership redirects the president's energy. Mutual respect and trust are further developed, and the president's position is enhanced overall.

The review of the governance structure of the institution can lead to improvement in overall management and oversight. The assessment of the president can take into account the effectiveness of the administrative team—how well its members work together with the president to pursue the institution's goals and implement policy. Also, conducting a board self-assessment simultaneously with a presidential assessment makes sense. Chapter Twenty outlines approaches to board assessment and makes suggestions for improving board leadership. It includes the responsibilities of the president and board chair in developing the leadership. A leadership assessment of the president, the administrative team, *and* the board supports the "exchange" relationship of interdependence among them. How well the board and the president work together is a predictor of other successes.

One of the most important purposes of presidential assessment is to review past and future goals. Strategic thinking calls for skills that take advantage of opportunities as they arise. Keeping the institution on track with its mission while looking for strategic opportunities to enhance the mission will become even more important during the retrenchment of the 1990s. Some critics of presidential assessment suggest that the word *assessment* be discarded in favor of *review*. Consider, however, that *review* means to look back on or to examine again; it does not convey the importance of setting goals. The pursuit of goals that are determined by the president and board nurtures shared governance and the mutual exchanges discussed above.

Although an assessment may be informal, determining its time and place prevents it from becoming a casual conversation among individuals. The assessment deserves a regular schedule for planning, implementation, and action. Kerr (1984) recommends that an informal review be conducted annually, with particular attention given to the reviews in the second and the seventh through tenth years. By the second year, the president has recruited an administrative team and begun to establish priorities for the institution. A review in the seventh or tenth year will reveal the long-term effects of faculty hiring, program development, and future plans.

Ideally, the search process would have included a set of priorities for the new president based on an institutional needs assessment. Ideally, the contract or letter of appointment would have enumerated those priorities, noting that they would serve as the criteria against which the president would be evaluated in one or two years. In this ideal situation, everyone knows what the expectations are, and this road map serves well for purposes of evaluation.

When the trustees think about goals after the president has been hired, the president and the chair of the board must determine a mutually agreed-upon set of criteria against which judgments about achievement can be made. The timing of the assessment should be mutually determined by the president and the board chair, with enough time given for the president to achieve the stated objectives and for the board to collect evaluative data. It is entirely proper for the president to take the lead in determining the nature and timing of the assessment. It is a good idea to have the president do a self-evaluation that is submitted to the board or committee doing the assessment. Most of the material in a written self-evaluation can be used for the annual report or interim report to the trustees. In addition to the president's self-evaluation, trustees will have information from the administrative team through the work of the president's senior officers with board committees and from other constituencies through general observation and informal means. The assessment conference, a private conversation between board or committee and the president, provides the opportunity to build mutual trust and guarantee shared authority.

Presidential Self-Evaluation

Central to the evaluation process is the statement of goals to be achieved. The president's self-evaluation should be guided by those goals, mutually derived by the president and the board at an earlier time. Each goal should be addressed by enumerating and describing achievements and outcomes. For example, if one goal expressed a need to increase enrollment, a response could include the actual percentage increase as well as a description of outreach efforts to targeted population groups. If another goal dealt with reallocating resources to begin new programs, a description of the strategic planning process that led to the discontinuation of some programs and the development of new ones would be in order. Timetables, processes for achieving goals, involvement of appropriate constituencies, and serendipitous outcomes should be encouraged.

Some goals will not have been met or will have changed. The self-evaluation should explain what intervened to either change the goal or cause a delay in achieving an outcome. Sometimes a goal cannot be met because of a lack of funding. Sometimes an unforeseen crisis causes a reordering of priorities. These are expected and should be included in the narrative. On the other hand, opportunities may arise that are only tangentially related to a goal. These should be described along with the rationale for dealing with them in a particular way.

To describe the intangibles of style, communication practices, and interpersonal relationships is often difficult. Every effort should be made, however, to include evidence of effectiveness and plans to work on areas that require improvement.

Personal and professional needs also should be addressed in the self-evaluation. Stress from multiple pressures and long working hours is a condition shared by many in leadership positions. An honest self-appraisal will recognize the need for professional renewal gained by attending meetings and symposia. Personal time for family and friends is often limited during semesters filled with college-related obligations. Vacations, travel, and time away can be encouraged by the board chair if the need is recognized and valued.

The written self-evaluation, which includes summary statements of strengths and areas of needed improvement, serves as a basis for developing future goals. As the board or committee discusses the assessment with the president, goals can be added, refined, sharpened, or deleted. Through this process of feedback and communication, mutually agreed upon goals and responsibilities are determined. The new goals become the criteria for the president's next assessment.

Recommendations and Suggestions

Presidential assessments, along with presidential selection and appointment, are major responsibilities of the governing board. In private institutions where the values of the president and board members are similar, where mutual respect and trust exists between board and president, and where open and regular communication exists, informal presidential assessment on an annual basis is recommended. Assessment must be conducted with the utmost sensitivity and care, remembering that the successful review will strengthen the president's position and improve performance, enhance the governance of the institution, and decide future goals for the college or university.

Steps in the Assessment Process

- Well in advance, a date is established for the assessment conference between president and board (or chair or committee).
- The president and the board chair agree upon the criteria to be used for the review.
- The president writes a self-evaluation and submits it to the chair.
- The board or a committee of the board meets to review the president's self-evaluation, the criteria, and its evaluation.
- An informal, private, and confidential conference is held by board members and president.
- The outcome of the assessment is shared with the full board.

Throughout their studies of the presidency, Kerr and Gade (1986, 1989) repeatedly state that the presidency is the most important position in a college or university, yet the position has become less attractive in recent times. As economic hardships now and in the future require difficult decisions about the reallocation of fiscal and human resources, realignment of programs, discarding of programs, and general retrenchment, the presidency is likely to see greater turnover than before. Support through systematic assessment should lengthen the terms of good presidents and shorten the terms of weak presidents. According to Clark Kerr and Marian Gade (1989), the board cannot be much better than its institution's president. Assessment, especially that which includes review of the board as well as the president, strengthens the entire governance structure of the institution.

Presidential assessment leads to support of the president in both personal and professional ways. Boards, aware of the demands on the president's time, should urge personal time, vacation, and sabbaticals for presidents. Salary adjustments and adequate staff support can be determined through annual reviews. Most important, as any president will tell you, words of encouragement and support count just as much if not more than financial rewards.

CHAPTER 9

Ensuring Sound
Financial and
Plant Management

John W. Pocock

It takes more than dollars to drive the higher education machine. The real but intangible assets of human intelligence and spirit and transforming vision are the roots of an outstanding educational system. However, dollars still make possible the envisioned programs and support each and every institution of higher education. Vision alone does little to pay faculty salaries.

Of all of the tasks assigned to the board of trustees, monitoring the financial affairs of the institution is the one most understood and accepted by the incoming trustee and has been through all the decades of American higher education. Understanding and accepting the task is one thing; executing it constructively is quite another, as the failed finances of many institutions amply attest. Some boards simply abandon this responsibility and let the administrators handle it without oversight. Some boards have trouble with the process of policy setting, monitoring, and correction. Many handle this process adequately but are behind the wave of events. Both the board and the individual trustee are at fault in failing to monitor the financial health and vitality of the institution.

The board as a whole bears the responsibility for the well-being of its institution's financial support, a responsibility assigned in private institutions by custom, bylaws, and enabling char-

139

ter. But each trustee, by virtue of his or her election to the board, accepts an individual fiduciary responsibility that cannot be avoided by simply keeping the mouth closed, the eyes averted, and the hands off important decisions. If this chapter can help to bring the individual trustee out of hiding and into full participation in financial decision making, it will have served its central purpose. The widespread myth that trustees often fail to understand fund accounting is no excuse. As will be demonstrated in the following pages, financial management is not accounting and, with proper interpretive reports and analyses, the accounting-illiterate trustee can make important and informed contributions to financial decisions.

The financial aspects of the board's duties will be assigned to a finance committee, which takes the lead in monitoring financial affairs. By delegation, this committee will serve as the main liaison with the president and administration, review financial reports and actions in detail, and bring recommended actions to the board for discussion and adoption. The finance committee is usually one of the largest board committees. It meets frequently and, because certain financial matters must be handled on schedule, it has considerable interim authority delegated to it by the board. The longer committee tenure of more financially experienced trustees will contribute to desirable continuity, but rotation of other trustees onto the committee is useful to bring other opinions into deliberations and to provide a bit of trustee education.

The chair of the committee will be required to be readily available and will spend more time on committee work than the chairs of most other committees. This work load should be understood and accepted by the selected chair. The finance committee should not only bring analyses and decision recommendations to the board but also undertake the orientation and education of individual trustees in the nature and practice of financial oversight.

Flow and Allocation of Resources

A simple way to bring coherence to the novice trustee's understanding of an institution's financial affairs is to picture a continuing pipeline of dollars through the institution, from the point of intake through the process of allocation to specific programs and projects, to expenditure in current operations or deposit in various capital accounts and reserves. In conceptually tracing this flow, the points of decision can be more directly identified and the effects of decisions clarified.

The central point to be remembered in all such analyses and decisions by the board is that dollars are generated by programs to support programs of the institution. Thus, committee and board discussions should focus on the policies and programs that are affected by the dollars rather than solely upon the dollars themselves. At every point of decision relating to the flow of funds, the question should be asked, What effect does this have on what programs? This question and its answers are really what financial management is all about.

Revenues

Dollars flow into the institution from various sources and in varying amounts. Student tuition and fees (net of unfunded student aid) are probably the major source of funds for most private institutions. Gifts and grants from private sources, grants from the government, income from investments, and income from auxiliary enterprises all add their portion. Each of these sources has its own controlling factors. Some factors, and therefore the intake flow, may be modified by board action. Shifts in sources that depend largely on factors outside institutional control must be accommodated by the board in its financial planning, sometimes painfully.

Tuition setting is one of the most harrowing financial decisions made by the board. The need to keep tuition low to make the institution affordable to students and their families must be balanced against the growing need for money to support institutional programs. Factors such as price competition with other institutions, historical precedent, and the economic environment also condition the decision. Despite all comparative statistics and budget projections, the decision is finally a judgment call—an informed judgment, but one that is still subjective. But this is typical of many of the most important decisions to be made in carrying out the financial management task.

The impact of student aid on the revenue derived from tuition and fees is something not well understood by many trustees. There are some student aid dollars flowing in from restricted gifts and endowed scholarships. These are real, spendable dollars. But much of the aid will probably be of the "unfunded" variety, which means that a discount on tuition is granted, thus cutting the full-price dollar revenue. Increasing the unfunded aid budget may be required to offset the economic hardship of rising tuition on some students deemed desirable by the institution. Student loan funds and student employment budgets may have to be increased. Thus a tuition increase may well bring in less revenue than expected because of the enlarged student aid requirements, a confounding addition to the already complex tuition decision.

Revenues from gifts and grants may have restrictions that compromise their usefulness in the current budget. They may well include "soft" money, generally a gift or grant for a specific purpose that can be withdrawn or expires after a specific period of time, which leaves the continuing funding of the sponsored program uncertain. What appears to be a generous contribution when it is first received can come back to haunt budgetary planning at a later date.

Payout from endowment may be forced up by board decision in order to increase stated current revenues. The remaining endowment shrinks, to the detriment of the institution's future. This is a questionable action that has been taken by some boards.

The monitoring of these various revenues and the projection of the future shifts in their flows is an important step in assessing the future health of the institution. Based upon such an analysis of future prospects, the board is in a position to take actions and set policies that may offset potential unhappiness or take advantage of foreseen revenue upswings.

Expenditures

Most boards center their financial management attention on the expenditure of dollars through the budget monitoring process. Approved outlays for current operations set the comparison base, and variations are cause for questions and budget revision. This monitoring is important, but without deeper probing, it may bypass significant problems that should be addressed by the board.

Program priorities should be discussed and established. Not every activity of an institution is of equal stature or need. The core academic programs should be high on the list. Some support and maintenance activities may be subject to modification when the institution faces financial pressures. Some peripheral activities may be niceties that are worthwhile but by no means central to the institutional mission. Many of these priorities will have been set in budget planning, but a trustee will do well to keep them firmly in mind and be prepared to reaffirm or alter program priorities as required.

Particular attention should be given to the proposed establishment of new programs. Questions should be raised about why the programs are needed and what they offer that is new or of importance. If funds are required, trustees should know where the money is coming from. And, most important, trustees should ask which current programs can be modified or eliminated when the new program is established. This last question is often avoided by trustees, administration, and faculty. Institutions have a ferocious attachment to their programs and shy away from discontinuing outmoded and unproductive programs. But for every new addition, some pruning of existing programs should be considered.

Cost cutting will inevitably arise as one of the onerous tasks of financial management. An alert administration will recognize the need and bring to the board its recommendations. If the administration neglects or is tardy in recognizing the need, the board should step in and request such recommendations. Across-the-board reductions are the easiest to mandate, but in these years of financial stringency, most of the easy cuts have already been made. Meaningful cuts now usually require the truncation or elimination of programs.

Even though the president and administration recognize the need and have candidate programs for reduction, the board may well be called upon to bear the onus of the final decision. The president and top administration officers are thus shielded from the unkindly reaction of those affected by the action. Though some may scoff, the board has a very real role in preserving executive effectiveness and campus acceptance of the president by asserting its responsibility for distasteful actions, even when the president is completely in accord with the action.

A continuing problem for boards, presidents, and administrations is the difficulty of evaluating end results and assessing the value to the institution of program results. A prime example might be the costs associated with maintaining a social sciences department versus the costs of a physics department in a liberal arts college. The social sciences department teaches far more credit hours, produces more degrees, and has relatively low expenditures per student served. The physics department teaches far fewer credit hours and produces few departmental degrees and yet, because of extensive equipment and laboratory space requirements, has high costs per unit served. Yet the liberal arts experience requires some exposure to and participation in a scientific discipline. Thus, the physics department must be evaluated in the context of its contribution to the total liberal arts experience. The only way to approach the problem of program assessment is to understand the amounts and purposes of the dollars expended and then to attend to the judgments of those involved in the programs and those responsible for managing the programs. Again, this is a matter of exercising informed judgement, and boards exist to render such judgments.

Loan Allocations

Some unrestricted revenue dollars may be allocated to a fund that provides loans to students. These funds augment the money received from donors that, under gift restrictions, can only be used for student loans. Such additions may be desirable in view of rising tuition and the need to provide some assistance to qualified students. The allocation is made to a capital fund that is part of institutional assets, and because the allocation is decreed by board action rather than by gift restriction, it can be reversed in changed circumstances and made available for other uses. The financial condition of the loan fund has been of increasing interest to institutions and to the government. The basic problem has been with the rate of defaults, with some institutions reporting a clearly unsustainable rate. The board is responsible for monitoring loan fund activity, including taking prudent action to increase collection efforts and tighten eligibility standards; otherwise, the loss of hard-won capital must be put at the board's door.

Plant Allocation

Most of the dollars invested in physical facilities and major equipment come from gifts and income restricted by the donor to plant use. Those dollars not already converted to bricks, mortar, and equipment are awaiting use for new construction, major repair, and plant loan repayment. However, allocating a portion of the current revenue to plant purposes may be desirable. Such an allocation thus joins the other plant capital funds, and because it is a trustee-designated allocation, it is reversible if the time comes when there are other priorities for the use of the designated dollars. The most frequent such trustee allocation is to provide additional funds to complete a building for which most of the funds have come from restricted gifts, to build small structures that do not attract private donors, to finance major repairs and rehabilitation, and to purchase equipment such as automobiles and trucks. Absent other donor sources, loans that have been taken to pay for plant and equipment needs are also paid by trustee allocation of current dollars. A more recent development has been the regular allocation of current dollars to a reserve fund that provides for the rehabilitation of buildings and equipment on a long-term, scheduled basis. This is discussed at length later in the chapter.

Quasi-Endowment Allocation

Much of the principal of the endowment will have come from gifts restricted to endowment and often further restricted to specific uses such as scholarships, support of endowed chairs, and support of designated programs. Except under extreme conditions and with the required legal releases, these funds cannot be used for any other purposes.

But more funds are usually required to increase the base value of the endowment and to maintain its purchasing power in the face of persistent inflation. The financially astute board will regularly add to endowment funds by retaining a portion of the earnings, by assigning unrestricted gifts and bequests to it, and by allocating current dollars coming from other sources. This trustee-designated portion of the endowment fund is known as quasi endowment and can be removed from the funds and used for other purposes solely by action of the board. The quasi endowment thus functions as a major catastrophe reserve that can add considerably to the perceived stability of the institution.

Restriction on Resources

The donor may mandate restrictions on the use of some funds. The most common restriction sets the purpose for which the gift may be used. Thus a gift to current operations may be restricted for use for scholarships or library operations. Or a gift to endowment is restricted for use in an endowed scholarship fund or an endowed chair. A less-common restriction mandates the time of expenditure by requiring that the application of the gift be spread over several years. Thus, not all revenues coming into the institution during a given year can be allocated according to trustee and administration desires, nor can they all be spent in the current year. While dollars are to a considerable degree interchangeable, in that dollars restricted to scholarships, for example, free up unrestricted dollars for other purposes, there have been cases in which the restricted income surpasses the need and so must be set aside and reserved for later expenditure. While the administration will be keeping a practiced eye on the restrictions, the trustees should be kept advised about the ratio of restricted versus unrestricted dollars in the budget.

Perhaps a more important figure in the appraisal of the institution's overall condition is the ratio of expendable funds to the annual operating requirement. Such available funds include the current excess cash in the current fund, unrestricted student loan funds sitting idle, unrestricted plant reserves, and the quasi-endowment. A high ratio suggests favorable financial security for the institution, but a very low ratio warns of the institution's vulnerability to financial stresses. Whether the figure is soothing or brings an unsettling message, it is a most important figure to be kept in mind.

Reporting That Aids Trustee Decision Making

The nature of the reports and the reporting system by which the necessary financial information is conveyed to the trustees can either ease or complicate the trustees' oversight role. For years, trustees have voiced complaints about the content and pertinence of financial reports; most reports furnished to them are simply a selection from the internal system that serves administrative financial information requirements. As such, these reports carry far more detail than is useful for trustee decisions, contain little interpretive or explanatory material, and employ technical features that can obscure the message sought by the trustee. Only in recent years have trustees begun to make known their confusion and identify the nature and content of reports they need. Financial officers of many institutions have moved to improve the situation, but there is still some distance to go.

A great deal of the trustee confusion can be traced to the fund accounting system, which is unique to the management of nonprofit institutions. The system stems directly from the requirements of the trustees' fiduciary function. Donations and revenues derived from various sources are often restricted to specific uses by the donor. The trustees are the designated stewards and are charged with seeing that these funds are used only for the designated purposes. Thus, funds are established that hold the money and assets for plant purposes, loan funds, endowment, and also current operations—with the "current fund" receiving all unrestricted revenues and revenues restricted to current operations use. Fund accounting thus provides a sort of asset inventory system, in which bins are provided for different types of assets and the flow into and out of, as well as the current level of, these assets can be measured directly.

The external auditor deals mainly with the conditions of these funds and thus attests to the board's stewardship. This external auditor's report is essential to portraying the financial condition of the institution but is far less useful to the trustee who is a financial amateur when he or she seeks information. Most of the basic information pertinent to operating effectiveness can be distilled from the fund accounting format, but doing so is awkward and requires some technical knowledge of the system.

Management reporting is distinctly different from fiduciary reporting, even though they spring from common data sources. Management reporting is a dynamic system that examines the results and implications, as measured in dollars, of actions and decisions made in the course of managing the institution. Such reports are essential to ease the trustee task of ensuring sound financial management. They are thus closely allied with business reporting because profit (or lack thereof) is the final measure. Purists often maintain that such an approach clouds the nonprofit status and denies the higher goals of the educational enterprise. Be that as it may, there is a bottom line to higher education financial operations. An institution cannot exist for long if it spends more than it receives—whether by loss, lack of profit, or excess (deficit) of income over expenditures.

The single most important report for the individual trustee is what I, a nonaccountant, choose to call the *operating statement*. This is similar to, and an extension of, the statement of current funds, revenues, expenditures and transfers (to use a common title) found in fund accounting system reports. A rearrangement or adaptation of this report can provide an operating statement that is more readable and understandable to trustees. Shorn of some detail, with some aggregation of line items, rearrangement into budget format, and addition of the current budget and last year's actual comparisons, the operating statement can look much like the corporate profit-and-loss statement. The details of the conversion can be left to the financial officer once he or she understands clearly what the board wants.

Trustees can use other reports to keep informed on the status of incoming gifts, investment performance, the endowment, and capital projects. Special reports can be compiled on areas of current interest and concern that should be discontinued when the need is past. For a more thorough discussion of management reporting requirements and suggested report formats, see *Financial Responsibilities of Governing Boards* published by the Association of Governing Boards of Universities and Colleges (1989a).

One caution should be noted here. The number of routine and special management reports requested by the board should be limited to those that clearly provide a core of financial management information to the trustees. Overloading the financial officer with requests for reports is easy to do, often because of the casual curiosity of only a few trustees. The financial officer has other things to do than supply trustees with information. He or she is charged with the operational management of the finances, which the trustees are monitoring.

Program Relevance

Dollars are spent to support programs. Expenditures are reported by object class (salaries, travel, books, paper, and paper clips) and by the functional or organizational unit that required the expenditures. Such reports are used by the administration as a part of the budget control apparatus and may be useful under certain circumstances to aid the trustee in understanding why and by whose authority the expenditures were made. But the trustees' main interest should be in the cost of the programs that affect the institution as whole and that cut across departmental lines and functional authorities. For example, an interdepartmental program in urban studies will require expenditures in several departments, which obscure the true cost of the program. First-year student seminars conducted by faculty from a number of departments fragment the expenditure and thereby distort the perceived costs of the program. In the past, identifying and aggregating program costs has been difficult and time consuming. With the help of computers, many institutions now include a program identification with each recorded cost, so they can provide program costing if requested. The initiative should be with the trustees to select and request reports on key programs of interest, again recognizing the danger of overloading the system with reports of minor consequence.

Depreciation

Institutions of higher education have been advised by the Financial Accounting Standards Board (FASB-93) that depreciation must be recognized in the case of long-lived tangible assets, such as buildings and equipment. The major effect of this advisory has been a substantial write-down in the former value of buildings and equipment and thus a sharp drop in the stated net worth (total of fund balances) on the institution's books. The decision as it now stands will have little effect on the current-funds statement. The intricacies of the change are best left to the accountants, but the decision does again point up a larger consideration long avoided by institutions of higher education.

Physical facilities have been deteriorating for years. This is the erosion of capital at its worst because it has been camouflaged by the convenient flexibility of higher education accounting practices. Dollars were directed to shore up sagging operating budgets, while the buildings continued to wear out unattended. Across the country, the cost of deferred maintenance is estimated in the tens of billions of dollars. And this estimate does not include the impending cases of like magnitude that will cover major rehabilitation of facilities long past their prime in condition and function. Gifts will not cover these specific needs. Major donors shy away from the honor of providing a memorial replacement roof to the chapel. For the most part, the monies will have to come from unrestricted operating revenue.

To begin to solve the problem, a growing number of institutions have established a cash charge, based on a variety of formulas, to the current operations budget, with the cash transferred to the plant fund as a reserve to accommodate future rehabilitation and repairs. In a sense, such charges are in lieu of the depreciation charges found on corporate operating statements, but they are fully funded and placed in reserve rather than being a simple bookkeeping entry. Many institutions now admit to the problem and would like to begin corrective action but are faced with a major drawback: such a forward-looking charge would throw the current operations severely into the red. Regardless of this unhappy result, the problem must eventually be faced. The financial vulnerability is growing and compounding year by year, and the ultimate impact could well carry an institution under. The board and the individual trustees should have a complete understanding of this peril and take actions to offset the debacle as financial opportunity permits. The classic study of this problem is found in Jenny's treatise *Hang Gliding or Looking for an Updraft* (1981). It is still completely relevant and worth an interested trustee's time.

Coherency of the Reporting Systems

A common complaint of trustees is that common line identifications have different meaning or contain different data on different reports. For example, the line item on the statement of current operations that reads "Gifts to current operations" may have a figure of $575,000, but the line item on the development report that reads "Gifts to current operations" has a figure of $690,000. The reports, prepared by different people, include only cash on the operating statement but include both cash and pledges on the development report. The explanation is understandable, but the reporting is still confusing to the trustee. There appears to be no real reason for such inconsistencies. Trustees should request that inconsistencies be eliminated. The result is what systems analysts would call a coherent system.

Accounting Creativity

A great deal of creative accounting can be and is practiced quite legitimately in higher education. The objective is to show a balanced budget. As Jenny (1981) puts it, the question is not, What is our bottom line? but rather, How can we arrange things to show a balanced budget?

The flexibility of fund accounting permits such legal artifice. Each fund is treated essentially as an individual enterprise. Although the consolidated fund balances tabulation is somewhat (but not completely) similar to a statement of net worth, the funds are treated separately as to their revenues and expenditures. The operating statement, based largely on data presented in the statement of current funds, revenues, expenditures, and transfers, can be enhanced by hiding some costs in other funds. Decisions to amortize costs over a period of years can bring relief to the bottom line this year and postpone the impact to later years. For example, although the cash has been spent, the start-up costs of a major fund-raising effort may be spread over the five years of the campaign, thus lightening the load on this year's budget but adding to the budgets of the next four years.

The desire to establish or maintain a positive image in the

eyes of a potential major donor, the attraction to a potential student of a stable institution "in the black," and the general public's perception of financial solvency are often understandable motives for such cosmetic reporting of financial results. The important thing is that the trustee recognize the process if such cosmetics have been employed and be fully aware of future implications.

Planning and Budgeting

The basis for board measurement and monitoring of the institution's financial affairs is the operating and capital budget. The budget should accommodate the institution's mission as endorsed by the board and should be consistent with the long- and short-term planning as approved by the board. This seemingly obvious point is made because too often I have seen budgets take on a life of their own that, after some years of free adaptation to events, no longer reflects the mission of the institution. Thus, as the sternly pure liberal arts institution competes for students, it may find its budget drifting through the years toward vocational programs in the competition for students, with no consideration of how the changes affect the institution's basic mission. This scenario is not a censure of the accommodation to budget pressures but rather a suggestion that a rational consideration of the change in mission and the long-term effects upon the institution should precede a changed orientation. The requirements for financial management and perhaps even solvency should not usurp the board's authority to clearly define a changing mission (prompted by whatever events) and evaluate the long-term consequences of such a change. The institution's financial managers do not have the prerogative to declare such change.

Operating Budget

The detailed budget will be prepared by the administration, with board input coming mainly from the finance committee. Normally, this process will bring the budget to the finance committee and the board several times. First, the board will see a planning budget or budget estimate that should include the assumptions underlying the budget figures and an invitation to comment on or question them. This step should come at least six months before the beginning of the budget year. Next, the board will review a proposed budget that revises earlier estimates and seeks board approval, pending more exact information on actual student numbers, gifts received, closing current year-end expenditures, and so on. This budget is usually presented near the close of the academic year. A third revision, adjusted to actual figures, should be presented to the board for approval as the final budget shortly after the beginning of the new academic year.

Control of the Operating Budget

Trustee control over the budget will be accomplished primarily by the nature of the questions trustees ask and their satisfaction with the responses. Casual and perfunctory questioning and the acceptance of half-answers does little to enforce the board's responsibilities. Basic assumptions should be questioned and discussed. Assumptions about student numbers and retention, inflation, interest rates, and many other items are the budget's base and should not be shaped to yield a "wished-for" budget result—a frequent human tendency. Trustee questions should uncover such wishful thinking and suggest more realistic assumptions. A good budgeting technique is to develop best-case and worst-case variations of the budget and thereby demonstrate the sensitivity of results to different assumptions. Many boards require such an analysis, which identifies the dominant influences and focuses discussion on the most important items.

A most important assumption concerns the amounts and types of revenue, an area where wishful thinking most often occurs. Even trustees, in their wish to see a balanced budget, are sometimes prone to force-fitting the revenue projections to the desired programs and facilities. The board should exercise a cool self-discipline at this point, being neither overly negative about nor swept along in the misplaced financial enthusiasm of administrators.

Questions concerning budgeted expenditures should be directed at major line items and the projected costs of programs. Tinkering with minor line items, which some trustees seem wont to do as a demonstration of the thoroughness of their examination, should be avoided as a misdirection of time and effort. If the budget is tight (and it always is), the trustees do well to ask the administration to once again review program priorities to be certain that top-priority programs are given the monies required to assure quality execution while low-priority programs take cuts or are eliminated. A simple percentage cut in every line item is not astute financial management. It implies an equivalence of all activities and material requirements that is patently not true in higher education programs. Forcing selective choices is one of the prime contributions trustees can make.

The board should also question the stability of income restricted to supporting specific activities. Budgets are often balanced with "soft" dollars that come from grants and gifts that are much appreciated but will not always be available. A foundation grant that subsidizes the initiation of a new urban studies program, for example, is great for launching a successful program. However, success brings the requirement to continue the urban studies program, but with what or whose dollars? Such soft money projects are a splendid way to rush into future budget deficits.

A most difficult decision at budget time is to balance today's needs against the needs of the future. Current requirements are often painfully obvious, and all have their supporting lobby. Faculty members press for postponement of major rehabilitation in order to provide funds for salary increases. Social sciences absolutely must initiate a new interdepartmental course with philosophy. Why not postpone maintenance? Why not increase the endowment payout for a year or two? This form of taking care of today's desires at the expense of the future has caused the erosion of the capital base of many institutions.

The Capital Budget

All institutions have their operating budgets in some form or another. Not all institutions have a formalized capital budget. Although its preparation may not be as procedurally complex as that for the operating budget, it is equally important to the financial discipline of the institution. The capital budget should look at least five years into the future and include the expenditure estimates for all major repairs, modifications, and rehabilitations of buildings. Major equipment replacements should be included also. A major one-time effort to catch up on all major deferred maintenance could be included. Routine maintenance and small purchases should be excluded. Anticipated sources of funds should be noted. Gifts may be sought for some of the new facilities and major rehabilitations, with expenditure authorizations to be given only after the arrival of such gifts. (But let it be noted that a distant pledge is of little use for building construction where the need is readily available money.) The plant reserve may furnish some funds. A direct allocation of current unrestricted funds, assuming that there is an existing fund balance, may be made. In some urgent cases, debt financing may be recommended.

The capital budget should be drawn up by the administration, often in consultation with the building and grounds committee, and submitted to the board for approval, as is the operating budget. Because of shifting priorities and the uncertainty of some funding availability, the capital budget will probably see many modifications as the months and years roll by. Because the capital budget does not have the same current-year focus as the operating budget, it should be reviewed, modified as necessary, and extended in time at least annually. The finance committee, assisted by the building and grounds committee, should monitor conformance with the budget and initiate corrective action if actual capital expenditures wander too far from the approved budget.

When the budgets and financial plans are established, the board takes up its monitoring assignment. Monitoring is more than just receiving reports. Questions should be asked continually and discussions held concerning the reported performance. The finance committee should follow the actual performance closely via phone, mail, and meetings that are scheduled between the full board meetings. If variances become too far out of line or new conditions arise, the finance committee and the board should move immediately to investigate and to institute changes if necessary. No trustee should silently accept obviously deficient financial performance.

Endowment Management

Investment policy and management are discussed thoroughly in Chapter Ten. But beyond the important matter of handling the investments most profitably are two fundamental decisions to be made by the board. The first is how much money to put into endowment funds. The second is how much of the earnings to take out. This again illustrates the tension of the future versus the present.

To the surprise of many trustees, the majority of private institutions have no or so little endowment that it is not a major factor in the financial affairs of the institution. As a practical matter, many institutions have erased endowment as a feature in their financial planning and look to current cash flows and donors' largesse to keep them solvent. Others cling to the notion of establishing and building an endowment, and many include such a need in their capital campaigns. Those institutions fortunate enough to have a substantial endowment still strive to increase endowment funds. If endowment is to be considered a major stabilizing factor in the future of the institution and through its earnings become a meaningful factor in institutional quality, the question becomes, how much? As much as possible may be the most correct answer, but it gives little planning guidance.

A common measure is the endowment per student, and a common goal aims at some target portion of the budgeted revenue, which can be roughly translated into a portion of cost per student to come from endowment. Thus, if the goal is 8 percent of a $15,000 per-student cost and the endowment payout is 5 percent, the underlying endowment required is $24,000 per student. Today, many substantially endowed institutions think in terms of $50,000 to $100,000 as per-student goals, with some of the most fortunate institutions already beyond the $100,000 mark. Each institution that seeks to establish or enlarge endowment funds must set its own goals based on a realistic assessment of budget competition within the institution for the dollars and the sources from which funds can come— probably a major capital campaign that highlights endowment needs to prospective donors.

At the other end of the endowment pipeline is the decision

about what the payout should be. In the past, the policy for many institutions has been to pay over all current earnings from the endowment funds. As the realization has come that inflation erodes the buying power of the endowment base, many institutions have adopted payout formulas that retain some portion of current earnings and capital gains (the total return) to offset this erosion of value. The formulas usually have the added advantage of stabilizing the annual transfer of funds into the revenue budget, which eases the financial planning task. Most formulas base the payout on the average market value of the endowment over a period of years, three years being the most common. The selection of the payout percentage balances the need to leave enough in the endowment to offset inflation with the demands of current budgets. Most institutions are found in the range of 5 to 7 percent, which usually does not leave enough to completely offset the endowment's erosion, although it does slow the erosion.

In the long run, it is financial discipline that matters. Once the board has set realistic goals for the creation or enhancement of endowment and a viable payout formula, the board must have the stamina to persist in the course adopted. Scarce dollars may force postponement of goal attainment and urgent current needs may suggest modification of the payout formula, but any such shifts should be made only with a full realization that the board is tampering with the future of the institution.

Plant Management

Plant management will normally fall under the oversight of a board committee that is usually called the buildings and grounds committee or the plant committee. This committee will have a close liaison with the financial committee. It should include, if possible, trustees with some plant, architectural, or engineering background. As it plans and monitors buildings, grounds, and equipment activity, the committee will watch the plant fund closely.

Facilities Planning

Facilities planning starts with a long-term master plan that spreads into detailed planning as the time for the execution of the master plan nears. The master plan may be developed by an outside consultant, but more often the capabilities of the institution suffice. The broad plan should stretch twenty years or more into the future and project new or expanded buildings; major rehabilitations; future facilities locations; modifications of utilities networks and installations; and layouts of walks, drives, and parking. The plan should obviously dovetail with the overall financial and program planning of the institution. Whether the plan is prepared by outside consultants or institution staff, the board's task, through the buildings and grounds committee, is to see that a viable plan is in place and kept up to date.

Assessment of the Condition of Facilities

The beginning of any facilities plan is an audit of the present condition of facilities. Many administrations (and therefore boards) feel that the conditions and needs are obvious; all that is required is money and time. It is surprising what faults and impending failures are overlooked by such a casual appreciation. A complete audit will cover all of the systems of every building in a standard analysis: exterior walls, windows, primary and secondary structure, interior walls, utility systems, and safety and handicapped access features, for example.

A major consideration in "time-to-replacement" estimates will be the life cycle of the buildings and each building's systems. Some buildings will be worn out. Others may well be outmoded and bypassed by the needs of the programs housed in them. Energy efficiency is a major concern, and there will inevitably be a few code violations, overlooked or given "grandfather" waivers, that will require updating in any major facilities renovation. Estimates of cost and priorities for accomplishment must be determined, and the source of necessary dollars must be identified in cooperation with the finance committee. The building and grounds committee has the responsibility of seeing that such a current audit is available and, if not, that one is undertaken.

New Construction

The anticipation of new buildings usually lights up the eyes of the trustees. New buildings imply forward motion. They suggest program renewal and modernization, and keeping up with the Joneses. But whether or not to build is a most central trustee decision. Funds so committed are locked into bricks, mortar, and equipment and are virtually irretrievable for any other purposes in the future.

Program needs and priorities should be given one more thorough review. Funding sources should be fairly well known and assured. Major gifts will probably be sought as part of a major capital campaign or as a special project. Whatever gift sources may be tapped, trustees must recognize that these gifts deplete the reservoir of dollars potentially available from donors for other purposes. In the absence of other sources and with a most critical need, debt financing may be required. Debt financing is considered by most institutions as a last resort. Not only are dollars locked into bricks and mortar, but future dollars are committed as well, therefore, the action prejudices future financial flexibility. If debt financing must be done, the board should identify the most probable sources for debt service funds, recognizing that debt service cannot be easily postponed and major donors do not flock to the opportunity to pay off debt.

The administration should take on the task of selecting the architects for the competition and should make its recommendation on the final choice. The decisions should be made in full consultation with the building and grounds committee, the chair of the board, and other closely interested trustees. Following the selection, the committee, in complete liaison with the administration, will be mostly occupied by monitoring the preliminary or concept phase. At this point, the standards of quality are set, the tone of the facility established, and the size of the facility finalized.

It should come as no surprise that once approval is given to proceed with preliminary drawings, faculty and administrative restraint can disappear, leaving the trustees to maintain the discipline that will put the available dollars to their best use. There will probably be some tension; after all, a department head will not soon again be the recipient of a new building and so moves to get everything possible while he or she can. But a "dollar saved is a dollar earned," and the building and grounds committee and the board have dollars to earn at this point.

Maintenance and Renewal

By this time, the educated trustee probably knows that higher education has a tremendous deferred maintenance backlog—some estimates are as much as $50 billion nationwide. The impact varies widely among institutions. The reason is no mystery. Deferred maintenance is a result of the gradual stealing of funds from future needs to provide for present needs and wants. Tuck-pointing can always be postponed. The failing roof can be given one last coating of tar. With luck, the old plumbing system will confine its leaks to places where damage is minimized. Most institutions are trying to catch up with repairs and preventive maintenance but costs keep rising as postponements continue.

The only way to get back on track is to assess the deferred maintenance needs, establish priorities and estimated costs, develop a plan, and then display the discipline to execute it. Funds may be scarce, but much deferred maintenance is to the point where it is just as emphatically a current need as the development of academic programs. In some cases, the facility may be so far gone through the lack of timely maintenance that building a new facility makes far more economic sense over the years ahead. It will cost more initially, but the opportunity to update outmoded features and the lower maintenance costs for years to come make it an opportunity to be explored. Again, the choice is often whether to plan for the future or limp along with inadequate facilities while trying to maintain acceptable academic and nonacademic programs today. Each institution has its own unique situation, and each institution should have a dedicated board that does not back away from hard judgment calls.

Plant Reserves

The place and growing adoption of plant reserves, which are built in anticipation of future major maintenance and rehabilitation requirements, has been mentioned earlier. Such reserves have an important potential stabilizing value, and boards should seriously consider creating such a fund. The allocation of an unrestricted bequest is a way of establishing a reserve that has been taken by a number of institutions. The discipline of making an annual charge to current funds is most helpful but should be entered into gradually to avoid disturbing current cash flows. And, once established, the reserve should not be considered a source for general contingency funds. The reserve fund has its own special dedicated purpose and the board must see that it is expended for that purpose and no other. An adequately funded and wisely used plant reserve can be one of the most important factors in stabilizing capital expenditures, so it contributes greatly to the superior management of the institution's finances through the years.

The Audit Committee

In keeping with its collective fiduciary responsibility, the board should see that the financial activities of the institution are subject to regular audit with respect to the validity of procedures and their conformance with donor restrictions, applicable laws and regulations, and board policies. Some larger private institutions have their own internal audit staff, but most combine the internal audit responsibilities with other functions. All institutions retain outside public accountants for the external audit. To oversee and conduct the necessary auditor liaisons, many boards are establishing an audit committee of the board. The committee is usually small, with five members being a common maximum. The committee may report independently to the board or may operate under the appointment of the finance committee, although the members need not be members of the finance committee. The board chair, the chair of the finance committee, and the president and members of the administration should be excluded from membership.

The committee's responsibilities should include being the liaison with internal auditors to discuss their procedures, findings, and recommendations. The committee should meet with the selected external auditors prior to the audit to discuss the scope and general procedures of the audit and to discuss areas where the board may desire a specific emphasis. Following the audit, the auditors should provide the committee with a detailed review of the findings, without administrators present. The committee should then review the findings with administrative managers and discuss corrective actions that may be necessary. The committee will report all of this activity to the full board and continue to monitor corrective actions. The committee will also make its recommendation to the board regarding the appointment or reappointment of the accounting firm to undertake the following year's audit.

Because of the continuing nature of audit procedures and programs of corrective action, the members of the audit committee may have somewhat longer tenure than members of other committees. It should be obvious, however, that some regular turnover is required to avoid any perception of an entrenched group of trustees that may be set in its ways and impervious to suggestions of possible new and productive avenues of review.

The overarching theme of this chapter has been that no trustee is exempt from the requirement to exercise fully his or her fiduciary responsibility and the responsibility to ensure that adequate financial policies and procedures are in place. The trustee should participate in the monitoring and discussions that are a part of the continuing evaluation of the financial outcomes of the institution's operations. Financial expertise is not a requirement. A seemingly awkward or inept question from a financial novice can force open matters that have been overlooked by trustees trained in traditional approaches and analyses. This is why having trustees from a variety of backgrounds on a board lends strength to the board. But every trustee, whether a financial amateur or trained professional, should get into the action. He or she can make a significant contribution to the successful financial management of the institution and so to the growing and enduring health of the institution that he or she has elected to serve.

CHAPTER 10

Setting Investment
Policy and
Monitoring
Performance

Louis R. Morrell

For some colleges and universities, the income from endowment is essential in supporting the operations of the institution while for others such income is supplementary, providing a margin of excellence in the academic program. Endowments are also critical in helping to offset the impact of economic downturns, times when donors might reduce gifts and parents and students might be less willing and able to accept rising fee levels. Thus, endowment funds provide a buffer that protects the academic program from the impact of cyclical economic conditions. In effect, the investment portfolio offers stability while it provides some degree of flexibility. The endowment also serves as a vehicle to transfer accumulated wealth from one period to the next. Unlike private foundations, which under current tax law must annually spend at least 5 percent of the market value of the investment fund, colleges and universities can accumulate all endowment growth. The probability of accumulating excessive levels of endowed funds is slight considering the ever-increasing need for more revenue to support the operating budget. Trustees must be concerned with balancing current financial needs with those of the future.

Establishing Investment Policies

One of the most important functions of the board of trustees is setting investment policies by working through its investment committee. That committee should make a series of investment-related policy recommendations to the board. Such policies, if approved by the board, form the framework under which the board fulfills its fiduciary responsibility with respect to the endowed assets of the institution. In addition to meeting the financial needs of the operating units within the institution, the board is responsible to external donors who have made gifts to establish or add to existing endowment funds. These responsibilities have traditionally been known as the stewardship function. Donors assume, and often demand, that the assets be well managed in terms of achieving a favorable amount of total return (appreciation and yield) while ensuring that sufficient economic value is maintained for the future. Each investment policy decision represents the position of the board on a specific aspect of the care and management of the endowed assets.

The broad overall investment policy of an institution might typically read as follows: "The investment policy of the institution is to place the endowed funds into a mix of asset classes in order to reduce market and inflation risk, to ensure a total return equal to or greater than the rate of inflation, to provide a steady and increasing stream of income for operations, to control the use of the endowment as a source of support for operations, and to retain asset value that is enhanced on an after-inflation adjusted basis."

Total return relates to achieving both current income and future capital appreciation from an investment. The two different kinds of return (income and appreciation) are combined to form the "total return" (Heerwagen, 1988, p. 5).

The establishment and acceptance of a broad investment policy is critical to ensure that board members agree about the board's objectives in overseeing the endowment assets and to ensure continuity of policies and practices over time (Ellis, 1985). Policies help to protect the investments against constant changes. Turnover in committee membership creates a special challenge to maintaining consistency. The key element is discipline that counters the tendency to take inappropriate action in response to short-term information and conditions. Members of investment committees are human and subject to decision making based partly on emotion. The true test of a committee comes when securities prices drop sharply in the market, a situation that causes anxiety. To counter this, members of the investment committee should be well informed about the realities of the investment world. A sound investment policy provides guidance both to the committee and to the portfolio manager. From the broad policy comes a series of decisions concerning the many aspects of endowment management. Each of the decisions is discussed in the following sections.

Endowment Management

Most institutions use the services of several outside investment managers because of the increased volatility of securities markets and the sharp increase in the number of investment vehicles now available. Individual managers specialize in one of several different investment styles, such as growth, value, and fixed income. Under this approach, the board or its investment committee no longer monitors individual holdings in the portfolio, but instead establishes performance goals and oversees the selected managers by gauging their ability to function in the changing environment. Personal meetings and regular communication with the managers are important. A committee should be in contact with all managers, whether they are performing well or not. This allows the committee to see its managers at all stages, thus gaining an understanding of their strengths and weaknesses (Rosenberg, 1986).

Balance of Return and Risk

The allocation of assets is a critical part of the investment committee's function. It involves both deciding which asset classes, such as domestic common stocks, international stocks, domestic bonds, foreign bonds, real estate, and cash equivalents, are to be included in the portfolio and the relative portion (weighting) of each. For example, an institution might wish to have 35 percent of its assets in domestic common stocks, 15 percent in international stocks, and 50 percent in domestic bonds. Some committees assign the allocation of assets to third parties, but most take action themselves. Before making a specific asset allocation decision, the committee must establish its investment objective, which can best be stated in real (adjusted for inflation) terms.

For example, a target return objective might be inflation plus 5 percent. In setting the target, the committee must be aware of the risk tolerance of the board. In general, the higher the return one seeks, the more willing one must be to accept risk. Thus, a key goal of the board is to find a balance between return and risk.

Many factors come into play when the return target is set. Institutions that rely on their endowment as a major source of income should be willing to accept greater risk in order to achieve a higher return. The total return of the endowment must be growing at a rate greater than the use of the endowment as a source of operating income; otherwise, the economic value of the endowment will decrease over time. At the same time, there is a natural tendency for those institutions that rely on endowment income to want to protect this important resource by minimizing risk and thus achieving lower returns.

Risk comes in many forms, and a key function of a board is to control it. One type of risk is called *price risk*. This is the danger that one will pay too high a price for a stock or bond. There is also *business risk* because the particular company in which one owns stock (or a bond) could lose profit or fail. *Interest rate risk* is the risk that higher interest rates will reduce the value of both stocks and bonds.

One factor to be considered in setting asset allocation is actions taken by other institutions of higher education. Each year the National Association of College and University Business Officers (NACUBO) publishes a study of investment performance that includes a section on asset allocation. Table 10.1 shows the asset allocation by size of endowment for the period that ended June 30, 1991.

As shown in Table 10.1, compared to smaller endowments, larger endowments tend to have smaller positions in fixed income and cash equivalents, and larger positions in equities, real estate,

Table 10.1. Asset Allocation by Colleges and Universities.

Asset Class	Size of Pool (in Millions of Dollars)			
	$25 and under	*$25 to $100*	*$100 to $400*	*Over $400*
Common stock	46.3%	49.6%	57.3%	52.5%
Fixed income	40.3	36.2	29.6	30.7
Cash equivalents	10.8	9.8	7.3	5.2
Real estate	1.2	1.5	2.5	3.0
Other	1.4	2.9	3.3	8.6
Total	100.0%	100.0%	100.0%	100.0%

Source: National Association of College and University Business Officers, 1992. Reprinted by permission.

and other assets (venture capital, oil, gas, leveraged buyouts, and distressed obligations).

Over long periods of time, equities have provided the greatest level of real (inflation-adjusted) return, averaging approximately 6 percent for the past eighty years. During the same period, bonds have provided only 1.5 percent return and cash, less than 1 percent. More recently, both equities and bonds have provided excellent real returns, with equities returning 12 percent and bonds returning 7.7 percent in real return in the 1980s. At the same time, equities have been more volatile than bonds or cash equivalents. Since 1960, stocks have experienced negative real returns in only seven of the twenty ten-year periods starting with 1960 to 1969 and ending with 1980 to 1989. Therefore, institutions that opt for asset mixes that offer relatively high returns must be prepared to accept periods of unfavorable investment results.

In general, the following assumptions can be made concerning asset classes:

1. Equities, both domestic and foreign, have average returns that are higher than those of bonds or cash equivalents. Volatility as measured by price fluctuation is greater in equities than in bonds. There is little or no volatility in short-term instruments, such as treasury bills or money market funds.

2. Foreign equities face a risk of loss of value from changes in currency rates. Such exposure diminishes over long time periods.
3. Bonds have higher returns than do cash instruments.
4. Venture capital, distressed obligation funds, and leveraged buyouts offer the opportunity for returns higher than stock and bonds but have higher volatility.

Asset Allocation

When the board selects the asset classes to be included in the portfolio, it should bear in mind that educational institutions are assumed to exist in perpetuity and have a limited need to withdraw funds. Both of these factors should lead boards to seek higher long-term returns and accept a relatively high degree of market-value fluctuation in the short term. Traditionally, the larger endowments with their greater concentrations in equities and nontraditional assets (venture capital, leveraged buyouts, oil and gas, and distressed obligations) have benefited from relatively high returns. For the ten-year period from 1980 to 1990, the average total returns of various asset classes have been as follows:

International equities	15.1%
Standard & Poor's 500 stocks	14.0%
Long-term treasury bonds	13.6%
Three-month treasury bills	8.1%

For the period 1947 to 1989, a portfolio of 70 percent stocks and 30 percent bonds would have had an annual return of 11.0 percent, in contrast to an annual return of 9.3 percent for a portfolio of 50 percent bonds and 50 percent stocks or a return of 5 percent for a portfolio of all bonds. A portfolio that invests only in bonds will gradually lose ground to inflation, which reduces the purchasing power of the interest income as well as the principal (Heerwagen, 1988, p. 12).

It should be noted that at one time, international equities were considered a nontraditional asset class. However, given the shrinking percent of global capitalization represented by the U.S. equities market, the diversity offered by foreign investments, and the

**Table 10.2. International Fund Returns
for Periods Ended December 31, 1992.**

	One Year	Three Years	Five Years	Ten Years
S&P 500	7.0%	10.8%	15.9%	16.2%
EAFE*	–12.2	–9.0	1.3	16.7

*Morgan Stanley Capital International—Europe, Australia, and Far East (EAFE) Index.

proven track record of investment managers dealing with foreign equities, there is a place in all college and university endowments for stocks of foreign countries. According to the Piper Index, international funds, in comparison to the Standard & Poor's (S&P) 500, had returns as shown in Table 10.2. Over long periods of time (five or more years) international funds have outperformed the S&P 500, but can be considerably volatile in the short run.

The board should set specific target ranges for each asset class, with a high and low percentage for each type of asset. The mix will depend on the desired reward or risk position of the board. For institutions that are not willing to accept the risk of nontraditional investments, such as venture capital, distressed obligations, oil and gas partnerships, and leveraged buyout funds, a typical allocation, with ranges, might be as follows:

Domestic equities	50 to 65%
Foreign equities	8 to 12%
Fixed income	33 to 38%
Cash equivalents	9%

Asset Repositioning

Asset mixes are constantly changing because of price fluctuations in the securities market. To maintain the predetermined mix, steps must be taken to periodically move assets among managers. Without the specific discipline reflected in the range for each type of asset, there can be a reluctance to reallocate assets. When assets are repositioned to stay within the predetermined range, a particular manager who has performed well and increased his or her share of the portfolio is penalized because fees are usually based on the market value of assets under his or her control. At the same time, with established targets, more funds would be assigned to a manager who has not performed well. However, such a system is essential to maintaining the proper asset mix and enabling the institution to dispose of assets at the upper end of the price range and acquire other assets at the lower end of the price range. This is a classic example of a sell-high and buy-low strategy.

Such periodic, relatively small repositionings within prescribed asset ranges should not be confused with market timing, which involves making large swings in asset mixes based on perceptions of market price movement rather than following a disciplined asset allocation policy. Many institutions do not view asset allocation decisions as a key trustee responsibility despite the evidence that trustee decisions may be at least as important as the quality of managers in determining the overall results (Academy for Educational Development, 1985).

A specific procedure should be established for asset repositioning. Too often, institutions rebalance assets only at the time the investment committee meets, which is not often enough and frequently at the wrong time. The cash equivalent account should be used as a residuary fund to balance the portfolio. So long as the target ranges of the noncash assets are maintained for a particular class, no repositioning would be required. Once the lower or upper limit of the range is exceeded, the assets should be moved. It is possible that more than one asset class will move in the same direction at the same time; in such instances, repositioning assets would not be necessary.

On the other hand, bonds and stocks tend to compete for the same investment funds, so it is possible that one class might become more attractive than the other with the result that funds flow to the more attractive class and prices change as the more attractive investment becomes higher priced. At some point, the price of the less-favorable asset will fall to a point at which the asset becomes a very attractive investment. The process of asset repositioning enables the institution to take advantage of such burgeoning opportunities.

I recommend that the institution's financial officer be given authority to reposition the portfolio to the midpoint of the asset allocation range whenever the upper or lower limit is exceeded. To do so, he or she should periodically monitor the asset mix. The institution should also have a policy concerning the receipt of funds from gifts. Such funds should promptly be assigned to one of the external managers.

It may be necessary to establish suballocations within an asset class. For example, if an institution has one "growth" and one "value" manager, it might wish to have a subtarget for each. Thus, when the overall asset mix is to be repositioned, to add to or subtract from the equities segment, the subtarget can be applied. There may also be times when the overall equity target is being maintained but the subtargets are out of balance. When this happens, assets must be transferred to keep the subtargets properly balanced.

Educational institutions with small endowments might opt to assign the asset repositioning task to a single balanced manager. Such managers invest in more than one asset class, at a minimum having both an equity and a fixed-income component. Generally, the balanced manager is free to move the funds between the two components based on his or her perception of relative value. There are two advantages to such an approach. First, there is greater flexibility; investments can be shifted quickly because they are being controlled by a single manager, which eliminates the need for a decision by the institution that would have to be conveyed to the manager. The second advantage is that management fees are reduced because employing one manager costs less, especially since fee schedules are usually of a pyramidal nature with the cost-per-thousand falling as the size of the fund increases. The disadvantage to the single balanced manager approach is that performance might not be as good as a multiple manager arrangement under which market segment specialization is present and more diversity exists.

Another alternative investment vehicle for boards who do not wish to deal with multiple external managers or use a single balanced manager is the Common Fund, a nonprofit corporation created to provide investment management services for educational institutions. The Common Fund follows a pooled approach, much like a mutual fund, in which the assets of the member institutions are combined. The operations are monitored by a trustee committee that selects and oversees the various managers. Within the Common Fund there are a series of alternatives, including equities, bonds, short-term instruments, and international investments. Participation in the Common Fund has the advantage of broad manager diversification, lower management costs, and oversight by a board that consists of investment professionals.

Selection of Managers

Evaluating and selecting managers can be a daunting task. The difficulty lies in the old warning that "past performance is no guarantee of future results." In fact, some people even suggest that an institution would be well advised to hire a manager whose performance in the recent past has been below average because performance generally moves in cycles. Market conditions change constantly. Moving money to managers who have the best recent records is likely to mean buying just before a fall (Rosenberg, 1986).

The first decision by the board of trustees is the style of the managers to be employed. *Style* generally refers to the characteristics of the stocks selected by the manager. There are a number of different styles, but the following are the most common.

Growth Managers

Growth managers seek companies that have rates of earnings growth higher than the market as a whole as measured by the S&P 500. Because stock prices generally reflect level and growth of earnings of a particular corporation, identifying those companies with above-average earnings growth should offer the opportunity for gain—the price of the stock should follow in the same direction. Most growth companies reinvest their earnings to provide additional working capital, so they usually pay low dividend rates to the shareholders. Because one cannot predict the future and unforeseen elements might adversely affect the earnings of the company, growth stocks are relatively risky, offering the possibility of both above-average gains and above-average declines.

Value Managers

Value managers generally seek companies that offer good value. The price of the stock may be low in relation to its earnings or the company may possess assets whose full value is not reflected in its share price. Such companies are often considered to be out of favor with the investment world. Unlike growth companies, which reinvest earnings, value companies generally pay out most of their earnings through high dividend rates. They are usually mature operations with more stable earnings.

International Managers

International managers specialize in foreign companies. Some managers select holdings that are international in scope, while others may concentrate in a particular region of the world. Portfolio size can often be a factor in performance because managers who handle large portfolios command additional resources that can be deployed to gather information on foreign operations that can be complex. In selecting an international manager, a board must decide whether to protect itself against changes in relative values between U.S. dollars and foreign currency by purchasing contracts with foreign exchange dealers ("hedging the currency"). Over extended periods of time, currency fluctuations tend to even out and thus provide higher return than hedged portfolios that pay fees for being hedged. Again, the board must decide how much risk it is willing to take.

Special-Situation Managers

Special-situation managers tend to seek opportunities where they can find them. They might concentrate on a certain industry that they feel will do well in a particular economic environment. They may identify a company that, because of extraordinary leadership or a unique product or service, might do especially well. Companies that are expanding product lines or are able to benefit from a particular circumstance might be identified and their shares purchased.

Bond Managers

Bond managers also have varying styles. There are basically two types of bond managers. One type uses an active managed approach, attempting to forecast interest rate movements. Doing so enables the managers to shift to long bonds before falling interest rates cause long-bond prices to rise and then back into shorter maturities before rising interest rates cause long-bond prices to fall. The other type of bond manager uses an indexed approach that reduces risk by spreading the mix of bonds over varying maturities. This second group strives for enhanced return by identifying companies or industries whose economic situations are improving, thus increasing the value of their bonds. The manager will buy and sell individual bonds in the expectation that other investors will recognize a change in the quality rating of the bond.

Performance Benchmarks

At the time a manager is selected, establishing a performance benchmark is essential to ensure that there is an understanding between the institution and the manager as to what is expected in terms of performance. The total return (appreciation and yield) of each manager should be monitored and compared to the benchmark.

In the area of equities, the most common benchmark is the S&P 500 index. All managers are expected to add value in the sense of achieving total returns, adjusted for their fees, that over time exceed the performance of the S&P 500. This expectation is based on the rationale that the institution could simply invest in an index fund that mirrors the S&P 500 and thus save investment management fees. Therefore, to make the use of individual managers worthwhile, the managers must be able to achieve performance that exceeds an indexed S&P 500 fund. Generally, value managers are expected to provide downside protection to a portfolio; that is, when the overall market falls in price, the value manager is expected to outperform the S&P 500. But in rising markets, the value manager would most likely have a gain smaller than that achieved by the S&P 500. On the other hand, growth and special-situation managers should achieve returns greater than the S&P 500 on a long-term basis while doing significantly better in rising markets and offering less downside protection than value managers.

For the bond portfolio, there are a number of benchmarks, such as indexes provided by Moody's, Merrill Lynch, Salomon Brothers, and Lehman Brothers. There are also indexes for international equity and bond portfolios. When using such indexes as benchmarks, noting portfolio weightings by country as a factor in determining return is best. Each country has its own performance return, and how well a portfolio does in comparison to an index depends on the asset mix of the portfolio. For example, an index with a large percentage of its assets in a high-performing country will attain a higher return than an individual portfolio with a small percentage of its assets in the high-performing country. A specific objective in terms of total return plus management fees should be stated as the performance standard for the bond manager to achieve.

In the case of balanced managers whose portfolios contain both stock and bond components, it is best to use a weighted average based on the target allocations for each asset class. Thus, if the asset target were 50 percent stocks and 50 percent bonds, one would compute the return based on a model portfolio that contains one-half of the S&P 500 and one-half of the bonds found in an index such as the Shearson Lehman (Corp/Govt). The actual result would then be compared to the benchmark performance.

When considering investment return, boards need to review performance over intervals that include a complete market cycle. Many successful managers underperform the market during brief periods, so their performance should be evaluated on the basis of longer intervals. Again, it is best to have an understanding with the outside managers and the investment committee as to the interval to be used for the evaluation of performance.

Reporting Practices

Members of the investment committee should receive monthly reports on the investment portfolio. The report should contain results and information for the current month and the fiscal year to date for the portfolio as a whole. It should also identify gift additions and appreciation or depreciation to date. Asset mix information that compares the target allocations with the actual mix at the end of the month should also be available. Performance by individual managers should be included, along with the indexes serving as benchmarks. There are a number of other supplementary items that can be included in the report: the largest holdings in the portfolio, major purchases and sales in the reporting period, analysis by industry group in comparison to the S&P 500, annualized management fees, and turnover by manager. Because it bears fiduciary responsibility for the institution, and overseeing the endowment assets is part of meeting such responsibility, the board should receive periodic reports as to the performance of the portfolio.

In addition to internal reporting, documents should be prepared for external parties such as donors. When resources are made available through gifts to the college or university, there is an obligation to provide donors with information on how well those assets are being managed and the level of resources being applied for the purposes for which the gifts were made. Institutions with large endowments might prepare special reports, and colleges and universities with smaller endowments might include a section on investments in its annual report or financial report. The information should include a description of the institution's investment policies and method of operation in the management of the portfolio. Performance information for the most recent year as well as for five- and ten-year periods is helpful. The content and format of the investment information should be created in consultation with members of the institutional advancement staff to ensure that the information being provided is clear to external parties. Donors want to know about the institution's endowment spending policy. They frequently have a preconceived expectation as to the effect their endowment contribution will have on the operating budget (Academy for Educational Development, 1985).

Risk Management

In overseeing the investment assets of an institution, a board of trustees exercises what could be called risk management. It must develop policies and take steps that enhance the return from the assets while maintaining risk at acceptable and reasonable levels.

Factors that influence success include the types of assets held, the mix of such assets, and the managers selected. College and university portfolios are exposed to three types of risk. There is no way to avoid one kind of risk, but the other two can be and should be avoided because the school is not rewarded for being subjected to such risk. The type of risk that cannot be avoided and for which one can expect to be rewarded is "market risk" (Ellis, 1985, p. 43). Prices of securities move up and down and so long as one invests in securities, one must accept such risk. However, it can be reduced by proper management.

The second type of risk is that linked to a particular stock, and the third type is related to a group of stocks. These two types of risk can be eliminated by designing a portfolio that replicates the market, called an "index fund." In minimizing the risk by investing in an index fund, the institution may achieve a reduced return.

For those who are willing to accept risk from a group of stocks or an individual stock, there are steps that can be taken to reduce the risk. One strategy involves diversification. Table 10.3. shows investment return relationships over the long term. Negative numbers indicate that returns should move inversely, and a zero indicates no particular relationship. For example, dollar bonds and U.S. stocks are more closely tied (rating of 4.5) than dollar bonds and real estate (rating of 2).

Risk can be further reduced by rebalancing the portfolio to

Table 10.3. Asset Risk Correlations.

	U.S. Stocks	Foreign Stocks	Dollar Bonds	Nondollar Bonds	Real Estate	Cash
U.S.	10.0	6.0	4.5	2.5	3.5	-1.0
Foreign stocks	6.0	10.0	2.5	6.0	3.0	-1.5
Dollar bonds	4.5	2.5	10.0	3.0	2.0	-0.5
Nondollar bonds	2.5	6.0	3.0	10.0	1.5	-1.0
Real estate	3.5	3.0	2.0	1.5	10.0	2.5
Cash	-1.0	-1.5	-0.5	-1.0	2.5	10.0

Source: Brinson Partners, Inc. (formerly First Chicago Investment Advisors). Reprinted by permission.

preset targets. Success in portfolio diversification comes from mixing assets that do not move in tandem and adjusting the mix to attain the original desired blend of different asset classes. Such diversification reduces risk that comes from a single stock and from a single sector or industry group.

Stewardship

In carrying out their fiduciary responsibility, boards of trustees must seek ways to achieve the highest possible rate of investment return within an appropriate level of risk or predictability. The investment goal is to achieve a return (yield and appreciation) equal to or greater than a combination of inflation plus the withdrawal of funds to support the operating budget. To achieve this goal, it is essential that the institution have clearly stated investment objectives and policies to guide the process of attaining the goal in a disciplined fashion. The process involves establishing guidelines, selecting asset classes to be included in the portfolio, designating investment managers, developing a means of repositioning assets, and creating a system to measure the performance of the overall portfolio and the individual managers.

CHAPTER 11

Clarifying the Fund-Raising Role

John W. Pocock

Trustees of private institutions have always had a central role in the fund-raising activities of their institutions. In 1636, the twelve overseers of fledgling Harvard University found the acquisition of the resources necessary to establish and maintain the institution high on the list of those tasks assigned by the Massachusetts General Court. Trustees may try to avert their eyes from the task or turn a deaf ear to the call for action, and many do. To do so is to deny their role as trustees. There simply is no place to hide.

Since the time of the earliest colonial schools, private dollars contributed by interested and discerning donors have meant the difference between meager survival—even extinction—and enriched performance for private institutions. Until the establishment of land-grant institutions in the mid-nineteenth century, private support kept the entire higher education establishment afloat. The history of private giving to higher education is long and enlightening but need not be recited in detail here. Suffice it to say that such voluntary giving came largely from the better endowed members of society until the early days of this century, when the private giving contingent began to grow and broaden rapidly. Following World War II, the apparatus of fund raising began to be refined and extended to become the highly organized and sophisticated process we

179

find in higher education today. The passive tin cup held out by the hopeful supplicant has been replaced by the well-planned and well-orchestrated programs that seed and reap the private giving required today.

The total voluntary support of American higher education, both public and private, in 1989–90 has been estimated at almost $10 billion by the Council for Aid to Education (1991). Twenty years earlier, the estimated total was slightly under $2 billion (Council for Aid to Education, 1972). Since 1983-84, contributions have grown three times faster than inflation as measured by the consumer price index and slightly more than twice as rapidly as the higher education price index, which mirrors the costs of goods and services purchased by higher education institutions. Clearly, many dollars are available to higher education from prospective donors. Reaching these donors and inspiring them to give to one's institution is a most competitive task in today's giving environment. Trustees must understand that they are at the head of this undertaking and that the effort can succeed or fail based on their commitment of time, talent, and treasure.

Why trustees? The simple answer is that the board is the ultimate seat of power in the private institution and therefore ultimately responsible for everything that happens within the institution. Adequate resources to maintain and forward institutional programs are at the heart of institutional health. The dominant resource is money. Trustees sit at the highest level of institutional governance and are presumably knowledgeable about the plans and needs of the institution. Furthermore, they are responsible for expending funds to best support the programs of the institution. Prospective major donors wish to deal with the people in whose hands lies the present and future health of the institution. Only the president can match the trustees in this respect, and the president simply cannot cultivate all prospective major donors.

The individual trustees were appointed to the board because they are recognized for their personal achievements and are respected role models and pacesetters in their communities. Most trustees know important people and move easily in their professional and social worlds. Their personal ties and relationships can be drawn upon to steer people into the institutional orbit and into an interest in the programs of the institution.

For all of these reasons, trustees have the clear potential to be the most productive participants at the highest level of the fund-raising program. Despite initial reluctance on the part of some trustees, personal satisfaction and a sense of personal fulfillment, both as a donor and a successful solicitor, are the greatest rewards cited by the trustees who make the effort and do the job. For many reasons, trustees must be full participants in fund raising if the goals sought are to be achieved.

A Fund-Raising Program Is More Than a Campaign

In the last several decades, the completely fleshed out fund-raising program has arrived as a central, ongoing function of a higher education institution. Many private institutions are only now recognizing what a total fund-raising approach involves and are still coming to terms with the requirements. The effective total fund-raising program builds on the proclaimed institutional mission, anticipates the short- and long-term needs of the institution, is supported by meaningful research, and brings a variety of fund-raising mechanisms into an orchestrated endeavor overseen by a trained professional staff. The annual campaign for current operating funds, the periodic capital campaigns, and ongoing special projects are merged into a well-balanced program.

Each component feeds on and nourishes the others. Donor prospects are identified according to their interests and the probability that they will make a major gift now or later. Then they are appropriately introduced to those institutional programs most likely to kindle their interests and draw their support. All of the means of contributing are selectively involved: for example, cash gifts, pledges, deferred gifts, pooled income funds, trusts, and bequests. Meshing all of these elements of the complete program is mainly the task of the professional fund-raising staff. Trustees need not understand all the details of the various undertakings, but they should grasp the complexity and the main elements of the entire adventure and so better pick up and execute the trustee role.

The trustees should make sure that the entire campus community and all of the off-campus constituencies—alumni, parents, friends, the community—understand the need for and accept the goals of the fund-raising program. Some people cling to the notion that funds should flow into the coffers of the institution through the natural charitable instincts of the human race. Such an idealistic scenario is not and has never been the case. The glow of institutional merit will not of itself attract the supporting resources required today. A gentle and continuing educational effort is necessary to maintain the awareness of and interest in the ongoing fund-raising program among faculty, students, alumni, parents, and prospective donors near and far. Trustees can help in this educational process. By spoken and written word and by actions, the board and individual trustees can assert their own acceptance, support, and leadership of fund raising. No group can bestow a higher credibility.

Where Funds Come From

Maintaining a competitive edge in fund raising starts with knowledge of the primary sources of gift support. It also requires knowledge of who competes for the same support, and effective presentation of the institution's uniqueness and distinctiveness.

Sources

Most of the gifts and most of the dollars come from individuals. A survey of the fund-raising activities of private institutions sponsored by the Association of Governing Boards of Universities and Colleges (1989b) showed that in 1985–86 individual institutions received a mean of 52.6 percent of their dollars from individuals, and the total rises to 60.5 percent if bequests are included. Other less comprehensive surveys confirm the figures, which have long been accepted as benchmarks by professional fund raisers.

Corporate sources rank second to individuals in dollars contributed and totaled more than 18 percent of gift receipts across all higher education institutions, private and public, according to the AGB survey. But private institutions should be cautious—corporations direct their dollars heavily toward the public sector and large institutions. Private institutions report a mean of 13.5 percent, with the smallest institutions receiving only about 10 percent of their gift dollars from corporate sources. This skewing of corporate giving should be noted when the fund-raising plans of private institutions are being developed.

Foundations rank third as sources for all higher education gift dollars, but here the climate favors private institutions, which received 15.2 percent of their dollars from foundations, as opposed to 10.4 for public institutions.

Religious groups have in the past been a supporting force in higher education, but this participation has lessened in the past few decades. Thus, the dollars coming from all other sources including religious groups has fallen to 11 percent, but the figure varies widely according to the unique circumstances of the receiving institution.

These figures are indicative only and should not be used as standards in establishing fund-raising goals. Although they may serve as useful guides, each institution has its own source pattern that should be explored and regularly compared with that of like institutions to ensure that source balance goals are realistic and do not overlook opportunities for expansion.

Competition

There is heavy competition for the billions of dollars offered each year by Americans in support of their favorite causes—over $90 billion in recent years to orchestras, museums, ballet companies, churches, and education. About 9 percent of this total comes to higher education. The whole higher education community and all individual institutions are engaged in this broader competition and would do well as a group to deport themselves so as to heighten public appreciation for their efforts.

Within the higher education community, the competition is direct and specific. Large research institutions compete with one another for the big supporting dollars. Liberal arts colleges compete among themselves and as a group compete with the more vocationally oriented institutions. Within a given geographical area, all causes compete for local dollars.

In recent years, the entry of public institutions into the search for private dollars has further complicated the competition. To date, the public institutions seem to be developing their own natural constituencies and attracting dollars from sources that have never been strong givers to the private sector. While it is too early to draw conclusions on the private/public contest for funds, probably more could be gained by joining forces to educate the citizenry in the growing needs for all higher education institutions than in quarreling over just who deserves the private dollar.

Institutional Uniqueness

To succeed in this competition, the institution must carefully assess its own particular attractions and strengths in its own educational niche and then lay out a basic competitive strategy that emphasizes these unique characteristics and provides a theme for the total fund-raising program. Trustees should help to develop such a strategy, monitor its effectiveness in practice, and urge modification when necessary.

Factors Beyond the Campus

The general condition of the external environment and thus of the donors' receptivity to institutional entreaties is always of concern to the fund raiser. Social and economic factors can and do alter the climate for giving. Yet what specific factors and to what effect is not all that clear. Government support of higher education has lessened in recent years and may not rebound soon. This puts pressure on the requirement for private giving that may or may not evoke a strong response from private donors. The general public disenchantment with higher education and its foibles in recent years would perhaps suggest a diminished public support, but this seems not to be the case according to available giving statistics. Detrimental tax legislation may be a forceful drag on donor ability and willingness to give, but the exact effect of this penalty has not yet been fully illuminated.

Economic Climate

The prevailing economic climate has always been a major factor in the discussion when a major campaign is contemplated. Some campaigns have been postponed in the face of economic downturns, while others have been launched during the same period and have achieved considerable success. The evidence suggests that although economic recession may generate a gloomy outlook among some people, it does not critically affect the giving patterns of most, especially major donors.

Major donors usually have well in hand the assets from which their gifts will come and a passing economic downturn does not seem to blunt their incentive to give. A number of surveys that deal with the interests of major donors report that economic and tax factors rank low on the donors' list of motivating factors. Rather, matters of perceived social responsibility, personal fulfillment, and individual recognition are a far higher priority and go far in offsetting local economic constraints. While such external factors exert some pressure on fund-raising results, the major determinants of the successful fund-raising program are clearly internal.

Public Image

Accepting all of the above, the perceived public image of an institution can critically temper the outcome of a fund-raising program for better or worse. A poorly informed or misinformed public does not rise eagerly to the opportunity to give. If the institution's image, for whatever reasons, has deteriorated in whole or part, the trustees should be among the first to grasp this truth and move to set perceptions right. Shifting or repairing the image of an institution takes time and effort and may well require a reconstituted and redirected public relations program. No fund-raising program will achieve full success if burdened by a negative public image. More often than not, the negative perception may be projected by only one or two areas of institutional activities. Damage control and repair may be carried out in a relatively short period of time. But it should be undertaken and positive results demonstrated before the board puts its imprimatur on a major fund-raising effort.

Preparing the Organizational Base for Fund Raising

The preparation of a sound organizational base would seem to be axiomatic as a requirement, but it is surprising how many institutions relatively new to major fund-raising efforts fail to prepare fully for the undertaking. The need for funds is always urgent, but the history of fund-raising failures cautions that trustees be certain that all groundwork is laid before embarking on a major fund-raising effort. Better to delay for success than to rush into failure.

Composition and Preparation of Board

The composition of the board itself is the first item to be considered. With so much dependent upon the board and the individual trustees, it is critical that the board understand and accept its central role and that the individual trustees can contribute to the task at hand. When asked what is the most common root failure in fund raising, most knowledgeable professionals and consultants agree that a poorly composed, uneducated, and confused board will almost guarantee failure. There are ways to check this matter out. A growing number of private institutions have developed a board profile that specifies the individual and group talents and characteristics they wish to have included in the makeup of their board. High on the lists is fund-raising competence.

There should be no mystery as to the requirements. Accepting the fact that all trustees should be socially responsible, personally committed to the institution, and willing to undertake all tasks of the board as called upon, there is an urgent need for trustees who have the talents and assets required and who will devote a major share of their board time to fund raising. These trustees will help organize and take leadership positions in the fund-raising efforts. They will have friends and contacts in circles that influence the flow of philanthropy. They will enjoy working with people and developing new friendships, and they will have the patience and be willing to undertake the cultivation so important in acquiring major gifts.

Further, there is no dodging the requirement that a good number of board members possess the personal resources that will enable them to make sizable donations to the institution. To some trustees, such a specific requirement is deemed impolite and even mercenary. They will point out that wisdom, too, is a useful requirement. Yet as has been pointed out elsewhere, wisdom and wealth are not necessarily mutually exclusive. No board member can escape the requirement to give and give generously, and no board can escape the requirement to attract members who can give.

The requirements of fund raising should be important criteria in the selection of board leadership. The board chair will be carrying a considerable load and occupy a highly visible position in any fund-raising program. He or she should be selected with this requirement strongly in mind and should understand just what is required in terms of time and energy to do justice to the position. The development committee should have among its members trustees with leadership skills in fund-raising, and the chair of the committee should be appointed with the understanding that he or she will be the deputy of the board chair in all fund-raising activities. The development committee should bear the major burden of orienting and educating all trustees as to their fund-raising responsibilities. While all of the foregoing may seem obvious to the experienced trustee, it remains a fact that the most prevalent flaw blocking successful execution of fund-raising programs is the inadequacy of the board and its individual members in meeting their fund-raising obligations.

Responsibilities of Professional Staff

Just as no institution can expect success in fund raising without a well-selected, educated, and energetic board, no board can undertake its mission without the presence and support of a competent professional staff. The professional staff is the core of operations and provides the creative ability to articulate the entire effort and to manage the ongoing enterprise in detail. Trustees should be convinced that such a competent staff is in place and has the personnel capacity to carry the responsibility adequately.

The president is always the chief fund raiser for the institution and will be most involved in the building and maintenance of the professional staff. According to a survey of the Association of

Governing Boards of Universities and Colleges (1989b), the president spends about one-third of his or her time raising funds. During major campaigns, the private institution's president may find this requirement moving up to one-half or more of his or her time. The president's ever-present leadership role in fund raising should be one of the major selection criteria, and the president should understand and accept this role.

The president will nominate or select a vice president for development or advancement as the first lieutenant in fund raising. The vice president is the tactical leader of the operational program as well as a participant in the strategy and policy determinations. This key staff appointment can make or break the effort, and the vice president's mental capabilities and physical stamina should be judged fully acceptable before moving into a major effort. The president certifies the vice president, but the board should keep its collective eyes open for any signs of a performance problem and consult with the president before significant damage is done.

Beyond the positions of president and vice president, the board should not become involved in personnel selection except as specifically requested. Trustees should be assured that all of the basic functions of fund-raising programs are covered and that the size of the staff is adequate. While no precise standards can be suggested in view of the diversity of institutions and their programs, the annual gift intake per professional staff member ran from about $400,000 for the smaller institutions to almost $1,200,000 for the largest (Association of Governing Boards of Universities and Colleges, 1989b). Although these figures may suggest a reasonable magnitude for staffing, gift totals do not rise automatically with the addition of staff.

It is worth noting that the general admonition to trustees to keep their individual and collective fingers out of institutional operations is breached in the case of development. As a participating member of the fund-raising organization, the trustee becomes quasi staff at a high level and must be brought into the operational details to be effective. Beyond this, trustees are well advised to restrain their supervisory instincts while monitoring staff performance. There can be only one operational boss in the fund-raising program, and that is the vice president for development, who reports to the president for guidance and direction.

Planning the Program

Successful development programs do not rise full-blown. They must be planned, and the planning should be directly linked to the mission statement of the institution and the long-range plans derived from it. The mission statement is the philosophical charter of the institution; it describes the type of education to be offered, how and to whom this education is to be offered, and what the essential services and goals are. By postulating the unique interests and concerns of the institution, it sets the basic tone and appeal of the entire fund-raising effort. It gives a special answer to the question, Why give? Trustees should be certain that a meaningful mission statement is in place.

The long-range plan delineates the specific programs and needs that will translate the mission statement into action. The fund-raising program should mirror the long-range plan by laying out the funding amounts and their timing to make the long-range plan a reality. A good development program that defines both the needs and the actions required to fulfill these needs brings a coherence to the entire undertaking. Such a program will include considerations of the feasibility of meeting the level and timing of the gift intake and may well cause a modification of the long-range plan if its feasibility is questionable.

Any plan should lean heavily for its appeal on the unique characteristics, purposes, and goals of the institution—those things that make it stand out in the company of its peers and competitors. Some of the unique features of the enterprise will warm the interests and hearts of prospective donors more than others. The real question is which characteristics will appeal most strongly to which type of donor and how plans can be shaped to emphasize these appealing characteristics. Trustees must also consider what can be done to raise the appreciation of all donor constituencies for such uniqueness—this is the unending task of donor education.

The plan will address the time required to cultivate donors and the likelihood of their gifts arriving in keeping with the schedule. Annual campaigns must be scheduled to work with the periodic capital campaigns so that previous donor relationships are not confused and overtaxed. Building needs, scholarship needs, academic program needs, and endowment needs must be balanced and viewed against the variety of prospective donor interests and capabilities. Most of this planning will be handled by the professional staff under presidential guidance and with the approval of the board. Despite the self-evident value of such long-range fundraising planning, the survey of the Association of Governing Boards of Universities and Colleges (1989b) uncovered the absence of such planning in many institutions.

The Board's Planning Role

As the program or campaign moves into action, the board has a few matters that it alone, as a governing body, can discharge. Presumably the board has followed and participated in the development of the plan as previously described. Curiously, there is considerable evidence that many boards leave the development of the plan almost entirely to the professional staff, with little or no input. Such a hands-off approach denies the staff the board's perspective, which should be most useful, and it violates the spirit of a team effort. Further, the lack of participation in the development of the plan costs the board a good opportunity to educate itself in the entire undertaking, an education that can inspire trustees to put their maximum effort into the fund raising.

Regardless of its degree of participation in plan formulation, the board should formally approve the planned program or campaign before the specific action begins. Each element of a total program should be examined. The annual campaign should never be taken for granted, although most boards leave the annual effort almost entirely to the professional staff. This is unfortunate because the annual campaign is the foundation of the entire fund-raising program. It develops giving attitudes, identifies potential upscale donors, is a part of major prospect cultivations, trains and identifies the most productive volunteers, gets the board involved, and sets the stage for the major campaign.

Program and Campaign Authorization

The authorization to move into a major program should be granted by the board only after a thorough discussion of the program's magnitude, timing, and costs and the feasibility of achieving the level of gifts sought. Initially, the board may wish the authorization to be provisional to wait the results of more detailed research and testing. The final plan can then be modified as the results suggest and as authorized by the board.

The board should look for balance between the several campaign modes and purposes, the feasibility of achieving the targeted level of funding, and the existing capability of the institution (staff, officers, and board) to undertake a successful effort. If there are questions or obvious gaps in the program, the board should refuse authorization until such questions have been answered and gaps filled to the board's satisfaction. For example, deferred giving is becoming extremely important as its effectiveness over the years is increasingly demonstrated. There are many discrete mechanisms by which deferred giving is encouraged and accomplished. The board should thus assure itself that an effective and well-balanced deferred giving program is included in the plan.

The need for such an in-depth examination is stressed because the emotional wave generated by the contemplation of a major fund-raising program or campaign can sometimes sweep away rational examination to the later distress of all concerned. A half-cocked send-off practically guarantees failure, as countless fund-raising horror stories attest.

Use of Consultants

The use of outside consultants should be considered by the board. Many institutions have found consultants useful in assessing the institution's public relations and assisting in the development of programs aimed at improving the public's perception of the institution. A consultant is often called in to advise on the design or strengthening of either the entire fund-raising program or parts thereof. The most common use of consultants is to study the feasibility of attaining the gift goal sought in a campaign or to suggest a realistic goal. About two-thirds of all the private institutions that responded to the survey of the Association of Governing Boards of Universities and Colleges (1989b) had used consultants for a feasibility survey, and almost all reported favorably on the results. A few major institutions with considerable experience and in-house staff may opt to carry out their own feasibility study, although even the largest are turning more often to outside consultants. Smaller institutions with neither the experience nor the staff will inevitably turn to an uninvolved expert to render an unbiased and professional judgment. Many institutions also retain the outside consultant to follow the campaign and advise them on strategy and tactics.

The talents and capabilities of consultants vary considerably. The important thing is to choose a consultant who has experience with comparable institutions that have comparable programs. The experiences of other client institutions with a specific consultant should be sought. Several consultants should be interviewed before selecting one.

The size of the consulting firm should make little difference if the experience and favorable client reviews are present. Although the larger firms may have more assembled background data and more minds to call upon, the single operator's continuing personal attention may be the more valuable asset. Small institutions have very often found the small firm or single professional most fitting to their own needs.

The board should make sure that the personal chemistry between the consultant and the institutional staff is positive. Good ideas cannot be transferred intact if they face emotional rejection. The purpose, means of conduct, results expected, and financial arrangements should be agreed on before starting work. Any reputable consultant will also want to establish such arrangements.

Needs List

The list of specific needs that the campaign seeks to satisfy should be prepared not only for the major campaign but also for the annual campaign for operating funds, even if the list is short. Few institutions issue much more than a general overview, unchanged from year to year, as to how the annual funds will be used. Because the ongoing regularity of the annual appeal may dull the enthusiasm of donors, a simple focus on a different specific requirement each year can freshen the approach, intrigue standby supporters, and attract new ones.

Whether for the annual campaign or for the much more comprehensive needs of a major campaign, the list will probably be assembled by the president and the professional staff for discussion, modification as necessary, and approval by the board. The list should present true needs, not wishes—it will be large enough without inflating it with unwarranted dreams. Priorities must be set and reliable estimates of cost prepared for each item. Donor attractiveness should be assessed and approaches developed to maximize prospective donor appeal. In the end, there should be something on the list to excite everyone who might be moved to give to the institution. The final list should be completely consistent with the long-range plans of the institution and capable of being adapted to campaign strategies.

Goal Setting

Goal setting is complex for the extended capital or combined capital and operating funds campaigns. The overall goal may be set with the assistance of the feasibility consultant, but there are a number of subgoals that must be set in order to measure the pace and balance of the campaign as it moves along.

For private institutions, a common campaign lasts about five years, which includes the "quiet" period. The quiet period begins the campaign: major gifts are sought to provide a nucleus fund that can be announced when the campaign "goes public." This fund excites the large population of potential donors that will be brought into play. The length of the quiet period varies among institutions and is often based on their actual success (or lack thereof) in bringing in the funds, but a good mean time seems to be two years of a five-year campaign. The quiet-period goals range from about 25 percent to 40 and even 50 percent of the total goal for the campaign. Lack of full success during the quiet period may well indicate that the total goal should be cut back or the entire campaign reassessed. High success and oversubscription during the quiet period has caused many institutions to increase their total goals. Thus, the quiet period should be deemed a test for the goals and strategies of the campaign.

Subgoals should be set for the various constituencies—alumni, foundations, corporations, community, and any other group—that will weigh substantially in the achievement of the goal. A goal must be set for trustee giving as well. The portion of the goal expected to come from trustees will vary according to the circumstances of the institution and the affluence of the board. Trustee giving goals reported by respondents to the survey by the Association of Governing Boards of Universities and Colleges (1989b) ranged from 10 to 50 percent, with most institutions reporting achievement. The final tally across all private institutions showed actual results running well in accord with the goals, with the mean being 16 percent of all dollars coming from trustees. This said, it should again be emphasized that the amount of giving potential of trustees will vary greatly and must be carefully assessed before setting the trustee goal. As they see it, most boards set very high goals for themselves, and most boards that set challenging goals surpass these goals in a significant way. Trustees do warm to the heat of the quest and regularly surprise themselves with what they really can do.

Budgets

The fund-raising budget will have been prepared by the staff and presented to the board for discussion and approval as part of the normal budget process. But as concern over the fund-raising needs of the institution rise, the board should discuss and question the budget to satisfy themselves that it is indeed adequate to support the fund-raising program being contemplated. A sign of the economic times in higher education is pressure to hold back on development and advancement office budgets while at the same time reaching out to attract more private gifts. There is no reason to be spendthrift, but bringing in money does cost money.

The exact manner in which costs of fund-raising activities are recorded varies considerably between institutions and could stand improvement if only to inform boards more succinctly where the money goes. Accepting such inconsistencies, the AGB survey mentioned above showed that the portion of the annual operating budget devoted to the core development functions—the hands-on fund raising—ran from 2.8 percent in the smallest institutions down to 0.5 percent in the largest. If other advancement costs of alumni and public relations and publications are included, the total runs from about 5.8 percent for the smallest institutions down to 0.9 percent for the largest. Clearly, the economy of scale is at work.

Most of these costs underlie the total ongoing fund-raising effort and continue whether or not a major campaign is in progress. In fact, indications from the more successful fund-raising institutions are that the added costs of a major campaign are nominal if the basic program has been funded and executed properly. Campaigns may add some staff, travel, and publications costs, but extensive travel, publications, and major public relations events should continue between campaigns so that the base is maintained for the campaigns themselves.

A special note should be added about the need for "front end" money as an investment in the program. If a new fund-raising program is being established, an existing one raised to a higher level, or a major campaign planned, some considerable allocation of budget dollars will most probably be required to get things moving. Some boards have appeared reluctant to appropriate and spend money for anticipated results a year or two down the line. While a successful program cannot simply be spent into being, the funds must be provided by a board with the faith that a well-developed program supported by adequate funds will bring successful results. If such faith is lacking, it is probably because the necessary preparations have not been made.

Board Organization

The board should review its own organization and assignments in accordance with its leadership role in fund raising. The president will probably spend 50 percent or more of his or her time in active fund raising during the course of a major campaign. The board and individual trustees should clear their decks to support the president and be prepared to take on the individual assignments generated by the president and the heightened activity of the professional staff. In particular, the board chair will assume a visible role and should be available to address assignments that the president simply does not have time to handle.

While some boards assign campaign leadership to the board's development committee, perhaps expanded with a few appropriate nontrustee members, a far more common practice is to establish a separate campaign committee to undertake the overall leadership. The campaign committee will have trustee members and a number of nontrustee members who have an interest in and avenues to specific constituencies. More than two-thirds of the institutions responding to the survey by the Association of Governing Boards of Universities and Colleges (1989b) had opted for using a campaign committee. Interestingly enough, the large institutions have almost universally adopted the campaign committee approach, with great success reported. Smaller institutions seem to cling hopefully to the board structure, perhaps not recognizing the special leadership values of a group that maintains the focus of the entire endeavor. A successful practice has been to establish several committees under the campaign committee to deal with specific constituencies: alumni, parents, students, foundations, corporations, and the essential major gifts committee. Although most members may be nontrustees, some trustees should be members of these committees to make evident the board's leadership participation. The committee on foundations and corporations and the major gifts committee should have substantial trustee membership, and their members will have direct participation in the cultivation and solicitation of the constituencies under their care.

Regardless of the pattern of board organization and trustee assignments, somebody or some group should be assigned to monitor board and trustee performance. Not all trustees will prove to be proficient in their assignments. Workloads may be too great for some trustees to carry with good results. Some trustees may wear out over a five-year campaign period. In such cases, the situation should be recognized and trustee assignment shifts made with grace and understanding. The chair of the board is the obvious candidate for this task, quietly and unobtrusively informed by committee chairs and observant professional staff.

The Trustee as a Fund Raiser

Effective trustee participation in fund raising begins with a significant personal gift and ends with appropriate acknowledgment of
donors' gifts. In between, good research on and cultivation of prospects are essential, together with "closing" the request for support.

The Personal Gift

First and foremost comes the trustees' responsibility for their own
gifts. Gifts should be in keeping with trustees' economic capability
but should stretch the trustees' commitment and dedication to the
institution. This absolute requirement has been regularly stressed
by fund raisers, and one would suppose that by now all trustees
would have gotten the message. The facts are otherwise. Some trustees do not give, for whatever reasons. Successful fund-raising institutions report no such withdrawals; they expect and get 100 percent
support at the first call. But in the AGB survey (Association of
Governing Boards of Universities and Colleges, 1989b), institutions
that reported some problems in attaining their goals also reported
a somewhat haphazard pattern of trustee support, some with only
half of their board contributing.

The reasons for the requirement are quite simple. First, failing to make a donation indicates that the trustee has little dedication to the institution he or she serves and would therefore not make
the effort to solicit other donations. Second, major donors, whether
individuals, corporations, or foundations, want to know that the
board of the institution for whose support they are being solicited
has shown its enthusiastic commitment to the cause by early and
unanimous support from its own pocketbooks. Why give to an
institution whose own trustees seem to vacillate in their support?

Boards should take care of their own solicitation; this is not
the task of the president or the professional staff. If the board cannot
carry out the solicitation of its own members successfully, there is
reason to question the effectiveness of the board's leadership of the
overall effort. The methods of board solicitation may vary, but all
successful solicitations seem to hinge on one central factor: each
trustee should be approached and cultivated as would any prospec-

tive major donor. The simple announcement by the chair that donations are expected will not do the job.

Trustees are people, too. They have their own egos, quirks,
and phobias. They have their preferences for the object of their gift.
They may need a bit of education in giving methods to fit their
circumstances to the most generous donation. All of this is recognized when outsiders are approached. The trustee prospect should
receive the same courtesies.

As with all donors, giving is its own reward. But this is even
more so for the trustee who serves the institution as a contributing
steward and reinforces that stewardship with a meaningful donation of personal resources to further the institution's future. This
sense of satisfaction and personal fulfillment is regularly cited as the
highest reward for the trustee's gift.

Identification of Prospects

With his or her own gift committed, the trustee should turn to
identifying and qualifying prospects who are capable of making
major gifts. Trustees move in circles where there are such persons,
and trustees have avenues by which to introduce themselves to these
people and cultivate them. Trustees do not, as a whole, get good
marks for such identification. Perhaps they have a normal human
hesitancy to identify friends and acquaintances for such a purpose.
Or perhaps an overly casual approach is taken to solicitating such
suggestions from trustees. A general request at a board meeting will
not suffice. It is far better for the chair or a member of the board's
development committee to sit down with each trustee for an extended discussion and draw out the names of prospects and the
reasons they qualify. Possible avenues of approach should be covered and the trustee's willingness to participate in the cultivation
ascertained, recognizing that the trustee making the suggestion may
not be in a position to participate for any of several reasons.

Cultivation

The major gifts committee should develop a strategy for the approach and cultivation of each major prospect and then monitor

that cultivation. A common procedure is to assign each prospect to a committee member for monitoring even though the committee member may not personally be participating in the cultivation. The single most important point to be remembered is that people give to people, regardless of whether the prospect is an individual. an executive of a foundation, or corporation staff. Accordingly, the purpose of cultivation is to build on existing relationships, develop personal rapport with new prospects, and establish a personal conduit through which the institution's interests and needs may be presented and the gift solicited.

Even under campaign pressure, cultivation takes time to produce results. Not all trustees are truly capable in cultivation, and some who have demonstrated their abilities will be called upon more than others. But every trustee should be included in some cultivation effort, no matter how minor, to promote a sense of personal participation. Not all cultivations will be carried on by trustees, but a trustee should be identified with each cultivation to add the prestige of the governing body to the effort. In all of this, the guidance and support of the professional staff is most important. The staff should follow every cultivation and be the control point for the actions. They should indicate when a cultivation is going nowhere and should be cut off or approached differently. They should have a sense from their experience of when to move to a specific request and so bring the cultivation to its final point, the closing.

Closing

Not many trustees are good askers. If possible, the president should be brought in as the closing request approaches, but a few trustees should also be readied for this role. In every case a specific proposal, based on the knowledge of interests and capabilities gained during the cultivation period, should be prepared for presentation. The proposal may be prepared by or with the assistance of the professional staff. Regardless of how it is prepared, the proposal should be reviewed and endorsed by the staff to ensure that no awkward conditions are proposed, that any giving method included is valid, and that the proposal is in keeping with the stated needs of the institution and campaign. Usually, more than a single person should be present when the specific request is made. This adds to the perceived importance of the occasion and brings more than one mind to answer questions and resolve final doubts. The presence of the president, if he or she is not making the solicitation, or a senior member of the professional staff adds to the ceremonial nature of the proceedings and confirms the institution's commitment to continue the relationship with an important donor.

Acknowledgment of Gifts

It should be unnecessary to include among trustee tasks the extending of a simple thank-you for the major gift. The requirement to major donors goes beyond the thank-you of the moment or the ceremonial dedication of a building or a chair. It should continue through the years, and trustees are good people to do it—a short note or phone call, a brief lunch to repeat once again how much the gift has meant to the institution. This sort of continuing follow-up does not come spontaneously. It must be scheduled and the professional staff should be responsible for such scheduling and control. The reasons for such a continuing thank-you are based on simple common courtesy and appreciation of a gift that made a difference. But beyond this, satisfied donors are good people to suggest other prospects and assist in their cultivation, and the thoroughly satisfied major donor may well return with another gift.

Evaluation of Outcomes

A major campaign may be over and the goals achieved, but the fund-raising program continues and another campaign is probably in the not-too-distant future. The lessons learned during the completed campaign are as important or more important than the achievement of the goal. In this era of computers, there is little reason why the statistics of the campaign results cannot be recorded in detail during the campaign and be available for later analysis. Trustees should be assured that such a capability is in place before the campaign begins.

    The performance of the giving constituencies should be reviewed for goal achievement, gift size, and preferences for a certain type of gift purpose or method. Some analysis of the effectiveness of various solicitation techniques can also be worked into the well-considered computer program. Such a detailed review is important because each constituency has its own unique pattern of giving, and the planning of all fund-raising efforts should be guided by these patterns. The lack of such an evaluation capability discards the lessons of experience and so invites a repetition of past errors and missed opportunities to increase effectiveness.

Perhaps the most telling management indicator in the last analysis is the cost of raising funds. Institutions vary in the manner in which they record their fund-raising costs, so direct comparisons, while useful, do not necessarily provide precise final grades for the effectiveness of fund-raising management. The comparisons do send signals as to the general placement of the institution's programs in relation to the competing institutional community. The figures submitted by participants in the AGB survey (Association of Governing Boards of Universities and Colleges, 1989b) put the average of the core development costs at 8.6 cents per operating and capital dollar received during the year, ranging from about 13 cents for the small institutions down to about 6.9 cents for the largest. If all advancement costs (including alumni and public relations and publications) are included, the average rises to about 22 cents per dollar received, ranging from 28 cents for the smallest institution to 12 cents for the largest. While the costs reported by large institutions showed remarkable consistency, the costs among smaller institutions varied widely—some went well over 50 cents per dollar raised.

What were the key factors in the fund-raising effectiveness of the most successful institutions? As an approach to such a reckoning, the average cost of funds raised for a random selection of private, four-year, single-campus institutions responding to the AGB survey was ranked from lowest to highest cost. The top half of the institutions was used to compare a number of subjectively selected causative factors. The values of the selected factors are compared in Table 11.1. Although the comparisons in Table 11.1 are by no means conclusive, they do raise some points for trustees to ponder.

Table 11.1. A Comparison of Key Factors in Fund-Raising Effectiveness.

	All Institutions	Top Half
Size of board	30.1	41.7
Percent of trustees with business background	54.0	63.0
Percent of annual fund dollars from trustees	13.0	14.5
Percent of operating budget for advancement office	3.0	4.1
Size of professional development staff	5.7	7.9
Percent of operating budget from gift support	7.7	9.6
Cost per dollar raised—all advancement	21.8	14.4

Source: Association of Governing Boards of Universities and Colleges, 1989b.

- Large boards have more hands and minds to bring to fund raising, and a business background may add some highly useful pragmatic skills.
- Boards that give more from their own resources seem to be part of the more successful fund-raising efforts.
- Successful institutions spend more on advancement and have larger staffs, but they also bring more funds back to the institution.
- The most successful institutions spend less of their gift dollars on acquiring funds.

    The central theme of this chapter and one most important for today's trustees to understand is that successful fund raising in higher education commands an extended apparatus, all components of which should be in place and working well to assure achievement of the goals sought. The trustee's personal gift and personal participation in the actual fund raising remain critically important. But these personal contributions and sacrifices can be lost in any failed fund-raising effort unless all of the preceding and surrounding components of the endeavor are present and well. Perhaps the greatest responsibility of the governing board is to assure itself that all of the pieces are indeed in place, so that the board's own giving and personal participation become the fuse that lights a successful program to build the future of their institution.

CHAPTER 12

Communicating with Campus and External Constituencies

Samuel Reid Spencer, Jr.

Old maxims die hard. So it is with the statement, repeated by trustees over the years with complacency and a large measure of good-humored satisfaction, that a board's sole function is to hire and fire the president. Only in relatively recent years have college trustees abandoned this "absentee landlord" theory in favor of responsible participation in college affairs.

Like many outworn maxims, the statement had enough truth in it to guarantee its persistence. That the choice of a president can make or break an institution is still true, but the concept lived on primarily because it was indeed possible, until recent years, for a president to run an institution as a benevolent dictator. Trustees could and did assume that if they chose the right leader, he or she would manage the institution without the necessity of their being deeply involved. The president was given the authority to allocate resources, make changes in programs, and appoint or dismiss personnel.

In this context, trustees left decisions on curriculum and campus affairs to the president and faculty, interesting themselves only in institutional matters, such as athletics, finance, and the physical plant, with which they felt comfortable. They accepted, as a corollary to the "hire and fire the president" maxim, the theory

204

that trustees had no need to concern themselves with educational matters. Because educational issues not only lie at the center of the collegiate enterprise but also drive institutional decisions, such a distinction makes no sense today—if, indeed, it ever did (Nason, 1982, p. 32).

Shared Governance

The advent of shared governance, spawned by the academic revolution of the 1960s and 1970s, dramatically altered the roles of both presidents and trustees. Even if they had wanted to, presidents could no longer govern their institutions on their own terms; hemmed in by explicit restrictions on their authority, they had to consult others and learn to operate by suggestion and persuasion rather than direction.

The public, too, had been accustomed to the idea that a college or university president ran the institution and spoke with complete authority on campus affairs. The upheavals of the Vietnam-War era, with embattled presidents locked out of their offices, shook this image to its foundations. Trustees could no longer sit back in the comfortable assurance that presidents had matters well in hand. As events on-campus increasingly engaged the attention of the public, the fact became painfully clear that trustees themselves could not avoid involvement. Faced with increasingly complex problems, boards had to develop an overarching concern for all aspects of their institutions' operations and activities. Although students and faculty rather than trustees were the activists, the campus revolution triggered a new era of active concern and involvement by college and university boards. Their revised role demanded something that the passivity of an earlier era had not required: the necessity to communicate board decisions, actions, and policies to the varied constituencies of their institutions.

There was no escape from this new assignment of duties. Education has become, and rightly so, a matter of great public concern. For a variety of reasons, colleges and universities are news; events that involve them—sports, of course, but other things as well—crowd the pages of the press and claim a considerable share of television coverage. Especially when controversial issues on-campus catch the public eye, trustees are seen by alumni, friends, and the media as desirable sources of information. The telephone rings, and the trustee must answer.

Sometimes, another type of caller may be at the other end of the line. Because trustees are people of some prominence, they are seen not only as sources of information but also as sources of influence. People who want to bring some weight to bear on the decisions or actions of an institution are legion. The caller might be an alumnus arguing for the admission of a son or daughter, an insurance agent asking for business from the college, a parent concerned about safety on campus, or a neighbor of the institution wanting to block a change in zoning. The trustee must be prepared to handle such approaches in an appropriate, if usually noncommittal, way.

Although today's trustees find the role of communicator thrust upon them by outside pressures, they should neither resent it nor try to escape it. Indeed, having grown out of the absentee landlord role, boards should recognize and accept the responsibility for becoming active interpreters to the general public and to their institutions' multifaceted constituencies.

Trustee Education

To do so requires educated trustees. Such education begins at the time of election in a process that the president and the board itself normally provide (see Chapter Sixteen). Beyond this, however, board members should consider a continuing process of self-education a duty. The relatively new view of trustee responsibilities has brought forth a welter of material on trusteeship. The Association of Governing Boards of Universities and Colleges (AGB) publishes continually updated guides to board responsibilities and functions. Especially helpful are the AGB workshops, which feature experienced leaders and offer trustees opportunities for discussions with their counterparts from other institutions. For keeping current on issues in academe and the context in which colleges and universities operate, the weekly *Chronicle of Higher Education* is highly useful. Some institutions provide subscriptions to all members of their boards.

Without question, trustees should stay fully informed about the lore and current state of the institution they serve. The annual "profile" of a college or university gives essential information such as enrollment, student credentials, faculty statistics, financial figures, and fees. Trustees need to have such information at their fingertips and be able to use it in their deliberations with one another and with the many constituents of the college or university.

The self-education process should also include conscientious preparation for board meetings; merely a cursory glance at presidential and staff reports on the assumption that the appropriate committees will deal with anything important is not sufficient. Regular reading of the campus newspaper and other publications will give insights—sometimes surprising—into matters of which trustees should be aware.

The trustee who is a good communicator serves the institution well. At its best, the role of trustee requires an alertness to opportunities for interpreting campus issues in a way that promotes understanding, if not always approval. The role also requires a willingness to take the initiative in that effort when appropriate, and on the other hand, the good judgment to know when silence is preferable.

Campus Constituencies: Administration, Faculty, Students

In terms of its constituencies, a college or university stands out as one of the most complex institutions of society. Built into the structure of an educational institution are a number of constituencies of different kinds, varying interests, and often diametrically opposed views. The problem of dealing effectively with this congeries of groups, each with its legitimate claims on the attention and consideration of the institution, places special demands on presidents and trustees.

The board must be flexible enough to relate to these varied groups in different ways appropriate to different situations. To the internal constituencies (faculty, staff, and students), the trustees loom as authority figures—understandably, because the board is the source of ultimate power in the independent college or university. To external but college-related groups, such as alumni and parents, trustees are sources of information and influence. To funding-related constituencies, such as foundations, corporations, and in some cases the church, trustees appear as advocates and often suppliants. To the general public, including the media, they are seen as knowledgeable sources of information and opinion on institutional and educational issues.

No trustee can be expected to fathom the intricate relationships in the academic community without understanding the changed structure of campus governance resulting from the events of the 1960s and 1970s. This structure differs markedly from the corporate model with which most of the public and a preponderance of college and university trustees are familiar. Given the fact that college boards are studded with business executives and that colleges and universities are indeed corporations, it is not surprising that many trustees still assume that an educational institution should follow the corporate example.

Earlier, when university presidents had what approached absolute authority, this was a logical expectation. As chief executive officer, the president could take command, exercise the necessary authority, and manage the enterprise in accordance with the directives of the board. However, no element within the business corporation compares with the modern college or university faculty. As faculty members rightly insist, they are not employees but professionals whose special status entitles them to meaningful participation in institutional governance. Federal courts gave this position legal status in the Yeshiva University case (*National Labor Relations Board* v. *Yeshiva University*, 444 U.S. 672, 1980) ruling against faculty unionization on the ground that faculty members have a significant part in management decisions.

We commonly refer to the campus upheaval two decades ago as a student revolution, and students were of course the most numerous and visible participants. Not so apparent to onlookers was the parallel revolution in campus governance, led primarily by faculties, which produced new models of organizational structure to replace the old corporate one.

Strains of faculty thinking crystallized in the *Statement on Government of Colleges and Universities* formulated under the auspices of the American Association of University Professors (AAUP)

(1966). Although this document recognized the president's position as leader of the institution, it assigned to the faculty primary responsibility for curriculum, methods of instruction, and areas of student life related to the educational process. Significantly, it firmly insisted that the ongoing operation of an academic institution is a joint effort in which faculties should have an explicitly participatory role.

The ferment of that era produced a variety of efforts to codify this participatory role. Some faculties pushed for representation on boards of trustees, an effort that the Carnegie Commission on Higher Education (1973) helped to scotch by an unequivocally adverse recommendation. Some institutions experimented with all-campus councils or assemblies made up of representatives from faculty, administration, and student bodies, but this model ran counter to the awakened consciousness of faculty prerogatives and proved ephemeral at best.

At the urging of faculties, institutions either wrote new constitutional documents or revised existing ones to incorporate the principles of the AAUP statement. Fundamentally, they increased the power of the faculty at the expense of the president, a process not unlike the English Parliament's progressive limitation on the power of the king. In some instances, the new documents went to the opposite extreme from the corporate model. From their days in elementary school, Americans acquire almost by osmosis a reverence for the checks-and-balances system of the United States Constitution. In fashioning new institutional arrangements, it was only natural that some proponents designed structures containing, in effect, an executive (the president and administrative staff), a legislative body (the faculty), and a supreme court (the board of trustees) to adjudicate differences between the first two.

However, a chartered independent institution is not an entity made up of equal parts but a system of delegated authority. Only when the board delegates its authority to the president, who in turn passes elements of that authority on to the faculty and students, can an essential line of accountability exist. This structure, with built-in provisions that guarantee to the faculty primary responsibility for the educational program and participation in campus decision making, is a unique model that lies between the corporate and government models. Today's trustees must understand and be prepared to interpret it to the constituencies of the institution.

Administration

One of the truisms of trusteeship is that the job of trustees is to set policy and the job of president and administrative staff is to manage. As long as the pattern of powerful presidents and passive trustees prevailed, this distinction was easy to maintain. However, as trustees became more active in overseeing of their institutions, the line between policy and management or administration began to blur. This has made it necessary for boards to try to determine different levels of policy and decide on corresponding degrees of appropriate involvement (Chait and Taylor, 1989).

A second truism is that the board and its members relate officially to the campus through the president and only through the president. This implies that no one on the campus except the president should report independently to the board (Nason, 1982). Only if this principle is honored can the board hold the president accountable for the overall management of the institution.

As valid as these two maxims of governance are, they put trustees on their mettle to make sure that their personal relationships with faculty, staff, and students are conducted in an appropriate way. This is especially true when individual friendships are involved, as they often are. Many trustees are alumni who studied with members of the faculty and consider them good friends. It is natural that these friendships not only continue but deepen when trusteeship creates a new link with former teachers.

Board procedures often produce even stronger ties between trustees and members of the institution's administrative staff. Virtually all boards work through a system of committees, each dealing with a specified area of operation, such as academic affairs, finance, buildings and grounds, and so on (see Chapter Seventeen). Because the president obviously cannot direct the work of all committees, each committee has the appropriate administrative officer as a member. Because trustees tend to gravitate to committees in which they have some expertise, they are likely to develop a natural link with an administrator who shares the same interests. Thus, a banker and the chief financial officer get together, an educator becomes friends with the academic vice president, and a sports enthusiast seeks out the athletic director.

Such individual relationships between trustees and faculty or staff members can and should be very constructive. They heighten the feeling that the board and campus are working together for a common cause. Mutual confidence builds a base for understanding institutional problems and the cooperation to work them out. The expertise of individual trustees and the outside perspective they bring can be very helpful for those responsible for dealing with internal management issues.

At the same time, close personal relationships can produce serious difficulties. The temptation to use a friendship, consciously or subconsciously, to advance a personal agenda is ever present, and it may move in either direction. Through a friend on the faculty or staff, a trustee may promote a cherished idea, push for appointment of a favorite individual to a staff post, or attempt to influence a tenure decision. An administrator may use his relationship with a committee member to bring indirect pressure on the president, especially when there has been disagreement between the administrator and the president on a particular issue. A faculty member may exploit a friendship to promote a cause in which she has a special interest.

What protection is there against such misuse of personal relationships? The board itself has the responsibility, through its nomination and evaluation procedures, to select members whose good judgment and integrity can be counted on. If individual trustees then abide by the principle that they relate officially to the institution only through the president, the risk of problems is slight.

There is greater risk, especially in committee work, that board members will cross the line between policy and management. The line is, after all, difficult to discern at times. When a trustee has more knowledge and experience than the staff member working in the same area, advice can easily become direction. This is even more likely to happen in an area to which the president seems to give little attention. In such instances, trustees may act with the best of intentions, not realizing that they are overstepping the bounds of accepted practice.

Faculty

Of all the constituencies to which trustees must relate and with whom they must communicate, the faculty is the most important and at the same time the most difficult. To an unfortunate degree, trustees have not understood the faculty and faculty members have not understood the trustees. Traditionally, the two groups have started from different sets of attitudes.

College faculties pride themselves on being professionals, not employees. The pride is justified. They have gone through long, rigorous, often difficult years to earn the credentials that qualify them for the classroom. Despite these qualifications and despite the important service faculty members perform, they receive meager material rewards in comparison with the compensation of comparable professionals in such fields as medicine and law. They are told that the faculty is the heart of a college or university, but until recent years they had little opportunity to influence the many institutional decisions that affect their lives.

Such circumstances have understandably shaped faculty attitudes toward trustees. Because the board holds ultimate power over the world in which faculty members live and move, there is an understandable tension that sometimes slides into resentment and hostility. How can trustees, outsiders who spend a day or two on the campus several times a year, possibly know or care enough about the institution to justify the power vested in them? Because most board members live and work in a world that does not seem to place great value on intellectual pursuits, how can they understand the dynamics of an academic community? In view of these attitudes, it is understandable that the central objective of faculty members in the campus revolution was greater participation in the governance of their institutions.

Trustees have traditionally held corresponding notions about faculties. To some of them, faculty members are seen as impractical theorists who never met a payroll and want the freedom to do as they please without accountability. At best, they demonstrate minimal loyalty to the institutions that pay their salaries; at worst, they make speeches and take positions inimical to their institutions' interests. To many trustees, the tenure system is the bête noire; it guarantees a lifetime job to individuals who have no further obligation to perform. Contrary to faculty characterization of them as occasional visitors with unjustified authority, trustees consider themselves unpaid volunteers who freely give both their service and financial support and bring a valuable perspective of the "real world" to institutional affairs.

All of the faculty and trustee stereotypes go back a long way. Unfortunately, the drive for faculty prerogatives and participation did little to help eliminate the stereotypes on either side; in fact, the events of the 1960s and 1970s exacerbated the tendency to indulge in them. As trustees moved toward a stronger and more visible role in institutional affairs, faculty lumped them together with administrators, who were the target of much of the movement. Consequently, the natural tension between faculty on one hand and administration and trustees on the other became increasingly adversarial. To board members whose business connections tended to shape their attitudes toward labor unions, the growth of faculty unionization in the same era did not help matters.

All institutions and their constituent elements have a strong stake in overcoming these adversarial attitudes. Unquestionably, better communication can help to bridge the gulf between on-campus and off-campus bodies, especially that between faculty and trustees. Spurred by new concepts of constructive trusteeship, boards are encouraging their administrations to bring groups together in a search for common ground and mutual interests.

A number of these efforts promote informal contacts. Social events for faculty, staff, and trustees in connection with board meetings are nothing new, but there is a conscious effort to increase the number of receptions, parties, and meals together where the atmosphere is clearly not confrontational. Occasional off-campus retreats offer opportunities for faculty and board members to know one another better and to discuss in a relaxed atmosphere institutional matters of mutual concern.

While such informal occasions are valuable, they also have limitations, and faculty members sometimes see them as superficial attempts at fellowship. More substantive, partly because they can be built into the system of regular procedures, are formal provisions for faculty participation. As noted earlier, some faculties twenty years ago urged the most obvious and visible means, faculty membership on the board. The basic objection to this idea is that having a representative of any particular group on the board—a pleader for a special interest, in the eyes of many—contravenes the concept that all trustees should serve in the interest of the institution as a whole (Carnegie Commission on Higher Education, 1973).

A good many institutional leaders have followed the advice of the Carnegie Commission on this matter, rejecting board membership for their own faculty members but electing as trustees professors from other colleges who bring a faculty point of view to board deliberations. Other leaders have provided for a member of the institution's own faculty to attend board meetings, although the faculty member has the privilege of the floor but not the power to vote.

Because committees do much of the work of the board and often serve as de facto decision-making bodies, some boards have added faculty members to their committees even though these members do not attend plenary sessions. Still other boards have adopted a system under which board committees meet at least once a year with their corresponding campus committees. The creation of trustee-faculty task forces to carry out specific assignments is an increasingly common practice.

All such devices for communication between boards and faculties help to satisfy legitimate faculty desires for three things: direct access to the board, a voice in institutional decisions, and information about trustee thinking and actions. As to the third desire, many institutions have adopted a standard procedure of reporting directly to campus constituencies the results of every board meeting. While this is usually done by the president of the college or university, the report may also include a statement from the chair of the board as well as the text of resolutions and motions acted on. These various channels of communication, especially when they are viewed as two-way, also help to educate trustees about campus issues and give them important insights into faculty opinion.

Trustees can further bridge traditional differences by appropriate words of praise and encouragement to individuals on campus. A major award to a faculty or staff member may well merit a formal expression of congratulations by the board. Individual trustees, simply by observing the campus and scanning college publications, can learn of achievements by campus personnel that merit commendation. In such instances, a phone call or letter can warm the heart of any faculty or staff recipient.

Students

As the somewhat amorphous student revolution took shape in the 1960s and 1970s, it articulated two distinct and seemingly unrelated objectives. The first was to free students from both curricular requirements and rules of conduct characteristic of most college campuses. The second was a congeries of societal issues, especially the Vietnam War and matters related to it. By the time the attack of that era had run its course, students had in effect achieved both objectives. Most curricular requirements and parietal rules had disappeared, and American troops had left Vietnam. The old in loco parentis stance of institutions toward their students had been consigned to history.

Because students and faculty members worked in tandem during those years, and because students tend to take their lead from faculty in campus issues, it is no surprise that students' attitudes paralleled those of their mentors. Like the faculty, students saw themselves as an important—perhaps the most important—campus constituency; consequently, in addition to sweeping away requirements, they also demanded more participation in institutional affairs.

Student government until the 1960s was a well-established concept, having come into general practice before World War I. It included both constitutional documents and a full-blown organizational structure. However, student government powers extended only to peers; student government constituted an *imperium in imperio* at a lower level than and essentially unrelated to the government of the institution. Its disciplinary sanctions worked because students were willing to enforce the rules of campus conduct laid down by the institution.

The revolution put different ideas into students' heads. Following the faculty lead, students sought a similar participatory role in college and university governance. In company with the administration, the board of trustees became the object of insistent proposals. Students viewed the trustees much as faculties did: boards were outsiders whose lack of knowledge and understanding of the campus disqualified them from exercising the absolute authority they apparently possessed.

To many students, the obvious solution was student representation on the board. In response, a number of state legislatures mandated such representation in public institutions (Millett, 1980b). Here again, however, the argument against including any "special pleaders" as trustees came to the fore. Even more persuasive to students themselves was the fact that no single representative could adequately speak for a student body of hundreds or thousands. While most colleges and universities rejected the push for student trustees, a number made concessions to it. The bylaws of a number of boards now specify that one or more trustees must be elected from the graduating class or from recent classes. At some institutions, student officers attend board meetings, make reports, and speak to issues under consideration, though without the power to vote.

Except when they had to act as a last court of appeal in exceptional cases, trustees traditionally assumed that college officials and faculty would deal with all matters involving students. That is still generally true, but today's trustees rightly recognize that even entering students are of voting age and must be considered young adults rather than children. Enlightened boards now provide students with both formal and informal opportunities for contact, often inviting them to some of the board's social occasions and consulting them about the work of appropriate standing and ad hoc committees.

Trustees also have to deal on occasion with one student agency that has no faculty parallel: the campus newspaper. Educational institutions that urge students to think critically, examine the fine print, and look at statements or issues from all sides should not be surprised when students apply this teaching to their own institutional environment. Just as the general press sees itself as a critic of society, the student newspaper sees itself as the campus critic. Because of this view, the newspaper attracts to its staff those students most attuned to the critical role. Especially during the student revolution, the campus press led the charge, often not only with attacks on issues but also with personal attacks that could easily have qualified as libel or slander. Trustees did not escape; indeed, along with presidents, they were the objects of some of the heaviest barrages. As unwelcome and sometimes outrageous as personal attacks can be, due regard for First Amendment rights should remain uppermost in the minds of presidents and boards.

While the virulence of such attacks subsided as campuses returned to a more peaceful mood, student newspapers still serve the critical function, and justifiably so. Student reporters who view Woodward and Bernstein as models are likely at any time to bombard trustees with questions—often blunt ones—and criticisms on institutional or societal issues.

Several issues are current counterparts of the concerns of the 1960s: divestment of stocks in companies that operate in South Africa, the environment, nuclear power, and so on. Students and faculty pressure boards to take public stands on whatever may come to the fore on their particular campuses. In responding to such proposals, trustees do well to hold firm to principles and steer clear of committing an institution to positions that are clearly political. Admittedly, drawing a line between principle and ideological committment is often difficult and requires the best judgment that board members can bring to their deliberations. Above all, with controversial matters, a board must uphold the principle of free expression and maintain the campus as an open forum where proponents and opponents of all sides can air their opinions.

Finally, in dealing with students, trustees should avoid even the appearance of being condescending or patronizing, even when what is said or done seems classically sophomoric. Patience, calmness, and a genuine desire to understand student positions are invaluable assets. So is candor; students especially appreciate straight answers. In all situations, it pays for trustees to consider that, after all, the students may be right.

External Relationships: Alumni,
Parents, Church, Public, and Donors

Beyond the campus, the trustee role shifts from that of authority figure to interpreter, troubleshooter, and advocate. Two of the external constituencies with whom trustees must be prepared to communicate, alumni and parents, have a direct relationship to the institution. A third for many independent colleges is the church with which the institution is affiliated. Other constituencies to which board members must speak on behalf of their institutions are the general public, including the media, and foundation and corporate donors.

Alumni

Of all of these constituencies, alumni are the most significant. Among them are the most critical and the most supportive of constituents, the most and least objective about the institution, the most interested and the most apathetic. They are rarely monolithic in their attitudes. A nucleus of alumni tends to be more vocal than their numbers warrant; others never respond to letters, appeals, questionnaires, or any other communication. Alumni have the capacity to do great good or great damage to their alma maters.

Even when they are not emotionally involved, they have a stake in the current and future status of institutions they attended. The validity of the degrees they earned depends on the public appraisal of their colleges and universities, and the perceived value of their degrees can affect their standing in the workplace and in their communities. That is why published ratings of educational institutions, fallible and inaccurate as they often are, command such high interest.

Alumni feel the same sense of ownership that faculty and current students do. Not only do they belong to the college; the college belongs to them. They are as eager to influence its decisions as members of the faculty are. Because of their genuine interest and willingness to give time, effort, and money, many of them become trustees. In many institutions, bylaws specify that the alumni association nominate or elect a number of board members, but the ones chosen in this way are rarely the only alumni who serve.

The fact that alumni associations elect trustees seems to run counter to the principle that boards should not include representatives of any particular constituent group. The practice can be defended, though not with complete satisfaction, on two grounds: first, that alumni, above all other constituencies, are likely to act in the interest of the institution as a whole, and second, that the alumni body is so numerous and diverse that no one can truly represent it.

There are two areas in which the interest and involvement of alumni often translate into trouble for their institutions. The first is athletics. An overwhelming percentage of all press coverage of colleges and universities appears on the sports pages. It is no accident that much of a sports-minded public judges the prestige of colleges and universities by the success of their teams.

Alumni share this attitude to an extent that concerns those who see education in quite different terms. The concern is justified. Alumni pressure on trustees, presidents, and athletic personnel to produce winning teams has led to unpardonably corrupt practices in higher education. Even in the absence of corruption, the passion for winning teams opens the door to meddling in the management of college affairs. In no other area is there such a great temptation for alumni to try to influence policy decisions and personnel appointments. Unfortunately, some of the pressure in the realm of athletics comes from alumni who serve as trustees. Even when this is not the case, boards have often bowed to outside pressure in the recognition that, as someone has said, sports represent the lowest common denominator of alumni interest.

To combat undue influence in this area, trustees must be convinced, and hold fast to the conviction, that teaching and learning are the primary responsibilities of an academic institution. Despite the pleasures of victory on the playing field, nothing does more for campus morale, and especially faculty morale, than firm adherence to this tenet. Trustees have a responsibility to see that resources are allocated in accordance with this principle, not skewed in favor of sports or any other peripheral element of the institution's operations. They can perform a valuable service by interpreting, especially to alumni, their conviction that educational concerns must remain central to the enterprise.

A second area in which pressure from alumni and friends often reaches individual trustees is that of admissions. The board, usually on the recommendation of the administration, sets admissions policy, but within this broad framework, the infinite variety of applicants' credentials makes setting firm guidelines on individual decisions impossible. Understandably, however, these decisions on individual applicants become the pressure points for trustees. The extent of outside pressure relates directly, of course, to the size of the applicant pool and the corresponding degree of selectivity of a given institution. Presidents and trustees of colleges at the upper end of the prestige scale are inevitably the target of the most vigorous appeals.

Even in less selective institutions, however, the pressure exists. Selectivity is a relative matter. Except for the few colleges that practice open admissions and accept all candidates who apply, there are inevitably some students whom campus authorities judge to be below their standards or, at best, marginal. Consequently, almost no trustee is immune to the letter or phone call that asks for help in having an applicant with questionable credentials admitted.

That being said, college admissions officers would be unhappy if alumni did not want their sons and daughters to attend their alma maters. For many institutions, this is the nucleus group for each incoming class, and almost universally children of alumni get special consideration if not outright favorable treatment. Because most alumni know or assume this, rejection of a "legacy" can be an especially traumatic experience for such applicants and their families. At this point, the trustee usually gets the call for help.

Responding to such appeals sympathetically but noncommittally takes tact and skill, because the way the case is handled can be very important to an institution. Parents rarely view their children with a rational eye. If the son or daughter has marginal credentials, there are always explanations: personality conflicts with teachers, illness, the inability to test well, a language "block," the time spent on a job or outside activities. The student is often characterized as a late bloomer who has just learned how to study.

What can trustees say to such appeals? There are of course

standard replies. First, that although trustees establish admissions policy, they have no part in decisions about individual applicants. Second, that the issue is one of fairness; it would not be fair to intervene on behalf of one candidate when there is no way for a trustee to compare that applicant with others. Third, that admissions officers are professionals, and if they have doubts about accepting the candidate, that person would probably have serious academic difficulty.

Valid as they are, such explanations rarely satisfy alumni eager to continue the family tradition. Trustees can legitimately offer to make sure that the admissions office knows of a candidate's connections with the college and that candidate's strong desire for admission. With the knowledge and permission of the admissions office, trustees can also pass on to the parent information about the status of the candidate's application and the timetable for notification. However, because even an inquiry from a trustee might be considered pressure, trustees are wise to have clear-cut ground rules for board relationships with the admissions staff.

Parents

On occasion, trustees must also deal with parents who have no connection with the institution except through sons and daughters. As with alumni parents, the contact may come at the admission stage and ordinarily requires the same kind of responses. More likely is a situation in which a parent of a current student seeks out a trustee because a son or daughter is in academic difficulty, has run afoul of college regulations, or needs a special dispensation of some kind. Common sense should be the guiding principle. Because trustees should rarely become directly involved in student matters, the best course is to steer parents to the appropriate on-campus source.

Church

Beginning with Harvard University, most independent colleges owe their origins to churches or church people. Above the gate to Harvard Yard, founders of the university noted their intention to provide a learned ministry to posterity "when our present ministers shall lie in the Dust." Although the bonds between college and church have always varied widely, relationships in many cases remained especially strong until after World War II. Charter and bylaw provisions distinguished the church colleges: required attendance at worship, required courses on the Bible, and careful observance of the Sabbath. Conduct codes were strict, and students broke them at their peril. Governing bodies of the churches nominated or elected trustees who were expected to share the faith.

Two developments loosened the ties. One was money. Despite the extent of the control they exercised, churches had rarely provided overwhelming or even substantial financial support. As colleges increasingly sought funds from private sources and government, they felt less allegiance to the churches that established them. The second development involved culture. Required worship and Bible instruction began to seem inappropriate in an increasingly diverse and pluralistic society. When the student revolution swept away virtually all the old rules of campus conduct, church institutions became indistinguishable from their secular counterparts.

Despite the changes, many colleges still value their connections with their founding churches. Some preserve strong ties and without apology offer education in a context that combines faith and learning. Trustees of these institutions have special responsibilities. As colleges have followed changes in societal attitudes, reflecting the natural tension between young and old, boards of these institutions have had a difficult task. In most instances, they have acted as brakes on the departure from traditional requirements and practices. At the same time, they have had to interpret to their churches a series of campus developments that church constituents often find unsettling.

In carrying out these sometimes unenviable duties, trustees do well to see themselves as a bridge between the college and its church. Doing so requires a knowledge of and sensitivity to the positions of both sides in a conflict. The job is easier and more effective if trustees keep in close touch with the church constituency. At all times boards have the responsibility of faithfulness to the mission of their institutions; in the case of church-related colleges, carrying out this responsibility implies commitment not only to the demands of effective trusteeship, but also to the basic values of the sponsoring church bodies. Interpreting the church to faculty, staff, and students is therefore an important part of the task of church-related college trustees.

General Public

The public and the media agencies that influence public opinion increasingly call on trustees as sources of information. Although the college administration normally speaks for the institution, the press and the public may well look to the ultimate source of power for authoritative statements when campus issues become public controversies. Such issues range over a wide spectrum: national ones such as military training on college campuses, local ones such as the closing of a street or a change in zoning, campus ones such as the distribution or sale of condoms. If a fraternity party gets out of hand, a professor writes a letter to the editor that raises the hackles of some of the citizenry, or a tragedy such as a rape or murder raises questions about campus security, such events are likely to trigger trustee involvement.

In instances that affect institutional welfare, the board must develop or define policy and make sure that both the campus and the public understand it. With regard to public statements on controversial matters, the board should speak with one voice through one person—ordinarily the chair or the president—designated to undertake that responsibility. An individual trustee who cannot accept the position of the board as a matter of principle even after the issue is decided may feel that he or she should resign (Nason, 1980). However, because such an action in itself constitutes a public statement, it should be taken only in rare instances after the most serious consideration. When debating controversial matters that affect the institution in the public arena, boards should do everything possible to arrive at consensus.

When individual trustees are approached by the media, they should refer the inquiry to the person designated to speak for the board. If the issue is one that the board has not considered, trustees should make no comment without first learning the facts and checking to determine whether any statement has been or is being made by campus authorities. When the president has had to take an un-popular position on a serious matter on behalf of the board, trustees can perform a valuable service by helping to interpret the action to the public and sharing the burden with the administration.

Donors

Only in the past several decades has college and university fund raising developed into a systematic, sophisticated effort with in-creasingly large and specialized staffs. Before that, presidents per-sonally undertook the task of searching for outside resources, occasionally with the help of individual board members. Today, within the structure of fund-raising programs carefully organized by the staff, trustees are expected to play an active part as both interpreters and advocates to potential donors (see Chapter Eleven).

Trustees can be of special help to their institutions in the advocacy role because of their built-in relationships with a number of constituents from whom financial support must come. Alumni are a natural constituency for the many trustees who have attended the colleges and universities they serve. In institutions that receive church funds, trustees have a responsibility to make the case for their institutions with church members and official bodies, usually in a context of keen competition with other organizations in the ecclesiastical framework. Trustees from the business world can help significantly in the solicitation of corporations and foundations through their contacts on boards of these organizations. In relating to all such sources of support, trustees can serve their institutions best not only by standing ready to participate when called upon, but also by taking the initiative in identifying potential donors within their areas of influence. Chapter Eleven discusses fully the fund-raising responsibilities of today's trustees.

The way in which trustees deal with external constituencies, especially when campus issues become public controversies, can produce either positive or negative consequences for their institu-tions. So can the advocacy role with potential donors. The desirabil-ity of constructive relationships with all of these constituencies derives from the modern assumption that colleges and universities deserve concerned, informed, and active trustees.

CHAPTER 13

Responding to
Political, Social,
and Ethical Issues

Paul N. Ylvisaker

It has become a truism to start each decade with a declaration of impending change. But even if a truism, the statement still has to be repeated: each decade of this century has seen the pace of change speeding up. And trustees of colleges and universities will find in the 1990s another dizzying rearrangement of the social and institutional landscape, already nearly unrecognizable.

The most problematic aspects of this change are the causes and consequences of increasing diversity, the onrush of pluralism in every aspect of life and quadrant of the globe. Spirits and voices so long held quiescent by traditional constraints have shaken loose and been given expression and power by today's electronic and photonic magnifications of the printing press. Both globally and locally, the haunting question is whether the center can hold, whether any known or putative form of governance can contain, let alone harness, the centrifugal genie that modernization has freed from the bottle.

One can therefore expect leadership and decision making to become ever more precarious and diffuse. The law of negotiated consent within a constantly differentiating constituency fastens itself with titanic force to all social institutions, especially to the academy, where it has so long held sway. A second and possibly

225

countervailing force will also gain strength during the coming decade: the dwindling of resources and the cost-price squeeze. Higher
education has become a big and expensive enterprise, with essential
outlays needed for physical plant, staff salaries, complicated student
needs, and regulatory requirements. Fiscal constraints could invite
more decisive leadership; but leadership could also shatter against
the call for pluralism and negotiated consent.

Both these contending forces will be intensified in the 1990s.
Pluralism will intensify through the swirling mix of cultures, re-
ligions, and divergent interests, now global in their reach. It will
intensify through demographic shifts within our own and the
world's population that will steadily diversify applicant pools, faculties, and student bodies, and through the erosion by advancing
technology of the insulating barriers that have traditionally kept
academic and social communities as stable enclaves. Fiscal constraints will intensify as societies pay the accumulated costs of environmental damage, poverty, health deficits, and social insecurity
as the agenda of the cold war shifts to regional and internal conflicts
that are accentuated by struggles over diminishing resources. It is
not beyond imagination to see a human race—and the academy—
surviving and even flourishing in that contentious environment.
But the learning curve and the art of social invention will have to
move sharply upward for the continuation of progress and even for
survival.

Communications technology and global migration have
made all sorts of boundaries permeable and in many ways obsoles-
cent. The boundaries of the campus are no exception. No longer a
walled city, the academy is more liquid than fixed. Administrators,
faculty members, and students flow outward, and electronic mes-
sages, competing values, and social violence gush inward. No
longer is the academy a protected and exclusive terrain; and it becomes less so with each passing year.

So far, implosion is more evident than explosion. External
forces have had more of an effect on the campus than the campus
has had on the culture outside. There are exceptions: scientific and
technological discoveries, such as the discovery of DNA, that have
radically altered the thinking and agenda of the global community;
the ingenuity of "Sesame Street"; and the pedagogical artistry of

peripatetic scholars on television. But these are individual sorties rather than collective assertiveness on the part of the academy.

Governance in such a fluid environment, even establishing an identity, becomes all the more a mercurial endeavor. But that is the challenge of the 1990s and beyond. The challenge begins and ends precisely at the point of establishing an identity: a distinguishable and distinctive mission, a forceful statement of what colleges and universities are all about. Trustees bear the ultimate responsibility for ensuring that such a statement is made. The mission statement must be a declaration of the values that the institution stands for, values that must be conspicuously practiced amidst the swirling pluralism of the life surrounding the institution.

The irony of pluralism is that it simultaneously demands and resists efforts to reach consensus on values. It sheds light on our diversity yet resists the imposition of any one code. Anarchy reigns at one end of the continuum, authoritarianism at the other.

But trustees do not have to adopt either extreme. Pluralism admits of its own resolution. The resolution lies in nurturing diversity while professing and practicing one's own creed. And this is precisely what trustees and their institutions will be called upon to do in the years immediately ahead. The squeeze on resources will not allow institutions and individuals to be all things to all people; but the grounds for making choices—of general mission and particular stands—will have to be explicit and clear. This task will not be easy but it will be essential, especially as the din of conflicting voices becomes ever louder and the issues to be settled grow even murkier.

The primary thrust will have to be on campus: campus leaders, including trustees, will need to define and model the behaviors they believe are critical. But no such candle can or should be hidden under a campus barrel. Those values need also to be extended into the world beyond.

Guiding Principles

In responding to political, social, and ethical issues, trustees have three essential responsibilities. First, they must discern critical influences in the external environment. Given their growing intrusion, external factors, such as demographic shifts, economic trends, social forces, and cultural tensions, need constantly to be identified and assessed by trustees. All of these factors occupy center stage and require far more attention from trustees than the casual reading of relevant newspaper articles. Trustees need to examine these factors at periodic retreats that feature, at least in part, the scanning of the future and involve faculty members and experts skilled in such assessments.

Second, trustees need to translate an understanding of the significance of external developments into campus policy and prac- tices. Being aware is half the battle; the rest is a matter of making certain the college or university is prepared to deal with what lies ahead. Presidents, administrators, and faculty members need to be regularly questioned as to whether they have anticipated and laid the groundwork for handling selected issues as they emerge.

Third, trustees should monitor the social, political, and eth- ical performance of the institution through recurrent questioning and discussion. It is one thing to profess the virtues of good citizen- ship, quite another to live up to those ideals. Trustees bear the ultimate responsibility for institutional performance; their own ex- ample sets the tone and the standard. Simply by raising concerns regularly and insistently, trustees can effectively discharge that responsibility.

Values to Uphold

Governing boards, together with campus leaders, should periodi- cally take inventory of their values. What do we and the institutions we serve stand for and strive to advance? There are many possible answers, of course, but here are five to help start a conversation with other board members.

Academic Freedom

The signal contribution of any institution of learning is to ensure society access to "the independent voice," that is, to be a forum for persons given freedom and sanctuary to address problems and issues—sometimes with detachment, sometimes with passion, but always unfettered by chains of enforced conventionality. That freedom is not simply the function of tenure, which seems often to be more the ultimate fringe benefit than the guarantee of an independent voice. It is, or should be, the value pervading the entire institution and the essential contribution of that institution to society.

In the coming decades, society will badly need the independent voice: for its creativity, criticism, advocacy, and challenge. During times of turmoil, as clearly the 1990s will be, society tends to close in on such freedom, just at the time such freedom becomes more essential. So, unfortunately, does higher education. Witness the constricting response to McCarthyism in the 1950s and the current wave of "political correctness" now insinuating itself on so many U.S. campuses. Commandment number one for trustees will be to preserve academic freedom, often against the odds and at heavy cost.

Excellence and Equity

In the years ahead, with rapid demographic shifts producing rising proportions of minority members in the actual or potential applicant pool for higher education, the two academic values of excellence and equity will have to be considered in tandem. There is evidence of success and ingenuity in dealing realistically with these values. The Algebra Project in Cambridge, Massachusetts, has demonstrated the capacity of minority students to achieve high levels of competence in mathematics, and the relatively new notion of multiple intelligences has challenged the myopic insistence on IQ as the single indicator of human potential. But colleges and universities will have to stretch their imagination and energies to create new approaches to the resolution of tensions between the twin values of excellence and equity. In the process, they must make a greater commitment to K-12 educational reform and to improving their own recruitment, counseling, and curriculum.

Tolerance and Caring

The decade of diversity will put a premium on the virtue of tolerance. Tolerance has always been considered the cornerstone and product of higher learning. It is the essential capacity to understand not only the human condition that gives rise to diversity but also to appreciate the extraordinary human benefits of diversity. Whether colleges and universities can maintain this tradition of tolerance in the face of expanding differences, challenging so much of the status quo, is a central question. Crimes of hate are rising across the country, and tension and violence already abound on U.S. campuses. More than tolerance will be required. An atmosphere of caring is needed, to assure those who are different that they and their education are treasured by everyone associated with the institution.

Academic Accountability

Academic freedom carries with it the reciprocal obligation of being accountable to the constituencies of higher education and to the general public that has ensured the freedom the academy enjoys. The boundaries of accountability are constantly and progressively being expanded through laws and regulations; an enlarging conception of the social and ethical role and responsibility of higher education; more explicit definitions and expectations of institutional performance, output, and value added; and ever more sophisticated consumer demand. Trustees will often find this complex environment of expectations perplexing. But failing to study it assiduously will place them and their institutions in peril.

Institutional Neutrality: A Value Open to Exception

It has been persuasively argued that institutions of higher education ought generally to remain neutral on controversial issues. This argument posits that colleges and universities should encourage individuals within their orbit to express themselves freely and vigorously but refrain from taking institutional stands that could inhibit the freedom of individual expression and mire the institution in prolonged, acrimonious, and divisive debate. Colleges and universities, it is contended, are not public legislatures; they should not become partisan but should seek to enlighten public debate by providing access to the independent voices of individual members of the academic community.

So far, so good. But as a rigid orthodoxy applied to every political, social, and ethical issue, this rule would morally cripple higher education. Too many institutions have hidden behind the rule, dodging the responsibility of wrestling with the knottier and more troubling issues that confront them and of giving force to the ideals they profess. Colleges and universities with religious affiliations and more codified sets of values usually find it easier to take positions on difficult issues. But even they find the going rough, when, for example, campus dialogue centers on such issues as abortion. More and more, they, like their secular counterparts, will find themselves pressed to declare institutionally where they stand on issues such as investments in South Africa, U.S. participation in regional and global conflicts, the implications of genetic engineering and biotechnology, race relations, and the allocation of social energy and resources.

There is no general formula for resolving the question of whether to remain institutionally neutral or to take a stand. But there is the imperative of regularly confronting the question and determining openly whether this is the place, this is the time, to say as Martin Luther once did, "Here I stand; I cannot do otherwise."

The Art of Defining Whether an Issue Is Political, Social, or Ethical

If one could clearly distinguish between political, social, and ethical issues, it might be easier to sort out which issues should find their way onto trustees' agendas and how trustees should respond to those issues. For example, issues judged to be purely political in nature might appropriately fall under the rule of institutional neutrality and be left to the tug and pull of individual opinion and partisan interplay. But most issues are not so unambiguous. What may begin as one development, for example, the widening of social disparities, quickly takes on the coloration of politics and the suspicion of ethical impropriety.

Weighing the response to such issues is exceedingly difficult. When and how should the debate continue as essentially a matter for individual expression, and when and how should the institution intervene? How a response is arrived at is often as critical as the response itself. Should it be proactive or reactive? Determined in open debate or behind closed doors? Made by the entire academic community or only a ruling segment? Arbitrary, or in some way honoring the academy's credo of converting each provocation into a learning experience?

Trustees are likely to face ambiguous political, social, and ethical issues frequently during the next decade. Trustees would do well to anticipate and lay the groundwork for their responses. Their rule should be: no surprises.

Critical Issues and Likely Provocations

Several issues are likely to seriously affect college and university campuses in the next decade. These include globalization, equity and social justice, integrity, due process, and ethics.

Globalization

Driven by technology, especially communications, the world is rapidly converting, as Marshall McLuhan said it would, into a global village. Already we have an instantaneous global market, a global political forum, a globalizing consciousness and response to a deteriorating environment, and a nascent world order evolving through a reaffirmed United Nations. That all this might be undone by a proliferation of isolated tongues, the collapse of another Tower of Babel, is entirely possible. But either alternative will be played out on a global stage. And higher education cannot avoid the consequences nor stand aside as an uninvolved observer.

The consequences of globalization will be both positive and negative. Just as with *Sputnik,* a powerful set of stimuli will be applied to all of U.S. society, and the responses will be varied: to reach out, to be part of, to compete, to learn, to grow. On the other hand, conflict will be universalized. Disputes outside the campus— whether in adjacent or distant communities—will be replicated within the campus, particularly as campus populations increasingly represent diversities of class, race, and national origin. Curiosity about people from other cultures and backgrounds will grow and produce healthy innovations in curriculum, research, and outreach. Fear of others will also grow, hopefully not apace. This fear will result in tensions and even violence flaring both on and off campus.

Those contrasting trends are already visible. Stanford University and Connecticut College are expanding their curricula sympathetically and constructively to be more global in content and perspective. The campuses of the universities of Michigan, with heavy Arabic concentrations, reflect the tensions of the Persian Gulf War. Brown University and scores of other institutions are scarred by hostility and campus violence inflicted upon them both from within and without. In the swirl of these developments, colleges and universities will be hard pressed to mediate conflicts of culture, politics, and values; to accept differences without surrendering their own distinctive values and rules of conduct; to prepare the campus and surrounding community so that the ground rules for handling disputes and resolving differences are understood and agreed upon; and to make of each controversy an opportunity for learning.

In the 1990s, conflict will be especially likely over military operations and service. Another debate may arise over the social role of both higher education and government. What should the response of higher education and government be to poverty, both local and worldwide, environmental degradation, the ethics of competition, and other accumulating dilemmas of moral choice?

Each of these issues will provoke trustees to consider whether to adopt an institutional position or follow the rule of neutrality. If there is any general principle that may help resolve the question (and ultimately there may be none, only personal and collective judgments), it is that institutional stands should be taken when basic values are challenged and the very survival of the institution and what it stands for are in question.

Equity and Social Justice

Higher education will find the century-long tension between elitism and equality exacerbated in the years immediately ahead, for a number of reasons. Demographic shifts are producing a population that is increasingly minority, poor, and less prepared for higher education than students of the last several decades. Harold Hodgkinson, the Paul Revere of educational demographers, has been sounding the warning (1990, p. 1): "At the moment, over 30 percent of our youth are at risk of school failure when they show up at kindergarten on the first day." A 1989 report of the U.S. House of Representatives Select Commmittee on Children, Youth, and Families cites the following statistics (p. 2): "Athough the number of children has fallen since the 1970s, the size of the overall population has continued to increase. Thus, children now make up a smaller fraction of the total population—26 percent—than they did in the past—36 percent in 1960. By 2010, children will represent only 23 percent of the population. Minority group members will continue to grow as a proportion of all children, comprising one in three children by 2010."

The more exclusive U.S. universities and colleges might be able to conduct their business as usual, comforted by the fact that their applicant pools, even when shifting toward greater proportions of minorities, will always yield enough students to sustain both their present numbers and standards. "There will always be," as one institutional officer remarked to me nonchalantly, "the number we need of our kind of students." But most colleges and universities will not have the luxury of standing aloof, and even those who presume to do so will not be immune to confrontations erupting over the social, political, and ethical issues arising from demographic shifts.

An even more fundamental reason for heightened tension is higher education's inherent identification with the current and emerging elite. Not only are colleges and universities dependent financially and otherwise on the more favored and affluent members of society, but it is also their declared purpose to produce those who will exercise leadership. And now that knowledge has become sine qua non for success in this age of information, higher education will become ever more the gatekeeper for entry into and progress in lucrative professions, particularly the professions that are the aristocracy of the service economy. Access to higher education is critical. But access will not be easily ensured for the growing pool of disadvantaged and less prepared members of the population, not with rising costs and declining student aid and the pressure and need to raise standards to meet the requirements of economic competitiveness and the general sophistication of modern life.

There are some ameliorating influences. The need of many institutions simply to fill classrooms to survive will make entry into college easier. But what implications does this easing of standards have for quality and financial aid? As a result of the Persian Gulf War, another influx of veterans with another GI bill can also be expected, and with greater numbers of minority applicants. One can find encouraging signs of institutional sensitivity, given the determination of leading colleges and universities to be more aggressive in recruiting less privileged students and making the necessary accommodations in financial aid, instruction, and counseling.

Trustees will need to attend to the issue of equity and social justice, anticipating the effects of the issue not only on institutional practice but also on the larger society. The cause of social justice will be a constant provocation during the 1990s because of imbalances of opportunity within the United States and globally, the reverberating disparities between populations in the Northern and Southern hemispheres, and the haunting predicaments of foreign populations seeking refuge and a better life in the United States. It would be surprising if trustees were not called upon to engage themselves personally as well as institutionally in these issues.

Integrity

The first victim of increased competition among colleges and universities is likely to be truth. Institutions will be tempted to advertise falsely, misrepresent what they can actually provide, cut corners and engage in cutthroat competition, allow inequities in faculty and staff compensation, tilt financial aid packages toward favored clientele, bury deferred maintenance under accounting covers, profess one set of ideals and ignore them in practice, and withhold from recruited presidents and faculty members the harsh realities they will discover when appointed. These practices are, sadly, already in evidence. And if truth becomes the victim, what is left of the soul of higher education?

Above all else, trustees have to be the guardians of truth. They do so, first of all, by insisting on and practicing integrity in their own relationships and deliberations. Second, they need to assure the campus community that truthfulness will be honored rather than penalized. Third, they will have to monitor the institution's performance in every aspect of its work and processes, asking hard questions and being willing to face equally hard answers. Fourth, they need to examine their institution's external relations and communications, to make as certain as they can that the general public's rightful expectation of academic integrity is being satisfied.

Now that the age of big higher education has arrived, the most predictable and most damning scandals will involve the loss of integrity. What has happened in collegiate athletics, scientific research, the advertising of academic wares, financial aid, and all too many other areas of higher education are all indications of what may follow and recur. Trustees should see these events as warning signs and move aggressively to prevent them from recurring.

Due Process

In recent decades, the public has increasingly insisted on fairness in every facet of institutional life and on governmental response to unfairness through increased regulation of vital academic processes that were long carried out without public scrutiny. For example, the public has become concerned about affirmative action, research on human subjects, facilities for the handicapped, genetic research and engineering, environmental impact, sexual harassment, and financial aid and repayment. The lengthening list shows no signs of shrinking, despite recent moves toward deregulation in the general economy and spreading resistance to regulations within the academic community.

Fairness is a powerful concept. Whether it is realized through governmental action or the voluntary response of colleges and universities, it will continue to be high on the agenda for higher education. Much of the agenda will be defensive, that is, simultaneously resisting the further intrusion of regulation while fighting counterattacks by those who would do away with innovations that on balance have advanced the cause of fairness. Affirmative action will continue to engender debate. So will judicial entry into tenure-granting processes, interinstitutional communication of policies of financial aid, secrecy in standardized testing, and confidentiality in a wide variety of traditional academic practices.

Knottier than any of these issues may well be the growing concern over freedom of expression on campus. Will equal opportunity and equal protection be given to views, either from the right or from the left, contrary to those prevalent (the current term is *politically correct*) on campus? What provisions or constraints should govern the appearance of outside speakers on campus? What latitude should be allowed for the unpopular, the unconventional, even the obscene?

Although these concerns involve the substantive aspects of due process, they also directly raise the question of fairness: equity among the various claimants and fairness in the procedures by which policies are adopted and carried out. Trustees will obviously have to familiarize themselves with the law and make certain they have sound legal advice. But they will also have to make certain that their institutions take the initiative in ensuring fairness and anticipating and containing the disputes that are bound to arise.

Ethics

Everything that has been discussed thus far has an ethical dimension. Still, there are other domains in which trustees will increasingly face ethical dilemmas that will demand a constant consideration and restatement of moral standards and values.

Science and technology, particularly biotechnology, will be the focus of many ethical concerns. The possibilities of altering reproductive and emotive behavior, of expanding the whole range of human choice in which divine or statistical law once prevailed, are bringing on a new age of ethical debate. Equally provocative are the exploration of space and consequent issues of priorities; revolutionary developments in communication, raising privacy questions; and environmental research that will force a rethinking of cultural norms and possibly the entire premise of economic development and the social order.

Higher education should be a major forum for such debate, divisive though it will surely be. The fact that the top two campus life issues of concern to college and university presidents are substance abuse and student apathy suggests that the academic forum is far from realizing its potential and responsibility (Carnegie Foundation for the Advancement of Teaching, 1989).

Being a trustee is no longer a passive exercise in civic distinction. It is a demanding role that requires focused attention on emerging issues of global scale and consequence. The campus cannot be isolated from the contentious questions that will be placed on society's agenda. It will in all likelihood be center stage, where most of these dramas will be played out. And trustees will bear the ultimate responsibility for making certain that the debate will be conducted openly, fairly, and with enlightenment and reason.

What will be expected of trustees is due diligence, the honoring of higher education's fundamental values and traditions, and a very healthy dose of self-education. One wonders whether there is in Oklahoma's recent legislation requiring governing board members to enroll in continued education an augury of what is to come.

CHAPTER 14

Setting Tenure and Personnel Policies

Richard P. Chait

This chapter highlights some key issues and policy options that should concern governing boards.

Why Are Academic Personnel Policies So Important?

Faculty members are the heart and soul of academic institutions. Their motivation, working environment, morale, and productivity depend on effective and enlightened policies that are properly administered and monitored.

Heart of the Enterprise

Colleges and universities offer students academic programs staffed by faculty. These academic programs largely define the mission of the institution, and the faculty largely determine how well that mission is fulfilled. When we list the great universities or the strongest departments, our judgments are inevitably assessments of the caliber of the faculty. Thus, although administrators, architects, athletic directors, and even trustees sometimes like to think otherwise, the quality of the faculty and the quality of the university are very nearly synonymous. Because professors are so crucial to the success of an institution, an essential responsibility for trustees is to understand the policies and practices that govern the employment and influence the performance of faculty.

Bulk of the Budget

The direct relationship of the faculty to the reputation of an institution might be reason enough to carefully consider policies and practices that affect academic personnel. There is, however, an equally powerful economic argument. Faculty compensation and related instructional expenses consume on average more than 25 percent of the budget for private colleges and universities (Taylor, Meyerson, Morrell, and Park, 1991). Over the long term, the compensation package (salary and benefits) for a faculty member tenured at age thirty-five could easily exceed $1,250,000 in the equivalent of today's dollars by the time the professor elects to retire. In that context, faculty are expensive and tenure decisions are costly. A decision to tenure five faculty members, for example, could represent a $6.25 million obligation. Colleges and universities need to be as attentive to tenure decisions as they are to construction decisions that entail a comparable capital outlay.

Proliferation of Procedures

Sometime in the late 1960s, American higher education entered an era when a spate of externally imposed rules and regulations started to prescribe and proscribe the behavior of academic institutions. Examples are plentiful: legislation for the handicapped, the Family Educational Rights and Privacy Act (Buckley Amendment), and even decisions by the Environmental Protection Agency.

Although many kinds of regulations have had an impact on colleges and universities, the most dramatic effects can be observed in the area of personnel administration. In 1968, President Johnson signed Executive Order 11246, which, together with Titles VI and VII of the 1964 Civil Rights Act and Title IX of the 1972 Education Amendments Act, provides the basis for affirmative action. Other prominent examples of such regulation include the Equal Pay/Equal Work Act and the Occupational Safety and Health Act. The Age Discrimination in Employment Act was amended to prohibit mandatory retirement by colleges and universities effective January

1, 1994. These statutes and orders govern the recruitment, appointment, promotion, compensation, and retirement of faculty.

In many ways, independent colleges and universities enjoy
greater latitude than public institutions do. For example, few independent colleges and universities are constrained by faculty unionization, especially since the United States Supreme Court decided in
National Labor Relations Board v. *Yeshiva University,* 444 U.S. 672
(1980) that full-time faculty members functioned essentially as managerial employees and were, therefore, ineligible to unionize under
the National Labor Relations Act of 1935. The benchmark cases for
procedural due process—*Board of Regents* v. *Roth,* 408 U.S. 564
(1972) and *Perry* v. *Sinderman,* 408 U.S. 593 (1972)—set constitutional requirements for public universities, and these requirements
may serve as guides for procedural safeguards to be established as
a matter of local policy by private institutions (Kaplin, 1978).

Increase in Litigation

Not unexpectedly, the proliferation of procedures and statutes has
spawned a noticeable increase in litigation. A casual observer may
wonder whether academics spend more time in the courtroom than
in the classroom. Between 1970 and 1984, there were 160 cases of
academic employment discrimination decided on the merits on matters ranging from appointment to promotion to pensions and retirement. Of these cases, however, only one-third occurred at independent
institutions. In the same period, there were 156 decisions at public
and private colleges on procedural and jurisdictional issues (LaNoue
and Lee, 1987). Perhaps of some solace to boards of trustees, plaintiffs
have enjoyed only modest success. As LaNoue and Lee reported (1987,
p. 30), "Of the 156 procedural/jurisdictional decisions, 58 have been
in favor of the plaintiff and 77 for the defendant, and 21 have been
split decisions in which both parties have won and lost on different
issues. On the other hand, plaintiffs have won only 34 of 160 decisions
that reached the merits (6 were split)." Even though colleges prevailed
in nearly four of every five substantive cases, few organizations relish
the prospects of a court appearance and, in any case, the costs in time,
money, morale, and goodwill are often substantial. Therefore, boards
of trustees should ensure that their institutions have clearly defined,

broadly disseminated, and faithfully followed policies, procedures, and performance criteria for personnel actions.

Scarcity of Resources

As tuition and expense levels increase and the competition for private support intensifies, independent colleges confront a difficult environment. Between 1963 and 1988, the market share of enrollments for independent institutions dropped from 35.5 percent to 22.1 percent, although there was a 70 percent increase in actual numbers of students (National Center for Education Statistics, 1990, p. 168). Almost 60 percent of all independent colleges enroll one thousand or fewer students (American Council on Education, 1989, p. 32); few, therefore, achieve economies of scale and many are financially fragile. Indeed, 285 have closed over the past thirty years (National Center for Education Statistics, 1990, p. 231).

For most small colleges, personnel decisions are critical and mistakes are costly. The same proposition applies to larger institutions, especially during a time of equilibrium or retrenchment. The academy can no longer hide mistakes with more people and more money. There will be far less flexibility to change people and hence programs exactly at a time when the ability to respond to changes in student demography and interests may be crucial, particularly for small independent colleges where each enrollment makes a difference.

The importance of the link between people and programs in higher education cannot be overstated. In higher education, product changes almost always require personnel changes. Unlike auto assembly line workers, who can turn with relative ease from producing one model to producing another, few classicists could shift from a course on Plato to a course on pollution. In other words, because there will probably be limited opportunities in the short term to change people or expand programs, each personnel decision will assume added significance and each mistake will be magnified. Now, perhaps more than ever before, human resources must be managed effectively.

Scarcity of Faculty

While estimates vary about the supply and demand of faculty over the next twenty years, the disagreements focus on the magnitude, not the certainty, of a shortage of qualified faculty. Bowen and Schuster (1986, p. 186) forecast a 4-to-6 percent yearly attrition rate of full-time faculty between 1990 and 2010: "At the annual rate of 4 percent, over ten years about 32 percent of all faculty positions would become vacant through attrition, and over twenty-five years 70 percent would become vacant." Recent turnover rates at private colleges fall close to the predicted range: 5.7 percent. In 1990, administrators at these institutions anticipated that over the next two years searches would have to be conducted for about 9 percent of all currently occupied full-time faculty positions (El-Khawas, 1990).

With limited financial resources and an expected shortage of faculty, the competition for academic personnel will be keen and intense. Already, 63 percent of the institutions surveyed by the American Council on Education (ACE) reported "difficulty in getting top applicants to accept positions" (El-Khawas, 1990, pp. 21–22). This concern was less pronounced at private institutions, where 48 percent of the respondents expressed concern about the predicted shortage of faculty, compared to 74 percent at public institutions (El-Khawas, 1990).

Colleges and universities will need, therefore, some comparative advantages to recruit and retain the best teachers and researchers. The competitive environment for faculty will only heighten the need for personnel policies and practices that are workable, attractive to faculty, and conducive to productive careers. In this regard, independent colleges and universities have a very powerful competitive advantage. Boards of trustees of state institutions frequently lack the authority to determine crucial personnel policies, which are set instead by a state agency or through a collective bargaining agreement. To compound the problem, public college boards frequently have limited control over the volume and flow of financial resources. In contrast, private colleges are free to develop, with faculty input, the most effective blend of employment policies and practices and the most appropriate allocation of resources. Guided by the president and chief academic officer, private colleges should exploit the potential to tailor policies that meet self-determined objectives and priorities and also reinforce institutional values and culture. In doing so, the college will create a better working environment and a competitive edge in recruiting and retaining a talented faculty.

Managing Human Resources

Most boards of trustees of independent colleges and universities recognize the need to manage their physical and fiscal resources. Capital and operating budgets are developed routinely, and three-to-five-year fiscal projections are hardly uncommon. Although the management of human resources also requires planning and monitoring over the short- and long-terms, many institutions fail to carry out these tasks.

Nearly all boards annually receive a balance sheet and a statement of changes in fund balances. The balance sheet presents a financial picture at a particular moment, and the statement of changes helps a board to compare current circumstances with conditions of the previous twelve months. But how many boards receive similar information about personnel in general and faculty in particular? Planning for the management of human resources might begin with an inventory of current staff. With faculty, for example, the data might be arrayed by department or school, age, sex, race, salary, work load, tenure status, degree attainment, and retirement date.

There are a number of computer-based programs to store and display these data (Nevison, 1980). More important, the models permit simulation exercises based upon various policy assumptions made by the institution. One can manipulate the policy variables that affect faculty, such as rates of promotion and tenure, length of probationary periods, retrenchment plans, and voluntary attrition. Through the application of these models, a college and its board can routinely examine historical patterns and trends, compile an up-to-date profile of the faculty, and forecast the likely effects of contemplated policy or environmental changes.

Placing a particular college within a larger context can easily be accomplished. The American Association of University Professors (AAUP) annually publishes a compendium of salary levels and tenure ratios. Other valuable statistical summaries issued annually include *The Condition of Education* by the National Center for Education Statistics and *Campus Trends* by the American Council on Education. In addition, many private colleges participate in consortia and data exchanges with a group of similar institutions. In any case, trustees should ensure that their institution has an appropriate faculty data base, periodically conducts projections and simulations, and monitors the condition and performance of the college against comparative data from similar institutions. For a superb guide to the scope and use of comparative data, trustees should consult *Strategic Analysis* (Taylor, Meyerson, Morrell and Park, 1991), which has special sections on faculty and instruction as well as three case studies on private colleges and universities.

With respect to the faculty and the curriculum, trustees worry most—and occasionally too much—about institutional flexibility. Despite all the expressed concerns, very few institutional leaders attempt to measure or gauge flexibility except to monitor the tenure ratio. This barometer may communicate something about flexibility if the bases for the calculation are sound. Trustees should understand whether, for example, the denominator of the ratio includes research and teaching assistants, librarians, and part-time faculty.

There are some other useful measures of flexibility that might be charted. Colleges can calculate the percentage of instructional salary dollars committed to tenured and untenured faculty respectively. This would give some sense of the financial flexibility necessary to achieve curricular flexibility. Faculty turnover rates should also be monitored. What are the average employment periods for tenured and untenured faculty members? How have these rates changed over the past five years? How do they compare with similar colleges? Because more program changes and innovations may have to be generated from within over the short-term, boards might ask how often courses are substantially revised, replaced, or discontinued.

To summarize, the effective management of human resources requires that a personnel data base be maintained; that appropriate data be regularly presented to the board; and that the board analyze the data retrospectively and prospectively, mindful of both local and national conditions. With this information at hand, a board will be better prepared to contemplate policy changes.

Contemplating Changes in Personnel Policy

Before considering changes in personnel policy, the board should ask a crucial question: Does the problem derive from an inadequate policy or from the ineffective administration of a sound policy? Obviously, a college should not change policies when it should change people or, conversely, change people when it should change policy. Sometimes both may need to be changed.

A simple illustration may suffice. Among private colleges, the percentage of tenured faculty varies considerably. Some institutions are below 50 percent; others are above 75 percent. The average tenure ratio in 1987–88 was 64.9 percent for all colleges and 58.4 percent for private four-year colleges and universities (National Center for Education Statistics, 1990, p. 227). The variations are attributable not so much to dissimilar tenure policies—most colleges have broadly similar policies—as to different standards, expectations, and related matters of policy implementation.

If a policy change seems advisable, the president and the board, as noted above, need as much hard data as possible to supplement ever-present opinions, impressions, and intuitions. Moreover, the board should ask the administration to articulate the problem to be resolved or the objective to be achieved by a policy change. Chait, Mortimer, Taylor, and Wood (1985, p. 6) outline the questions the board (or the appropriate board committee) should use to actively engage in discussions about policy objectives:

- Does the weakness lie with the policy or with its implementation?
- What are the main purposes the policy is intended to serve?
- Is the proposal aimed at a new objective, or is it a new approach to an established goal?
- Are there any conflicts among various policy objectives?
- How will we know whether our purposes have been realized?
- How will we monitor and evaluate the impact of the policy?

The administration should then explore with the faculty policy alternatives congruent with the objectives of the board and periodically update the board as a preferred course of action emerges. Eventually, the administration should present a draft policy for discussion by the board or the designated trustee committee. The board should not draft, edit, or revise personnel policy statements. Reservations should be expressed and, as necessary, the administration may be directed to rewrite the policy in a way that satisfies the board's concerns.

Where policy changes will affect faculty directly, the faculty should be consulted for three reasons. First, faculty may have some valuable ideas to contribute to the discussion. Second, consultation suggests that the board and the administration respect the legitimate role of the faculty in the process of shared governance, a central tenet of most institutions. Incidentally, "meaningful participation of faculty in the governance process" has a very positive effect on faculty morale, stronger even than "institutional financial support and faculty salaries" (Anderson, 1988, p. 6). Third, consultation improves the likelihood that change will be effective, especially in those instances, such as promotion and tenure reviews or curricular changes, where the faculty will actually be called upon to implement the new policy. At a minimum, the board should understand, preferably firsthand, the dominant sentiment of the faculty about the issue under consideration. Many private colleges also adopt procedures, such as multiconstituency task forces, faculty representatives to trustee committees, and regular reports from the leadership of the faculty senate, that are coordinated by the president.

When the moment arrives to write the final version of a new policy, language should be chosen that is appropriate to the institution and its distinctive aims. The board of trustees should seek assurances that the proposed policies have not been borrowed wholesale from other colleges or from professional associations without very careful analysis of each and every provision. Furniss (1976, 1978), for example, questions the status of policies on tenure and retrenchment recommended by the AAUP and cautions institutions not to adopt the Association's policies word for word.

Although policies are enormously important, personnel actions speak louder than personnel policies. To whom a college awards tenure communicates far more about institutional standards than does tenure policy. To whom a college awards a promotion, a merit increment, or a sabbatical leave communicates far more about institutional values than do policy pronouncements. In that sense, personnel decisions are clear signals widely broadcast, and the actions of the board should closely fit the intended message.

Understanding Academic Tenure

Few faculty personnel policies are more perplexing to trustees than those surrounding the institution of academic tenure. The first step in reducing the confusion is for trustees to understand the origins and purposes of tenure.

Definitions

Among personnel policies and actions, none looms larger than academic tenure. As noted earlier, tenure decisions involve substantial economic and contractual commitments to individuals and programs. Despite the central importance of tenure, many trustees (and some academics) are uncertain about the provisions and purposes of tenure policy. This confusion adds to the larger controversy over the value and wisdom of a tenure system.

Some definitions may help to minimize the confusion. Traditionally, the academic community has regarded the 1940 AAUP Statement on Academic Freedom and Tenure as the definitive exposition. In part, that statement declares: "Tenure is a means to certain ends—specifically, (1) freedom of teaching and research and of extramural activities and (2) a sufficient degree of economic security to make the profession attractive to men and women of ability. Freedom and economic security—hence, tenure—are indispensable to the success of an institution in fulfilling its obligations to its students and to society" (American Association of University Professors, 1984, p. 3).

As much a characterization as a definition, the AAUP statement might be compared to a more operational definition offered by the Commission on Academic Tenure cosponsored by the AAUP and the Association of American Colleges (1973). The commission defined tenure as "an arrangement under which faculty appointments in an institution of higher education are continued until retirement for age or physical disability, subject to dismissal for adequate cause or unavoidable termination on account of financial exigency or change of institutional program" (p. 256).

Taken together, these statements provide a useful definition of academic tenure. However, trustees should remember that general definitions by associations and commissions do not supersede the specific policy provisions adopted by a board of trustees, enacted by a legislature, or negotiated by a faculty union. Academic tenure will be neither more nor less than what official institutional policy stipulates, although absent any specific institutional statement, national norms may be brought to bear (*Krotkoff* v. *Goucher College*, 585 F. 2d 675, 1978). With these caveats in mind, we can speak broadly of the primary purposes of academic tenure.

Purposes

As the 1940 AAUP statement suggests, tenure aims to safeguard academic freedom and ensure a measure of economic security. Like academic tenure, the term *academic freedom* enjoys no common definition. To critics, the term suggests a license to speak irresponsibly on any issue. To defenders, academic freedom represents a hallowed doctrine and a prerequisite to the practice of the profession. In fact, academic freedom has three essential components:

1.   The freedom to conduct and publish research.
2.   The freedom to teach and discuss issues pertinent to a course or subject without introducing into the classroom irrelevant matters.
3.   The freedom to speak or write as a citizen without expressly speaking or writing on behalf of the institution unless authorized to do so.

In short, academic freedom is meant to provide an atmosphere conducive to the open and unfettered pursuit and exchange of knowledge. Some people argue that tenure safeguards academic freedom because the award of tenure formally and explicitly confers the three privileges mentioned above. Tenured personnel are thereby assured that their research and teaching can be guided by their best professional judgments, not by outside pressures or concerns for continued employment.

Unlike academic freedom, economic security is a well-established and easily understood concept. By carefully specifying the grounds and procedures whereby tenured personnel may be dismissed, tenure protects against arbitrary and capricious personnel actions, and thus provides significant job security.

As originally conceived, tenure was to benefit the institution as well as the individual, and many proponents of tenure argue that the benefits are indeed mutual. These proponents traditionally hold that tenure creates an environment that encourages faculty to undertake long-term and high-risk projects. Further, the presence of a tenured faculty helps develop a coterie of professionals loyal to the college yet sufficiently secure to act as constructive critics. Finally, and perhaps most important, the very nature of a tenure decision presumably forces the institution to assess each candidate carefully and thus to exercise quality control. Board members must understand the espoused goals and objectives of tenure policies; only then can trustees examine actual tenure practices fruitfully.

Prevalence

Formal academic tenure in the United States is a product of the twentieth century. Although various forerunners were available to some faculty in the 1800s, academic tenure as a systematic policy was not well established until the early 1900s when universities such as Harvard and Johns Hopkins adopted the policy. It was not generally accepted as a fundamental precept of the profession until the 1915 Declaration of Principles by the then newly formed AAUP.

Today, however, academic tenure operates on almost all college campuses. About 85 percent of all colleges and universities have a tenure system, and these institutions employ about 95 percent of all full-time faculty. All universities, nearly all four-year colleges, and some two thirds of all two-year colleges have a tenure system.

While nearly all institutions have tenure systems, obviously not all faculty have tenure—only 64.9 percent in 1987–88, virtually the same percentage reported in 1980–81. Seventy percent of all male faculty members and 50 percent of all female faculty members were tenured (National Center for Education Statistics, 1990). In all, a good many faculty hold tenure; a reasonable estimate might be about 317,000 of the some 489,000 full-time faculty. Slightly more than half (54 percent) of all faculty surveyed in 1989 considered tenure more difficult to achieve than five years previously, although that figure represents a steep decline from 1975, when 73 percent of the respondents believed the chances for tenure were dimmer than five years earlier (Carnegie Foundation for the Advancement of Teaching, 1989).

Procedures

Although the criteria, standards, and procedures for the award of tenure differ from college to college (and often from school to school within a university), there are enough commonalities to construct a generalized description of the bases and processes that govern tenure decisions.

How do tenure decisions arise? Normally, a faculty member automatically stands for tenure at a fixed time, generally one year before the expiration of the probationary period. In exceptional cases, a candidate may be considered a year or two earlier, and in rare instances, a college or university may offer an extremely well-established scholar at another school an appointment with "instant tenure." Denial of tenure at the end of the probationary period almost always means that the unsuccessful candidate *must* leave the institution after a terminal year of the contract. Such provisions are referred to as the "up or out" rule.

Tenure decisions typically reflect assessments of performance and judgments about potential. Minimum eligibility requirements usually include:

1. *Service in a probationary period.* The probationary period which normally lasts three to seven years (although exceptions exist at both ends of the range) offers the faculty member an opportunity to develop and refine the skills necessary for the position, and it offers the institution a chance to observe and evaluate the faculty member's performance. Service elsewhere may be counted toward fulfillment of the probationary period, although credit for prior service usually does not exceed half the total probationary period. Satisfactory completion of the probationary period represents one measure of professional experience.

2. *Attainment of appropriate academic credentials.* This would usually mean attaining the highest degree, such as a Ph.D., that is normally awarded in one's discipline. Currently, four-year colleges and universities usually tenure only faculty who already possess a terminal degree.

3. *Appointment to an appropriate academic rank.* Most commonly, to be considered for tenure, faculty must hold or be qualified to hold the rank of assistant or associate professor. It is

commonplace, but by no means required, to link the tenure decision to promotion in rank.

4. *Successful past performance.* This is normally assessed in three broad areas: teaching, scholarship (or research), and service to the college and the profession. Depending on the institution or the department, these criteria are weighted differently. While some institutions require excellence in all three areas, more often institutions require excellence in one or two areas with solid performance in the other(s).

5. *Growth potential.* An individual's capacity and ability to continue to develop as a teacher and scholar are also considered. Most often, these forecasts are based on past performance and the value attached by students and colleagues to work done thus far by the faculty member.

Although tenure decisions are ultimately subjective in nature, a body of evidence is usually assembled to inform the deliberations. A typical dossier includes letters of recommendation from students and campus colleagues; letters from outside references (usually from colleagues in the same or an allied field) that address the quality of the candidate's scholarship, the candidate's publications and scholarly reviews of these works, student evaluations of teaching, course syllabi and examinations, and a self-evaluation or personal statement that includes the candidate's goals and objectives for the future. Not all institutions collect all these materials and each institution obviously assesses the evidence differently.

As a matter of procedure, the review process typically entails a sequence of deliberations and recommendations that often begin at the departmental or program level. In many universities and some liberal arts colleges, the recommendations of the department and department chair carry great weight. Beyond the department, the process moves to the dean, a school- or collegewide committee, the academic vice-president, and the president. In nearly all cases, the president eventually places a recommendation for action before the board of trustees.

Because the board bears ultimate as well as legal responsibility for the adequacy and equity of the process, it should determine that the procedures are fair, reasonable, manageable, comprehensive, and structurally appropriate to the mission and structure of the institution. From time to time, the academic affairs (or equivalent) committee should ask the dean or provost to "walk" the committee through the process. En route, trustees might ask questions such as:

- What documents do faculty receive that explain the process?
- Does the process allow an evaluative record to be constructed from the start of the probationary period?
- How do the procedures guarantee faculty due process? Are the procedures acceptable to a large majority of the faculty?
- Are there any significant differences in procedures across academic units, and if so, why?

The committee's role is not to write procedures but rather to ensure that there are procedures that are widely understood and appropriate to the task.

Establishing Tenure Policy

Although boards should be generally acquainted with the procedures that govern tenure reviews, the more important aspects of the process for the board are establishing tenure policy and making tenure decisions. Before embarking upon a consideration of tenure policies, a board should first recognize that these policies exist within a larger institutional context. Thus, the board must have a working knowledge of the following documents and how they interrelate: existing bylaws, rules, regulations, and relevant state statutes; the affirmative action plan; the operating budget; strategic priorities and mission statement; and a profile of the institution's faculty, as described earlier.

Tenure policies and practices are unusually sensitive issues for faculty. Therefore, the need to be clear on policy objectives and consult widely with faculty is especially acute. Moreover, certain aspects of tenure policy involve contractual obligations between the institution as employer and the professor as employee. Changes in policy may require that some faculty be "grandfathered," that is, exempted from any change.

What tenure-related policies should a governing board establish? With appropriate and substantial participation by the college community, a board ought to set policies that govern the probationary period, credential or degree requirements, and rank requirements for tenure. On the advice and recommendation of the faculty and academic staff, the board should also set general guidelines on the relative importance of teaching, scholarship, and service. Criteria that affect judgments of past performance and future contributions are best determined by faculty peers and academic administrators, although the board should insist that such criteria be plainly stated and clearly supportive of the mission of the institution.

Among the questions the board might raise are:

- Does the probationary period provide adequate time to evaluate a faculty member's performance?
- Are assignments sufficiently varied during the probationary period to test a faculty member's abilities in all areas of responsibility?
- Are the degree requirements appropriate to the mission of the institution and the conditions of the marketplace?
- Is the relative importance assigned to teaching, research, and service consistent with the mission of the institution? Is there sufficient latitude to accommodate faculty with different interests and strengths?
- What policy statements do faculty receive? How are standards and expectations communicated to the faculty? Have they changed over the past five years?
- Are institutional needs, strategic priorities, and affirmative action reflected in appropriate criteria for promotion and tenure decisions? If not, why not?

Making Tenure Decisions

Individual tenure decisions, at one level, require considerable familiarity with an individual's qualifications. The decision requires a sophisticated assessment of the candidate's professional expertise—an assessment best rendered by other experts. Yet, at another level, a tenure decision requires familiarity with institutional needs and priorities. Trustees are more likely to be acquainted with the institution's needs than with the individual's strengths. A governing board should consider the fit between individual merit, as judged by academic professionals, and institutional needs, as judged by the board in consultation with the academic administration. Such a role implies that, compared to the faculty and to a lesser extent to the administration, the board will ask a somewhat different set of questions and will require a somewhat different set of materials to make an informed decision.

With a perspective focused on institutional needs, a board may ask questions such as:

- Do we have the financial resources to support these tenured appointments?
- Are these permanent appointments consistent with the strategic priorities, curricular needs, and affirmative action plans of the institution?
- Will these decisions unwisely constrain institutional flexibility or unduly bind a particular department?
- Do enrollment and placement patterns warrant a permanent appointment?
- Will these decisions foreclose even more attractive appointments to tenure within the foreseeable future?
- If tenure were denied, would the dollars "saved" be allocated to the same position, another program, or a different department?

These questions start to suggest the kind of data that a board requires to participate effectively in tenure decisions and, for that matter, in the review of tenure policies. All too often, administrators furnish boards with the very same information provided to faculty and deans even though trustees have (or should have) a markedly different set of concerns. If trustees receive only information about the individual merit of a candidate, how can the board help but dwell on that aspect of the decision? If the board receives information on enrollments, placements, finances, faculty flow, tenure levels, and affirmative action, however, a very different discussion might ensue.

The division between individual merit and institutional need can be too sharply drawn. Surely, faculty deliberations on merit should be made within the context of institutional needs, and conversely, trustees should be acquainted with the qualifications of tenure candidates. In general, however, the board should concentrate on the extent to which individuals with strong credentials for tenure meet institutional needs.

As a rule, if the board feels assured that the prescribed process has been followed and the appropriate criteria applied, it should rarely have cause to review tenure recommendations for individual merit. A fair question might be whether a president or a board *can* determine the academic quality of highly specialized experts working in so many diverse fields. The board may receive these assurances formally or informally from the president or from its normal review of faculty portfolios. On occasion, the board or one of its committees may elect to review a tenure recommendation more meticulously than usual solely to ensure that the prescribed process has been followed, the proper documentation collected, and the appropriate criteria applied. Carefully limited to questions of procedure and discreetly conducted, such a spot check would probably not be seen either as an intrusion on faculty prerogative or as lack of support for the president.

So far, we have identified two reasons why a board should review recommendations for tenure: to determine the fit between the individual and the institution and to ensure procedural regularity. Other circumstances that may warrant an in-depth review by the board are widely disparate evaluations of the same candidate or a conspicuously disproportionate number of either positive or negative recommendations, either overall or by race or sex.

While a board may be tempted to investigate the merits of recommendations from the president that generate an uproar on campus, the board should be careful to review only cases where there is reason to believe that established policy has been violated. In other words, unless state policy or a labor contract requires otherwise, a board should not serve as a court of last resort for faculty members considered talented by some but found wanting by others when established policies and procedures have been equitably applied. The risks associated with a review on merit by the board are substantial. Very likely the action of the board will be perceived by faculty as an intrusion on their autonomy. Morale may sink as tension heightens. The president, too, may regard the review as an inappropriate interference or as a vote of no confidence. Thus, such reviews should be conducted only rarely and even then with great care.

In certain cases, institutional bylaws, state policy, or a labor contract may *require* that upon petition the board review a tenure decision or hear a grievance. Boards should have guidelines that anticipate and address these circumstances—guidelines that include a clear statement of the board's authority to render a final decision; a review procedure that assures due process and respects confidentiality; assignment of the responsibility for review to an appropriate board unit, such as the education or faculty affairs committee; a description of the range of sanctions and remedies that can be applied; and a description of the general circumstances, such as a charge of unlawful discrimination, under which the board might consider questions of individual merit.

Prior to undertaking any review, the board and the president should consider the need for legal counsel to assist them in such matters as due process, need for transcripts, sources and uses of evidence, and personal liability. However, with respect to all personnel policies or individual personnel actions, the board should first ask itself if they are "fair" and *then* ask university counsel if they are legal. What is legal is not always fair, but what is fair is almost always legal. Institutions that are consistently equitable and fair-minded are less likely to encounter lawsuits and more likely to win the few cases that do arise.

Revoking Tenure

As difficult and unpleasant as a decision to deny tenure may be, any attempt to revoke tenure will prove doubly so. Because tenure policies are designed to guard against capricious and arbitrary dismissals, such proceedings are typically cumbersome and weighted to favor the tenured faculty member. In general, tenured faculty can be dismissed for three reasons: adequate cause, financial exigency, and program discontinuation. In all three cases, the burden of proof rests with the institution and due process must be provided.

Dismissal for *adequate cause* traditionally encompasses professional incompetence, acts of moral turpitude, neglect of duty, insubordination, and dishonesty in teaching or research. Dismissals for cause are rare not so much because colleges and universities have no incompetent faculty but because the political costs of such proceedings are steep and few administrations systematically document inadequate performance over time. Usually, the problem is not with the policy per se—most schools have reasonable statements about adequate cause—but with policy execution. With the end to mandatory retirement, the need for methodical, longitudinal data on faculty performance will become even more critical, lest some unfit professors continue to serve.

Until the 1970s and the onset of a no-growth era, policy statements about dismissal due to *financial exigency* were little more than boilerplate buried deep within the faculty handbook. More and more, however, colleges and universities have been compelled by financial stringency, which returned in the early 1990s, to exhume and apply the policy. As a rule, tenure policy permits the dismissal of permanent faculty when fiscal conditions are so severe that institutional survival requires the release of these persons. Independent colleges may, however, set a different standard; for example, one that permits layoffs due to chronic financial stress across campus or solely within a particular department or college (*Scheur v. Creighton University*, 260 N.W. 2d 595, 1977; Furniss, 1976). In most instances, the dismissal of untenured faculty within a program or department precedes the dismissal of tenured personnel, although boards enjoy wide latitude to determine the criteria that govern layoffs (*Johnson v. Board of Regents of the University of Wisconsin System*, 377 F. Supp. 230, 1974).

There have been numerous court cases on the issue of retrenchment generally and the dismissal of tenured faculty more particularly (Kaplin, 1978, 1980). On the whole, these cases suggest that the administration and board of trustees have the authority to determine whether or not true financial exigency exists and considerable discretion to determine the most prudent means of reducing expenses. Unless in violation of institutional policy, contrary to state or federal law, or a matter of subterfuge, the courts have preserved the authority of the administration and board to select the programs and personnel to be terminated.

The federal courts have required that state institutions ensure due process under such circumstances. These requirements for state institutions are a useful guideline for private institutions. The court held that the university must provide a written statement of the basis for the decision to lay off employees; a reasonable description of the manner in which that decision was reached; reasonable disclosure of the data the decision makers used; an opportunity for terminated faculty to argue that the decision reached was arbitrary, capricious, or unlawful; and adequate notice and appropriate compensation to terminated employees (*Johnson* v. *Board of Regents of the University of Wisconsin System*, 377 F. Supp. 230, 1974).

Tenured faculty may also be dismissed when an institution elects to discontinue or curtail a particular program or department. Very often, dismissals due to *program discontinuation* relate closely to financial considerations. However, the decision may be motivated solely by a department's quality or the centrality of the department to the institution's mission.

From all the court cases on retrenchment and layoffs, one extraordinarily important principle emerges, a principle that simply cannot be overemphasized: "Each case is subject to its own contractual provisions" (*Lumpert* v. *University of Dubuque*, 255 N.W. 2d 168, 1977, p. 10). What a college can or cannot do within the broad confines of the law depends chiefly on the stipulations of relevant institutional policies.

Whatever the substance of the retrenchment policies of an institution, the policies ought to be adopted in advance of the need to use them. The moment of crisis is not a particularly opportune time to formulate policy, least of all retrenchment policy. Moreover, as a matter of sound practice, academic personnel and programs should be evaluated periodically. Such evaluations will help identify problems early, establish a history and habit of review, and provide valuable data to inform retrenchment decisions should cutbacks someday be deemed necessary.

Considering Modifications and Alternatives

Although a well-established concept and a widespread practice, academic tenure has always been subject to criticism, most especially in the last decade or so. Briefly stated, these criticisms are:

1. *Tenure reduces accountability.* Critics argue that tenure is a one-sided contract binding the institution to the teacher, but not the teacher to the institution. With a "lifetime contract," a tenured faculty member is effectively removed from accountability and the performance incentive implicit in periodically having to seek contract renewal.

2. *Tenure constrains flexibility.* Each time an institution confers tenure, it makes a long-term financial and program commitment. Because these commitments are not easily withdrawn, the institution becomes that much more rigid and less capable of making commitments to other individuals and programs.

3. *Tenure impedes affirmative action.* Tenure removes positions from the job market for extended periods of time. The larger the percentage of positions filled with tenured personnel, the fewer the vacancies. Consequently, the institution must wait for retrenchment, death, or dismissal for cause before it can diversify the faculty.

4. *Tenure establishes a class system.* Tenure policies limit academic freedom and other privileges to the tenured faculty. If academic freedom is essential to the profession and tenure is essential to academic freedom, how can untenured faculty successfully practice the profession?

5. *Tenure duplicates other protection.* Critics of tenure maintain that state and federal law and numerous court decisions afford faculty all the freedom needed to teach, conduct research, and speak out.

Whenever the demographic and economic trends are unfavorable, criticisms of tenure seem to intensify. Thus, colleges tenured to capacity are searching for a way out and colleges not yet tenured to capacity are looking for strategies and policies that will enable them to stay that way. From these efforts, some alternatives have emerged that either introduce modifications to a tenure system or replace tenure with a contract system. Treated at length by Chait and Ford (1982), these variations arise most often at private colleges, which have the flexibility to experiment, innovate, and adapt. The new wrinkles include the following.

The simplest, although not always most desirable, modification is a *tenure quota*—that is, the establishment of a ceiling on the percentage of faculty who may hold tenure at any given time. The only options are to waive the quota or wave farewell. Tenure quotas or guidelines do ensure some flexibility and the introduction of new blood. They also force hard choices, because the fixed number of tenure slots available means that only so many among those eligible can be accommodated. However, because only untenured faculty are adversely affected in a direct manner by tenure quotas, the burden of resolving an institutional problem falls unevenly on one constituency. Moreover, junior faculty, faced with bleak prospects for tenure, start to think more of enhancing their mobility than of serving the campus community.

More and more institutions have elected to *extend the probationary period* that faculty must serve to qualify for tenure. Extended probation affords a longer time to observe and evaluate untenured faculty. Of course, the longer an untenured faculty member remains at an institution, the more likely that his or her anxiety will increase and the more difficult the decision to terminate the faculty member will become. Although the AAUP sets seven years as a standard, numerous institutions, particularly research universities, have longer probationary periods.

A modification related to extended probationary periods is a *waiver of the "up or out" rule.* Several independent colleges no longer require faculty to either earn tenure or leave the institution at the conclusion of the probationary period. Instead, faculty may be retained without tenure on renewable multiyear appointments. These so-called tenurable faculty may be considered for tenure at some future date should a tenure slot open.

While retaining the essence of traditional tenure policy, the modifications discussed thus far do alter the notion of tenure as originally conceived. The *periodic evaluation of tenured faculty,* however, is not inconsistent with conventional policy. More and more institutions now evaluate tenured faculty intermittently, perhaps every four or five years, absent an evaluation for some other purpose such as promotion or sabbatical leave. Although few colleges have used these assessments as a means to terminate weak faculty members, the process, at its best, may lead to improved performance (Licata, 1986).

For colleges that wish to abandon rather than modify conventional tenure policies, *term contracts* represent the only alternative. Although contract systems operate on relatively few campuses, most notably two-year colleges, each system has a different name and at least one different wrinkle. There are, for example, growth or learning contracts, rolling contracts, and variable length contracts. Despite the different catchwords, all these systems share a common element: an appointment for a specific and limited time period with no assurance (or proscription) of continued employment beyond the expiration date of the contract.

In most cases, initial contracts are for a relatively brief period—usually one to three years. As a contract term draws to an end, the college evaluates the candidate's performance to date, and the candidate presents a prospectus or statement of goals for the next contract period. Under the rolling contract system, the faculty member's multiyear contract extends, or rolls, at the end of each year as long as favorable evaluations continue. Should there be a negative evaluation, the faculty member has a fixed period of time to remedy the deficiencies noted.

In theory, contracts offer opportunities to exercise discretion, cut losses, minimize long-term commitments, maximize institutional flexibility, and make personnel changes. But clearly, not many institutions exercise these opportunities; almost all institutions renew nearly all their contracts (Chait and Ford, 1982).

Thus far, we have considered some modifications *of* tenure and some alternatives *to* tenure. Another option would be some combination of modifications and alternatives. In some ways, the "peaceful coexistence" of tenure and nontenure systems hardly represents an innovation. Nearly all institutions have had part-time and adjunct faculty in nontenure positions working side by side with tenured and tenure-track faculty. Now, however, there are more appointments of full-time faculty to positions expressly designated as outside the tenure track where service does not apply toward fulfillment of the probationary period. Limited-term, off-track positions do ensure some turnover, although the same turnover could be achieved by nonreappointment of a probationary faculty. However, the off-track policy does not raise false hopes of tenure and does not leave any ambiguity about long-term prospects.

To summarize, there are numerous modifications and alternatives to tenure. Each entails some trade-offs that need to be assessed within a specific institutional context. All changes in tenure policy should be approached carefully and investigated thoroughly. No other issue touches so many nerves and spawns so much controversy.

Administering Promotion and
Tenure Policies Effectively

Among all the alternatives to tenure, the most obvious option is often easily overlooked: to administer current policy more effectively. As noted earlier, many institutions are able to make discriminating and discerning judgments and thereby hold tenure ratios to a reasonable level, perhaps between one-half and two-thirds of the full-time faculty. While one cannot generalize too broadly, colleges and universities that do exercise selectivity share certain common policies and practices.

First, these institutions approach faculty excellence as a matter to be judged, not measured. Though some aspects of performance can be quantified, most cannot; therefore, parties to the tenure process collect and review evidence appropriate to the decision at hand. Something of a judicial model applies. To begin the process, a jury of peers, usually at the department or college level, examines the evidence and offers a judgment, sometimes unanimous and sometimes divided. These recommendations are often appealed, reviewed, and even reversed at higher levels. Ultimately, however, informed professionals reach a decision.

Second, the judgments are based on clear criteria that are spelled out to the faculty member at the time of appointment. Again, clear criteria do not necessarily mean mathematically measurable criteria, although there may be some quantitative data to support the criteria, such as effective class presentation or scholarly productivity. Whatever the particular criteria applied, they normally do not change between the time of appointment and the tenure decision. Standards of performance may change—the institution may expect more from a full professor than from an assistant professor—but the bases of judgment remain relatively constant.

Third, the criteria are not limited to individual merit; institutional priorities are also considered. As suggested earlier, college presidents and boards of trustees must make tenure decisions against a backdrop of institutional priorities, such as financial equilibrium, affirmative action, and enrollment patterns.

Fourth, there are usually interim evaluations that are more frequent at the earlier stages of a candidate's progress. Many colleges employ, either formally or informally, a threshold or breakpoint evaluation at or near the halfway point to tenure and again one year before the candidate's current appointment expires. (Untenured faculty normally have one-to-three-year contracts renewable at the institution's option up to the end of the probationary period.) These more comprehensive evaluations are clearly understood by all to be a significant hurdle en route to tenure. At the conclusion of this assessment, the appropriate academic officer informs the weakest faculty members that their probationary appointments will not be renewed. This process is colloquially referred to as "weeding out."

Fifth, nearly all institutions with well-managed tenure practices require multilevel reviews at the time of the tenure decision. Each level introduces a somewhat different perspective. To maintain institutional quality, a department must be answerable to a larger constituency; for example, colleagues at the same institution but in allied fields, peers in the same field but at other institutions, or perhaps both. Divisional or collegewide committees can actually serve to protect strong departments against weak departments with lesser standards.

Finally, these institutions employ someone at or near the top who is able to say no on close votes if institutional priorities so dictate. To retain the confidence and goodwill of the faculty members who are party to the decision and to ensure the integrity of the process, however, the president or provost shares his or her thinking with the collegewide committee, the dean, and the department head.

These policies and practices are by no means surefire solutions to the tenure problem. Much depends on the institutional context, local tradition, and individual leadership. But any steps taken to administer tenure policies more effectively are likely to have a more immediate, positive, and pragmatic effect than rhetorical assaults against the concept.

Auditing Promotion and Tenure Policies

To audit promotion and tenure policies, a board of trustees or its academic affairs committee should ask the administration a series of questions every year or so. Some of the inquiries concern the faculty evaluation process that underlies promotion and tenure decisions; others concern the outcomes of the review process.

With respect to evaluation, the board might ask:

- What are the paramount purposes of faculty evaluation?
- What areas of responsibility are evaluated and what criteria are applied?
- Are the standards based on performance relative to others on campus, national norms, or the achievement of certain objectives?
- What evidence does the college gather from whom?
- How are student evaluations incorporated into the process?
- Who participates in the evaluation? What role, if any, do students, peers, administrators, and outside experts play in the decision-making process?
- How often do evaluations occur? Are all faculty, tenured and untenured, evaluated regularly? Who manages the process?
- How are faculty informed of the results?

The board should be satisfied that the faculty and the administration together have articulated reasonable purposes and areas of evaluation as well as suitable criteria, standards, and sources of evidence. From time to time, professors and administrators may suggest that the work of an academic, especially a teacher, simply cannot be evaluated. Trustees should be skeptical of such assertions. There are numerous volumes available that describe in detail workable, sensible faculty evaluation programs as well as tools and techniques that can be used to collect valid data from students, colleagues, and administrators in order to gauge faculty performance in teaching, research, and service (see, for example, Seldin, 1984; Centra, 1979). The failure to adopt a well-designed, comprehensive faculty evaluation system may reflect, therefore, a lack of political will and desire more than the absence of sound evaluation methods.

In order to understand the results of the promotion and tenure process, the board should request certain outcome data on a regular basis, probably once a year. While these data should not be construed as indicators of quality, the information will familiarize the board with the results of the process and the data should provoke a discussion with faculty and staff about the effectiveness of the tenure system and whether the objectives of the institution are being met. The data presented to the board should answer these questions:

- What percentage of a faculty cohort (people appointed in the same year) reached the point of having a tenure decision?
- What percentage resigned and why? (Absolute numbers may be more informative for smaller colleges.)
- Of those considered for promotion or tenure, what percentage were successful?
- How many promotion or tenure decisions led to a grievance on substance? on procedure?
- Are there any marked differences in success rates among various academic units?
- What is the tenure ratio and how is it calculated?
- What percentage of the instructional payroll is committed to tenured faculty?
- What is the projected tenure level five and ten years from now?
- Are there any marked differences in the success rates of women and minorities compared with other faculty?

Although not immediately germane to the promotion and tenure process, trustees concerned with the capacity of the institution to recruit and retain a talented and diverse faculty might also ask:

- How many appointments offered by the college were declined, and why?
- How many faculty whom the college would have preferred to retain resigned, and why?
- Were women and minorities disproportionately represented among these categories?

- What steps can the college take to reduce the number of rejected offers and unwanted resignations?

Questions about promotion and tenure success rates and the inability to attract or retain faculty should be a critical concern of trustees as regards the faculty generally and women and minorities more particularly. Despite some twenty years of formal affirmative action programs on almost every campus, the statistics reveal little progress. African Americans constitute little more than 1 percent of all full-time faculty at public colleges and universities, exclusive of historically black colleges, a proportion virtually unchanged over the past decade. The percentage of African American faculty (4.1 percent) nationwide has actually dropped somewhat since 1977. Hispanics compose about 1.6 percent of the full-time professoriate. Although the proportion of women has increased very slightly over the past thirty years to about 27 percent, women represent only 11 percent of full professors and 23 percent of associate professors. Furthermore, not only do women at all ranks earn less than men, but the overall salary gap has actually widened (National Center for Education Statistics, 1990, Association of Governing Boards of Universities and Colleges, 1990).

Policy recommendations to advance affirmative action are not in short supply (Washington and Harvey, 1989; Blackwell, 1988; Brown, 1988) and have not changed dramatically over the past fifteen years (Carnegie Council on Policy Studies in Higher Education, 1975). Boards of trustees should be especially mindful that successful affirmative action programs require a very visible commitment by the leadership of the college, which surely includes the board. Evidence of that commitment includes heartfelt rhetoric as well as concrete actions, such as the recruitment and advancement of a multicultural faculty (Hyer, 1985; Washington and Harvey, 1989). Boards and administrations committed to affirmative action should vigilantly audit the effects and results of promotion and tenure policies on efforts to diversify the faculty.

Personnel policies extend well beyond promotion, tenure, and affirmative action. There are, for example, the questions of salaries, work loads, benefits, and professional development. Not all of these issues can be addressed in a single chapter, perhaps not even in a single volume. Yet, policy formulations on all of these issues can be approached in a similar manner. Above all else, there should be a clear understanding on the board's part of the purposes to be served and the goals to be attained by a particular policy or practice. Against that backdrop, the administration should draft policies in concert with the faculty and then seek the counsel and reactions of the board. Once adopted, the effectiveness of a policy—the degree to which it attains the stated objectives—should be monitored by the administration and reported periodically to the board, with changes recommended as necessary.

Sound personnel policies and procedures are neither a panacea nor a substitute for talented faculty and adequate resources. However, poor policies or ineffective policy execution can reduce motivation, provoke dissatisfaction, and waste human as well as fiscal resources. By contrast, well-reasoned and well-administered policies can help to create an overall environment that is conducive to bringing out the best in people—and is that not another way of stating the principal goal of education?

CHAPTER 15

Defining, Assessing,
and Nurturing Quality

E. Grady Bogue

Conventional assumptions about collegiate quality often appear in the conversations of academic leaders, board members, and civic leaders. Consider, for example, the following:

Only high-cost colleges have quality.
Only large and comprehensive colleges have quality.
Only highly selective colleges have quality.
Only nationally recognized colleges have quality.
Only a few colleges can have quality.
Only colleges with impressive resources have quality.

This cluster of assumptions evokes a pyramidal image of quality: older and larger research universities cluster at the apex; former teachers' colleges (now universities) reside in the middle; community colleges dominate the base; and liberal arts colleges are sprinkled throughout, depending on their perceived attributes. Is this pyramidal structure a narrowly conceived model of collegiate quality that fosters an unnecessary and unhelpful arrogance? As the Association of Governing Boards of Universities and Colleges notes, it is a model "driven by the prestige of research" and designed "to stoke academic egos instead of students' dreams" (1992, p. 22). Let us consider a contrasting image.

Peter Senge (1990) offers this conviction: "I do not believe great organizations have ever been built by trying to emulate another, any more than individual greatness is achieved by trying to copy another 'great person'" (p. 11). Under this assumption, quality results not from imitating another institution or individual, but in reaching for and discovering one's own promise and distinction, whether personal or organizational. Our assumptions, our "mental maps," may be both confining and facilitating as we attempt to impart meaning to the world about us. The purpose of this chapter is to open our curiosity about the nature and nurture of college quality.

Questions of Quality

What do we hope to achieve and how good a job are we doing? These questions of purpose and performance are fundamental leadership questions for any organized enterprise, corporate or collegiate. These questions of quality are surely critical to board members and others who hold institutions in trust. In this chapter, I hope to expand the reader's understanding of how collegiate organizations define, assess, and nurture quality. A second purpose is to identify a cluster of "governing ideas" that will enable the board member to evaluate both the intent and the impact of campus quality assurance programs and policies.

To recite here the evidence of our national concern with quality in both the business and the government sectors is unnecessary. This concern is equally active in American colleges and universities, as evident in a review of newspapers, magazines, contemporary books, and electronic news media coverage. The board member interested in specific citations of such evidence should refer to Resource F. The current national debate on quality has opened for public and collegiate inspection a range of questions and issues:

- Is quality in limited supply? Can only a few institutions have quality?
- Is quality to be expressed in a single performance indicator or is more data needed to illuminate organizational performance?

- How can the definition and assessment of collegiate quality recognize the diversity of institutional missions and simultaneously respect meaningful performance standards?
- To what extent should information on quality be subject to public disclosure?
- Are quality and funding always linked in positive and direct correlation? What variables, other than money, directly affect the quality of programs and services?
- What is to be the primary purpose for the assessment of quality—improvement or accountability?

With the last question in mind, the question of purpose, let us begin with a story that highlights the issue of accountability and reveals the most fundamental purpose of our quest for quality.

The First Accountability

Years ago, I agonized over the performance of a graduate student, an incident I described in *The Evidence for Quality* (Bogue and Saunders, 1992, pp. 5–6) as follows: "A thirty-year-old woman enrolled in a graduate course has submitted a major paper. This paper is not just grammatically incorrect; it is incoherent! Her performance in the course has been marginal on every dimension, culminating in this disappointing and heartbreaking final paper. Any reasonable standard of acceptable performance would not encourage a passing grade for this paper, much less for the course. It might be argued that each person contributing to the meaning of this student's bachelor's degree has committed an act of malpractice, cheating this woman of her potential and dignity."

How could this happen? This woman was a graduate of an institution that is regionally accredited and of a program that is professionally accredited. Think of how easy it would have been to discover whether this student could write a grammatically correct sentence, a coherent paragraph, or a sensible essay. Think of the prescriptive and corrective action that could and should have been taken early in her collegiate career. I went on to write, "This example illustrates a mind left wasted, a mind left dispirited and disengaged. To know that this student has been exposed to a lower quality climate requires no great philosophical agony in defining quality nor any technological feat in measuring it" (pp. 5-6).

Is not our first accountability to our students? Board members can and should ascertain whether any campus within the circle of their care is meeting this first accountability. Conversations built on hazy and narrow notions of quality should yield to more thoughtful and substantive exchanges. Having in hand a consensus definition of quality is an essential first step.

A Definition of Quality

Few themes have occupied the attention of such a diverse array of minds over such a long period of time as the theme of quality. Poets and philosophers, executives and employees, scholars and statesmen, those who teach and those who are taught will see that the quest for quality is an unfinished journey.

Although defining quality is a first-order challenge for higher education, we should not believe that it is a challenge unique to colleges and universities. Philip Crosby, a widely recognized writer on the corporate sector, defines quality simply as "conformance to requirements" (1984, p. 60). *I Know It When I See It: A Modern Fable About Quality,* a book published by the American Management Association, touts customer satisfaction as the principal indicator of quality: "Customers aren't interested in our specs. They're interested in the answer to one simple question: Did the product do what I expected it to do?" (Guaspari, 1985, p. 68). In *Managing Quality,* David Garvin (1988) describes the multiple dimensions of quality as follows:

- *Performance*—The "fitness for use" test: Does the product do what the consumer wants?
- *Features*—The "bells and whistles" that supplement the basic functions and add competitive edge.
- *Reliability*—How long until the first failure or until service is needed?
- *Conformance*—The extent to which the product meets established specifications and manufacturer standards.

- *Durability*—The length of product life.
- *Serviceability*—Speed, cost, and ease of repair.
- *Esthetics*—A highly subjective but measurable aspect of product appeal.
- *Perceived quality*—Is a Honda built in America perceived as a Japanese car? Of higher quality than a car built by an American company?

The service spirit of those who put heart and meaning into our organizations, whether corporate or collegiate, and the importance of the quality "reality" they create is nicely presented by Scandinavian Airlines System (SAS) President Jan Carlzon (1987, p. 2): "But if you ask our customers about SAS, they won't tell you about our planes or our offices or the way we finance our capital investment. Instead, they talk about their experiences with the people of SAS." Think about the thousand collegiate "moments of truth" created in any week through the interaction of students with faculty and staff. Here is an important governing idea of collegiate quality: our people, our faculty and staff, give operational meaning to the word quality.

W. Edwards Deming, the man who gave impetus to the rapid enhancement of quality in Japanese industry and perhaps the most renowned and oft-quoted American authority on the issue of quality, furnishes still another definitional priority. The first item in Deming's list of fourteen points for management is to "create constancy of purpose for improvement of product and service" (1986, p. 24). The essence of quality, from Deming's perspective, is the commitment to constant improvement—a second governing idea and theme to which we will return.

Are academic definitions of quality different from those cited for the corporate sector? There are similarities and serious points of departure. Among the leading researchers and writers in American higher education is Alexander Astin, who gives this definition of quality: "The most excellent institutions are . . . those that have the greatest impact—add the most value, as economists would say—on the student's knowledge and personal development and on the faculty member's scholarly and pedagogical ability and productivity"

(1985, p. 61). This definition moves away from an emphasis on size and selectivity and accents results rather than reputation.

Another statesman of American higher education is Lewis Mayhew. He and his coauthors offer a slightly different definition in *Quest for Quality*: "Quality undergraduate education consists of preparing learners through the use of words, numbers, and abstract concepts to understand, cope with, and positively influence the environment in which they find themselves" (Mayhew, Ford, and Hubbard, 1990, p. 29). This definition, while useful, fails to acknowledge the idea that education at every level in our society is a moral enterprise, and whether it acknowledges the role of passion, appropriately celebrated in such books as Peters and Austin's 1985 book, *A Passion for Excellence*, is another question. The role of passion in the nurture of quality is a matter to which we will return.

In *The Evidence for Quality* (1992), Saunders and I ventured this definition: "Quality is conformance to mission specification and goal achievement—within publicly accepted standards of accountability and integrity" (p. 20). What we hoped to achieve in this definition was to recognize, respect, and reinforce the concept that there are varieties of excellence in American higher education, from Stanford University in the West to Samford University in the South, from the University of Michigan in the North to the University of Montevallo in the South, from Centenary College to Central Piedmont Community College, from the Air Force Academy to Antioch University. Anyone who takes in the grand sweep of American higher education will immediately and intuitively sense the folly of the pyramidal image described earlier, an image that so often fashions our notions of quality. Respect for the diverse varieties of excellence is another governing idea essential to an effective quality assurance program.

A second of our aspirations was to ensure that our definition of quality embraced an ethical test. Contemporary news coverage, several book-length reports and critiques on higher education, and conference themes on public trust in higher education highlight current concerns with performance integrity issues in higher education. We have seen a pattern of unfortunate administrative and faculty behavior that is leading to what some commentators describe as a "loss of sanctuary" for higher education. Though any one of these ethical abuses may be seen as an exception to a more general reality of integrity, we do not believe that quality associates well with duplicity: we cannot claim to be nurturing quality while stealing from our institutions, our governments, and our clients.

A definition of collegiate quality, then, requires assumptions. These assumptions shape the reality in which we seek to nurture quality. For example, the belief that quality is in limited supply contradicts the idea that quality is attainable and essential to each and every campus for which a board member is responsible. This belief argues against the idea that quality will always be related to mission and that the mission of any campus, no matter how comprehensive, will always be limited. A campus or system of campuses that has units and programs with differing missions is understandable. A campus or system of campuses with "second class" units and programs is more difficult to defend.

A preference for closure and a discomfort with ambiguity might urge the selection of a "best" definition of quality from among those presented here. There are, however, informing and helpful elements in each of these definitions. Astin's definition, for example, suggests that a college making no developmental contribution, no value-added contribution, to its students would hardly be considered a quality institution. Mayhew, Ford, and Hubbard's definition affirms that a college not equipping its graduates to cope with and positively influence the environment would hardly be considered a quality institution. Saunders and I urge that collegiate quality must be related to mission and goals, to the educational and ethical performance of the institution. The complex nature of quality requires a multifaceted approach to the assessment of quality, a matter to which we now turn.

Assessment of Quality

Can we trust the assertion, cited earlier that customer satisfaction is the primary indicator of quality (Guaspari, 1985)? Perhaps under some conditions. But we can do better than that. We can assemble concrete and specific evidence on quality. We can, and should, know as much about our students on exit as we do on entry—about changes in their knowledge, skill, and attitudes.

There are several questions that can inform and focus discussions on assessing quality.

1. How can we improve decision making? In the corporate world, we make design, production, and marketing decisions. In the collegiate world, we make decisions to implement, revise, and terminate programs, and to admit, place, advance, suspend, and graduate students. Such decisions should be informed by assessment. A simple decision model suggests that most quality decisions in collegiate work turn on the need to offer accountability support for programs and services, and to support action that leads to program or service improvement.

2. What indicators will we accept as evidence of quality? Earlier we noted David Garvin's citation (1988) of such factors as "fitness for use, reliability, conformance to specification, [and] durability" for use in assessing the quality of industrial products. American higher education has fashioned a wide array of evidence for quality that includes

- *Accreditation:* the test of mission and goal achievement
- *Rankings and ratings:* the test of reputation
- *Outcomes:* the test of value added
- *Licensure:* the test of professional standards
- *Program reviews:* the test of peer review
- *Follow-up studies:* the test of client satisfaction

Each of these evidences has strengths and liabilities. Perhaps the oldest and best-known seal of collegiate quality, accreditation, is built on the premise and promise of mission integrity and performance improvement, but it has been accused of many imperfections—for example, that it is a periodic exercise in professional back scratching. Ranking and rating studies, including the well-known *U.S. News and World Report* and media ratings of "America's best colleges," keep quality conversations alive, but offer little help in efforts to improve quality and are often referred to as "quantified gossip." Student satisfaction is a legitimate and essential evidence of quality; however, student satisfaction may be inversely related to quality in educational settings. A more detailed evaluation of these different types of evidence can be found in *The Evidence for Quality* (Bogue and Saunders, 1992).

Let us close this discussion on evidence with another governing idea. To the importance of relating quality to mission, we add the importance of assembling multiple instances of evidence on quality. The nature of both personal and institutional performance is too complex and diverse to be captured in a single data point. Consider the leadership and educational posture of the accounting department chair who knows that her students have the highest pass rate of any institution in the state on the certified public accountant examination, who has a trend line of high satisfaction from graduates over recent years, whose files are filled with a clear majority of complimentary letters from employers of her graduates, whose stuents regularly perform better on campuswide assessments of communication and critical thinking skills, and whose department was praised by a recent program review panel of accounting faculty from other institutions. This chair has a cluster of evidence, of performance intelligence, useful in making both decisions and improvements. Just as physicians do not have a health meter in their offices but assess our health by examining a cluster of medical evidence, so do we need a cluster of performance evidence to make quality judgments about our students, programs, and institutions.

3. What standard of performance will be acceptable? Identifying performance evidence raises the question of standards; will we employ criterion standards that compare performance to a predetermined criterion level, comparative standards that judge performance against a "normed" population of students or programs, or connoisseurship standards that evaluate performance via the opinions and values of a panel of judges?

As an evidence of collegiate quality, for example, accreditation and program reviews rely heavily on the connoisseurship standard, in which the evidence on quality is evaluated according to the knowledge, values, and experience of the visiting team. Whether a program or an institution gets a pass or fail, an excellent or unsatisfactory rating, depends on the judgment of the team. This situation leads to our final question,

4. Who will make the judgments of quality? In the early years of the *U.S. News and World Report* studies, college presidents

were asked to rank institutions. A decent argument could be made
that the president of Vanguard University may know little about
Coastal College beyond his or her friendship with the president or
limited anecdotal evidence. Of such tangential knowledge can come
reputational rankings circulated over the land. To the credit of *U.S.
News and World Report,* later rankings revealed increased sophistication of criteria and judges. A single rater using a global criterion
was replaced with multiple raters using multiple criteria. Both campus officers and board members need to know whether those making quality judgments of programs and services have sufficient
knowledge and experience to warrant their confidence.

Let us close this exploration on the assessment of quality
with a note on another governing idea. Quality assurance is an
exercise in decision making. The principal reason for an aggressive
quality assurance program on any campus should be to inform the
decisions made about students, policies, and programs—the call of
"first accountability." Unfortunately, too many campuses still require assessment exercises that have no utility or application what-
soever. We recall, for example, a two-year college and a university
that had required their graduates to take a test of general education,
in this case the ACT COMP battery. Neither institution used the
results for program or student performance decisions. It would not
be a difficult task for a board member to discover whether a campus
was using quality information in its policy and program decisions.

However, quality assurance is more than an exercise in decision making; it is also a venture in discovery. The search for truth
certainly involves the theoretical, but it can involve empirical and
accidental elements as well. Does the spark of creativity favor those
folks standing or sitting, or those in motion? Reflection and action
are complements in the search for truth, and quality assurance
should venture into learning and discovery.

Nurturing Quality

What questions can board members use to evaluate quality assurance policies and programs on the campus or campuses for which
they are responsible? Here are themes and questions to help exam-

ine campus commitment to quality assurance—a summary look at the governing ideas we have been advancing.

Distinctive Mission

Does the campus have a distinctive mission statement? Questions of ends encourage questions of beginnings. Inquiries of performance will eventually lead to inquiries of purpose. The campus mission furnishes an essential foundation for an effective quality assurance effort. Does the campus have a crisp statement of mission and values, a statement that clearly and forcefully reveals what the campus stands for? If the mission statement is so vague and undistinctive that it could describe a hundred other campuses, you might have the origins of a quality problem.

Evidence of Improvement

Can the campus offer evidence of improvements that have been made to program and policy as a result of assessment and quality inquiries? The improvement question is one that should be posed to and answered by every organized unit on campus. A campus or program unit that cannot offer a reasonably prompt and substantive answer to the question, "What did you do with what you found out?" deserves skepticism about the strength and substance of its quality assurance efforts.

Links to Teaching and Learning

How have quality activities been used to improve teaching and learning, to enhance student, faculty, and staff growth and development? Are quality assurance and assessment activities perceived by the faculty to be "user friendly, appropriate, and sensible? Board members will not have to search their memories very deeply to remember who the primary architects of quality are. They are the faculty who elevated our vision, lifted us from the poverty of the commonplace, and pushed us to fulfill our potential. Assessment and quality assurance exercises unconnected to improvements in teaching and learning are empty exercises.

Multiple Indicators

An effective quality assurance program will involve the acquisition of evidence on both student and program performance. Does the campus have a variety of quality evidence—conventional tests, program reviews, accreditation, licensure results, client satisfaction and follow-up, and perhaps more innovative intelligence—that facilitates assessment?

External Standards

In the early history of American higher education, one of the principal board member roles was to "examine" the proposed graduates. Thus, to the judgments and standards of the faculty was added the "external standard" of the board. The use of such standards continues to be found in externally referenced assessment exercises and the use of external teams in accreditation and program review. There is a philosophic tension inherent in this governing idea. Some contemporary philosophies of quality—total quality management, for example—justifiably insist that those responsible for the product are responsible for quality. Is trust misplaced if a third party or an external standard is inserted into the quality assurance process? I think not. An essential feature of the academy is the testing of ideas against the larger community of scholars. The results of our work must come into public forum at some time.

Strategic Perspective

Does the campus have a strategic and unifying vision of quality? This vision will be built on the idea that there is no policy, no behavior, no practice that does not influence quality; moreover, there will be a coherent and logical system of interactions among the various institutional approaches to quality assurance. The philosophy and components of the quality assurance system will be characterized by awareness and allegiance that is known and owned by faculty and staff.

A campus whose quality assurance efforts salute these governing ideas will have experienced the renewal power of these ideas.

Such a campus will have rediscovered purpose and priority, promoted the development of its faculty and staff via continued learning, and strengthened community. There can be no quality in an educational enterprise without caring, and there can be no caring without community. With this note on community and quality in mind, let us examine a concept currently in management vogue, that of total quality management (TQM), and ask what potential it offers for collegiate quality assurance.

Total Quality Management

The term *total quality management* (TQM), also referred to as strategic quality management, has emerged from the work of a cluster of writers that includes W. Edwards Deming, W. A. Shewart, Philip Crosby, Joseph Juran, and David Garvin. An informing and integrating work, one offering a favorable treatment of TQM as applied to higher education, is Daniel Seymour's *On Q: Causing Quality in Higher Education* (1992). Seymour is "convinced that accrediting agencies, program reviews, standing committees, control-minded governing boards, and the occasional well-intentioned task force" will not be the instruments for causing quality in higher education (1992, p. x). He offers TQM as an answer to his question, "Is there a better way to manage higher education?"

Seymour identifies these principles as the operational embodiment of strategic quality management:

> Quality is meeting or exceeding customer needs.
> Quality is everyone's job.
> Quality is continuous improvement.
> Quality is leadership.
> Quality is human resource development.
> Quality is in the system.
> Quality is fear reduction.
> Quality is recognition and reward.
> Quality is teamwork.
> Quality is measurement.
> Quality is systematic problem solving.

Most of these principles are not inimical to the governing ideas discussed earlier. Although Seymour's commentary on TQM is friendly to what we have built thus far, his advocacy of TQM warrants thoughtful review. Seymour suggests that current and conventional quality instruments, such as program reviews and accreditation, make little significant contribution to college quality. He sees these instruments as occasional devices that convey the appearance of quality and that establish a "good enough" mindset. Those who have been on both the giving and receiving end of program and accreditation reviews will know the liabilities of these and other "evidence" of quality previously cited in this chapter. Both these instruments are built, however, on the premise and promise of improvement, an idea central to TQM and one of the governing ideas of quality emphasized in this chapter.

Is it necessary to deprecate the contributions of quality assurance instruments already in place in order to appreciate what TQM has to offer? I think not. Space constraints do not permit the scrutiny of all the principles of TQM. Having accented the principle of continual improvement, we elect to examine two additional ideas from TQM. With respect to the driving principle of TQM, that of client satisfaction, few would argue that we listen enough to our students and other clients. There are, however, critical differences between corporate and collegiate settings in the application of this principle. Any faculty member who has found that caring for students is in tension with caring for standards knows the limitation of this quality test for colleges and universities. Students do indeed, as Seymour suggests, vote with their feet. It is sad when they occasionally vote for shoddy and shallow options; when they do, the ideal of quality should not be exchanged for the notion of satisfaction.

A point in passing: Seymour offers a chapter in his book, titled "Choosing to Be Distinctive," which is a clarion call that opens with this painful but accurate note: "The reason so few people have a clear understanding of their institution's vision is because there is really nothing in it worth remembering" (1992, p. 62). As Seymour notes, the more "filler" and generalities one can find in a mission or vision statement, the less likely a campus can translate that vision into a quality reality. Linking quality to mission first involves a thoughtfully constructed mission statement, as we affirmed in one of the governing ideas.

Now a word on problem solving. Many campuses are trying TQM. For most, it has offered an exciting and renewing agenda. While some faculty and administrative officers see TQM as appropriate for improvements in the admissions office, the business office, the facilities maintenance office, the campus security office, or other administrative settings, others note, as does Seymour, that these are not the only settings where "we degrade, we hassle, and we ignore" (1992, p. 115). Will we be as quick to see opportunities for listening to our clients, for continuous improvement, for problem solving in the academic heart of colleges and universities— where students can be harmed by low and empty expectations, by assessment exercises that have little or no decision utility, or by a vision of quality that depends more on faculty publication counts than teaching and caring for our students? This is a question that board members can legitimately explore.

Whether the initial euphoria and subsequent quiet passage of some previously heralded management concepts will, in retrospect, also describe the fate of TQM in colleges and universities remains a test of time. An argument can be made that many of the philosophical principles cited for TQM have been at work in academia for some time. The quest for quality will always remain an unfinished journey, and there is no reason to neglect any conceptual tool that will aid us in that quest. As with any tool, the effectiveness of its application turns on the artistry of its user in ensuring that it fits the time, task, and place.

Heart First: A Vision of Quality

Boards can ascertain whether the campuses under their care can offer a range of evidence of quality; whether these campuses can furnish evidence on policy, program, and personnel improvements that have been made as a result of quality inquiry; and whether educational and management decisions are being informed by quality information. These are conceptual or "head first" concerns, and they are among the most important governing ideas of quality cited in this chapter.

But the principal guarantor of quality is not "head first" concerns but "heart first" actions of caring and daring. Academic leaders and trustees should care enough for truth, service, and human growth and dignity to ensure that their vision of quality pervades the campus. This vision should call students and colleagues from the poverty of the commonplace, through higher standards, consistent encouragement, active compassion, respect for diversity, and renewed dedication to the highest ethical standards. Such a promise can be realized if we conceive of academic quality as synonymous with the campus as a community of caring (Bogue and Saunders, 1992).

In *Sand and Foam*, Kahlil Gibran wrote, "Your heart and my mind will never agree until your mind ceases to live in numbers and my heart in the mist" (1973, p. 30). Not all that is real, not all that is meaningful, not all that is beautiful in colleges and universities, or any other learning organization, will yield to numbers. There are, however, governing ideas that encourage colleges and universities to engage performance questions more effectively—questions as legitimate and essential to collegiate organizations as to others. No, more legitimate and essential! Are a mind and heart cheated of promise and potential not a more painful mistake than a faulty computer or car?

In commending these governing ideas of quality to the attention of trustees, we seek not so much consensus or closure as to promote a more open curiosity about the nature and nurture of quality, to encourage a vision of collegiate quality assurance as a venture of both decision and discovery, and to promote an action agenda of caring and daring.

PART THREE

Developing the Board

Governing boards are only as effective as their individual members: how trustees conduct themselves in meetings, how they educate themselves and are educated by their leaders, how well they are led, and how well they are served by their chief executives and staffs. None of these matters should be left to chance or to ad hoc attention.

The five chapters in Part Three are devoted to the process of developing effective trustees and ensuring that good boards are on the path to becoming better boards. Offering suggestions on subjects ranging from new board member selection, orientation, and in-service education strategies to the responsibility of boards to study their performance periodically, these chapters provide practical guidelines for trustee and staff leaders.

Two individuals bear most of the responsibility for developing the board: the board chair and president. Their relationship is addressed, along with the principles that contribute to good board structures and to effective board and committee meetings.

In sum, Part Three suggests a variety of options available to governing boards and their leaders to strengthen their abilities to meet the high expectations held for them by so many. Effective trustees and governing boards are the result of good planning, teamwork, and focused attention on their education and development.

CHAPTER 16

Selecting, Orienting, and Developing Trustees

Robert L. Gale

There are two vital ingredients in building a strong board of trustees: selecting good people and educating them early and well. No amount of orientation or information can make an outstanding board out of a poorly chosen group. Conversely, outstanding trustees may be wasted if they are not properly motivated. This chapter offers suggestions on how to identify, properly enlist, and effectively deploy board members, emphasizing sound trustee orientation and the development of trustee leadership.

Selecting Trustees

The mission, direction, and needs of the institution should strongly influence selection of trustees. These are concerns that the president and board should examine together. Once they agree on the fundamentals of their joint enterprise, the board and president can move to the nominating committee stage and begin considering board composition. In so doing, they should proceed in four steps: decide what specific skills are needed on the board, establish a search-and-recruit procedure, develop an orientation process, and create a procedure for terminating service.

In theory, the self-perpetuating boards of the some 1,600 independent colleges and universities in the United States are able to control their own appointment procedures. In practice, however, something else happens. Many boards thoughtfully consider the mix of skills and backgrounds needed among trustees; many other boards do not. Some boards have an effective and conscientious nominating committee; many others do not. Some boards give total responsibility for trustee selection to the president; many others give the chief executive no responsibility at all. It is also noteworthy that although private institutions tend to have the largest boards, their membership is least diverse as measured by various demographic characteristics.

As one of the most vital of the standing committees, the nominating committee (more appropriately called the committee on trustees, given its broad responsibilities) should have a clear statement of purpose in the bylaws or other policy document. Its first task is to evaluate the composition of the board in terms of skills, background, residence, age, sex, ethnicity, and other factors. The qualities needed in new board members will become apparent. Nominees should be welcomed from all the key constituencies of the institution, and the committee should actively solicit candidates from other board members. Nominating committee members should face up to the fact, however, that in practice most candidates will inevitably be identified by the committee itself. The committee should check the credentials of candidates, cultivate good prospects, and, for those selected to join the board, issue the invitation in an appropriate fashion.

In recent years, the nominating committee also commonly takes responsibility for orienting of new members, recommending board officers, reviewing the performance of trustees eligible for reelection, and recommending committee assignments.

It is vital that the chair of the nominating committee be one of the most respected, dedicated, and thoughtful board members. No other standing committee is as important to the long-range development and viability of the board. Very often, the chair's competence will be the decisive factor that affects the future composition of the board. The size of the committee should be small, with membership made up of those who have demonstrated distinctive service to their institution and who have access to good prospects.

Even a good nominating committee with well-defined duties

will not operate satisfactorily unless a set of clearly written policies is adopted. These should include the minimum number of meetings to be held each year, the process by which the names of prospective nominees are solicited, the method of checking qualifications, the way in which recommendations are brought to the full board, and the process by which newly elected board members are oriented. Recommendations for board office and committee assignments are usually determined in consultation with the chair and president and forwarded along with the names of new nominees to the board.

The committee should meet each time the full board meets, even when vacancies do not exist, to expand and keep current the pool of potential nominees. If an unexpected vacancy occurs or if an unusually capable person is identified for possible nomination, the committee should be prepared to call a special meeting. The solicitation of nominees from the various constituencies of the institution should also be formalized. This process will vary from institution to institution, but at least once a year key groups should be encouraged to make suggestions. Because the committee must be prepared to find most of the prospective candidates itself, however, careful planning is necessary to ensure an adequate list of top-notch prospects.

Among independent institutions, approximately three thousand board seats are estimated to be unfilled at any given moment. This large number of vacancies may result in part from confusion about the most effective procedures to identify candidates, but it is good practice to have one or two vacancies in case exciting prospects should suddenly appear. Methods of checking on the qualifications of potential board members should parallel those used by corporate management in considering prospective high-level employees. Special care should be taken to ascertain how candidates have performed on other volunteer boards.

Recommendations for election to the board should never be presented at a board meeting without prior notification to all trustees. Candidates' names and biographical information should be supplied in advance of the board meeting, when the meeting's agenda and supporting materials are mailed. If nominating committees are charged with the additional duty of orienting new trustees (with staff support), a formal procedure should be in place.

Board Composition

Board composition should be viewed in two separate dimensions: first, what we usually call balance or diversity—that is, personal characteristics such as age, sex, ethnicity, residence, and alumni status; and second, the individual talents or professional backgrounds that a board needs for good balance.

An important question the board should consider is, are we a local, regional, or national institution? The answer to this question will help a board determine how widely to recruit. For a small college that gets the lion's share of its students and financial support from a limited area, trying to achieve a wide geographic representation on its board makes little sense. However, a regional or national college or university should recruit more broadly.

There is universal agreement on the need to expand efforts to recruit women and minorities. A 1991 survey by the Association of Governing Boards of Universities and Colleges (see Resource B) showed some gain for women (to 23 percent), but minorities remained at 9 percent in independent institutions.

The first thing most boards and administrators want and need among their trustees is the ability to give and to get money. Close behind is the ability to deal effectively with the money raised, whether from tuition, endowment income, gifts, or government grants. These two talents are not always found in the same person, however. Another characteristic that a board should find among some of its members is a broad knowledge of and interest in higher education. The obvious source for this type of trustee is the faculty or administration of another institution.

Some board members fear that placing a president of another institution on their board will cause difficulties for their own president, but this is unlikely. On the contrary, a president as board member can be very helpful to the institution's president, because he or she will often raise issues that should be discussed but that the institution's president may hesitate to raise. For past presidents of institutions to be made trustees is not usually desirable, however, because they are unlikely to bring to their new role sufficient objectivity. This also argues against selection of a president from an institution that competes for the same students or gift dollars.

Some board members should be knowledgeable in marketing—a word we hardly dared apply to education just a few years ago. Today's institutions must be able to determine their markets and use sound marketing principles to attract potential students and donors. Once the market is determined, the college or university must be able to reach it effectively. In admissions marketing—finding the right students for a given institution—an ethnically diverse board can be of considerable help in recruiting a varied student body. If an institution has a natural Hispanic constituency, for example, Hispanic board members can help to relate the capabilities of the institution to the needs of the constituency.

With pressing public policy issues affecting higher education in local, state, and the federal government, it is helpful to have a few trustees who know their way around the state capital and Washington, D.C. The escalation in the number of lawsuits brought against institutions and their governing boards in recent years also makes legal expertise a desirable board skill. Trustees who are attorneys should not, however, serve as institutional counsel, with or without remuneration—to avoid even the appearance of a conflict of interest and to ensure that free service does not mean poor service to the institution. Finally, recruiting members who have expertise in real estate and physical plant management is an excellent idea. The plant is generally the institution's biggest financial asset, and a good board should have the competence to protect it.

Faculty and Student Trustees

The pressure to include faculty and students on boards has diminished, but some institutions are still considering such a policy despite what most students of governance consider an unresolvable conflict of interest. A faculty member from another institution, however, can provide a useful perspective without creating such a conflict. Recently graduated alumni can also bring important points of view to bear on board deliberations. In any event, faculty and student leaders from the institution can be more helpful and effective on certain board committees, where most of the work of the board is centered, than as trustees, especially when *all* trustees are expected to serve the institution as a whole.

With respect to board composition, the Carnegie Commission on Higher Education suggests, "Board membership should reflect the different age, sex, and racial groups that are involved in the concerns of the institutions. Faculty members from other institutions and young alumni should be considered for board memberships" (1973, p. 35).

Identifying Prospects

To evaluate a board's composition, it is worthwhile to create a profile of the board's current membership and make a list of current board members' characteristics, such as age, sex, ethnicity, occupation, location, alumni status, and length of service. This will show where the board is strong, where it is adequate, and where it is weak.

If the board profile shows that existing needs are fairly well covered, the board should consider whether there is a new category that should be added. For example, is there reason to think that money could be raised with help in New York, Chicago, or Dallas? Would having someone from one of these areas on the board be helpful? Could the board use a person who is knowledgeable about athletic programs, medical programs, or risk management?

Does the board depend too heavily on alumni? Because they have a built-in interest, alumni and parents tend to be overrepresented. Church-related institutions naturally consider church leaders as possible trustees, but every such board needs to recruit outside its own religious community and even its own faith. The local community also presents fertile ground for possible nominees because local people are likely to know about the institution and its value to the community. However, boards must be wary of choosing members who would simply like to add the distinction of trusteeship to their vitae. Instead, boards must try to determine how an individual stands in the community and in his or her business or professional field. Is this person a leader or potential leader?

Generally speaking, it is not advisable to try to recruit someone who has already reached the top of the career ladder unless he or she is a graduate of the institution. Even if such a person accepts the invitation, he or she is likely to be too busy to contribute to the responsibilities of the board. It is better to look for persons who are

on their way up and willing to work. A valuable talent for nominating committee members is the knack for identifying "comers"—
those who are moving up rapidly. Such persons, committed to the
institution before they reach the top, become investments in the
future.

The overcommitted person often proves to be a particular
disappointment; yet often it is the busy person who will take the
additional time to serve well. Again and again the complaint is
heard, "So-and-so was on four boards, so we were sure he would be
good. But when he got on our board, he didn't do anything." My
response is, If you had called the executives of those other four
boards, you would have found that the reason he could join your
board was that he wasn't doing anything on theirs. The time to find
that out is before an invitation is offered. Check volunteer references
as carefully as if a chief executive were being selected.

Because the need to raise money is so central to most private
institutions today, the following caution was expressed to me by
Edward G. Wilson, longtime member of the Earlham College
board: "Trustees must have deep emotional commitment to the
institution to guarantee fund-raising success. Thought must be
given to financial power in selecting trustees, but take a man or
woman who knows what a commitment is rather than a rich person
without commitment" (personal conversation, March 1985).

Cultivating and Enlisting Prospects

Once prospective board members have been identified, how do you
approach them? The first thing to do is determine whether the
prospect is well-enough acquainted with your institution to become
a trustee immediately or whether additional time and cultivation
are necessary. If the latter is the case, a good approach is to assign
an active board member, if possible an acquaintance of the prospect,
to familiarize the person with the school. Even board members who
are not at home in fund raising or other areas are nearly always
happy to do this kind of job. Cultivation can involve many things,
including taking prospects to lunch with the president, inviting
them to campus events, and giving them a tour of the campus.

When it comes time for the formal invitation, do not make

the mistake of being too casual. Depending on the telephone or a letter may risk the loss of a good prospect. Make a personal call and use the best team that can be put together—perhaps the president and either the board chair or the nominating committee chair, or the president together with a board member who is a friend or business associate of the prospective trustee. Only in a somewhat formalized setting can it be made clear that something more is wanted from the person than the use of his or her name on the letterhead. If a false impression is given, subsequent assignments for committee work or requests for giving or fund raising may cause the new recruit to feel misled and to think, "That isn't what I was told when I was invited to join the board." A simple and effective way to minimize misunderstanding is to give prospective board members a written statement of what is expected of the board and its trustees. Every board should develop its own document. Resource A offers helpful guidance.

Orienting New Trustees

Once a new board member has been enlisted, a well-conducted orientation is essential. When new board members have been made aware that there are defined responsibilities attached to their trusteeship, they must then be shown how to discharge these responsibilities. Too often a good person spends two or three years on a board without ever really coming to grips with what is going on. Such a waste of time and talent is inexcusable. Because new trustees are alike only in their newness, however, orientation programs should be personalized as much as possible to take advantage of the member's unique interests, whether vocational or avocational.

Orientation should normally be the province of the nominating or membership committee. The committee need not conduct the orientation but should oversee it. An officer of the college may be the best person to coordinate the job, with the aid of appropriate materials and one or more trustees, including the president and the board chair. Avoid overloading new trustees with literature that looks like the *Encyclopaedia Britannica*.

The new trustee should learn the campus as soon as possible. An orientation session in conjunction with the first board meeting is a practical possibility. At minimum, the president, the board chair, and the chair of the nominating or orientation committee can conduct a tour of the campus that includes meetings with student and faculty leaders. A few institutions have a trustee-in-residence program open to all trustees, new and old, but with emphasis on the new trustee, who is required to stay overnight on campus sometime in the first six months of his or her tenure. This orientation should include spending a night in a student residence and meeting with students, faculty, and key administrators. One technique that some boards use for orientation is the "buddy system," whereby each new member of the board is assigned to a trustee who knows the ropes, can answer questions, introduce other members, go over the agenda of the upcoming meeting, serve as campus guide, and generally help break the ice and encourage participation.

Capitalizing on the Talents of New Trustees

New trustees, excited about being on the board of a college, may experience a sense of anticlimax if they find themselves with nothing to do. A good solution is to assign new members immediately to active committees. An ideal assignment might be an ad hoc committee that has just been organized to tackle a problem on a six-month or one-year basis.

If such a committee is not currently at work, take a good look at the new recruit before assigning that person to one of the standing committees. The obvious choice may be the wrong choice. For example, bankers almost invariably get assigned to the finance committee. They may belong there eventually, but it is often better to start them out on the academic affairs or student affairs committee where they will get a sense of the institution and exposure to some new issues. Once the committee assignment has been made, the committee chair and the staff member assigned to the committee should be alerted to ensure that the new recruit is quickly involved. Generally, some task needs to be done. The staff member should give the new trustee a briefing on the past and current activities of the committee so that he or she feels confident to join discussions quickly.

Because private college boards tend to meet only three or four times a year, keeping in touch with new trustees between meetings is especially important. One good idea is to have the president or chair, or both, talk with each new trustee on the phone or over lunch. Time should be found to tell the new members about current activities and plans and to listen to their questions about the institution or their role as a trustee. This is also a good time to do a little sounding out. A new trustee should not be pigeonholed on the basis of insufficient information; additional areas of interest may emerge with better acquaintance. New trustees should also be given a chance to volunteer for something. Because board members and the chief executive have limited time, capable staff should be enlisted to help involve new trustees. Once new trustees have become partly acclimated, it may be helpful if they complete the trustee audit found in Resource C in this volume.

Special Problems and Opportunities

Finally, let us turn briefly to some special areas in building and maintaining a strong and effective board.

Church-Related Colleges

Church-related institutions continue to involve nonclergy in their work. One way to do this is through an institutional advisory committee. The president and one or more trustees should work closely with such a committee, so that the members feel that what they are doing will have some impact on policy, even though they have no legal authority. Such an advisory committee can make a real contribution if given a clear purpose, good membership, staff support, and a sense of genuine importance.

When they serve on a governing board with large numbers of the religious community, lay members may need some encouragement before they will voice their views. If the president and board chair help the lay trustees to feel that the institution is theirs too, the trustees will join more fully in discussions and become more active. When a fixed percentage of religious community trustees is required by policy, it is usually possible to increase the overall size of the board so that enough lay members can be recruited to perform essential tasks, including fund raising and public relations. However, they need to be meaningfully involved in other areas of board responsibility as well.

Dealing with Weak Trustees

One of the most difficult problems for many boards is how to weed out people who have lost their effectiveness or who perhaps never should have been asked to serve in the first place. The best solution is to have a chair who is strong enough to ask such a person to step down. This difficult but necessary conversation on the eve of a renewal of term may begin this way: "We know your business has required much of your time and attention for the past couple of years, John, but I've been asked by the nominating committee [or committee on trustees] to ask you if you see the possibility of your giving the college and board more of your time." Sometimes the result is that an inactive trustee is galvanized into useful activity; sometimes a resignation results. Either way, the institution and board win.

Age and term limitations are sometimes easier solutions, though they involve the risk of losing good members. A mandatory retirement age of, say, seventy-five, coupled with a limit of three consecutive three-year terms, can be provided in the bylaws. A trustee emeritus category in the bylaws may help. When particularly effective members come to the end of their final term, they can be quietly told (in advance) that they will be reelected to the board after a year's absence. Even this creates some risk of losing a good person, however, because the chair or nominating committee of another board may "pirate" a trustee on sabbatical. All of these practices are judgment calls by the board.

Rewarding Outstanding Trustees

Although trustees do not expect recognition for unusual effort on behalf of their institutions, certain courtesies are often overlooked. At a minimum, a board could be recognized through an attractive brochure that provides a picture and biographical sketch of each trustee, including terms of office and committee assignments. Updated annually, it can also be an effective aid to public relations or development activities.

An occasional award, plaque, gavel, or testimonial dinner can be provided, always from the perspective of recognizing the contribution of the board itself first and of a particular trustee second. The danger lies in overlooking someone who should not be overlooked; thus the need for a sense of proportion and propriety. Unusual investments of time should be recognized as much as monetary contributions or willingness and ability to solicit funds.

Recognition in the form of a board resolution may also be appropriate, if it is used sparingly. Outstanding trustees can also be saluted in a dignified way through announcements at institutional functions. An annual award from the board of trustees might be established for the person or persons—an administrator, faculty member, student, and occasionally a trustee—who (for example) demonstrate unusual initiative and leadership. The nominating committee can consider other ideas that are tasteful and timely.

In-Service Education and Development

New trustees, as well as those with many years of service, need to learn to work together for a board to function as a group and not as a collection of individuals. The best way to develop a good working relationship is through periodic workshops and retreats. All boards need the opportunity to step away from the usual board business to assess their performance as individuals and as a whole. Workshops and retreats also offer an opportunity to look in-depth at the future of the institution, which is hard to accomplish during the press of business at regular board meetings. Regular board business should rarely be part of such a workshop or a retreat; if it is, keep it to a minimum.

Developing Goals and Objectives for a Retreat

If a board, which is made up of individuals who have other full-time responsibilities, is going to take the time necessary for a retreat or workshop, the objectives should be clear, goals should be set, and a plan should be in place to accomplish these objectives. What might some of these goals be? Here are a few:

1. *Improving the organization of the board.* Is the committee structure functioning well? Are there too few committees, or too many? Are the committees too large or too small? Do they function effectively and reduce the amount of in-depth discussion at the regular board meetings? Is staffing what it should be for each committee? Most boards of independent colleges and universities function most effectively through committees (see Chapter Seventeen). Another area of concern might be the selection of board officers, the length of their terms, and the effectiveness of their performance. Usually such questions are or should be within the nominating committee's portfolio. A strong and effective nominating committee is a must to secure appropriate new board members and assure strong board leadership.

2. *The effectiveness of the board in fund raising.* Most board work does not require the kind of direct and sustained involvement of trustees that fund raising does. Fund raising is also a role that trustees tend to avoid unless they are motivated, provided with good leadership on the board and staff, and given clear expectations. Often an open and in-depth discussion at a retreat can make a great difference in the participation of the board. Invited outside facilitators or fund-raising consultants can be very helpful (see Chapter Eleven).

3. *Strategic planning.* Too few boards spend enough quality time looking at the future of the institution. This is clearly one of the major roles that a board should play, and time must be made for such discussion. A well-designed board retreat along this line can help focus the thoughts of the administration and the board to ensure that the trustees have a genuine sense of ownership for the new plan and its priorities (see Chapter Five).

4. *Improving board/president relations.* Before agreeing to serve on the board of a college or university, candidates should feel comfortable with the general direction in which the institution is heading and with the president's leadership. Nevertheless, especially in times of stress, communication sometimes breaks down and minor differences occur. It is when such problems are nonexistent or minor that such concerns should be discussed in the re-

laxed atmosphere of a retreat. Again, sometimes a trusted third-party facilitator, through his or her objectivity and professionalism, can help everyone concerned (see Chapter Eight).

5. *Board self-assessment.* At least every five years, the board should assess its own performance and take a serious and thorough look at how it is functioning as a board. Sometimes an apparent problem in the presidency is really a problem with the board. An outside consultant can help a board to assess its strengths and needs and help it significantly increase its effectiveness. This is also a time to look at the membership composition and organization of the board (see Chapters Seventeen and Twenty).

Mechanics of a Retreat

It is important to remember that a retreat takes the valuable time of many busy individuals; every effort should be made to see that the event is held at a time convenient for most members, that an appropriate place is chosen, and that arrangements for the meeting are as perfect as possible.

Obviously, a two- or three-day retreat demands a great deal of advance planning if it is to take place when especially the key members of the board are able to attend. Frequently, a Friday to Saturday format works best because only one day is taken from business and one day away from a weekend. The days should be discussed during a regular board meeting when retreat plans are underway. Ideally, a place should be chosen away from the board-room and the institution—one that provides a comfortable and relaxing atmosphere with appropriate facilities and equipment.

Once the site has been selected, it is important to find the right room for the meetings and to have it set up in such a manner as to make relaxed discussion easy. At minimum, the main meeting room should have windows, plenty of space, and comfortable chairs. Appropriate resource materials, audiovisual equipment, if needed, and appealing but not lavish meals all help to set the stage for a productive retreat.

If the cost of such a workshop is a problem, frequently a local foundation or corporation, a particularly interested board member, or an assessment of all trustees can help to defray costs, which include lodging, meals, and speaker expenses.

Using an Outside Facilitator

Frequently, an outside facilitator, if carefully chosen, can add objectivity and insight that would not be available from within the board and the administration. Such an individual might be a trustee or president from another institution, or, more probably, one of a number of consultants who are experienced in this kind of sometimes delicate work. The advantages that can accrue from such objectivity are significant. The AGB has a cadre of experienced facilitators available to its member boards through its on-campus and board-mentor programs. For more advice on the use of board retreats and workshops, see Chapter Twenty.

What makes a good board member? The most important ingredients are intelligence, good judgment, commitment, and the ability to ask the right questions. Persons with these and other qualities along the same line, fortified with effective orientation and in-service programs, will make a difference. An alert chief executive and board chair and an effective nominating committee chair—together with good strategy, patience, and time—are key to building an effective board.

CHAPTER 17

Organizing
and Staffing
the Board

Richard T. Ingram

No compelling empirical data exist to support the contention that how a governing board is organized significantly determines its effectiveness or the institution's performance. And yet, intuitively, students of trusteeship—including presidents and trustees themselves—believe that such matters as the board's size, trustee terms of office and rotation, committee structure, officerships, how meetings are conducted, staffing, and other processes typically provided for in bylaws have much to do with how well the board will perform.

To assume that such matters might directly influence how the college or university performs may be a stretch, but few doubt that how a board is organized and conducts its work strongly influences the effectiveness of the board: boards can be too large or too small; they can have too many trustees in service for too long; executive committees should not meet six times a year when the board only meets twice annually; board chairs should not have limitless terms; boards should not have excessive numbers of committees, and so on. Although such matters are not empirically verified, they are logically and experientially linked to such diverse consequences as trustee morale, the ability of the president and staff to serve the board well, trustee meeting attendance, and even the personal giving and fund-raising record of the board, to cite a few. A poorly organized board is potentially an unhappy and inefficient board, and such a board is likely to be mediocre in its commitment and effectiveness.

The thesis of this chapter is that how a board is organized and served by staff determines how it functions. Much has been learned in recent years about which strategies work better than others, but there are still no absolute rules. Nearly every guideline or principle has its "proven" exceptions somewhere in the wonderful kaleidoscope of independent higher education. There are only two basic routes to making a good board better: strengthen the membership of the board over time or strengthen the structure of the board and, therefore, the way the board conducts its business. Better yet, employ both routes! This chapter discusses several of the bumps, curves, and potential dead ends on the latter route, although, in the end, only good judgment will determine what is best for a given institution. Some general principles of good board organization are highlighted in italics throughout the chapter.

Avoiding Dead Ends

Every board of trustees has its own personality, style, and traditions that are reflected in its composition and structure. Although none of these are easily changed even when they should be, it is possible to make major changes in the structure of a board and thus begin new traditions that will ultimately be seen in the personality, style, and performance of the board. All that is required is a chief executive, board chair, and at least a few key committed trustees to decide that the time has come to try something new. Some boards simply need some fine tuning, whereas others need major overhaul, but all will benefit from thoughtful consideration of their structures in light of the experience of others. The *process* of involving the entire board in exploring options can rejuvenate trustees because it helps everyone to assume ownership over the results.

Several organizational problems deserve particular attention. Mindful that there are exceptions to every rule, these illustrative and commonplace practices are normally counterproductive:

- Board memberships that exceed forty or forty-five individuals.
- Executive committees that consistently meet more often than the

board and are perceived to (or do in fact) make most of the important decisions.

- Board standing committees, most especially finance committees, whose members presume they have the power to make decisions for the board rather than to consider options and recommend courses of action to the full board.
- Excessive numbers of "ex-officio" trustees (with or without the power to vote), "life" or "emeritus" trustees, and faculty and student trustees.
- Nominating committees that fail to assess the performance of incumbent trustees eligible for reelection to new terms or to otherwise grasp the fact that their responsibilities are critical to the effectiveness of the board (and ultimately the institution).
- Unlimited trustee terms of office, in practice if not in policy.
- Unlimited board officer terms, in practice if not in policy.
- Failure to groom talent and plan for succession to board officerships or to periodically rotate committee leaders.
- Failure to periodically use ad hoc committees to address special opportunities or problems.
- Failure to bring nontrustee talent periodically to the work of certain board committees, which would secure needed talent and prospective future trustees.
- Inadequate staffing of the board and its committees, including failure to integrate committee work—particularly the work of academic affairs and finance committees.

These practices and others like them are addressed in this chapter as we look at what constitutes optimum board size, trustee and board officer terms, special trustee categories, board standing committees (especially the role and function of the executive and nominating committees), advisory committees, councils and boards adjunct to the board of trustees, the importance of good staff work, and what constitutes a good set of bylaws.

Sizing Up the Board

Large boards generally wish to be smaller and small boards larger, but there is as yet no compelling evidence that the size of the board has much to do with its effectiveness (Chait, Holland, and Taylor, 1991). There is, however, some evidence that larger boards tend to be associated with institutions that are the most successful at fund raising (see Chapter Eleven). Pocock's study for the Association of Governing Boards of Universities and Colleges (1989b) reveals that independent colleges and universities found to be more successful in fund raising have an average size of forty-two trustees, whereas all of independent higher education has an average of about thirty-one trustees—eleven fewer trustees, on average. Although we should avoid any conclusion about cause and effect from this finding, bigger *can* be better.

It is a standard myth that larger boards (in excess of, say, forty trustees) are mostly confined to the larger, selective, research, and doctorate-granting independent universities—particularly those colleges and universities with national reputations. It is equally fictitious that prestigious universities are more likely to have exceptional boards of trustees whose structures should be emulated. What, then, can we conclude?

In the absence of convincing evidence to the contrary, these general principles should guide decisions about the size of the board.

Be flexible. Bylaws should specify a minimum (say, twenty-one) and a maximum (say, thirty-five) number of members. Far more important than the number are the needs to maintain room to expand so that promising new trustees can be cultivated and recruited to the board, to systematically assess incumbent trustee performance to minimize the number of ineffective and uncommitted trustees, and to motivate and educate incumbent trustees so that they enjoy their experience and remain committed to the institution. We should work as hard at retaining good trustees as we do at retaining students.

Because most of the work of the board should be accomplished in standing committees, determine the size of the board after deciding the number of essential committees needed. Thus, the number of trustees should be determined by the number of committees that are *required* for the board to meet its responsibilities. The sections in this chapter that address related considerations, such as the number of committees on which trustees should serve and the ideal number of trustees for committee membership, should guide this decision. To maintain a basic committee structure of at least five active standing committees, at least twenty-one board members are probably required to share the workload.

Do not expand the board because there is reluctance to discontinue the service of unproductive, uncommitted trustees. There is considerable anecdotal evidence that many boards have grown larger primarily because of the perfectly human tendency to avoid being judgmental of others. Such avoidance is detrimental to the board and the institution it serves. Boards can become too big, too unwieldy, too difficult to serve well—just as they can be too small in light of the much higher expectations held for boards and trustees today.

In the end, good judgment must prevail. There is much to be said for an exceptionally large board to downsize, for an exceptionally small board to expand, and for every board to expect commitment from all members. The process of expanding or contracting also brings with it opportunities for all trustees to assess how good they really are and for everyone to test the viability of the structure of the board. Kicking the tires occasionally is healthy.

Terms of Office for Trustees

The average term of independent college and university trustees is four years, but the most typical (median) term is three years. An AGB survey (Taylor 1988) also reveals a definite trend toward limiting the number of consecutive terms: at least 42 percent of all private institutions have set a maximum of three consecutive terms in their bylaws; a one-year hiatus or "sabbatical" is required before the possibility of reelection beyond nine years of total service.

With regard to the ideal length of term, there is none, but three years seems about right. The principles are as follows.

Trustees should serve terms that enable both incumbents and the institution to cancel the social contract that binds them when either party wishes to do so. Thus, three-year terms seem fair to both sides of the equation. However, too few institutions set clear standards for what is expected of trustees to encourage systematic review of those eligible for reelection; this, unfortunately, causes the need to provide a safety net in the form of a maximum number of consecutive terms (to force performance assessment by the appropriate board committee).

Even at the risk of losing valuable trustees during the one year hiatus, assessing the value of each trustee's service at least at the end of nine years of service is better than not doing any assessment at all. But the far better practice is to set reasonable expectations for all trustees so that the nominating committee is enabled to systematically review the performance of incumbents at the end of their renewable terms. In the end, both systematic review and a maximum period of service are probably desirable. There are creative ways to keep exceptionally committed trustees involved with the institution during their sabbaticals.

Term of Office for the Chair

An AGB survey (Taylor, 1988) reveals that 22 percent of all independent institutions set a limit on the number of years the board chair may serve; responding institutions also reported that their incumbent chairs had served an average of four years. How long is long enough and how short is too short? This decision, like so many others, depends on many, often contradictory, factors.

Relatively few trustees have the leadership traits, stamina, capacity to renew enthusiasm in themselves and others, time, commitment, fund-raising expertise, and clear and consistent understanding of the distinctive leadership roles shared with the chief executive for many more than, say, five years. But some have it all—I know a liberal arts college trustee who served with distinction as board chair of his alma mater for seventeen years and made at least two presidents and the board very happy with his leadership and his generosity. He even served as capital campaign chair at the same time. But such persons unfortunately are rare indeed.

Able and committed trustees naturally aspire to the top post on their boards. Is damage done to their aspirations, commitment, and morale if the position seems to be "locked up" by the same trustee for exceptionally long periods (even by someone who may be a, or *the*, major donor and proven fund raiser)? How can we stay with the "winner" trustee who commands the respect of the majority of the board through a very flexible policy, without violating the principle of succession planning? Some precedents or traditions can be very problematic. There are no easy answers, but the following guidelines together with the illustrative bylaws in Resource D may help.

The board chair and, by extension, all board officers, should have renewable one-year terms with suggested minimum and maximum periods of service (see Resource D). The word "ordinarily" is very useful in bylaws and other board policies; for example, "The chair and vice chair shall be elected annually upon nomination by the committee on trusteeship and shall ordinarily serve for at least three consecutive years but not more than five years." Thus, we have a safety net (annual performance review) and flexibility for longer service when the truly exceptional leader is found.

Boards need to plan for succession to the top leadership role, preferably through the position of vice chair. Too few boards plan for succession at their, and their institution's, peril. To retain flexibility, the illustrative bylaws in Resource D do not *require* that the incumbent vice chair succeed to the top post, but the assumption of succession is there. The office of vice chair is typically more honorific than substantive in role and responsibilities, but the individual who holds the position on the eve of the incumbent chair's stepping down should be acknowledged by all trustees as their appropriate next leader. The board chair and chief executive should consistently bring the vice chair into their deliberations.

Ex-Officio, Honorary, Life, and Emeritus Trustees

Most boards have at least one special category of trustee, such as ex-officio, honorary, life, or emeritus. Such trustees may or may not vote. Some boards, unfortunately, have most of these categories. Some boards have more of these trustees than regular, voting trustees, and deciding what to do with them is a problem. There is much to be said for having *one* trustee category for those truly deserving of a continuing relationship with the board and institution under certain circumstances, but *honorary* and *life* labels should be avoided or discontinued. A single emeritus category should do nicely, as suggested below and in Resource D. And there may be need for one, two, or three ex-officio ("by virtue of position") trusteeships, limited largely to church-related or special-purpose institutions, but care should be taken not to have too many. The following principles should guide the decision.

Trustees who have served with distinction for some minimum period of service, whose commitment to the institution remains strong, and who cannot or should not be expected to meet the same obligations as regular trustees, should be eligible for election to a special trusteeship. The *trustee emeritus* label is my choice, but there are more important considerations. The position should have fixed and renewable terms to avoid the practice of lifetime appointments; these individuals should continue to *do something* of note to justify the distinction bestowed upon them. There should be a limited number of such trusteeships to encourage thoughtful consideration of candidates. Not everyone who retires from the board deserves to be given the title, and the position should *mean something special* to everyone. All special trustees should be encouraged to serve on board committees, for example, and all should feel free to participate in board meetings (thus the need to avoid having too many such positions). They should not vote, however.

Ex-officio positions (with or without vote) should be reserved for the fewest possible number of leaders. Among these are the chief executive, top church leaders in church-related institutions (who should be discouraged from sending their "representatives" lest a "watch dog" psychology prevails), and a very few others for whom a clear and compelling case can be made. Having too many such trusteeships conveys the perception that the board is organized more as a legislative body of special interests, thus violating what a board of trustees should be. Even in the case of the alumni who have distinguished themselves, it is probably better to ensure through consistent practice their inclusion in the ranks of trustees than to designate a certain number of alumni positions, although a possible exception is the elected leader of the alumni association.

About 62 percent of independent academic institutions provide for the chief executive to be a voting member of the board (Ingram, 1988). Whether this is a good or inappropriate practice and if the chief executive benefits from or should wish this arrangement has been debated for a very long time. In any case, the for-profit, corporate model clearly prevails in a majority of institutions.

Faculty and Student Trusteeship

Should students and faculty have representatives on the boards of the institutions where they study or teach? The vast majority of independent colleges and universities do not think so (see Resource B). Many institutions include their own students and faculty on certain board committees, however (Ingram, 1988).

Although there is anecdotal evidence that the experience of boards with student trustees is largely salutary, there are justifiable philosophical and practical concerns about the practice. A case can be made for student service on boards on the grounds of consumerism, increased openness, and especially direct educational benefit to those elected or appointed. But student trusteeship contradicts the notion that *all* trustees have an obligation to be and remain independent of special interests or groups. On the practical side, furthermore, it is difficult to support the contention that the same performance standards expected of all trustees can apply to students—including personal giving and active participation in fund raising. Delicate personnel, legal, real estate, and financial issues require a measure of confidentiality that may be awkward for everyone if students (or faculty) are present. Although nonvoting student trustees can be excused or excluded from certain parts of board meetings, this makes no one happy. Trustees should never be made to feel reluctant to speak or ask questions because of the presence of students.

With regard to faculty trusteeship, the most compelling argument against the practice is that it is a prima facie conflict of interest because the faculty receive their incomes from the institution; furthermore, faculty presumably have their own organizational forums to provide advice and counsel.

Much good can come from including student and faculty leaders as full partners on appropriate board committees where their advice and counsel can be especially helpful. There is also room for educators on the board from other, peer institutions to bring faculty perspectives to the table, preferably from institutions that do not compete for the same sources of students and money. Boards are not legislative bodies. Classified employees (administrative staff) and other groups could make the same claim as students and faculty that they, too, are entitled to board membership.

Thus the principle: *trustees can benefit from access to student and faculty leaders, but this access is best and more appropriately secured by means other than through voting or nonvoting trusteeship.* The conventional wisdom that the chief executive should be at the center of the board's communication with faculty and students is sound.

Standing Committees

Most boards have too many committees rather than too few. And too few trustees and chief executives are satisfied with the quality of committee work, a problem shared by trustees and management. What constitutes a sound committee structure and how can committee work be made more rewarding and useful? There are as many answers as there are institutional settings and leaders, but form should always follow function.

Space does not permit addressing each of the nine typical standing committees, although woe unto the board and president who have all of them! The executive committee is mentioned briefly in the next section of this chapter because of its unique role, and Chapter Sixteen addresses the nominating committee, which has a central role in organizing the board and is more appropriately named the "committee on trustees" or "committee on board membership." AGB maintains a set of pamphlets for each of nine standard committees, and *Making Trusteeship Work* incorporates all of them in a single volume (Ingram, 1988).

The following principles provide a checklist of options to consider:

For effective problem solving and the greatest sense of achievement, the optimum group size is five. This consistent finding from social science research (Mueller, 1984) argues for most committee memberships to be about seven (to allow for some absenteeism).

Every committee should have a board-approved statement of

its role and scope of responsibilities. The statement can be included
in or separate from the bylaws of the board, but annual review by
the committee is important to ensure that it is clear, current, comprehensive, and compelling.

*Committees should be consolidated rather than expanded in
number.* Thus, the academic and student affairs realms can be combined; the audit and investment agendas can be addressed in separate subcommittees of the finance committee; the responsibility of
the board for ensuring good institutional planning can be vested in
the executive committee, where the key leaders of the board are
assembled; and so on.

*Committees will only be as effective as their leaders and the
staff persons assigned to them.* Staffing issues are discussed later in
this chapter, and Chapter Eighteen addresses the importance of
meeting agendas and related matters. All committees should have
designated vice chairs to ensure that leadership is available and to
groom new chairs. Customary and appropriate practice is for the
board chair and the chief executive to jointly choose committee
leaders and make committee assignments, but the chief executive
has the prerogative to decide who should staff each committee.

Committee chairs and members should rotate periodically.
The aim should be to give deserving, committed trustees opportunities to lead. It may be counterintuitive and illogical, especially for
new trustees, to place the banker on the student affairs committee
and the educator on the finance committee, but it works! Every three
years, at most, ask all trustees for their first three ranked committee
preferences and grant most of them their wishes.

Committee work should be integrated as much as possible.
For example, the academic affairs committee should meet at least
once each year with the finance committee to discuss shared issues.
Budget projections cannot be reviewed by the finance committee
completely independently of faculty and academic program priorities. Such joint meetings can be energizing for everyone.

*The most rewarding and productive committee work often
comes from ad hoc committee assignments* (Wood, 1985). All boards
should have at least one active ad hoc committee with a very particular assignment to accomplish within a specified time period.
Large and pressing issues that the institution confronts in the short-

or long-term future and that cut across standing committee job descriptions can make for exciting committee work. For example, reorganizing the structure and bylaws of the board, deciding whether or not to build a new library, or determining the appropriateness of moving from a club sports to an intercollegiate sports program lend themselves to such committee work.

Nontrustees who have special expertise can bring needed talent as full committee members. They can bring some fresh perspectives, useful information, commitment to the institution, and the possibility of their own future trusteeship. Committee work is a good place to identify prospective board members.

Most regular committee meetings should be scheduled on the eve of board meetings (with the exception of the executive committee, for reasons elaborated later, or perhaps the finance committee, which may need to meet more frequently). This eliminates the need for formal committee minutes, because the highlights of the meetings of each committee can be captured in the minutes of board meetings. Multiple committee assignments can be a problem in adhering to this principle, but careful scheduling of meetings and assignment of trustees will help; for example, two meetings can be scheduled concurrently provided the committee memberships do not overlap.

Maintaining committee meeting attendance records can be motivational, especially if they are regularly distributed to all trustees with board meeting attendance records. Consistent absentees should be given opportunities to move to other committees.

Committees recommend and commend; boards determine and decide. Except for the executive committee, which has certain specified authority delegated by the bylaws of the board, committees are responsible for studying and recommending options. Unless specifically delegated authority in the board minutes, committees should avoid unilateral decision making.

There is ample room for experimentation with regard to the committee organization of a board. Periodic change is often uncomfortable, but it is usually healthy and helps to avoid the lethargy that accompanies routine. The chief executive and the board chair must take the lead in suggesting changes; the potential rewards in rejuvenated board members almost always justify the effort required. Third-party consultation to look at options can be very helpful by bringing objectivity and experience to the process of board reorganization and bylaw revision.

Executive Committee

Virtually all boards of independent institutions have executive committees, but these have widely varying sizes, membership composition, purposes, and consequences. Because the executive committee is the only committee vested with broad authority to make, rather than recommend, decisions—a power normally delegated by the board in its bylaws—no other standing committee has greater potential for good or harm. Thus, it is a key committee whose role and scope of responsibilities should be reviewed periodically. What follows is a case for a new, or at least redefined, set of purposes that bear directly on the organizational effectiveness of the board.

The membership composition and purposes of the executive committee should be clarified in the bylaws of the board, as suggested in Resource D. These purposes are twofold. The first is that the committee serves at the pleasure of the board as its agent in helping the president to address nonessential business between regular board meetings and thereby conserve board meeting time.

The second purpose is to assist the chair and president in their joint responsibility to help the board function effectively and efficiently by suggesting board meeting agenda items and periodically assessing the quality of committee work. The executive committee should have authority to act for the board of trustees on all matters except for the following, which are reserved for the board: presidential selection and termination; trustee and board officer selection; changes in institutional mission and purposes; changes to the charter or articles of incorporation; incurring of corporate indebtedness; sale of institutional assets or tangible property; adoption of the annual budget; and conferral of degrees. The bylaws or other board policy may reserve other powers for the board of trustees, including, for example, final approval of the chief executive's total compensation package. In addition to its authority to take action on emergency matters that cannot or should not be deferred to the next scheduled meeting of the board, the executive committee oversees the work of board committees, the institution's planning process or progress on planning goals, the responsibility of the board to support the president and assess his or her performance, and annual review of the president's compensation and conditions of employment. (For more information on this subject, see Resource D)

These two purposes suggest that the committee has a central role in helping the president and board chair to fulfill their leadership roles and also in helping the board meet its responsibilities. Its special functions are made possible in part because of its unique membership composition and delegated authority. The committee should also hold itself and be held accountable to the full board; many boards require distribution of committee minutes to all trustees, and some require ratification of its minutes at the subsequent board meeting. With regard to its membership composition, here are some rules of thumb:

An ideal composition includes all board officers, the chairs of all (or specified) standing committees, and one or two at-large trustees. Thus, the key leaders of the board are gathered together to enable the committee to be a dependable source of counsel to the board chair and president, and to oversee institutional planning through its involvement in the process.

The number of committee members should be approximately one-third of the total number of trustees on the board. To be much larger would be contradictory to the committee's important purpose of conserving the time of the majority of trustees; to be much smaller would violate the principle that the executive committee should consist of all of the key leaders (not just the officers) of the board to maintain its credibility.

The board chair should also chair the executive committee. Some boards have experimented with asking the vice chair of the board to preside at executive committee meetings with less than happy results. There can only be one board chair.

To avoid or reduce perceptions that the committee is presuming the functions of the full board, it is important for the committee not to meet more often than the board meets, except in unusual circumstances. Nor should it meet the same day or the day before board meetings lest it convey an unintended message: that the important decisions to be brought up at board meetings have already been decided by board leaders. Promptly sharing its minutes with all trustees is an important protocol that acknowledges accountability to the full board. These and other issues concerning the committee are elaborated in an AGB pamphlet, *Executive Committee* (Ingram, 1985).

Adjunct Advisory Groups

Many colleges and universities have established institution-wide advisory committees, councils, and boards that consist of highly visible men and women. In addition to being a good source of future trustees, such groups can help to strengthen outreach or public relations initiatives and fund-raising programs, as well as serve a variety of other institutional purposes. The record of success for such groups is mixed, however, even when planning has been sound. They require considerable presidential and staff attention, and they too often function without apparent governing board interest in or appreciation for them. Setting them up is relatively easy; making them work effectively is difficult. When they do not work, they can be literally and figuratively rather expensive propositions.

Nevertheless, such enterprises are worth considering as part of the structure of a college or university, because they can be immensely helpful when they work well. The ingredients for success are fivefold: providing a good statement of the scope, purpose, and organization of the group; providing good staffing to ensure a stimulating agenda; involving the personal attention of the president and at least a few trustees as members; selecting the most committed members and especially the right chair who may or may not be a trustee; and providing opportunities for the group to meet with the board of trustees at least once every year or two. For a fuller treatment of this subject, see the AGB pamphlet *Making Advisory Committees and Boards Work* (Ingram, 1989a).

Good Staffing Is Everything

Clark Kerr remarks in his study of the academic presidency that "few presidents can be much better than their boards; none can be much worse—at least not for very long" (Commission on Strengthening Presidential Leadership, 1984). But Kerr would also agree that the converse is true. Few boards can be much better than their presidents enable them to be.

The extent to which a board serves its institution well is a direct function of how well it is served. The president and other senior officers have almost everything to do with determining how effectively the board functions. How the board is organized is important, but how well that organization is served by the professional and administrative staff is even more important.

Most experienced presidents learned a long time ago that other officers must help with committee work, because in committees most of the responsibilities of the board are addressed. The logical assignment of staff by function needs no discussion here, but there are some related matters that can make a difference in how staff think about and act on their responsibilities. We begin with some advice for the president or chancellor.

Because the chief executive needs all the help he or she can get, it is common practice to designate a single individual to coordinate development of committee and board agendas as well as supporting information, logistics, minutes, and all the rest. There is in fact an emerging new higher education profession in the large private and public universities and multicampus systems: the university or board secretary. Leaders of smaller institutions are also recognizing that the attention trustees and boards require argues for at least a half-time professional with an appropriate position title. Space does not permit elaborating a job description for this increasingly important position, one that includes a number of significant institutional duties, but see Resource F for two important sources of information.

But what else beyond having a clearly designated coordinator can the president do to help the chief finance officer, academic officer, advancement officer, and others to do a better job of serving the board, especially through their committees? Training. Much can be gained from bringing everyone who has committee staffing responsibilities together periodically for the purpose of learning and sharing what is known about group psychology and behavior, how to work with committee chairs in shaping the meeting agendas, how to present data and information in interesting and useful ways, what to do when the unexpected happens, when to consult with the president, the importance of follow-up, how to help the committee chair to make effective (terse) reports to the board, and so on.

Every staff member should be encouraged to read *Process Consultation: Lessons for Managers and Consultants* (Schein, 1987). It elaborates the concepts of process, managing change, intervention strategies, and managers as helpers. Even a few hours every quarter devoted to discussions of these and related topics, taking turns leading discussions of some of Schein's chapters, selected chapters in this volume, or how committee and board meetings seem to be received by the trustees can be very useful. Another excellent reference is the last chapter, "What's a President to Do?" in *The Effective Board of Trustees* (Chait, Holland, and Taylor, 1991). Best of all, invite a qualified consultant to facilitate a staff meeting or to work with the president and staff periodically over a period of several months. Creative ideas on how to strengthen the structure of the board and how to improve the quality and presentation of information for the trustees will flow more easily.

And for the staff officer who works with one or more board committees, these tidbits may be helpful. First, convince your president or chancellor to convene the officers for a candid discussion of how the board can be served better through its committee and board meetings (see Chapter Eighteen), how communication between meetings can be improved, and how institutional data and information can be presented in more interesting and useful ways. Begin with a debriefing immediately following a board meeting: How did our meeting go today? How did our trustees seem to respond to our preparations? How can we help the committees to function better?

Second, read the Schein (1987) and Chait, Holland, and Taylor (1991) books. Suggest that your colleagues also do so to set the stage for a series of discussions about the relevance of the ideas in the books to your board. Assign chapters for presentation in the context of what is useful to all of you.

Third, consider having each officer prepare an "executive summary" that covers most of the detail in his or her area of responsibility. This summary reduces or eliminates time that staff spend talking about past activities. Distribute the summaries with the committee agenda and other supporting materials, and keep the committee agenda oriented to current and future issues. Make it more interesting and more fun for everyone.

Fourth, help your committee chair to be an effective presiding officer and discussion leader. That means visiting in advance of meetings to discuss the agenda, recent events, and data and information in support of the agenda to help stimulate discussion in meetings. Consider preparing a comprehensive, but terse, set of meeting highlights for the committee chair's report at the following board meeting.

Some Concluding Thoughts

A longtime observer of corporate boardroom behavior through his service on many for-profit boards and as a management consultant offers a useful perspective: "the difference between a smart board and a dumb board isn't that smart directors don't make mistakes; they just don't keep making the same mistakes over and over" (Mueller, 1984, p. 213). One of the many jobs of president, board chair, and staff officer is to help the board learn from its mistakes, look occasionally in the mirror, experiment with adjustments to the structure of the board, and to ask the right questions. All of this and more is called *process*. We are all at the same time teachers and learners.

Organizing and properly staffing a board is a collegial process, whether it amounts to fine-tuning or major overhaul; either, but particularly the latter, can bring a tremendous sense of personal (and organizational) achievement and renewal. But making changes is difficult even when they are necessary or when everyone except the board's key leaders seem to see the need for them: thus the strategy of "bylaw revision." Under the nonthreatening guise of bringing (perhaps antiquated) bylaws up to date, much can be accomplished that goes well beyond tinkering with a few bylaw provisions. The process can breathe new life into even the most lethargic of boards if planned and conducted properly. The ownership by the board of both process and outcomes is critical.

The illustrative bylaws for independent colleges and universities in Resource D represent the accumulated experience of many people over many years. They provide the basis for assessing the provisions in the bylaws of your board. The greater the discrepancy in substance between the two sets of provisions, the more likely that your board would benefit from the process of revising them.

Setting an opportunity for your board to discuss its job description (the "powers" of the board), membership composition (what does "balance" mean for this institution?), board officerships (what do we expect of them and they of us?), committee structure (including executive and nominating committee responsibilities), and related matters works. Several hundred boards have conducted self-studies using AGB's Board Mentor Program or other sources of qualified facilitators with very successful outcomes. Many such programs have been scheduled as board workshops or retreats to guide a small committee of trustees charged, with the president, to draft a new set of bylaws, which is a means to a much more important end.

CHAPTER 18

Making Board
and Committee
Meetings Work

Richard T. Ingram

Meetings are an essential part of trusteeship, and we should like them more than we do. Trustees understandably expect their time to be used well, especially the time they devote to meetings, but complaints are commonplace. The purpose of this chapter is to suggest improvements for those who organize board meetings, preside over them, and participate in them. By applying some commonsense rules, experimenting with new approaches to agenda development, and expecting those who lead discussions to prepare adequately for them, meetings can be made much more satisfying and useful.

These quips illustrate the cynicism many feel about meetings:

- At board meetings, the one unmatched asset is the ability to yawn with your mouth closed.
- Meetings are events at which minutes are kept—and hours are lost.
- When all is said and done in the boardroom, there is much more said than done.
- A board meeting is an unnatural act performed in public by consenting adults.

- At board meetings, the president is supposed to talk, the trustees are supposed to think, and the chair's job is to keep the trustees from talking and the president from thinking.
- The degree to which an agenda item is understood is inversely proportional to the amount of paperwork connected with it.

At their best, board meetings are opportunities to make good decisions based on good information, stimulate creativity, use the skills and talents of participants, instill camaraderie and common purpose, build understanding, educate, and renew trustee commitment. The best meetings and presiders discourage domination by one or two personalities, encourage open and honest exchange, build trust, and contribute in significant ways to building an effective board.

Good meetings are not accidents. They are an art form; good theater when in the hands of able leaders. Every committee or board meeting is a stage that sends its players home feeling either good about themselves and their institution or empty and disappointed. More meetings should be stimulating and fun, and they can be with good planning and leaders who understand the psychology of group behavior.

Like everything else having to do with the conduct of trusteeship, the search for balance is necessary. Boards can meet too often or not often enough. Trustees can be given too much paper and data but not enough information to prepare for meetings. Too many issues may be on a given meeting agenda, resulting in little or no accomplishment at all. Boards can have too many committees for the number of trustees, resulting in "meeting burnout." Trustees can be asked to sit in meetings that extend beyond human endurance, or the meetings can be so short that they mock board responsibility. Balance and periodic experimentation with everything from when and where the board should meet to the form and substance of agendas are worthy goals. The humdrum of routine can be avoided.

If a board seems to be lethargic or ineffective, it is likely that its meetings are at least part of the problem. This chapter is about options that can help to make board and committee meetings better, based on these assumptions:

- *The style and substance of meetings are the inevitable consequence of tradition and the chief executive's expectations.* That is, meetings reflect the institution's culture and values, which extend over many years, and the incumbent chief executive's expectations of the board's role in helping to lead the institution.
- *Meetings reflect the structure of the board.* The number of trustees and how the board is organized to conduct most of its work through committees affect the quality of board meetings.
- *Meetings are more than the sum of their parts.* Because meetings are a mix of process and content, they are influenced by many different factors, such as their frequency and length, the issues that constitute their agendas, the quality of information prepared in advance, the availability of conscientious staff help, and the personal style and capacity of trustee leaders to preside over them. These matters, and the important logistical details that can make or break meetings, are addressed here.

How Often and for How Long Should the Board Meet?

Boards should meet only as often and as long as necessary to do their job. The boards of independent colleges and universities typically meet quarterly, whereas the boards of public institutions meet much more frequently. According to a recent national survey reported by Taylor (1988), community college boards typically have monthly meetings, state system and multicampus boards meet nine times a year, and other public colleges and universities meet seven times annually. Independent colleges and universities rely much more on executive committees, which meet an average of five times annually between regular board meetings. But the boards of private institutions depend much more on committee meetings between regular board meetings than do their public counterparts, and typically they have longer board meetings; there is an inverse relationship between number and length of meetings. Furthermore, private boards are free of legal mandates that often require public boards to approve certain routine matters that private college and university trustees would consider inappropriate or unnecessary.

It is difficult to imagine how a governing board can meet less than quarterly and still meet its responsibilities, however. Boards that meet twice or three times annually are likely to have executive committees that meet at least quarterly or more, but such boards also run the risk of having morale and motivational problems among trustees who do not serve on the executive committee, where so much of the action may seem to take place.

There is a strong trend for private college and university boards to dedicate one of their board meetings to an annual retreat where normal business agendas are made secondary to other special purposes important to trustee education, board development, or some other pressing institutional need. These special meetings usually constitute one of the quarterly board meetings, or a fifth meeting. Either way, it is a good practice.

The individual human brain can absorb and retain only so much at a time even under ideal circumstances, but in a room with many others—all connected to vocal cords—attention span inevitably diminishes. Meetings should be as short as possible and highly focused in their content. They are best held in the morning; the worst times are the period immediately following lunch or after a full day at the office.

Logistics

Common sense calls for meetings to be conducted in facilities appropriate to the seriousness of their purposes. Everything from the table, chairs, and what adorns the walls contributes to or detracts from how participants feel about themselves and their institution. Trustees should be able to see one another without gymnastics. Participant names should be clearly visible on large place cards set in advance; this helps new trustees to connect names with faces, conveys the seriousness of purpose, and makes possible the advantage of mixing seating arrangements from meeting to meeting. Individuals customarily park themselves in the same place at the table from meeting to meeting if seats are not preassigned, and research tells us that compatible personalities tend to sit together while antagonists tend to sit across the table from one another. Random, preassigned seating helps to counteract such phenomena and enables trustees to get to know each other more easily over time.

Basic audiovisual equipment (overhead projector, newsprint on easels, video camera recorder) should be readily available, and the importance of good ventilation and lighting are also obvious but sometimes neglected. Because so many uncontrollable forces converge in the normal course of meetings, those responsible for organizing and conducting meetings should take advantage of at least the environmental variables that can be controlled.

Setting the Agenda

All meetings typically have three functions: to inform, to explore ideas or options (discussion), or to request a formal action of some kind. Agenda items should indicate to participants what is expected along these lines. Action items that require the adoption of resolutions, for example, should have a notation to this effect and draft wording should be prepared and distributed with the agenda in advance. The agenda is a map that guides preparation and participation.

Good agendas have many other characteristics. They should:

- Look different from one meeting to the next.
- Be issue-driven rather than report-driven.
- Include brief (one- or two-sentence) narrative statements with items to provide context for the items and to clarify what the intent is: information, discussion, or action. Reference to accompanying background information should be made.
- Suggest time limits for specific items or groups of items.
- Require executive summaries of activities from senior staff.
- Minimize the need for additional written material to be distributed at meetings.
- Reflect the work and recommendations of board committees.
- Consistently provide for trustee education with in-depth reviews of major academic programs, schools, or departments; discussion of one or more external forces that affect the institution; occasional presentations by faculty or student leaders; periodic discussion of articles that bear on trusteeship or some aspect of board responsibilities; periodic presentations by guest speakers external to the institution, and the like. Be relevant and creative!
- *Always* be distributed at least seven to ten days in advance.

Board and committee agendas are appropriately prepared by the chief executive and staff, but should be cleared with the board and committee chairs as a matter of simple courtesy. This also helps chairs to prepare for the meeting and enables them to suggest improvements.

Executive Session

There is much to be said for the practice of having at the end of *all* board meetings executive sessions in which only the chief executive and trustees participate. Boards and executives need some private time together where either party can ask questions, share opinions more comfortably on delicate or especially confidential matters, dispel rumors, or address issues that might not otherwise be raised. Such a practice promotes honest and useful communication. Many boards routinely provide for such sessions on their agendas even though neither the president nor the trustees may need the session for more than the few minutes required to decide that is the case.

Minutes are necessary only when an official action is taken by the board or executive committee. If an action is especially confidential and the best interest of the institution is not to record it in the minutes, the chief executive should prepare a separate memorandum of record for distribution to the board chair and other board officers, at minimum, and perhaps to all trustees—both present and absent. This is a matter of judgment, depending on the issues involved.

Some presidents have also found that leaving the boardroom toward the end of the executive session, to give the trustees some private time, is useful. Such a practice instills in trustees a genuine sense of ownership and responsibility, and it can help to ensure that little problems that may involve board-president relationships do not become big ones. This is not for all presidents and all boards, and such a practice should be the president's call. At minimum, it requires a high level of trust, a very self-confident executive, a board chair who understands the delicacies involved and handles them properly, and two basic rules: such a practice should be routine, not sporadic, if it is done at all, and the chair extends to the president the courtesy of an immediate debriefing following the session. The doctrine of "no surprises" works both ways.

Providing and Presenting Information

The form and substance of agendas and supporting materials say much about how well a board is served by its chief executive and staff. Especially because a large number of corporate executives serve as trustees and are accustomed to professional presentation of data and information in their boardrooms, a high level of sophistication is expected. Thanks to the personal computer and new software technology, the presentation of data can be made much more interesting and useful. The use of color, graphs, and charts to present otherwise boring numbers can make a big difference. But the distinction between data and information needs to be made; what numbers reveal is what really matters in the boardroom.

Numbers should never be presented without interpretation and analysis: thus the need for concise narrative summaries. Trustees most appreciate help in seeing *trends* (current facts with comparable data from prior years), *ratios* (for example, expenses to revenues), and *projections* (extrapolations based on current trends together with clearly stated assumptions).

The chief executive and staff should periodically discuss the quality of the what and how of reports and presentations to the board. The advice and counsel of the board should be sought in the process. It may be helpful to develop a comprehensive "trustee information system" that includes periodic and regular reports according to a management calendar and the availability of data throughout the academic year. Updating becomes an easy matter once a good system is in place.

Periodic use of overhead slides and other visual aids is also important in boardroom presentations. Like anything else, this can be overdone, but staff should periodically evaluate one another's use of such devices and their manner of presentation. Seek the advice of individual trustees whose judgment would be helpful.

What is needed is more experimentation, a willingness to try new approaches to the presentation of facts and information. Whether the trends and projections are encouraging or discouraging, the first step to helping a board meet its responsibilities is to help it see what management sees. Of course, the dictum of "no surprises" should prevail; for example, anticipated board resolutions and specific actions should always be drafted and distributed in advance.

Conducting the Meeting

The tone and style of meetings are set by their leaders. Although institutional tradition influences the meetings, they directly reflect the chair's personality and ability to conduct them. Consequently, meetings may be largely informal or formal, focused or unfocused, tense or relaxed, boring or fun, and they are often a mix of all of these. The minutes of meetings often reveal how discussion flows from the presentation of information or proposed actions. Some meetings reflect a "Quaker consensus" tone and style, while others emphasize voting and strict adherence to *Robert's Rules of Order* (Robert, 1971).

The important conclusion is not that one meeting style is superior to another, although some are more effective in motivating volunteers than others; rather, it is that the board and committee chairs and the chief executive should periodically consider the tone and style of meetings to determine whether they are what is desired. Disappointing attendance, for example, may indicate a problem. Many factors, including the experience and expectations of participants, affect meeting environments.

Consistently starting meetings on time sets a certain tone, just as always starting them ten or fifteen minutes late sends certain signals. Opening the meeting with a humorous statement reflects a certain style, while a strictly businesslike posture reflects another. Letting discussions ramble has the same deleterious effect as cutting them off too quickly, but balance between these extremes sets yet another atmosphere. The person who presides has almost everything to do with how satisfied meeting participants feel about themselves and the use of their time. Effective chairs tend to

- Keep discussion focused.
- Gracefully but effectively disengage those who would otherwise

dominate discussions. It is not always the silent person who does not have anything to say.

- Understand that individuals and groups tend to avoid complex issues and prefer to dwell on easy and less consequential matters.
- Know that precisely stating the problem is the first step to resolving it.
- Synthesize and summarize apparent consensus.
- Encourage reticent participants to express themselves.
- Know the chief executive's position and recommendation concerning delicate issues in advance and ensure that he or she has an opportunity to be heard.
- Know when issues should be tabled for more thought and study or when the time has come for a vote.
- Display a sense of humor.

Experienced presiding officers know that they need not completely sacrifice their own views on important issues to be good facilitators, but they know that their advocacy should be used sparingly and timed carefully. They best serve the board by disclosing their own views later in discussion rather than too early and speaking on the heels of someone who has just expressed a similar perspective rather than contradicting a preceding speaker. Restraint is necessary because when the chair speaks on a matter of importance, his or her opinion is likely to be very influential.

Self-indulgence has no place in the chair's style. The voices of neither the chair nor the chief executive should be heard more often than those of others around the table. Both share responsibility to see that candor is not sacrificed to dysfunctional politeness, that collective good judgment is not sacrificed to expediency, and that frankness does not become incivility. Most of all, trustees look for enthusiasm and competence in their leaders. Leaders promote the sense of belonging sought by board members.

Warren Bennis and Burt Nanus (1985) point to the need for "emotional wisdom" and the following "people skills" in leaders: the ability to accept people as they are; the capacity to relate to people and issues in terms of the present, not the past; the ability to treat people with whom you are close with the same respect and attention extended to strangers and casual acquaintances; the ability to trust others even if the risk is great; the ability to find personal reward in the knowledge of a job well done rather than through the constant approval of others.

Kieffer's Laws of Meetings

George David Kieffer (1993) offers four insights about meetings to consider:

1. *Meetings tend to fail in direct proportion to the number and variety of tasks being undertaken.* Getting groups to think is difficult enough without trying to cover too many large issues and tasks. Reduce the number of issues and tasks to the smallest number possible.
2. *Meetings tend to fail in direct proportion to the number of people participating.* Each member of a group brings certain needs, aspirations, personality characteristics, and talents to the team. Thus, large groups depend more on committee work. The leaders of the board should decide when complex issues should be at least initially explored in smaller group settings.
3. *Meetings tend to fail in inverse proportion to preparation time and in direct proportion to meeting time.* The most important work for meetings is often done before the meeting, because once the meeting begins, options become limited. Meetings should be kept as short as possible because the attention span of most individuals is quite short. Ironically, short meetings often require more preparation time.
4. *Meetings fail when the environment is inconsistent with their purposes,* thus the need to provide appropriate settings to avoid distractions and promote the accomplishment of group tasks.

Minutes

Writing a good set of minutes is an art that most of us avoid at any cost. Yet they are very important as both a legal requirement and as a symbol of the accomplishments of the board. Fortunate are the board and chief executive who have someone on staff with the sustained enthusiasm and competence to draft a good record of board and executive committee proceedings. We should express our appreciation to him or her more often than we do.

The chief executive, board chair, and board secretary (whether trustee or staff member) have a joint responsibility to see that minutes are accurate and written to encourage reading, strike a balance between too much and too little detail, and convey the flow and substance of discussion without being verbatim transcripts of "who said what." A sense of the major pros and cons should suffice.

There are other characteristics of a good set of minutes. Listing all attendees *and* absentees is good practice. Having the list in minutes helps to maintain accurate attendance lists for use by the nominating committee, and it helps to focus attention on any chronic absenteeism. And it is important to refer specifically to appropriate documents provided to the board before or at the board meeting, especially if they support a particular point of information, conclusion, or board action. For example: "Referring to the quarterly balance sheet for the period ending June 30, *as previously distributed to all board members,* the treasurer stated that . . ." If formal votes are not taken on specific actions, but there is a clear sense of unanimity on whether or how to proceed, the record might read like this: "Following discussion, *it was the sense of the board that* . . ." Citing the names of specific individuals except for those who make and second motions is not necessary and, in fact, is usually undesirable.

Rarely does the person who drafts the minutes sign them. Both the chief executive and the signer should see the draft before it is placed in final form for distribution. The aim should be to distribute the minutes of board and executive committee minutes to all trustees within thirty days. A second set of minutes is provided to trustees as part of their subsequent board meeting materials.

Finally, because written documents outweigh oral testimony in the eyes of the courts, having legal counsel periodically review the adequacy and style of minutes is sensible. Minutes should be permanently maintained and safeguarded. Meetings should not be tape-recorded, in my opinion, and probably in the opinion of most attorneys. Good minutes are written all the time without depending on tape recording, which can be very distracting to participants.

Besides, most writers of minutes would wish to be spared having to "sit" through the same meeting a second time!

There is, unfortunately, little or no room for humor in minutes. But trustees and those who prepare minutes should enjoy this verse from the 1971 *Standard Manual* of the London Institute of Directors (cited in Mueller, 1984, p. 235):

> And while the Great Ones repair to their dinner,
> The secretary stays, growing thinner and thinner,
> Racking his brains to record and report
> What he thinks they will think
>   that they ought to have thought.

It's Your Meeting

Decide what you want to get out of a meeting; meetings will be much more rewarding and satisfying if you know what you want to accomplish before you take your place at the table. If more of us devoted more time to prepare for meetings, deciding in advance how we could make our best contribution to them, choosing even one significant issue that would particularly benefit from our expertise or perspective, meetings would be more productive for everyone. There is a time to follow and a time to lead, but there is much to be said for the strategy of deciding in advance how we can make our best contribution to every meeting as participant leaders.

Most board members, regardless of the institutional setting, behave differently in the boardroom than they do outside of it. An unfortunate truism is that we tend to take ourselves more seriously than we should. We should balance our individual need to make a difference with the overall need of others to enjoy their volunteer service.

CHAPTER 19

Understanding Chief Executive and Board Chair Responsibilities

Richard T. Ingram

The relationship between chief executive and the chosen leader of the board has almost everything to do with how well the governing board will perform. The synergy between these two individuals can make possible what neither could accomplish alone. Whether the gap between the leadership potential and actual performance of the board is narrow or wide inevitably reflects how they work together.

The purpose of this chapter is to explore the special relationship between the chief executive and the board chair within the context of helping the board to do its job well. Although the president is responsible for managing the institution, the chair is responsible for managing the board, and they are jointly responsible for the leadership of the board and the institution. There are times when the president takes the lead and times when the board chair does so; certain prerogatives are reserved for the board chair and others are reserved for the president. Understanding the difference between their roles marks an effective relationship, but no less than knowing when they must act jointly.

An Appropriate Relationship

The prerequisites of an ideal relationship include having a board chair who is the clear choice of the large majority of trustees, does not serve for too little time or too long, has earned the respect of trustees and administrators alike, understands fully the commitment required of the position, and has proven ability to preside at meetings. There are others, of course, but we begin with these.

The chief executive should appreciate the chair's responsibility to serve the institution and public trust first and the president's needs second, to manage the affairs of the board, to speak for the board in certain situations, and to see that the board does its job. The president and chair must trust one another and realize that one can be only as effective as the other.

Personal style complements substance and competence. The multitude of personal qualities and interpersonal skills that make or break would-be leaders are a crucial determinant of the relationship. This is not to suggest that executive and chair styles must be alike, but they should not conflict with one another. Mutual respect, adjustment to one another's style, clear understanding that there can be only one chief executive and only one board chair, keeping one another informed and aware of travel schedules, all make for an ideal relationship.

When the chair–chief executive team is what it should be, new opportunities present themselves: trustees and staff are motivated to higher expectations and, therefore, better performance; the board is much more likely to function as a team rather than as a collection of individuals with their own agendas; a deliberate strategy for strengthening the performance of the board is more likely to develop; ambiguities between board and management roles are reduced; institutional priorities are more clearly identified and more quickly addressed; confidence in the board and institution by external and internal stakeholders is enhanced; trustee and staff morale is bolstered as trusteeship becomes more fun than drudgery; and the president is made to feel comfortable in seeking advice from the chair on any matter, personal or institutional.

There Can Be Only One Chair

Among the more important personal qualities to be sought in the elected leader of the board are listening, communication, objectivity, sensitivity and decisiveness, influence, foresight, and presiding skills.

Listening

An effective leader should consistently demonstrate not only the ability to listen to but also to *hear* the views of others. The chair understands that personal views on issues must often be modulated and sometimes sacrificed to those of others. Expressing personal positions after everyone else has had their say is nearly always better.

Communication

Trustees appreciate hearing from their chair directly from time to time. Along with the occasional memo or fax, the personal phone call goes a long way toward establishing and maintaining rapport and the flow of information. This takes time, but it is always a good investment. They want to hear from their president or chancellor, too, of course, and thus coordination is important. The chair should remember that good communication with the president is a two-way proposition; there is room for initiative here as well.

Objectivity

Ideology, arrogance, or insensitivity, especially on the part of the chair, have no place in the boardroom. The chair should be seen as having a sense of fairness and openness on all the issues and information that come before the board. This is especially important in maintaining good rapport with the chief executive and staff. How the chair treats the receipt of "bad news" or rumors, for example, has much to do with building trust.

Sensitivity and Decisiveness

Boards need strong leaders and so do chief executives. When the time comes to make difficult decisions among competing options and when these decisions are within the chair's prerogatives, the chair must take the lead. This can be done without sacrificing sen-

sitivity to the opinions of others, most especially the chief executive's views. Trust is built on the chair's ability to explain his or her
position clearly, decisively, and consistently once discussion is
concluded.

Influence

The chair should be well connected with those outside the institution or system who can do it some good. This circumstance argues
for the careful selection of the chair, but he or she must also be
willing to use such influence when it best serves the interests of the
institution.

Foresight

Fortunate are the chief executive, board, and institution when they
have a chair who possesses the ability to predict likely consequences
of proposed actions or a decision not to act. The chair's ability to
read the likely reactions of the trustees, for example, can be immensely helpful to the president.

Presiding Skills

The chair accepts the responsibility for helping the board to accomplish its aims. Such leadership is exercised particularly through
his or her ability to conduct good meetings. Chapter Eighteen provides some useful advice about conducting meetings.

There are several other qualities to be sought in the chair.
The chief executive normally has only one place to look for dependable and consistent support in his or her increasingly difficult role
and that is to the board. And the elected leader of the board bears
much of the responsibility on this score. Ideally, the chair is capable
of being a trusted adviser and even friend. He or she must be accessible to the president and alert to his or her professional and personal
needs, morale, health, and welfare. The board chair should likewise
be concerned about recognizing any and all special contributions of
the president's spouse. Keeping confidences and willingly taking
some of the heat off the president are also among the chair's respon-

sibilities. The chair should likewise take the lead in acknowledging the appreciation of the board for a job well done. Trustees should be loving critics. But there is also much room for praise. Chapter Eight elaborates how a board can support its chief executive, especially through its chair.

The Chair's Responsibilities

Most of the chair's responsibilities fall into four broad categories. They are to be knowledgeable about the institution in all of its complexity, to develop ways to strengthen the effectiveness of the board, to speak for the board when appropriate, and to serve as the conscience and disciplinarian of the board. In sum, the chair's job is to motivate trustees and lead the board in partnership with the chief executive.

To Be Knowledgeable

A common lament of chief executives is that their boards are more comfortable with immediate, short-term matters than with helping to shape a vision for the long term. The chair should be the most knowledgeable of all trustees about the institution as a prerequisite to helping the board hold a fix on the horizon. Maintaining a sense of direction and clear purpose is a difficult but essential responsibility.

First, being knowledgeable means having a command of the information—the statistics, the strengths and weaknesses of major programs and services, the senior officers, the condition of the physical plant, and so on. But it also means keeping abreast of demographic trends, emerging issues and trends in higher education, the changing political landscape, economic developments, and so on. The chair must be a voracious reader.

Second, the chair should perennially ask these two questions: Are we addressing the *real* issues that set, affect, and maintain the course of the institution? Are we making the best use of our time and energy? The chair should help the board and president to see themselves as others see them.

The university is an exceedingly complex web of traditions, values, decision makers, constituencies, and individual faculty entrepreneurs, and it has enormous resistance to change. The university has been likened to a giant super tanker that requires considerable time and space to change course—the secret of the academy's strength for centuries and, some would argue, its weakness. The chair's ability to explain and defend the institution's uniqueness and complexity enables him or her to help the president navigate the institution through troubled water.

To Strengthen the Effectiveness of the Board

The chair and president should periodically discuss how the board is doing in meeting its responsibilities. All boards can be and do better. A thorough and candid diagnosis may follow along these lines: On what specific dimensions is the board especially strong and weak? Are the committees functioning well? Which are and are not, and why? Are board agendas and supporting materials on target? Do the trustees likely share our assessment or do we need to test our conclusions with them? The next order of business is for the chair and president to develop a strategy to fix what may be broken by setting a strategy with specific goals and objectives within a realistic time frame.

Chapter Twenty addresses the need for all boards to periodically conduct self-assessments, but the process begins with private and candid deliberation between the board chair and chief executive. The fact that only about 42 percent of all types of independent boards of higher education reported conducting a self-study of their performance within the past five years is discouraging (see Resource B).

The chair has a key role in new trustee orientation as well; first by insisting that a solid and interesting program be designed, and second by actively participating in it. Surprisingly, a recent survey by the Association of Governing Boards reveals that about 25 percent of all independent boards still do not provide such programs (see Resource B).

To Speak for the Board

The chair will be called upon to explain, defend, or advocate a variety of board deliberations, decisions, or institutional actions.

Reporters love ambush interviews and know how to use the telephone. Faculty and student leaders understandably like to hear from a board spokesperson from time to time, as do alumni leaders, athletic boosters, and civic leaders. This responsibility should be understood and accepted by board chairs in concert with chief executive encouragement and guidance.

Who should take the lead depends on the situation, the issue, and the anticipated reactions of those most directly affected by what is said and by whom. This is a matter that calls for good judgment by the chair and president, however. The best rules of thumb are to remember that the integrity of the institution and the presidency must be first priorities, to avoid speaking about a matter that is clearly within the president's portfolio (except in the most compelling or unusual circumstance), and to fully disclose what is or should be in the public domain. One mark of an effective board is the tradition or practice accepted by all trustees whereby inquiries or requests for comment are referred to the board chair or president.

To Be the Conscience and Disciplinarian of the Board

Another characteristic of a good board is its ability to keep its house in order—no small task if some trustees believe, mistakenly, that they have legal rights or responsibilities as individual board members. They do not.

Occasionally the chair must admonish, cajole, or take the misguided or inexperienced trustee to the woodshed for a private and candid conversation. The need for such initiatives will be infrequent, but the chair should not be reluctant to meet this responsibility. There is no place for factionalism among trustees or grandstanding by the occasional trustee who may believe he or she has a corner on wisdom. How the chair handles such delicate situations determines the measure of respect earned from the trustees and president.

Furthermore, there is justifiable concern about the decline in ethical standards in academe, about conflicts of interest in the boardroom, and about violations of individual rights to privacy. In serving the public trust, the board and president look to the chair to help them balance what has been labeled a trilemma: the mandate of the institution and board to do their job, the right of the public to know, and the individual's right to privacy (Cleveland, 1985). The chair more than any other trustee or institutional officer serves as gatekeeper in matters of organizational conscience. He or she sets the moral, ethical, and legal tone for the entire board through personal example and by being its conscience.

There Can Be Only One Chief Executive

The academic presidency is increasingly beleaguered, according to the report of the Commission on Strengthening Presidential Leadership (1984). The ever-increasing multiplicity of expectations from group and individual stakeholders has taken its toll on the president's ability to provide academic leadership, and one of the sources of pressure is the board itself.

Trustees understandably expect a great deal from their president or chancellor; their own effectiveness is determined in large measure by the president's competence, after all. Successful presidents spend a large measure of their time with trustees, for trustees, and on trustees. Chief executives accept the fact that their and their institution's effectiveness will be little better than the effectiveness of the board. Thus, trustee education and board development is a presidential responsibility.

On a few basic matters there should be no ambiguity between board and chief executive. There can only be one chief executive; neither the chair nor the board are capable of substituting their judgments on matters properly reserved for the president or chancellor. While the chair must manage the board, he or she must have sustained and committed help from the chief executive. Finally, although the chair and the president share responsibility for leading the board, there are some particular expectations of the president in this regard.

The Chief Executive's Responsibilities

The president should accept responsibility for educating the board, keeping the trustees promptly informed to avoid surprises, preparing the board and its committees for their work, and implementing the policy decisions of the board with dispatch. All of these matters require help, which has led to an emerging profession. The professional staff position of board secretary continues to develop within the field of administration (Smotony, 1993).

To Educate the Board

Whether the board gives a clear mandate for the president to be or not to be the chief educator of the board, he or she should assume the role. Virtually every board meeting should have an educational component in one of three categories: in-service trustee development, academic programs, and trends and issues in higher education that are especially relevant to the future of the institution.

This education calls for some reserved meeting time and creativity on the president's part. A timely article provided in advance for discussion; a faculty member who has just returned from participating in an exchange program; a guest speaker on the responsibilities of trusteeship, higher education finance, or fund raising; a student newspaper editor who can share student perspectives on issues confronting the institution—all are obvious ideas that can inform and engage the board.

Other ideas are distributing an informative set of multiple-choice questions (and answers) that cover basic institutional facts and characteristics to enable the individual trustee to assess his or her personal knowledge; asking a trustee who attended a regional or national meeting to report highlights to the board; and inviting a trustee to engage the board in a discussion of a subject related to his or her other volunteer or career experience that may have relevance to the institution. Board members will have other ideas.

Of special note is an apparent trend for boards to designate one meeting each year as a retreat or special workshop to address long-range issues that are affecting the institution. Such a meeting provides the opportunity to help trustees review their performance and renew their commitment.

To Keep Trustees Promptly Informed

The doctrine of "no surprises" prevails: bad news and good news must be provided to trustees as soon as practical before it is delivered by someone else. The need for confidentiality sometimes presents problems, but it should not be used to rationalize waiting for an executive session. The fax machine offers new opportunities, but the telephone works best in spite of the time it requires. Trustees like to hear their president's voice.

To Prepare Trustees for Their Meetings

Trustees expect their chief executive and staff to prepare good agendas with solid supporting material in advance of meetings. The president should solicit ideas from the trustees for future agendas and to otherwise help the board members to set priorities for the use of their time. While they do not mind occasional written materials distributed at committee and board meetings, these should be the exception rather than the rule. Financial data should *always* be sent in advance except in very unusual circumstances, particularly if action on them is required or expected.

Trustees often complain that they get either too much paper and information or too little, but they universally admire good presentation, occasional use of slides or other visual aids, tightly written executive summaries, information and analysis rather than raw numbers, and evidence of good proofreading.

To Implement Board Policies Promptly

Promptly implementing board policies is an obvious responsibility, but it sometimes becomes a source of needless tension between chief executives and their boards. The key to success is threefold: promptly and accurately capturing the board action, decision, or policy; giving good feedback as soon as possible, with information about how the implementation process seems to be going; and providing subsequent assessment of the impact of the board action.

Shared Responsibilities

In sum, the board chair and president share the responsibility for leading the board. Trustees, like any group in any enterprise, will rise only to the level of expectation held for them by their leaders.

Together, the chair and the president should clarify what is needed and expected; design a game plan to strengthen the effectiveness of the board; continuously discuss how the talents, experiences, and influence of individual trustees can be used to the advantage of the institution; and work together to motivate their colleagues to higher levels of performance. When trusteeship is rewarding, the chair and president have made it so.

CHAPTER 20

Assessing
Board Performance

Barbara E. Taylor

Colleges and universities depend on their boards for skilled leadership, and yet few boards operate as effectively as they might. Reflecting on this problem, researchers and practitioners have cited regular assessment as an essential tool for improving board performance.

The Case for Board Assessment

Alderfer remarked that "a key factor" of successful boards is the presence of "an active mechanism for the board to review its own structure and performance" (1986, p. 50). Studies of employees and groups have shown a connection between regular appraisal and improved performance (Lawler, 1973; Zander, 1982), and recent empirical research has demonstrated that one feature of effective independent college boards is their habit of engaging in self-reflection and seeking feedback on their performance (Chait, Holland, and Taylor, 1991). Houle emphasized this point by asserting that "the capacity for self-criticism is the surest impetus for improving the quality of the board and the work it does" (1989, p. 157).

There is little mystery to the connection between assessment and better performance. Skillful assessment produces systematic feedback on performance that boards otherwise would not receive.

As Zander (1982, p. 113) indicated, "when members get no feedback on their group's performance . . . they tend to believe that the output of their group has been good, that they can be satisfied the unit has succeeded. Members who get little feedback also expect their group will do well in days to come and do not fear failure. No news is good news." Few trustees have contact with a variety of boards, and so most lack broad experience on which to base comparative judgments about their accomplishments. What is experienced on a particular board is usually assumed to be acceptable performance.

As volunteer groups, moreover, college and university boards have a particular problem. A common view is that expecting boards to be self-critical and concerned about improving their performance is unfair because, after all, trustees are uncompensated volunteers with time-consuming professional and personal commitments that usually take precedence over board responsibilities. But board assessment need not be extremely time-consuming, and the improvements that may result from the assessment process are likely to make board service far more satisfying. (See Chait and Taylor, 1989, for a discussion of some of the frustrations that members of underperforming and dysfunctional boards feel.)

There are other reasons to take the need for board assessment seriously. Boards are usually involved in appraising the performance of the chief executive, and many also require that faculty and staff be evaluated regularly. It may strike constituents as unfair when a board that imposes assessment requirements on others is unwilling to evaluate its own performance.

Moreover, most boards of independent institutions are formally accountable to themselves alone (assuming that they act in accordance with the law and the charter of the institution). But if they are seen as ineffective or intransigent, they risk losing the support of donors, parents, prospective students, sponsoring churches, and other key stakeholders.

Finally, a board is a corporate entity usually composed of individual achievers. One of the most difficult lessons for any trustee to learn is that the activities of an individual board member, regardless of how valuable, are no substitute for group strength and success. Regular board assessment helps create a sense of collective responsibility and achievement, and the candor that honest self-reflection entails can help bind board members together in pursuit of common goals.

Assessment and Board Development

Assessment is just one facet of a continuing board development effort that all boards and their leadership, including the board chair and the president, should plan and undertake. Board development has both formal and informal aspects; that is, it includes specific activities aimed at enhancing board performance and it also emanates naturally from a board operating style that encourages openness to innovation, tolerance for diverse opinions, and an emphasis on trustee learning. Some aspects of this broad concept of board development include

- Orientation programs that inform new board members about the history, mission, and characteristics of the institution and about the role and responsibilities of the board.
- Continuing education in the form of workshops and conferences, common readings, issue-oriented discussions during board meetings, or board retreats aimed at learning about the institution or the responsibilities of the board.
- Periodic determination of goals and priorities by the board in support of its own responsibilities or the larger goals of the college or university.
- An environment of openness within the board and between the board and institutional leaders that encourages careful analysis of problems, brainstorming, receptivity to questions by trustees, and willingness to take constituent views into account.
- Regular opportunities for social interaction that help trustees know one another as individuals. This knowledge contributes to solidifying the internal relationships that bind trustees together as a corporate unit.
- Opportunities for social and substantive interaction between the board and important constituents such as faculty, students, alumni, and parents in order to reinforce the responsibility of the board to others and to keep trustees apprised of the needs and aspirations of other institutional stakeholders.

Conducting Board Assessments

The process of assessing board performance has been advanced significantly in recent years. Higher education boards probably have more experience with it than those of other enterprises. Many helpful lessons have been learned, and new tools are available.

Setting Goals and Standards for Achievement

A prerequisite for constructive board assessment is the articulation of standards and goals against which performance can be measured. Consider, for example, a few of the various possible indicators of success that might be taken as meaningful by individual members of a board: 100 percent attendance at board meetings, good relations with the faculty, lack of controversy within the board, lots of free exchange within the board, fund-raising success, never disagreeing with the president, and frequently offering the president candid feedback.

These indicators are diverse and some are contradictory, yet one or more might reasonably be held as valid by any given member of a board. Therefore, even if each trustee were willing and able to assess the performance of the board accurately, board members might well come to very different conclusions about the strengths and weaknesses of the board.

Setting standards and goals for board performance should be part of a long-term program of board development that requires free and open exchange within the board and between the board and the president. These exchanges should concern institutional priorities and the role of the board in advancing those priorities. For example, the role of the board may include direct involvement in goal attainment, such as helping attain a fund-raising goal, as well as participation in developmental activities that strengthen the ability of a board to function capably on behalf of the institution. Such activities may include, among others, efforts to interact more effectively with constituents or to enhance communication within the board.

Three views of what constitutes exemplary board performance are found in the literature, and embedded in each view are assumptions about the fundamental goals of a board. The first and by far the most prevalent of these centers on the responsibilities of boards, such as those outlined in Chapter Six. The prevalent as-

sumption with this view is that a board that performs these responsibilities well is effective (Paltridge, 1980).

The second view concentrates on satisfaction with internal
board operations such as meetings, active participation by trustees,
board leadership, bylaws, committee structures, attendance, and
quality of meetings (see Chapters Seventeen and Eighteen).

The third view considers board success almost entirely from
the perspective of group process—the *means* by which goals are
achieved. In this sense, process becomes as important as substance,
and performance is judged not only according to whether or not the
money was raised or the new program launched, but also by the
breadth of involvement by constituents and the satisfaction of stakeholders with the results (Chait, Holland, and Taylor, 1991).

In actuality, aspects of all three approaches can be combined
to reflect a particular board's understanding of what constitutes
exemplary performance. It is wise to think broadly about what success is and to consider seriously the proposition that satisfactory
performance includes tackling the right issues, using the right processes, and organizing the board in ways that support both good
substance and good process.

Before embarking on any board development or assessment
effort, it is important for trustees, with their president, to discuss
their assumptions about what constitutes effective board activity,
what the short- and long-term goals of the board are, and what
indicators would signify success.

Self-Assessment Instruments

Various self-assessment instruments exist to assist boards in gauging their performance. As valuable as such instruments can be as
springboards for discussion, most cannot claim to present an accurate picture of the performance of a board. Ashford (1989) found
that self-assessments of performance are rarely accurate because the
environment provides few unambiguous clues about what successful performance is, opinions vary so much about what constitute
valid indicators of success, and in order to maintain a positive self-
image, most people tend to reject or reinterpret negative information about performance.

In research focused specifically on independent college and

university boards, Chait and Taylor (1987) examined the results of self-assessments by sixty-one boards of public and independent institutions that had completed a frequently used evaluation instrument and found extremely small variations in responses across institutions and among individual board members. Although experience and intuition suggest that board performance varies considerably among institutions, most board members in this study reported that their boards were performing at an above-average level across the range of their responsibilities. In other words, there is serious doubt that these self-assessments provided an accurate picture of actual board performance.

However, it is important to note that a board does not need a perfect self-assessment instrument in order to benefit from using one. The key to the value of most instruments is found in the interpretation of what might seem to be rather fine differences in responses by individuals, the skill of a facilitator who can assist the board in understanding what the instrument might be reflecting (and not reflecting), and, most of all, the willingness of board members to reflect candidly on their performance and what can be done to improve it.

Perhaps the most frequently used board self-assessment instrument is the "Self-Study Criteria" of the Association of Governing Boards of Universities and Colleges (AGB) (see Resource C), which is intended primarily to be used in conjunction with AGB's board mentor workshop, a self-study retreat facilitated by a specially trained peer trustee. Fundamentally, the "Self-Study Criteria" ask trustees to rate the performance of their board across a variety of substantive areas, such as institutional planning, academic oversight, and fund raising, as well as with respect to the state of relations between the board and such significant constituents as the president, students, and faculty. Individual responses to the criteria are aggregated and used as a springboard for discussion at the workshop, where the facilitator encourages the board to reflect on reasons for variations in ratings of particular criteria.

Other board assessment instruments include

- A simple rating scale for boards developed by Houle (1989), which asks trustees to rate their board in twelve areas dealing with board structure, constituent relations, and goal setting.

- A board self-rating schedule developed by Savage (1982), which invites trustees to rate the structure, knowledge, practices, performance, relationships, and other qualities of their board.
- A questionnaire created by Chait, Holland, and Taylor (1991) in connection with an empirical study of board effectiveness, which is used to assess board performance in six competency areas, most of which concern board process. This questionnaire has been subjected to extensive field testing and revision and to date shows modest evidence of validity and reliability. However, the authors' less than spectacular success in this effort highlights again the difficulty of creating a self-assessment instrument that is capable of reflecting actual board performance.

Use of Outside Consultants and Facilitators

Board assessment efforts can profit greatly from the use of outside consultants and facilitators. The right person can bring important qualities to the effort. The first quality is objectivity. A skilled facilitator can listen objectively and reflect back to the board what is being said, noting areas of dissension and disagreement. If selected properly, the facilitator will not be seen as having a particular ax to grind, as might be the case if a board member or the president were to act as facilitator.

Another quality is the knowledge of board performance. An experienced facilitator should be knowledgeable about board performance and able to help a board understand how it might go about enhancing its efforts. Furthermore, the facilitator should have skill as a moderator. A capable facilitator can often read between the lines of a self-assessment instrument and help a board understand its own view of its performance, as well as help structure group discussions and exercises that encourage creative thinking and consensus building.

Consultants and facilitators can be used in a variety of ways in board assessment efforts. Most commonly, they are used to help plan and facilitate board retreats and other extended sessions aimed at goal setting, assessment, and board development. However, they may be used to lead shorter board development and assessment sessions during or in conjunction with regular board meetings at which board responsibilities, goals, and performance are discussed.

When relationships within the board or between the board and one of its constituent groups have broken down, a consultant can be retained to interview all parties and provide feedback to the board about the problem and potential solutions.

A consultant may be retained to conduct an assessment of board performance by observing the board, reviewing documents such as board and committee minutes, and conducting confidential interviews with trustees and constituents. This is done quite rarely, and it is not a substitute for honest self-appraisal by the board. However, as one part of a larger effort to understand as thoroughly as possible the performance of the board, an honest assessment by a knowledgeable outsider is likely to benefit a board.

Role of Board Leadership

The leaders of a board, particularly the chair and president, play a crucial role in board development and assessment activities. Essential to success in any form of board assessment is the ability of board leaders to create a climate in which candor and open discussion about the responsibilities and performance of the board can flourish. Board leaders do this by encouraging trustee participation and maintaining an environment in which there are few "untouchable" topics. While such practices encourage good decision making and a high level of trustee commitment, they are useful specifically in preparing a board to assess its performance honestly. In other words, the habit of candor, developed in other contexts, carries over to the self-assessment process.

Board leaders are especially central to encouraging ongoing and less formal approaches to board assessment. We tend to equate assessment with the periodic board retreat or appointment of a consultant to undertake a major study of the operations of the board. On the contrary, assessment should be a normal part of the regular operations of the board. Some useful approaches follow.

The chair can ask board members to complete a short questionnaire that inquires about desirable board goals, attitudes toward their trusteeship, and ways to improve the performance of the board. Or the chair, perhaps with the president, can seek responses to such questions by interviewing individual board members.

At the end of a regular board meeting, the chair can go around the table and invite trustees to comment orally or in writing on the meeting. Was it interesting and well conducted? Did the board consider issues of real consequence for the institution? Did trustees have on a timely basis the information that they needed to make good decisions? What could be done to make the next meeting of the board even more profitable?

At least one chair, with the president's assistance, prepares an occasional "pop quiz" that is distributed to trustees at a board meeting. The quiz might include simple multiple-choice or fill-in-the-blank questions about the budget, enrollments, or faculty of the college, or about the obligations and stated priorities of the board. Trustees complete the quiz individually and their responses are not collected, but the board has great fun hearing the correct responses to the quiz and comparing scores. The exercise reinforces in an enjoyable way the obligation trustees assume to be informed about the college and the board.

All boards make mistakes, but too few reflect on their errors and the lessons they learned. A chair can encourage the board to step back after a significant mistake and discuss what happened, why, and what lessons the board should draw from the incident. In this way, boards learn how to avoid similar errors in the future and, perhaps equally important, learn the habit of candor within the group.

It was argued above that a board must set goals for itself. Board leaders can reinforce the importance of these goals and the commitment of the board to them by leading trustees in an annual review of the successes and failures of the board in achieving its priorities.

With assistance from the president, the chair can lead the board in collecting periodic external feedback on its performance from senior administrators, faculty leaders, students, and alumni. While valuable, this exercise can be tricky for two reasons. First, it can be difficult for some constituents, especially senior administrators, to be completely candid. One solution is to ask a consultant or other neutral third party to interview individuals privately and report their comments anonymously. A second problem is that relatively few faculty, students, or nontrustee alumni know the work of the board intimately enough to comment knowledgeably on it. This suggests that the logical people to talk to are constituent representatives to the board or its committees, or student and faculty leaders who have regular commerce with the board, although in such cases the board should be careful not to assume that the opinions expressed are necessarily representative.

Board leadership should encourage the creation of a board committee on trusteeship that is charged with evaluating the performance of individual trustees and monitoring the achievements of the board as a whole. The committee, which in many cases replaces the nominating committee, helps plan orientation programs, retreats, and other board development activities and can advise the chair and president about areas of board weakness and suggested remedies.

Board Retreats

Periodic retreats can be powerful board development tools. Many boards recount as a watershed the experience of going away together as a group and spending a day or two discussing nothing but the goals, aspirations, and performance of the board.

For far too many boards, a retreat is the only setting in which open discussion is encouraged, larger issues are tackled, attention is given to the board as a corporate whole, and time is set aside for social interaction. Although most boards could improve their normal operations by adopting some of the features associated with retreats, the periodic retreat still provides an important opportunity to step back from the press of normal business and focus exclusively on the performance of the board. Capably handled, retreats can pay major dividends.

The discussion of retreats that follows draws on Savage (1982), which is the most thorough treatment available of the steps involved in planning and carrying out a board retreat. Primary leadership for proposing and developing a retreat should rest with the chair and the president. In the absence of individual and mutual support for the effort, a retreat is unlikely to succeed.

There is a lesson for presidents, in particular, in this emphasis on joint responsibility. Many chief executives, thinking that assessment is good for boards, go about planning and offering a retreat with token or no involvement by trustees. In the absence of real support for the effort by all or the vast majority of board members, the retreat will not succeed. If board support cannot be secured, the president and chair would do better to embark on a less intensive (and perhaps less threatening) series of board development and assessment activities, such as those mentioned earlier in this chapter, and accustom the board gradually to the idea of more thorough assessment in a retreat setting.

The steps involved in developing and conducting a successful retreat can sound time-consuming and onerous, but Savage emphasizes that "every step the board takes in this [retreat] process is a model of how the board should normally operate" (1982, p. 13). That is, what may look like an overly complex approach to securing board input into, support for, and involvement in the process actually reinforces the authority, accountability, and commitment of the board.

The following activities—agreement on shared assumptions, a profile of the board, formal action by the board, appointing an agenda committee, information gathering and agenda development, conducting the retreat, and postretreat action—form the foundation for a successful retreat.

Agreement on Shared Assumptions

At the outset, the chair and president should reach agreement concerning their assumptions about the board's role and goals, its relationships with important constituents, the function of board development and assessment activities, the qualities the institution values in its board members, the relationship between board and institutional priorities, problems the institution is facing, and any other matters that seem pertinent to setting the priorities of the board and analyzing its performance. Individuals hold such assumptions but rarely articulate them, and when the implicit assumptions board leaders hold are in conflict, a successful board development program is difficult or impossible to achieve. If necessary, other board members or an outside consultant can be brought in to facilitate agreement between the chair and president on issues deemed crucial to the success of board development.

After reaching general agreement about common assumptions, board development priorities, and the specific idea of a retreat, the chair should indicate to the board that a retreat is under consideration, explain its possible purposes, describe steps to be taken subsequently, and invite the input of trustees.

Profile of the Board

At this stage, alone or with a consultant, the board should conduct a preliminary review of its own goals, structure, and practices, both to test the group's readiness to undertake a more thorough analysis of its performance and to highlight issues that need further consideration in a retreat setting. The board chair, members of the committee on trusteeship, or a consultant, with advice from the president, might interview individual board members to inquire about their experiences as trustees; their perceptions of the board's strengths, weaknesses, and priorities; their impressions of the problems facing the institution; and their general interest in the idea of a retreat.

Formal Action by the Board

Once assumptions are clarified and a preliminary assessment of the board has been undertaken, the chair should ask the board for a formal resolution agreeing to proceed with plans for a retreat. If an outside facilitator is to be used, the resolution should identify the person, and, if possible, he or she should be present at the meeting and introduced to the board. The resolution should specify the purposes of the retreat, the time and commitment involved, and the obligation of board members to be present and to participate.

Although this step in the preparation process for the retreat may seem overly formal, it is important to ensure that no trustee is surprised by the retreat or its purposes and that all board members assume a sense of responsibility for the success of the retreat. Even if a handful of trustees remain unconvinced of the value of the effort, they should not feel that they were misled or hoodwinked into supporting it.

Appointing an Agenda Committee

At this stage, the chair appoints an agenda committee to prepare for the retreat, and if the board decides not to use an outside facilitator, this committee also prepares to conduct the retreat. The agenda committee may be comprised of members of the committee on trusteeship or it may be an ad hoc group. In either case, the board chair and the president should be committee members, and the facilitator, if any, should work closely with the committee to develop plans for the retreat. The major responsibilities of the agenda committee are to determine the specific purposes of the retreat, set its location and dates, develop the agenda, and issue invitations.

The site should be quiet and comfortable, located away from campus, offer overnight accommodations and dining facilities, and be accessible to as many trustees as possible. The dates of the retreat should be selected to encourage maximum participation, and the retreat should extend at minimum over a twenty-four–hour period to allow for sufficient meeting and social time.

The agenda for the retreat must be carefully planned, as detailed below, and the assistance of a skilled facilitator is strongly encouraged, especially for boards not accustomed to regular retreats. However, the agenda committee should resist the temptation to turn all further responsibility for the retreat over to the facilitator. If the board is to gain maximum benefit from the experience, its members must retain ownership of the planning effort.

In order to derive maximum benefit from a board assessment retreat, attendance should be limited to trustees and the president. The presence of spouses and administrators other than the president can be distracting and undermine candor. (Other retreats, such as those intended for strategic planning or board education, may profitably include spouses, administrators, faculty, students, and others.)

Information Gathering and Agenda Development

Boards and facilitators preparing for a retreat usually find it useful to gather detailed information about trustees' perceptions of the board's responsibilities, priorities, and performance. Available questionnaires were described earlier in this chapter, though the agenda committee and facilitator may wish to modify whatever standard instrument is selected in order to reflect the goals and priorities of a particular board.

Instruments should be completed privately and anonymously, and returned to the facilitator or to the institution so that responses can be aggregated. The facilitator and the agenda committee can then prepare a specific agenda, based in part on responses to the survey.

If possible, the proposed agenda should be shared with the full board for comments and modifications. If time prohibits this, the committee should circulate the agenda as widely as possible. Again, the idea is to enhance as much as possible the commitment of all trustees to the retreat process.

Conducting the Retreat

The facilitator or other individual chairing the retreat assumes responsibility for keeping the meeting on schedule, encouraging each trustee to feel a sense of ownership of the process and of the board's performance, and ensuring that the retreat concludes with specific suggestions for postretreat action.

The retreat and its agenda should be based on the following:

- A clear statement of the purposes of the retreat that are reasonable and achievable in the time allotted and at the board's current level of commitment and sophistication.
- Thorough discussion by the board of the results of the self-study instrument, if any. To facilitate this process, each trustee should be sent a copy of the survey results at least a week before the retreat.
- Small group sessions that encourage participation by everyone in devising strategies for enhancing board performance.
- Plenary sessions to enable small groups to report their findings and for the board as a whole to come to consensus about next steps.
- Leadership opportunities for as many trustees as possible. The

facilitator, president, and chair should not dominate the proceedings.
- Sufficient flexibility to accommodate unpredictable shifts in
  trustees' energy levels or interest in pursuing particular issues.
- Social time to enable board members to relax and build their
  relationships with one another.

The retreat should end with a reasonable consensus among
trustees about board goals, issues the board faces, priorities for improving group performance, and steps to be taken after the retreat
concludes. Trustees can be invited to complete an evaluation of the
experience that the chair, president, and agenda committee can use
in planning future board development activities.

Postretreat Action

On the basis of the discussions and recommendations from the retreat, the facilitator should write a report that summarizes the highlights of each session, the agreements reached, and recommendations
for further action. The agenda committee should review the report
for accuracy and completeness and prepare to commend it to the full
board for adoption. So that the entire board can be brought into the
spirit of the retreat, the chair or a member of the agenda committee
should contact trustees who were unable to attend the retreat and
brief them about it.

Once the report is reviewed and adopted by the entire board,
the chair should assign responsibility for specific tasks and priorities to the board, particular committees, or the president. The
board should be involved in monitoring progress toward achieving
the goals that were adopted at or subsequent to the retreat. Those
responsible for follow-up should report periodically on progress
achieved and seek advice on modifications. It is essential that the
chair and president demonstrate ongoing and visible leadership in
carrying out the board improvement strategies devised at the retreat.
Not holding a retreat at all would probably be better than failing
to follow up after the event is concluded.

Some boards wisely commit themselves to subsequent board
development retreats, both to monitor progress in achieving goals

set previously and to outline future priorities. This practice reinforces the idea that board development is not a one-time effort but an ongoing responsibility.

Assessment is an important tool for improving board performance and one that is even more useful when viewed in the larger context of an ongoing board development effort. The process of considering and discussing the responsibilities and achievements of the board on a continuing basis, as well as during periodic retreats, can be a powerful device for enhancing board learning and cohesiveness.

Board leaders, including the chair and president, have a special responsibility to educate trustees about the value of performance assessment and to create opportunities for the board to reflect on its aspirations and performance. The result will be a more able and committed board with the self-knowledge and internal strength required to provide skillful institutional leadership.

RESOURCE A

Statement
of Board Member
Responsibilities

Several important trends in the trusteeship of independent higher education have been observed in the past decade that help to explain its relatively good health. Those responsible for recruiting trustees are clarifying expectations for prospective nominees, rather than downplaying the commitment required. New trustee orientation programs have become more substantive, in-service education programs are provided more frequently, and periodic self-study programs to help the board examine its effectiveness are much more accepted practices. And, as difficult as it is, many more boards are assessing the commitment and performance of trustees who are eligible for reelection to the board. Nominating committees (or committees on trustees) are doing more than simply maintaining lists of prospective board members and automatically recommending incumbents for new terms.

Pro forma renewal of terms is still a problem in many institutions, however, and trustees remain reluctant to judge their peers. The fact that many more academic boards are setting a limit on the number of consecutive terms and requiring a one-year hiatus or "sabbatical" counters the earlier practice of, in effect, life terms. Given the importance of *every* trustee position, individual performance assessment and the safety net of a required hiatus are necessary. The health and welfare of the institution require that every board member be candidly assessed by a responsible group of trustees whose performance and commitment are well known and highly respected—but by what criteria?

Many boards have adopted statements of trustee responsibilities, which are their own definitions of stewardship, to serve multiple purposes. The process of drafting and adopting such written statements is by itself healthy and sends a clear signal to everyone that the bar is being raised. Statements of trustee responsibility clarify expectations for prospective board members (before they accept nomination) and provide criteria by which incumbents eligible for re-election can be assessed. Good judgment is still required by those trustees charged with the responsibility of ensuring an effective board membership, of course, but guidelines such as those in Exhibit A.1. can inform it.

Exhibit A.1. Statement of Responsibilities.

We, the members of the board of trustees of [*name of institution*] recognize that one of our responsibilities is to select our successors. These guidelines serve to clarify what is expected of those invited to join us in serving the university [*college, school, or seminary*] and the public trust we hold both individually and collectively.

We, each and every one, pledge:

Our Commitment by

1. Faithfully and consistently participating in board and committee meetings, other board functions, and as many campus events as possible. The institution asks for a small percentage of our time, and although it is a large gift, given the many other demands on us, our university needs all of it.
2. Preparing for meetings by reading the agenda and its supporting material, and participating in those meetings by sharing our experiences and skills and asking good questions. The chief executive and staff do their best to engage us in matters affecting the course of the university, and our responsibility is to make the best use of limited meeting time to make the best possible decisions.
3. Contributing to the annual fund and to capital campaigns to the very best of our ability. If we do not see the value of our university and help to meet its financial needs, why should anyone else?
4. Serving the university as a whole, rather than representing the interests of any constituency, according to our individual judgment and conscience.

Exhibit A.1. Statement of Responsibilities, Cont'd.

---

5. Helping to open doors on behalf of the university to secure the financial, human, and political resources necessary for the institution to accomplish its mission and purposes successfully.

6. Taking advantage of opportunities to say something good about the university to the various groups with whom we have influence. While we contribute much to the university, it also contributes to our personal growth; we are here to learn but also to teach the outside world enthusiastically about our institution.

7. Accepting leadership positions and other special assignments when asked. Our board is committed to periodically rotating leaders and asks that we each take our turn when it comes. Our work on behalf of the university between committee and board meetings can make an enormous difference.

Our Best Effort to Protect the Integrity of the University and the Board by

8. Avoiding situations that could cause even the appearance of a conflict of interest beyond those that may have been known to exist at the time of election to the board. It is binding on each of us that we make full disclosure of potentially problematic relationships, especially those that involve direct or indirect receipt of university funds. And we accept the possibility that disclosure alone may not be, in the judgment of the board, an adequate response.

9. Maintaining confidentiality of the executive sessions of the board that may involve sensitive personnel or other matters.

10. Speaking for the board or the institution only when authorized to do so by the board. Speaking for the board is the president's and board chair's responsibility.

11. Refraining from asking for special favors of the president or staff. The president reports to the board as a whole, and the staff to the president.

And Our Active Participation by

12. Keeping ourselves informed about the university and trends and issues in higher education that can affect its future.

13. Asking timely and substantive questions, without hesitation, based on our concerns, convictions, and conscience, while supporting the majority decision on issues that are finally reached by the board.

14. Avoiding judgments on the basis of information received from individuals or groups with real or perceived grievance. Substantive information should be referred to the president and/or board chair.

15. Asking for data and information through committee and board meeting work that help the board to address long-term strategies. The service of the university to future generations is being shaped on our watch.

Exhibit A.1. Statement of Responsibilities, Cont'd.

16. Recognizing that it is the board *as a corporate body* that approves university policies and monitors their implementation. The responsibility of the administration is to manage day-to-day business. As individual trustees, we have no special prerogatives except when we convene as a corporate body.
17. Respecting the presidency and publicly supporting the president.
18. Being a good listener and bringing a sense of humor to our deliberations, along with having the determination to say and do what is best for the university in the long haul.

Survey of Independent Governing Board Characteristics, Policies, and Practices

In 1991, the Association of Governing Boards of Universities and Colleges (AGB), with support from the Teachers Insurance Annuity Association–College Retirement Equities Fund (TIAA-CREF), conducted a survey of its member governing boards. Responses were received from 471 independent two- and four-year colleges and universities, theological seminaries, and specialized institutions.

This survey included a section on board composition that allows for comparison with data from other surveys dating back to 1917. However, survey methodologies and sample sizes vary considerably from study to study.

A summary of the major findings from the 1991 AGB survey is provided in Resource B. Because of space limitations, the summary includes some data that are not provided in the tables to follow. Where data are presented in accompanying tables, the summary cites table numbers. Although based on a sample of independent college and university governing boards, the data are believed to be a reliable and a valid representation of the independent sector of higher education. Percentages may not always total 100 percent as a consequence of rounding.

Diversity on Governing Boards

Early in this century, males dominated (97 percent) the membership of governing boards of independent colleges and universities (Nearing, 1917) (see Table B.1). A half-century later, males constituted 88 percent of all trustees (Hartnett, 1969). Female membership grew from 3 percent in 1917 (Nearing, 1917) to 12 percent in 1969 (Hartnett, 1969) to 23 percent in 1991 (see Table B.1). Among independent sector institutions, female representation is highest (26 percent) on boards of two-year colleges.

Whereas 1 percent of all independent board members were reported to be from minority groups in 1969, their representation is 9 percent in 1991 (see Table B.1). African Americans currently account for 6 percent of board members of independent institutions overall and 11 percent of board members of theological institutions (see Table B.1). In 1977, 1 percent of board members were from groups other than whites and African Americans; in 1991 that figure was 3 percent (see Table B.1).

Board Size and Composition

The independent college or university governing board has an average of thirty members. Fourteen percent of boards surveyed include faculty from within the institution as voting members, while 10 percent include students (see Table B.2). Boards of theological institutions include faculty as voting members with about twice the frequency of other independent institutions. Thirty-eight percent of the independent boards surveyed have members from their alumni appointed or elected by the alumni or an alumni association (see Table B.2). Thirty-five percent of independent boards surveyed have members elected or appointed by a sponsoring church body (see Table B.2).

Trustee Terms

The majority of all types of independent boards surveyed, except specialized institution boards, limit the number of consecutive terms that board members may serve (see Table B.3). Ninety-six percent of boards with term limits allow eligibility for reelection to the board after a one-year waiting period (see Table B.3). Board chairs surveyed have served in that position for an average of four years, but nearly one-third are limited to an average of five years as chair of the board.

Board Meetings

Independent boards meet an average of four times per year for four hours per meeting. On average, a board member devotes twenty-seven hours annually to board and committee meetings. Board members of theological institutions commit an average of thirty-one hours per year, whereas two-year board members devote twenty-one hours. (These figures do not include preparation time for meetings or account for other duties between meetings.)

Standing Committees

The standing committees used most frequently by governing boards of independent institutions are, in descending order, executive (81 percent), development (74 percent), finance (73 percent), and academic affairs (72 percent). Table B.4 shows the use of standing committees by type of institution. A typical board committee has eight members. The minority of boards surveyed include faculty and students as voting members of standing committees. Faculty are most frequently voting members on academic affairs (39 percent), student affairs (31 percent), and planning (28 percent). Students are voting members most frequently on student affairs (39 percent), academic affairs (20 percent), and buildings and grounds (15 percent).

Board Staff

Virtually all independent boards surveyed have a designated staff person to assist them with their responsibilities. However, in 94 percent of the cases these are part-time responsibilities combined with other institutional duties (see Table B.8).

Board Policies

About two-thirds of four-year and specialized boards and half of two-year boards surveyed have adopted statements that define what constitutes a conflict of interest for board members. This is an increase from the 48 percent of four-year boards and 43 percent of two-year boards that reported such policies in AGB's 1988 survey (Taylor, 1988). The percentage of boards whose members are required to file disclosure statements on their assets and business affiliations increased from 10 percent in 1988 to 16 percent in 1991. A formal orientation program for new trustees is offered by 75 percent of independent boards, an increase from 61 percent in 1988.

Chief Executive

Incumbent independent college and university presidents have served an average of seven years, whereas their predecessors had served an average of ten years. Table B.11 shows variances in length of service by type of institution or system. In 64 percent of independent institutions, the chief executive serves as a voting member of the governing board of their institution. In descending order, presidents have academic rank, tenure, or both in theological institutions (90 percent), four-year institutions (68 percent), specialized institutions (47 percent), and two-year colleges (27 percent) (see Table B.12).

Twenty-eight percent of four-year independent governing boards have established procedures and written policies to guide the presidential search process (see Table B.9). Thirty-five percent used an executive search firm or other outside consultant to assist in the selection of the current chief executive. Over half of all independent boards surveyed have adopted formal policies to guide the review of chief executive performance (see Table B.9).

Part I: Board Membership

Table B.1. Trustee Gender and Racial/Ethnic Background.

	Type of Institution				
	All Independents %	Two-Year %	Four-Year %	Theological %	Specialized %
Male					
1917	97	*	*	*	*
1969	88	*	*	*	*
1977	85	*	*	*	*
1985	80	79	80	*	*
1991	77	74	77	79	81
Female					
1917	3	*	*	*	*
1969	12	*	*	*	*
1977	15	*	*	*	*
1985	20	21	20	*	*
1991	23	26	23	21	19
White					
1969	99	*	*	*	*
1977	94	*	*	*	*
1985	91	83	98	*	*
1991	91	93	91	83	91
African Americans					
1969	1	*	*	*	*
1977	5	*	*	*	*
1985	6	7	5	*	*
1991	6	5	6	11	6
Hispanic					
1985	>1	0	>1	*	*
1991	1	>1	1	5	1
Other Minorities					
1969	>1	*	*	*	*
1977	1	*	*	*	*
1985	3	10	2	*	*
1991					
Asian	1	>1	1	1	1
Native American	1	2	1	0	>1
Other	>1	>1	>1	>1	>1

*Data not available.

Source: Data abstracted from Nearing, 1917; Hartnett, 1969; Atelsek and Gomberg, 1977; and an AGB survey conducted in 1991.

Table B.2. Institutions with Students, Faculty,
Alumni, and Ex-Officio Representatives as Voting Members.

	Type of Institution			
	Two-Year %	Four-Year %	Theological %	Specialized %
Student(s)	3	9	2	13
Faculty (within the institution)	7	13	29	15
Faculty (other institutions)	31	34	29	11
Alumni elected or appointed by alumni or alumni association	28	55	32	36
All other alumni	59	71	55	53
Members elected or appointed by a sponsoring church body, including ex-officio with vote	41	38	47	4

Table B.3. Trustee Term Limitations.

	Type of Institution			
	Two-Year %	Four-Year %	Theological %	Specialized %
Boards that limit the number of consecutive trustee terms[a]	59	60	61	38
Boards that permit trustees to be re-elected or reappointed[b]	100	96	100	91
Boards that have a mandatory retirement age for trustees	14	28	11	13

[a]The average number of consecutive terms is three for all institutional categories.

[b]The typical waiting period between terms for all institutional categories is one year.

Part Two: Board Structure

Table B.4. Board Committees.

	Type of Institution			
	Two-Year %	Four-Year %	Theological %	Specialized %
Executive	79	82	82	82
Academic affairs	72	74	63	64
Student affairs	55	68	29	40
Planning	21	22	29	38
Development	69	77	71	64
Finance	72	75	55	76
Investment	41	38	24	29
Buildings and grounds	41	54	37	46
Nominating	62	53	47	62
Trusteeship	4	23	29	16

Table B.5. Executive Committee and the Use of Executive Sessions.

	Type of Institution			
	Two-Year %	Four-Year %	Theological %	Specialized %
Boards whose nonexecutive committee members regularly attend executive committee meetings	9	13	7	7
Boards whose formal minutes of executive committee meetings are shared with the full board:				
Yes	92	78	65	75
No; minutes are taken but shared only with executive committee members	4	14	19	16
No formal minutes are taken	4	8	16	9
Boards that routinely use executive sessions (a portion of the meeting restricted to the board members and often the chief executive)	31	46	50	38

Table B.6. Open Meetings.

	Type of Institution			
	Two-Year %	Four-Year %	Theological %	Specialized %
Board meetings are open to the public and media	24	12	28	22
Committee meetings are open to the public and media	21	9	22	17

Table B.7. Board Self-Assessment.

	Type of Institution			
	Two-Year %	Four-Year %	Theological %	Specialized %
Boards that have undertaken a formal self-evaluation within the past five years	35	41	57	46
Boards with self-evaluation policies:				
Board policy requires periodic formal board self-evaluation	10	8	10	26
By tradition, the board evaluates its performance on a regular basis	10	28	14	17
Formal board self-evaluation occurs on an irregular basis	80	67	76	61
Boards that have undertaken formal self-evaluations using an outside facilitator	50	42	57	57

Table B.8. Board Staffing.

	Type of Institution			
	Two-Year %	Four-Year %	Theological %	Specialized %
Boards that employ support staff with the following titles:				
Secretary to the board/ university	4	21	3	6
Assistant to the president	11	22	21	30
Administrative assistant to the president	7	11	5	17
University counsel/ general counsel	0	1	0	2
Other titles	78	44	71	46
Boards with a designated staff person to assist them:				
Full-time	8	6	3	6
Part-time	92	94	97	94
Boards with a staff person who directly reports to the:				
Chief executive	83	91	91	84
Board chair	17	6	3	12
Other	0	3	6	4

Part Three: The Chief Executive

Table B.9. Search for and Assessment of the Chief Executive.

	Type of Institution			
	Two-Year %	Four-Year %	Theological %	Specialized %
Boards with a written board policy or an established procedure to guide the search process for the chief executive officer	21	28	38	27
Boards that used an executive search firm or other outside consultant to assist with the process of selecting the current chief executive	21	35	14	38
Boards with a written board policy to guide the comprehensive review of the chief executive's performance	52	45	65	61

Table B.10. Presidential Contracts.

| | Type of Institution | | | |
	Two-Year %	Four-Year %	Theological %	Specialized %
Boards whose incumbent chief executive currently serves under the terms of a written contract	62	63	43	75
Boards whose chief executive received a written contract at the time of appointment	52	62	61	73

Table B.11. Terms of Chief Executive Service.

| | Type of Institution | | | |
	Two-Year (years)	Four-Year (years)	Theological (years)	Specialized (years)
Average term of current chief executive	5	8	8	7
Average term of previous chief executive	7	10	9	10

Table B.12. Academic Rank and Tenure Status of Chief Executive.

	Type of Institution			
	Two-Year %	Four-Year %	Theological %	Specialized %
Boards whose chief executive officer holds academic rank or tenure:				
Both academic rank and tenure	3	27	49	17
Academic rank only	24	41	41	28
Tenure only	0	>1	0	2

Table B.13. Prior Position of Chief Executive.

	Type of Institution			
	Two-Year %	*Four-Year* %	*Theological* %	*Specialized* %
Positions held by chief executive immediately prior to the current position:				
Chief executive of another higher education institution	14	16	8	15
Administrator in this or another higher education institution	57	60	39	45
Professor in this or another higher education institution	4	7	31	9
Other position within higher education	4	7	0	6
Other position outside of higher education	21	10	22	25

RESOURCE C

Self-Study Criteria
for Independent
Colleges and
Universities

This survey is designed to be completed individually by the board members and chief executives of independent colleges and universities. Its purpose is twofold: to enable trustees to assess the relative strengths and needs of their governing board as a corporate entity and to test the breadth and depth of their knowledge of their responsibilities as individual trustees. Determining how trustees perceive the performance of their boards is a first step toward improvement—toward making a good board better.

This form and others like it, for different types of institutional settings, are available from the Association of Governing Boards of Universities and Colleges (AGB). A *User's Guide* is also available. AGB's Board Mentor Program provides access to qualified facilitators to enable boards to objectively discuss the issues suggested by a consolidated summary of the anonymous responses to the questions in this survey. For more information about this survey form or the Board Mentor Program, please telephone or write to the AGB.

Criterion 1: Institutional Mission and Educational Policy

No institution can be all things to all people. Each institution must decide what its particular mission—its real purpose—is if it is to have sound direction. The mission must be clearly defined so students will know the purposes and objectives of the institution, faculty members will know how to direct their efforts, and the several publics on whom the campus community depends will know what they are supporting.

An official statement that sets forth the specific mission of a college or university should be a cooperative effort of the administration, the faculty, and the governing board. Acting alone, the board lacks the professional experience to define educational goals in detail. Its role is to insure that the mission is clearly stated. Because it stands apart from day-to-day operations, administrative preoccupations, and faculty special interests, the board is in a unique position to lead, seek consensus, and stimulate action.

		Yes	*No*	*Don't Know/ Can't Judge*
1.	Is there a written and officially adopted statement of the mission or purpose of the institution?	___	___	___
2.	In your opinion, is this statement sufficiently clear and useful to serve as a guide to the board, administration, and faculty?	___	___	___
3.	Does the board periodically review its statement of purpose and educational goals, and examine the policies which implement them?	___	___	___
4.	Does the board assume a role in helping to determine whether educational programs are viable			

and consistent with the mission
of the institution?   ___   ___   ___
5. Do you feel that the institution
lives up to its stated mission?   ___   ___   ___

Summary: In relation to this criterion, I feel that the overall performance of the board has been

Very Good ___ Good ___ Barely Adequate ___ Poor ___ Don't Know/Can't Judge ___

Further comments or suggestions related to this criterion:

Criterion 2: Institutional Planning

In the difficult period stretching ahead for higher education, effective planning is increasingly essential. The number and future sources of students should be anticipated, projections of expenses and income need to be studied, the character of the educational program and student services must be considered, and the size of the faculty and its distribution by rank and tenured status are matters to be plotted carefully. The board should be involved in the planning process, and adopted plans should be used by the board as a guide to decision making.

	Yes	*No*	*Don't Know/ Can't Judge*
1. Does the board require, participate in, review, and/or approve comprehensive institutional planning regarding			
a. Enrollments?	___	___	___
b. Staffing?	___	___	___
c. Physical facilities?	___	___	___
d. Availability of resources?	___	___	___
e. Educational programs?	___	___	___

2. Has the board approved a comprehensive institutional plan
   within the past five years?   ____ ____   ____
3. Does the board have a schedule
   for reviewing and, if desirable,
   revising the plan at regular
   intervals?   ____ ____   ____
4. Was the faculty involved in the
   development of the plan?   ____ ____   ____

Summary: In relation to this criterion, I feel that the overall performance of the board has been

Very Good ___ Good ___ Barely Adequate ___ Poor ___ Don't Know/Can't Judge ___

Further comments or suggestions related to this criterion:

Criterion 3: Physical Plant

One of the responsibilities of the board is to create and maintain a
physical environment that is conducive to learning and consistent
with reasonable expectations of future funds and enrollment trends.
Decisions that involve the campus master plan and the capital outlay budget request are the major concerns. Prudence demands that
maximum use be made of the present physical plant before construction or remodeling is considered. And maintenance should not
be deferred to the possible peril of the institution's future. Efficient
use of the time and effort of the board requires that the board be
concerned only with those matters that cannot properly be delegated
to the staff.

	Yes	*No*	*Don't Know/ Can't Judge*
1. Has the board approved a master plan for the physical campus that includes both present and anticipated needs?	____	____	____

2. Within the past two years, has
   the board received and reviewed
   a report on physical plant utilization classroom, laboratory,
   dormitory, office, and other
   building space? ___ ___   ___

3. Prior to its consideration of re
   quests for remodeling or new
   construction, has the board satisfied itself that present spaces
   are being used effectively and
   instructional areas are sched-
   uled for optimum utilization? ___ ___   ___

4. Is the board satisfied that maintenance programs are adequate
   and that they are not being deferred unreasonably? ___ ___   ___

5. Do you feel that the board
   makes decisions on details relating to buildings and grounds
   that really should be delegated
   to the administrative staff? ___ ___   ___

Summary: In relation to this criterion, I feel that the overall performance of the board has been

Very Good ___ Good ___ Barely Adequate ___ Poor ___ Don't Know/Can't Judge ___

Further comments or suggestions related to this criterion:

Criterion 4: Financial Management

In the financial affairs of the institution, the board has a responsibility to ensure that there is a mechanism in place for prudent
fiscal management. This responsibility calls especially on the expertise of those board members who are experienced in devising

financial policies, managing investments, or who have other financial skills. The board must ensure that sound financial policies are followed, yet refrain from becoming involved in the execution of policies or their administration.

		Yes	No	Don't Know/ Can't Judge
1.	Does the board accept fully its responsibility for prudent fiscal management?	___	___	___
2.	Does the board carry out its responsibility for overseeing fiscal resources, particularly in the preparation and monitoring of an annual operating budget?	___	___	___
3.	Do all board members receive financial reports			
	a. In an intelligible and useful format?	___	___	___
	b. Often enough?	___	___	___
4.	Does the board have within its membership persons with special expertise who give their advice in the following areas			
	a. Long-range fiscal planning?	___	___	___
	b. Investment practices?	___	___	___
	c. Fiscal management?	___	___	___
	d. Budget review?	___	___	___
	e. Analysis of reports and recommendations?	___	___	___

Summary: In relation to this criterion, I feel that the overall performance of the board has been

Very Good ___ Good ___ Barely Adequate ___ Poor ___ Don't Know/Can't Judge ___

Further comments or suggestions related to this criterion:

Criterion 5: Financial Support

A board has the responsibility to ensure that sufficient financial resources are generated so that the institution is able to meet its mission and goals. Part of this responsibility is discharged through careful oversight of the financial affairs of the institution. Board members, however, also have a responsibility to give willingly from their personal means, to encourage others to do so, and to otherwise participate actively in the development program. The interest and efforts of others are affected by the example set by the trustees and the board as a whole.

	Yes	No	Don't Know/ Can't Judge
1. Do you feel that the development program is well organized into a continuing and coordinated effort of the board, the president, and the chief development officer?	——	——	——
2. Do you feel that the fundraising efforts of the institution are consistent with the stated mission and goals developed by the governing board?	——	——	——
3. Do you feel there is an adequate financial commitment on the part of individual board members to			
a. Give personally?	——	——	——
b. Influence other persons or organizations to give?	——	——	——

4. Does the board receive periodic fund-raising reports that include aggregate trustee giving as a separate category?   ___ ___   ___

5. Has the board established appropriate policies and guidelines for the various types of fund-raising activities (for example, annual fund, capital campaign, and planned giving)?   ___ ___   ___

Summary: In relation to this criterion, I feel that the overall performance of the board has been

Very Good ___ Good ___ Barely Adequate ___ Poor ___ Don't Know/Can't Judge ___

Further comments or suggestions related to this criterion:

Criterion 6: Board Membership

A primary requisite for effective governance is to be sure that the men and women responsible for the policy direction of the institution have the skills, knowledge, and background necessary for effective decision making. The complex operation of modern educational institutions requires that boards have available to them a wide range of experience and expertise. The larger society to which these institutions are now linked more closely than ever before requires that the membership of the board be more diverse in terms of geographic, social, or occupational origins and viewpoints. Such diversity does not require that members be representatives of special groups or interests unless this is specified in the bylaws or charter. Each member must be willing to serve the interests of the institution as a whole.

			Yes	No	Don't Know/ Can't Judge
1.		Do you feel that the board now contains a sufficient range of expertise, attitudes, and external relationships to make it effective?	___	___	___
2.		Does the board have a committee that assesses the qualifications of new members with respect to the needs of the board and that maintains a roster of prospective members?	___	___	___
3.		Does the board have a committee that reviews the performance of its individual members?	___	___	___
4.		Does the board have an established procedure for orienting new members to their institution and to their duties and responsibilities?			___
5.		Do you feel that the board should alter its policies and practices with respect to			
	a.	Size?	___	___	___
	b.	Length of term?	___	___	___
	c.	Number of successive terms?	___	___	___
	d.	Age limit or honorary retirement?	___	___	___
	e.	Age composition?	___	___	___
	f.	Sex composition?	___	___	___
	g.	Minority composition?	___	___	___
	h.	Geographical composition?	___	___	___
	i.	Persons with educational experience?	___	___	___

j. Persons with financial
    management experience?   ___ ___   ___
k. Requiring a minimum
    attendance record?   ___ ___   ___

Summary: In relation to this criterion, I feel that the overall performance of the board has been

Very Good ___ Good ___ Barely Adequate ___ Poor ___ Don't Know/Can't Judge ___

Further comments or suggestions related to this criterion:

Criterion 7: Board Organization

The effectiveness of a board depends greatly on the structure of the board's organization and the conduct of the board's meetings. A productive board is usually one that periodically takes the time to thoughtfully sort out its duties, critically review its organizational structure and rules of procedure, and update its bylaws and policy or operations documents. Committee structure depends on the board's size, the frequency of meetings, and the work load that can be placed on individual members. Periodic critical review should also determine, among other things, if a few persons in fact are making most of the decisions for the board, if responsible minority opinions have the opportunity for full board consideration, and if communication between the campus community and the public is open.

		Yes	*No*	*Don't Know/ Can't Judge*

1. Within the past two or three
    years, has the board in some
    formal way reviewed its organi-
    zation, committee practices, and
    bylaws?   ___ ___   ___

2. Do meeting agendas
   a. Put before you issues of
      policy for consideration by
      the board? — — —
   b. Include appropriate sup-
      porting information in the
      right amount? — — —
   c. Reach you sufficiently in
      advance of the meeting? — — —
3. Do you believe that the number
   and duration of board meetings
   are sufficient to properly take
   care of the institution's
   business? — — —
4. Are board meetings effectively
   conducted and reasonably
   stimulating? — — —
5. Do you feel that the present
   committee structure
   a. Handles the work of the
      board efficiently? — — —
   b. Gives the full board the
      opportunity to consider
      adequately all matters of
      key importance? — — —
   c. Allows constituencies to be
      heard before recommenda-
      tions are formed? — — —
6. Do board policies vis-à-vis
   board and committee membership afford sufficient opportunity for rotating leadership? — — —

Summary: In relation to this criterion, I feel that the overall performance of the board has been

Very Good ___ Good ___ Barely Adequate ___ Poor ___ Don't Know/Can't Judge ___

Further comments or suggestions related to this criterion:

Criterion 8: Board/Chief Executive Relations

Trustees and the chief executive officer share at least one major characteristic: they have a total institutional perspective. The quality of the working relationship between the board and the executive officer is of critical importance to the effectiveness of each. Although the board must take responsibility for basic policies and their consequences, it must also give the chief executive the authority and flexibility to act decisively.

    Selecting the chief executive officer is a major responsibility of the governing board, and the selection should be preceded by a clear definition of his or her qualifications and expected accomplishments.

		Yes	*No*	*Don't Know/ Can't Judge*
1.	Is there a climate of mutual trust and support between the board and chief executive?	____	____	____
2.	Have the board or some of its members counseled the chief executive to provide guidelines or strengthen certain areas of performance?	____	____	____
3.	Do you feel that the board has delegated to the chief executive the authority he or she needs to administer the institution successfully?	____	____	____
4.	Is there a written statement of role and responsibility for the chief executive that defines clearly his or her functions and the expectations of the board?	____	____	____

5. Is there a clear understanding
    of the respective responsibilities
    between the chief executive and
    the board concerning their
    fund-raising roles?   ___   ___   ___
6. Does the board or a board com-
    mittee formally assess the chief
    executive's performance in
    some systematic way from time
    to time?   ___   ___   ___

Summary: In relation to this criterion, I feel that the overall performance of the board has been

Very Good ___ Good ___ Barely Adequate ___ Poor ___ Don't Know/Can't Judge ___

Further comments or suggestions related to this criterion:

Criterion 9: Board/Faculty Relations

In academic affairs, a measure of the board's success is the nature
of its relationship with the faculty. Most lay board members lack the
professional expertise to legislate in this area, yet they share the
burden of responsibility for the quality of the institution and for
the manner in which the institution fulfills its academic goals.
Therefore, the board must trust the professionals for advice and
delegate to them authority to carry out educational policies and
procedures.

The line between governing policy and operating policy is
not easily drawn, but it must nevertheless be established with reasonable clarity. The institution needs to be given academic direction, but the faculty must be free to perform its professional work.

	Yes	No	Don't Know/ Can't Judge

1. Does the board have effective means of two-way communication with the faculty? ____ ____ ____

2. Does the board, through the chief executive, seek the advice and recommendations of faculty leaders in formulating basic educational policies? ____ ____ ____

3. Do you feel that the board exercises authority over
   a. More aspects of educational affairs than it needs to? ____ ____ ____
   b. Fewer aspects of educational affairs than it should? ____ ____ ____
   c. Neither; its participation in educational affairs is about right. ____ ____ ____

4. Does the board delegate to the chief executive and faculty full responsibility for implementing educational policies? ____ ____ ____

5. Has the board adopted adequate policies concerning
   a. Grievance procedures? ____ ____ ____
   b. Process for selection, promotion, retention, and tenure? ____ ____ ____

Summary: In relation to this criterion, I feel that the overall performance of the board has been

Very Good ____ Good ____ Barely Adequate ____ Poor ____ Don't Know/Can't Judge ____

Further comments or suggestions related to this criterion:

Criterion 10: Board/Student Relations

The board has the ultimate responsibility to protect the welfare of students and to provide a healthy campus environment that is conducive to scholarship and personal development. The students' health and comfort are essential to learning. The students' freedom to learn independently is a basic tenet of academic freedom, and like other freedoms it must be exercised under the obligation to protect the welfare of the community as a whole. The board should also assure itself of good communication with students.

	Yes	*No*	*Don't Know/ Can't Judge*
1. Does the board have a satisfactory means for continuing two-way communication with students?	___	___	___
2. Has the board approved policies that make adequate provision for the students' health, welfare, and noncurricular (cultural, educational, recreational) activities?	___	___	___
3. Has the board set adequate policies for student appeal of perceived injustices (academic or other)?	___	___	___
4. Are students and student organizations free to examine and discuss questions or issues of interest to them and to express opinions publicly, so long as the fact that they speak only for themselves is made clear?	___	___	___

Summary: In relation to this criterion, I feel that the overall performance of the board has been

Very Good ___ Good ___ Barely Adequate ___ Poor ___ Don't Know/Can't Judge ___

Further comments or suggestions related to this criterion:

Criterion 11: Court of Appeal

Governing boards may from time to time be called upon to fulfill a quasi-judicial function in the settlement of disputes that arise within the institutional community. As a general rule, however, disputes should be settled at the lowest possible administrative level to avoid inappropriate board involvement in operational matters. The board should delegate authority and develop carefully due process policies.

	Yes	*No*	*Don't Know/ Can't Judge*
1. Has the board developed procedural due process or "fair hearing" requirements that delegate the management of conflict situations to the chief executive and to academic administrators or faculty leaders?	___	___	___
2. Are the disputes that have been brought to the board			
a. Summarized accurately and concisely for your study?	___	___	___
b. Done so before they have escalated to crisis proportions?	___	___	___

   c.   Settled without unduly
      prolonged debate?   —— ——   ——

3.   Do you feel that disputes have
    been settled with sympathetic
    understanding of the human
    and institutional issues
    involved?   —— ——   ——

4.   Do you feel that the board has
    been called upon to adjudicate
    cases of conflict that should
    have been settled before they
    came to the board?   —— ——   ——

Summary: In relation to this criterion, I feel that the overall performance of the board has been

Very Good ___ Good ___ Barely Adequate ___ Poor ___ Don't Know/Can't Judge ___

Further comments or suggestions related to this criterion:

General Assessment

1.   What issues have most occupied the time and attention of the
    board during the past year?

2.   What were the one or two successes during the past year for
    which the board feels some satisfaction?

3.   What particular shortcomings do you see in the organization
    or performance of the board that need attention?

4.   Other comments or suggestions?

Trustee Audit

The responsibilities of individual trustees are different from those of boards as corporate entities. The following checklist is designed to help board members assess the extent to which they have absorbed the breadth and depth of their roles and institutions. The questions seem somewhat imposing, but they are not intended to cause acute trustee or presidential depression. A perfect score is an unreasonable expectation.

      Candid responses can be helpful to the design of orientation programs for new board members or future workshops and retreats. The checklist can also be adapted to the unique characteristics of your particular institution as a supplement to the preceding board self-study criteria. It was developed by Richard T. Ingram, president of the Association of Governing Boards of Colleges and Universities (AGB), as part of the *Handbook of College and University Trusteeship* (1980a). The questions are the result of the scrutiny of a number of chief executives and trustees.

	Yes	*No*	*Somewhat or Sometimes*
Background			
1. Do you feel you have adequate opportunity to understand your obligations, responsibilities, and opportunities for growth as a trustee?	___	___	___
2. Do you have a clear grasp of the responsibilities of your board?	___	___	___

3. If you have answered yes to
either or both questions, what
has been the primary source(s)
of your information (for example, an orientation program, a
particular individual, a book,
or prior service as a board
member)?   ___ ___   ___

4. Are you familiar with the stated
mission, institutional plan, and
current policies of your
institution?   ___ ___   ___

5. Do you stay abreast of higher
education trends, legislation,
and other public policy by reading AGB publications, the
Chronicle of Higher Education,
or other material?   ___ ___   ___

6. Have you taken an opportunity
recently to meet with trustees
and educators from other
institutions?   ___

7. Do you have adequate opportunities to know your fellow
trustees?   ___ ___   ___

8. Do you find any conflict between your responsibility for
the welfare and advancement of
your institution and your responsibility to the citizens of
your region, state, or nation?   ___ ___   ___

9. Please indicate with an "x"
your strongest areas of expertise
based on your background and
personal experience.

    ___ Budget/finance   ___ Student affairs

    ___ Investments   ___ Faculty affairs

    ___ Management   ___ Fund raising

_____ Planning   _____ Public relations
_____ Legal affairs   _____ Marketing
_____ Plant management _____ Government relations
_____ Real estate   _____ Other (please list)
_____ Education

10. Now go back and make a check
     mark at any areas of primary
     interest outside of your back-
     ground and expertise.

Knowledge of the Institution

11. Are you familiar with the recent
     history of your institution and
     what makes it distinctive from
     neighboring colleges and
     universities?   _____ _____   _____

12. Cite three special strengths of
     your institution
     a. _____
     b. _____
     c. _____

13. Cite three greatest needs of your
     institution
     a. _____
     b. _____
     c. _____

14. Do you feel well informed
     about the type and quality of
     educational programs at your
     institution?   _____ _____   _____

15. Have you attended a campus
     event within the past year?   _____ _____   _____

16. Do you read the campus news-
     paper or faculty or student or-
     ganization minutes?   _____ _____   _____

17. Do you know the names of your
     institution's

a. Key administrators? —— —— ——
b. Faculty leaders? —— —— ——
c. Student leaders? —— —— ——

18. Have you met some of the peo-
    ple in question 17 apart from
    board meetings? —— —— ——

19. Are you acquainted with the
    physical plant and maintenance
    needs of your institution? —— —— ——

Board and Committee Meetings

20. Are you satisfied with your at-
    tendance at board and commit-
    tee meetings? —— —— ——

21. Do you read the minutes of
    meetings to determine whether
    they faithfully represent the
    proceedings and decisions as
    you recall them? —— —— ——

22. Do you prepare for board meet-
    ings by reading agendas and
    supporting materials? —— —— ——

23. Do you suggest agenda items? —— —— ——

24. Do you help board and com-
    mittee meetings to steer clear of
    nonpolicy matters better left to
    the administration? —— —— ——

Fund Raising and Public Relations

25. Do you contribute a gift to your
    institution according to your
    means for
    a. Annual operations? —— —— ——
    b. Capital campaigns? —— —— ——

26. Within the past year or two,

have you helped secure a gift
from an individual, corpora-
tion, or other source?   ___ ___   ___

27.   Have you recently taken advantage of an opportunity to say a
good word about your institution to a policy maker or orga-
nization at the state level?   ___ ___   ___

28.   Do you take advantage of opportunities to inform other
groups or persons about your
institution or about higher education generally?   ___ ___   ___

Trustee Concerns

29.   Do you understand the concept
of fund accounting?   ___ ___   ___

30.   Do you find the financial statements of your institution to be
intelligible?   ___ ___   ___

31.   Are you mindful of the stated
mission, institutional plan and
goals, and current policies of
your institution when voting
on proposals presented to the
board?   ___ ___   ___

32.   Do you feel you are sensitive to
the concerns of students and
faculty while maintaining im-
partiality and a total institu-
tional perspective?   ___ ___   ___

33.   Do you help meet the needs of
your chief executive for occasional counsel and support in
his or her often difficult relationships with on- and off-
campus groups?   ___ ___   ___

34. Do you appreciate the importance of keeping your chief executive informed in the event
you establish personal communication lines with individuals on campus and of the need
to avoid prejudiced judgments
on the basis of such
relationships?   ___ ___   ___

35. Have you ever suggested to the
nominating committee or the
appointing authority of the
board someone who would
make an outstanding new
board member?   ___ ___   ___

36. Are you satisfied that there are
no real or apparent conflicts of
interest in your service as a
trustee?   ___ ___   ___

37. Do you avoid asking special favors of the administration, including requests for
information, without the
knowledge of at least the presi-
dent or board chair?   ___ ___   ___

38. If you have not already done so,
would you be willing to serve
as a committee chair or board
officer?   ___ ___   ___

Why or why not?

39. Have you found your trusteeship to be stimulating and re-
warding thus far?   ___ ___   ___

Why or why not?

40.   How would you rate yourself as
      a trustee at this time?

Above Average ____ Average ____ Below Average ____

RESOURCE D

Bylaws for
Independent
Colleges and
Universities

Few documents are read with less enthusiasm than bylaws, yet they constitute the most important legal document in the portfolio of the board, especially when they are well conceived and written. A good set of bylaws should

• Define the broad authority of the board by including an *illustrative* set of board responsibilities.

• Avoid legalistic language and detail that is best covered in other legal documents, such as employment contracts. Ambiguous language can invite otherwise avoidable litigation.

• Avoid provisions that pertain to groups or constituents other than the board (such as the faculty senate or advisory councils). The bylaws of the board should be reserved for the board only; other advisory or constituent groups that are part of institutional governance should have their own statements of purpose and organization.

• Be developed or revised with respect to other campus documents. Especially with regard to the authority and responsibility of the governing board, bylaws should clearly reserve final authority for the board on all fundamental campus policies, including the declaration and management of financial exigency and faculty tenure. Bylaws must clearly state that they take precedence over all other institutional documents, including the faculty handbook. (Such other documents and their revisions should ultimately require board approval to ensure that they do not conflict with the bylaws of the board).

• Allow for flexibility on appropriate matters. For example, the total number of board members should be allowed to vary between some set minimum and maximum, as should the size of board committees.

• Strike a balance between too much detail, which causes the need for frequent revision, and too little detail, which invites inconsistent interpretation and action.

• Set the broad parameters of how the board should be organized to maximize its effectiveness through good committee work (where most of the work of the board is likely to be done), but statements of committee responsibilities should be approved by the board and maintained separately from the bylaws. The exceptions to this suggestion pertain to the executive committee and the committee on trusteeship because their functions are linked so directly to bylaw provisions. In the conduct of committee work, it is important for everyone to remember that *all* committees *recommend* courses of action to the board unless the board (or its bylaws) clearly specifies otherwise.

• Clearly define the functions of the executive committee as being *the instrument of the board* for certain planning and oversight responsibilities rather than an independent decision-making group.

• Include provision on the indemnification of trustees and the definition of what constitutes a potential conflict of interest for trustees (preferably with reference to a fuller and separate board-approved statement on the subject).

• Be reviewed periodically by the secretary of the board and by legal counsel to ensure that they are consistent with state law. Such review by trustees and legal counsel must be taken seriously. The review process often opens opportunities to identify and fix certain problems and to renew the commitment of the board to meet its responsibilities—for example, by coming to grips with the possibility that the board has become too large, that the time has come to set a limit on the number of consecutive terms a trustee can serve, that officerships should have some outside limit on length of service, or that there are too many ex-officio trusteeships.

The illustrative bylaws in this section should be adapted to fit the particular cultures and traditions of the institution and board. They reflect many good practices and a number of choices among competing alternatives that *the board* should ultimately decide for itself in consultation with the president. There is an important role for legal counsel in the drafting or revising of board bylaws, of course, but such counsel should not dictate final choices except where state or federal law may be involved.

The following illustrative bylaws reflect several assumptions:

1. The board is entirely self-perpetuating (trustees select their own successors through a process defined in the bylaws).

2. It is preferable to avoid the cumbersome distinction between "officers of the board" and "officers of the institution." A bifurcated approach may be preferred by some but is rarely necessary.

3. Except for the executive committee and the committee on trusteeship, the role and scope of board standing committees are best defined separately from the bylaws. The Association of Governing Boards of Universities and Colleges offers a series of pamphlets on each of the typical standing committees to help guide the development of such committee "charges." Statements of committee purpose, role, and scope frequently require revision and are therefore best maintained separately. See Chapter Seventeen in this book and *Making Trusteeship Work* by Richard T. Ingram (1988) for additional resources.

4. The office of treasurer is held by a trustee rather than a member of the administration. The illustrative bylaw provision for this position attempts to avoid a common problem that many bylaws have—where the job description reads more like one intended for the chief financial officer of the institution.

5. The office of secretary is held by a trustee rather than a member of the administration. Although larger universities often reserve this position for a professional staff member, the majority of private institutions use it as an opportunity for trustee leadership.

6. The institution is nonsectarian and serves a broad constituency. Certain special types of academic institutions (for example,

single-sex or church-related) will require certain adjustments in some provisions.

7. The board maintains a separate and fuller statement on conflict of interest, along with a requirement for all trustees to complete an annual disclosure statement (see Resource E). Similarly, a separate statement on the prohibition of discrimination should be approved by the board and reviewed annually by legal counsel who can help interpret changing definitions and the most recent and relevant case law.

Illustrative Bylaws
Table of Contents

[Name of College or University]
Board of Trustees

Bylaws

Article I: Board Authority and Responsibilities

Section 1. The board of trustees shall have and exercise those corporate powers prescribed by law. Its ultimate authority is affirmed through its general, academic, and financial policy-making functions and its responsibility for the financial health and welfare of the corporation. The board of trustees shall exercise ultimate institutional authority as set forth in these bylaws and in such other policy documents it deems to be appropriate. These bylaws and other board policy statements shall take precedence over all other institutional statements, documents, and policies.

Section 2. The board of trustees shall have the authority to carry out all lawful functions that are permitted by these bylaws or by the articles of incorporation. This authority, in consultation with the president, shall include but shall not be limited to these illustrative functions:

1. Determine and periodically review the mission and purposes of the university.

2. Appoint the president, who shall be chief executive officer of the university, and set appropriate conditions of employment, including compensation.

3. Establish the conditions of employment of other key institutional officers who serve at the pleasure of the president (in consultation with the board).

4. Support the president and assess his or her performance.

5. Review and approve proposed changes in the academic programs and other major enterprises of the university consistent with the mission, plans, and financial resources of the university.

6. Approve institutional policies that bear on faculty ap-

pointment, promotion, tenure, and dismissal as well as personnel or antidiscrimination policies for other categories of employees.

7. Approve the annual budget and annual tuition and fees, regularly monitor the financial condition of the university, and establish policy guidelines that affect all institutional assets including investments and the physical plant.

8. Contribute financially to the fund-raising goals of the university, participate actively in strategies to secure sources of support, and authorize university officers to accept gifts or bequests subject to board policy guidelines.

9. Authorize any need for debt financing and approve the securing of loans.

10. Authorize the construction of new buildings, capitalization of deferred maintenance backlogs, and major renovations of existing buildings.

11. Authorize the purchase, sale, and management of all land, buildings, or major equipment.

12. Approve policies that contribute to the best possible environment for students to learn and develop their abilities and that contribute to the best possible environment for the faculty to teach, pursue their scholarship, and perform public service. These policies include the protection of academic freedom.

13. Approve all earned and honorary degrees through the faculty and president as they shall recommend.

14. Serve actively as advocates for the university in appropriate matters of public policy in consultation with the president and other responsible parties as the board shall determine.

15. Periodically undertake or authorize assessments of the performance of the board.

Article II: Membership of the Board of Trustees

Section 1. The board of trustees shall consist of not less than twenty-one (21) nor more than thirty-five (35) persons.

Section 2. New trustees and incumbent members of the board of trustees who are eligible for reelection normally shall be elected at the annual meeting of the board by a majority of the trustees then in office. Any unfulfilled term may be filled through a special election at any regular meeting of the board of trustees.

Section 3. Trustees shall serve for three-year terms and shall be eligible for reelection to a maximum of three full consecutive terms. Trustees who have served for nine consecutive years (exclusive of any partial term) shall be eligible for reelection following a one-year hiatus. The four board officers shall be exempt from this provision until at least one year has passed following completion of their term of office or until the committee on trusteeship shall otherwise determine.

Section 4. All trustees serve at the pleasure of the board. A trustee may be removed from office by an affirmative vote of two-thirds of the trustees.

Section 5. The committee on trusteeship shall recommend candidates for election or reelection to the board through procedures adopted by the board. A slate of candidates shall be provided to all trustees at least thirty days in advance of the annual or regular meeting at which an election is scheduled. Biographical information for each prospective trustee candidate will be provided as well.

Article III: Trustees Emeriti

Upon recommendation of the committee on trusteeship, trustees who have served with distinction for at least two terms may be elected by the majority of trustees as trustees emeriti. Terms shall be three years and shall be renewable provided the total number of trustees emeriti does not exceed one-third of the total number of regular voting trustees. Trustees emeriti shall be eligible to serve on board committees, except for the executive committee and the committee on trusteeship, with vote, and shall speak freely at all board and committee meetings. They shall not have voting privileges at board meetings and shall not be counted as part of quorum determinations. Trustees emeriti shall be sent notices and minutes of all board meetings and are encouraged to attend board meetings or otherwise accept special assignments that are helpful to the board of trustees and the university.

Article IV: Officers of the University

Section 1. The officers of the university shall be the chair, vice chair, secretary, and treasurer of the board of trustees, and the president and one or more vice presidents. All officers shall serve at the pleasure of the board of trustees except for the vice presidents, who shall serve at the pleasure of the president in consultation with the board of trustees.

Section 2. The chair, vice chair, secretary, and treasurer shall be trustees. The president shall be an ex-officio member of the board of trustees without power to vote, and his or her presence at meetings shall not be counted as part of quorum determinations. The other university officers shall not be members of the board.

Section 3. The terms of office for officerships will vary as provided elsewhere in these bylaws. The board may approve the appointment of other officers upon recommendation of the president.

Article V: Terms and Responsibilities of the Chair and Vice Chair of the Board of Trustees

Section 1. The chair and vice chair shall be elected annually upon nomination by the committee on trusteeship and shall ordinarily serve for at least three consecutive years but not more than five years. Vacancies may be filled at any time by a majority vote of the members of the board, but election or reelection shall normally take place at the designated annual meeting.

Section 2. The chair shall preside at all board and executive committee meetings, have the right to vote on all questions, appoint committee chairs and vice chairs, determine the composition of all board committees with the exception of the executive committee, and otherwise serve as spokesperson for the board. He or she shall serve as chair of the executive committee, ex-officio member of all other standing committees of the board, and have other duties as the board may prescribe from time to time.

Section 3. In the absence of the chair, the vice chair shall perform the duties of the office of the chair, including presiding at board and executive committee meetings. He or she shall have other powers and duties as the board may from time to time prescribe and may or may not be nominated to succeed the chair when a vacancy occurs in that officership as the committee on trustees shall decide.

Article VI: Term and Responsibilities of the Secretary

Section 1. The secretary shall be elected annually upon nomination of the committee on trusteeship and shall ordinarily serve for at least three consecutive years but not more than five years.

Section 2. The secretary shall ensure that the board of trustees is acting in accordance with these bylaws and bylaw amendments are promptly made as necessary, that minutes of board and executive committee meetings are accurate and promptly distributed to all trustees, that meetings are properly scheduled and trustees notified, and that board policy statements and other official records are properly maintained. The secretary shall perform other duties as prescribed from time to time by the board and may be assisted in all duties by a staff person designated by the president.

Article VII: Term and Responsibilities of the Treasurer

Section 1. The treasurer shall be elected annually upon nomination of the committee on trusteeship and shall ordinarily serve for at least three consecutive years but not more than five years.

Section 2. The treasurer shall ordinarily serve as chair of the finance committee of the board of trustees and otherwise serve as the key leader of the board on all financial management policy matters. He or she shall ensure that all trustees regularly receive appropriate and comprehensible financial statements from the administration of the university that include comparisons of revenues and expenditures with both the approved annual budget and the preceding fiscal year for the same time periods. The treasurer shall ensure that other financial reports, including those for special or major board-approved expenditures, university investments, and annual or special audits, are provided to all trustees in a timely manner for review and discussion as appropriate. He or she works closely with the chief financial officer of the university, the board-approved auditor, and the investment and audit committees of the board as appropriate or necessary.

Article VIII: Term, Authority, and Responsibilities of the President of the University

Section 1. The president serves at the pleasure of the board of trustees for such term, compensation, and conditions of employment as the board shall determine.

Section 2. The president shall be the chief executive officer of the university and the chief advisor to and executive agent of the board of trustees. His or her authority is vested through the board of trustees and includes responsibilities for all university educational and managerial affairs. The president is responsible for leading the university, hiring all vice presidents (in consultation with the board), implementing all board policies, keeping the board informed on appropriate matters, consulting with the board in a timely fashion on matters appropriate to its policy-making and fiduciary functions, and serving as the key spokesperson for the university. He or she has the authority to execute all documents on behalf of the university and the board of trustees consistent with board policies and the best interests of the university. The president serves as an ex-officio member of all board committees except the audit committee.

Article IX: Term, Authority, and Responsibilities of the Vice President(s)

The vice president(s) shall serve for such term(s) and have such authority and responsibilities as the president shall determine in consultation with the board of trustees. In the absence or disability of the president, the board of trustees shall determine which vice president or other individual shall perform the president's duties.

Article X: Meetings

Section 1. The board of trustees shall have at least four regular meetings annually on such dates and at such places as it shall determine. The annual meeting for the purpose of electing trustees, officers, and at-large members of the executive committee shall be the first board meeting scheduled after September 1 of each year.

Section 2. Special meetings may be held at the call of the board chair, the president, or any five trustees. Written notice of such special meetings shall be sent to all trustees by the chair or secretary of the board of trustees with a clear statement of purpose(s) at least ten days in advance. Business at such special meetings shall be confined to the stated purpose(s).

Section 3. A quorum for the transaction of business at meetings of the board of trustees or its executive committee shall consist of a majority of their respective regular voting member trustees. Except as otherwise provided in these bylaws or the articles of incorporation, a majority vote of those members present with a proper quorum shall constitute proper action.

Article XI: Action Without a Formal Meeting

Any action required or permitted to be taken by the board of trustees or by any committee thereof may be taken without a formal meeting. Meetings may be conducted by mail, fax, conference call, telegram, cable, or in any other way the trustees shall decide. A written consent setting forth the action(s) taken and signed by each appropriate member trustee shall be filed with the minutes of the proceedings as soon as practical.

Article XII: Committees

Section 1. The board shall establish such standing and ad hoc committees as it deems appropriate to discharge its responsibilities. Each committee shall have a written statement of purpose, role, and scope as approved by the board, and such rules of procedure or policy guidelines that it or the board, as appropriate, shall approve. Such statements shall be reviewed annually by each committee.

Section 2. The chair of the board of trustees shall have the responsibility of appointing the chairs, vice chairs, and members of all board committees except the executive committee. All committee chairs, vice chairs, and a majority of committee members shall be trustees.

Section 3. Each committee shall have a clearly designated officer of the university or member of the administrative staff as determined by the president to assist it with its work. Each committee shall meet at least three times annually and regularly report on its work and recommendations to the board of trustees. Except for the executive committee, whose minutes of meetings are required, other committees shall decide whether written minutes are necessary and desirable and whether they should be distributed to the trustees.

Article XIII: Composition, Purposes, and
Responsibilities of the Executive Committee

Section 1. The executive committee shall have ____ members, all of whom shall be voting trustees, except for the president of the university, who shall be ex-officio without vote and not counted as part of a quorum for the purpose of transacting business. The chair, vice chair, secretary, and treasurer of the board of trustees shall be members along with the chairs of all board standing committees [*or designated committees if the number of committees is too extensive*]. In addition, ____ [*one or two*] trustee(s) shall be nominated by the committee on trusteeship and elected by the board at the annual meeting to serve at-large on the committee.

Section 2. The purpose of the executive committee is twofold: to conserve time, it shall serve at the pleasure of the board as the board's agent in helping the president to address routine business between regular board meetings; and it shall assist the chair and the president in their joint responsibility to help the board to function effectively and efficiently by suggesting board meeting agenda items and periodically assessing the quality of committee work. The committee shall have authority to act for the board of trustees on all matters except for the following, which shall be reserved for the board: presidential selection and termination; trustee and board officer selection; changes in institutional mission and purposes; changes to the charter or articles of incorporation; incurring of corporate indebtedness; sale of university assets or tangible property; adoption of the annual budget; and conferral of degrees. These bylaws or other board policy may reserve other powers for the board of trustees. In addition to its authority to take action on emergency matters that cannot or should not be deferred to the next scheduled meeting of the board, the executive committee shall oversee the work of board committees, the university's planning process or progress on planning goals, and the board's responsibility to support the president and assess his or her performance, and it shall review annually the president's compensation and conditions of employment.

Section 3. The committee shall meet as often as necessary to conduct its business as the chair and president shall determine, and it shall ensure that minutes are taken and promptly distributed to all trustees for subsequent ratification by the board of trustees at its next regular meeting. A majority of voting trustee committee members shall constitute a quorum.

Article XIV: Composition, Purposes, and Responsibilities of the Committee on Trusteeship

Section 1. The committee on trusteeship shall have at least five members and not more than seven, all of whom shall be voting trustees. The chair, vice chair, and members of the committee shall be appointed for renewable one-year terms by the chair of the board of trustees.

Section 2. The purpose of the committee on trusteeship is threefold: it shall ensure that the membership and leadership of the board consist of highly qualified and committed individuals, it shall en sure that regular programs of new trustee and in-service education are maintained, and it shall periodically recommend initiatives by which the board shall assess its performance. It serves as the agent of the board in reviewing the performance of incumbent trustees and board officers who are eligible for reelection, maintains a list of qualified candidates for possible nomination, considers cultivation strategies for promising trustee candidates, and proposes and periodically reviews the adequacy of a statement of trustee responsibilities as adopted by the board. It shall establish its own rules of procedure in consultation with the board chair, president, and the board of trustees.

Section 3. The committee shall meet as often as necessary to conduct its business, but no fewer than three times annually. It shall seek the assistance of all trustees in the course of meeting its responsibilities in accordance with these bylaws and its own rules of procedures as adopted by the board of trustees. A majority of the members of the committee shall constitute a quorum.

Article XV: Indemnification

Each trustee and officer of the university shall be indemnified against all expenses actually and necessarily incurred by such trustee or officer in connection with the defense of any action, suit, or proceeding to which he or she has been made a party by reason of being or having been such trustee or officer. The university shall cover such expenses except in relation to matters where the trustee or officer shall be adjudicated in such action, suit, or proceeding to be liable for gross negligence or willful misconduct in the performance of duty. The university shall maintain appropriate trustee and officer liability insurance coverage for this purpose.

Article XVI: Conflict of Interest

A trustee shall be considered to have a conflict of interest if (1) such trustee has existing or potential financial or other interests that impair or might reasonably appear to impair such member's independent, unbiased judgment in the discharge of his or her responsibilities to the university, or (2) such trustee is aware that a member of his or her family, or any organization in which such trustee (or member of his or her family) is an officer, director, employee, member, partner, trustee, or controlling stockholder, has such existing or potential financial or other interests. For the purposes of this provision, a family member is defined as a spouse, parents, siblings, children, and any other relative if the latter resides in the same household as the trustee. All trustees shall disclose to the board any possible conflict of interest at the earliest practical time. Furthermore, the trustee shall absent himself or herself from discussions of, and abstain from voting on, such matters under consideration by the board of trustees or its committees. The minutes of such meetings shall reflect that a disclosure was made and that the trustee who has a conflict or possible conflict abstained from voting. Any trustee who is uncertain whether a conflict of interest may exist in any matter may request that the board or committee resolve the question in his or her absence by majority vote. Each trustee shall complete and sign a disclosure form provided annually by the secretary of the board of trustees.

Article XVII: Review and Amendment of Bylaws

Section 1. These bylaws may be changed or amended at any meeting of the trustees by a two-thirds vote of those present, provided notice of the substance of the proposed amendment is sent to all trustees at least thirty days before the meeting.

Section 2. These bylaws shall be reviewed periodically by the secretary of the board of trustees and the executive committee, who shall recommend any necessary changes to the board of trustees.

Adopted by the board of trustees on _____ .
Amended: _____ .
                    _____ .

RESOURCE E

Guidelines on Conflict of Interest and Disclosure Issues

Potential conflicts of interest and related ethical matters have become a source of increasing concern in the tax-exempt and for-profit sectors. Increasing numbers of college and university governing boards have adopted policy statements to make public their positions on these complex issues. Especially since Watergate more than twenty years ago, governmental reform has brought varying degrees of disclosure requirements to public higher education trustees in most states. In private higher education, definitions of and statements on conflict of interest have been largely a matter of voluntary initiative—initiative that is appropriately gaining in acceptance.

The Association of Governing Boards of Universities and Colleges is increasingly consulted by its members and the media on whether it has a position on specific situations involving a trustee or institutional officer that could be interpreted as being a real or perceived conflict of interest, and it is consulted on how these situations should be handled. Few inquiries are more difficult to respond to, because matters of conflict almost always involve caveats of one sort or another and extenuating circumstances that only the board can address and resolve. Such judgments by boards can be helped immensely by adopting guidelines such as those provided in this resource.

What is a conflict of interest and what is not? Why do real or perceived conflicts justify the concerns that accompany, or should accompany, them? When is a perceived conflict of such importance that it should be addressed as if it were real? How does an institution maintain a sense of balance on these matters given that the kind of people needed on boards of trustees may bring connections and relationships that could be perceived as problematic? Is it really possible or even desirable to avoid problems by articulating an institutional policy to cover most or all possible contingencies? These are among the questions that trustees and institutional officers should address.

Questions of conflict that involve institutional leaders are important because *all* volunteer and salaried leaders are trustees of the institution in the sense that they are acting on behalf of the public good—not for themselves, members of their families, or business associates. And as trustees, all institutional leaders have legal, moral, and ethical responsibilities to protect the institution's integrity and well being in serving the public's trust. Individual members of governing boards have a duty to protect themselves and fellow trustees from situations that can range from embarrassment to vulnerability to lawsuit. Thus, disclosure of potential conflicts is a reasonable step to be taken by reasonable persons in the best interest of everyone, most especially the institution.

These ambiguities are considerable because they occupy the "twilight zone" between explicit federal and state law and the freedom of trustees to define their own values and standards of good conduct. Academic institutions are expected to live by the highest possible ethical and moral standards. In the end, most matters of real or perceived conflict of interest must be resolved through the exercise of good judgment by the majority of trustees once full disclosure is made and considered. There is no place for dysfunctional politeness in the boardroom when the integrity of the institution or board is at stake.

A potential conflict of interest is a situation that involves a personal, familial, or business relationship between a trustee (or institutional officer) and the institution that can cause the institution to be legally or otherwise vulnerable to criticism, embarrassment, or litigation in the opinion of responsible stakeholders. Such situations involve ethical or moral values, to be sure, but they are distinguishable and much more visible because they (1) usually involve money or profit or otherwise bear on the fiduciary responsibility of the board to ensure that no trustee or institutional officer use (or be perceived to be using) his or her institutional affiliation for personal financial gain except as may be explicitly allowed by institutional policy and (2) usually involve one or more aspects of the programs, personnel, or auxiliary enterprises of the institution.

Some additional considerations may be helpful as the board of a private institution develops or revises its own guidelines. First, trustees must keep their own houses in order. The president's and administration's responsibilities are largely limited to calling problems or potential problems to the attention of the leaders of the board.

Second, policy guidelines and annual disclosure requirements should strike a balance between being overly prescriptive and so vague and general that they are easily ignored or ineffective. Nepotism, for example, is a practice to be avoided as a general rule, but should the guidelines be specific about it? Should a trustee be permitted to serve as the general counsel of the institution (even without direct compensation) when his or her firm receives periodic or substantial legal fees for services? Is it a conflict for a local bank president to serve on the board when all or most of the accounts of the institution are maintained in that institution (even though other banking facilities are also convenient)? Other illustrations of potentially troublesome situations involve the purchase of real estate owned by a trustee or relative of a trustee, and a trustee whose insurance business provides for all or most of the insurance needs of the institution.

Third, the bylaws of the board should provide a definition of conflict of interest and refer to a separate and more comprehensive board policy on the subject, along with the requirement of an annual disclosure by the trustees and institutional officers. These documents should be part of a portfolio of materials given to prospective trustees *before* they accept nomination and are considered for election to the board.

Fourth, specific conflict of interest situations that are deemed important enough to call them to the attention of the board should be documented in the minutes of the board or executive committee. The nature of the potential conflict should be elaborated in reasonable detail, and the fact that the trustee involved was properly absent from both substantive discussion and subsequent vote, and actions taken or the reasons why the board may decide that no conflict exists should be spelled out. This gives everyone a measure of protection.

Finally, whether a matter is of sufficient importance to warrant its being a conflict (or a perceived conflict of such importance) that justifies board action could be decided on this basis: is it a matter on which action or decision (or decision not to act) of the board would be easily defended or explained by the president or board chair in the event the local newspaper developed a story about it?

Illustrative Conflict-of-Interest Policy and Disclosure Form for Trustees and Institutional Officers

Scope

The following statement of policy applies to each member of the board and to all officers of _____ University [*or College*]. It is intended to serve as guidance for all persons employed by the institution in positions of significant responsibility including [*define categories of positions*].

Fiduciary Responsibilities

Members of the board, officers, and employees of the university serve the public trust and have a clear obligation to fulfill their responsibilities in a manner consistent with this fact. All decisions of the board and officers of the administration and faculty are to be made solely on the basis of a desire to promote the best interests of the institution and the public good. The integrity of the university must be protected and advanced at all times.

Inevitably, men and women of substance are responsibly involved in the affairs of other institutions and organizations. An effective board, administration, and faculty cannot consist of persons entirely free from possible conflicts of interest. Although most such potential conflicts are and will be deemed to be inconsequential, everyone has the responsibility to ensure that the board is made aware of situations that involve personal, familial, or business relationships that could be troublesome for the university. Thus, the board requires each trustee and institutional officer to annually review this policy; disclose any possible personal, familial, or business relationships that reasonably could give rise to a conflict involving the university; and acknowledge by his or her signature that he or she is in accordance with the letter and spirit of this policy.

Disclosure

All trustees and officers are requested to list on this form *only those substantive relationships* that they (or members of their family) maintain with organizations that do business with the university or that otherwise could be construed to potentially affect their independent, unbiased judgment in light of their decision-making authority or responsibility. In event a trustee is uncertain as to the appropriateness of listing a particular relationship, the chair of the board of trustees *and/or* the president should be consulted. They, in turn, may elect to consult with legal counsel, the executive committee, or the board of trustees in executive session. Such information, including information provided on this form, shall be held in confidence except when, after consultation with the trustee, the best interests of the institution would be served by disclosure.

The following definitions are provided to help the trustee decide whether a relationship should be listed on this form.

> *Business relationship:* A relationship in which a trustee or officer, or a member of his or her family as defined below, serves as an officer, director, employee, partner, trustee, or controlling stockholder of an organization that does substantial business with the university.
> *Family member:* A spouse, parents, siblings, children, or any other relative if the latter resides in the same household as the trustee or officer.
> *Substantial benefit:* When a trustee or a member of the trustee's family (1) is the actual or beneficial owner of more

than 5 percent of the voting stock or controlling interest of an organization that does substantial business with the university or (2) has other direct or indirect dealings with such an organization from which the trustee or family member benefits directly, indirectly, or potentially from cash or property receipts that total $10,000 or more per annum.

Restraint on Participation

Trustees or officers who have declared or been found to have a conflict of interest shall refrain from participating in the consideration of proposed transactions, unless for special reasons the board or administration requests information or interpretation. Persons with conflicts shall not vote or be present at the time of the vote.

Please complete the following
and return this form in the envelope provided

1. Are you aware of any relationships with the university between yourself or a member of your family, as defined by the letter or spirit of this policy, that may represent a conflict of interest?
_____ Yes _____ No
If Yes, please list or elaborate such relationships and the details of annual or potential financial benefit as you can best estimate them (please use the reverse side of this form if more space is needed).

———————————————————————————————

———————————————————————————————

———————————————————————————————

2. During the past twelve months, did you or a member of your family receive any gifts or loans from any source from which the university buys goods or services or otherwise has significant business dealings?
_____ Yes _____ No
If Yes, please list such gifts or loans here.

Name of Source   *Item*   *Approximate Value*

_____

_____

_____

     I certify that the foregoing information is true and complete to the best of my knowledge.

_____

Name (please print)

_____   _____

   Date   Signature

Exceptions: (If there are none, please write *none.*)

_____

_____

_____

Recommended Readings

Here are useful background readings for each of the chapters in this book.

Chapter One: Exercising Stewardship in Times of Transition

Gardner reminds us in *On Leadership* that leadership is ultimately "the accomplishment of group purpose" (1990, p. 42). The book is worthwhile reading for anyone who aspires to lead, whether as trustee, chief executive, or other institutional officer of an academic institution where policy decisions are made from the department level and up.

Mason's book *College and University Government* is a gem. Mason was professor and chair of political science at Tulane University and chair of the American Association of University Professors' committee on college and university government at the time the book was published. It is in handbook form and intended primarily "for those members of academic institutions who are devising a system of government for their colleges and universities" (1972, p. ix). Written from a unique perspective in a much different era, Mason's book makes a strong case for faculty participation in university government. The section titled "The Board of Trustees—

The Reality of Limited Power vs. the Myth of Unlimited Sovereignty" is especially provocative and useful reading.

Kerr and Gade's report card (1989) on the state of higher education trusteeship is also helpful reading, although most of it is oriented to the issues of public sector trusteeship. *The Guardians* concludes that, on the whole, the boards of private higher education function much more effectively than those in the public sector—in part because the independent sector has the freedom to choose its trustees more carefully and in part because it functions in a much less politicized environment.

Especially relevant to private higher education is *The Effective Board of Trustees* (Chait, Holland, and Taylor, 1991). Interviews with some one hundred trustees and presidents on twenty-two independent college and university campuses provide the basis for concluding that six distinct yet related skill sets characterize effective boards. It is a practical guide, as indicated by the title of its last chapter: "What's a President to Do?"

Chapter Two: The Demography of Independent Higher Education

Beginning with some history is useful, and trustees should make a point of reading the history of the institution they serve. For a more general introduction to the history of American higher education, the standard source is *The American College and University* (Rudolph, 1990).

A concise source of data and trends for independent institutions is the annual *Independent Colleges and Universities: A National Profile*, published by the National Institute of Independent Colleges and Universities in Washington, D.C. A useful analysis, with special attention to the different policies of each state, is the report by the Education Commission of the States Task Force on State Policy and Independent Higher Education (1990), *The Preservation of Excellence in American Higher Education: The Essential Role of Private Colleges and Universities*.

A helpful study of curriculum and institutional culture is *College: The Undergraduate Experience in America* (Boyer, 1987). The best text on assessing educational outcomes has been *What Matters in College: Four Critical Years Revisited* (Astin, 1992). *In-*

vestment in Learning: The Individual and Social Value of American Higher Education (Bowen, 1977) continues to be worth study by anyone seeking a guide to measuring the overall contributions of colleges and universities to our society.

Chapter Three: The Economics of Independent Higher Education

Until recently, there was a dearth of good reading for the layperson on the economics and financing of higher education, particularly for the private sector. However, the fiscal exigencies of the 1990s have produced a new interest on behalf of higher education researchers and a substantial increase in this literature. Jossey-Bass has a fine series called New Directions for Higher Education, which includes volumes on financial planning, new financing strategies, and making the budget process work. The Pew Charitable Trusts have funded the Pew Higher Education Research Program at the University of Pennsylvania, which publishes "Policy Perspectives," a series of very thoughtful and nontechnical essays about the changing condition of higher education and the environment. A third series, which is mostly numbers but an important resource in understanding the economic environment, are the annual statistical reports on the condition of higher education published by the National Center for Education Statistics of the U.S. Department of Education (1989a, 1990).

The Consortium on Financing Higher Education has embarked on a four-year project to study various aspects of the economics of selective private colleges and universities. This project will produce a series of papers written for a lay audience. Finally, the Forum for College Financing, housed at Stanford University, also produces an annual series of essays and papers that directly address the practical issues of the economics of higher education. This forum has a book titled *Productivity and Higher Education* (Anderson and Meyerson, 1991).

Chapter Four: Coping with a Litigious Environment

A valuable source on the broad range of legal issues facing both public and private higher education institutions is Kaplin's *The Law of Higher Education* (Kaplin, 1985a) and its 1985 to 1990 up-

date (Kaplin and Lee, 1990). This comprehensive work addresses
constitutional, statutory, and regulatory mandates as well as case
law that affects colleges and universities and their constituencies.

An excellent annual review of the most important judicial
developments relating to higher education, Dutile's "Higher Education and the Courts," is published in the *Journal of College and
University Law* each fall and covers the preceding calendar year.

A series of brief, concise reference guides on specific topics
and issues of interest to trustees, administrators, faculty, and legal
counsel alike is available from the National Association of College
and University Attorneys in Washington, D.C. Recent titles include,
among others, *Risky Business: Risk Management, Loss Prevention,
and Insurance Procurement for Colleges and Universities* (Bennett,
1990), *What to Do When OSHA Comes Calling* (Barber, 1991); and
*Crime on Campus: Analyzing and Managing the Increasing Risk of
Institutional Liability* (Burling, 1990). The 1985 article by Roderick
K. Daane in the *Journal of College and University Law* is the single
best analysis of the role of college legal counsel to date.

Chapter Five: Planning for Strategic Decision Making

George Keller's *Academic Strategy: The Management Revolution in
American Higher Education* (1983) continues to be one of the best
introductions to the subject of planning for colleges and universities. It describes the challenges facing institutions of higher learning in the 1980s (many of which still apply), the role of strategic
planning in higher education, and a planning methodology. *Strategic Management in Public and Nonprofit Organizations* (Bryson,
1989) is a more recent text that provides a detailed account of the
steps in the planning process as well as examples of successful and
unsuccessful efforts at several organizations. Firsthand accounts of
strategic planning by executives at seven colleges and universities
can be found in *Successful Strategic Planning: Case Studies* (Steeples, 1988).

Two popular authors have produced very useful guides on
planning and management. Although Michael Porter writes for a
business audience, many of the concepts he outlines in *Competitive
Advantage* (1985) apply to colleges and universities as well. His
thought-provoking books are required reading at many top busi-

ness schools, and they serve as good references for many of the planning concepts successful businesses use. In *Managing the Non-Profit Organization* (1990), Peter Drucker interviews executives and "thought leaders" in not-for-profit management on such subjects as managing for performance, building an effective board, and the importance of a mission statement.

Assessing how an institution is performing over time and in relation to its peers is an important component of strategic planning. *Strategic Analysis: Using Comparative Data to Understand Your Institution* (Taylor, Meyerson, Morrell, and Park, 1991) examines key strategic indicators in nine areas (students, faculty and administration, instruction, research, plant, tuition and financial aid, student support, giving, and finances) for more than five hundred colleges and universities. This framework can help planning groups assess the performance of their institutions in comparison to national norms.

Harvard Business Review often contains insightful pieces on strategic planning. Although most often their focus is on the business world, analogies can be drawn for colleges and universities. The thesis of Gary Hamel and C. K. Prahalad (1989) in their article "Strategic Intent" is that the companies that have risen to global leadership over the past two decades began with a goal or "strategic intent" that exceeded their existing resources. Chief executives then rallied the organization to close the gap. In "Crafting Strategy," Henry Mintzberg (1987) says that successful strategies emerge over time as organizations innovate and respond to their markets. He thinks that managers need an intuitive feel for their business as well as facts, figures, and forecasts. We think these ideas may prove useful for strategic planning in higher education as well as in the corporate world.

Change is often an outcome of the strategic planning process. Michael Beer, Russell Eisenstat, and Bert Spector (1990) studied organizational change at large corporations. They offer advice on managing change in their *Harvard Business Review* article "Why Change Programs Don't Produce Change."

The literature on the role of board members in strategic planning at colleges and universities is not extensive. However, one authoritative text on strategic leadership by governing boards is

John Carver's *Boards That Make a Difference* (1990). This book was written specifically for the governing boards of nonprofit and public organizations.

Chapter Six: Responsibilities of the Governing Board

Two excellent books on the structure and governance of colleges and universities, one by a trustee and the other by a president, are *The Governance of Colleges and Universities* by John J. Corson (1960, 1975) and *Presidents, Professors, and Trustees* by W. H. Cowley (1980). Corson's book is a classic, well worth any trustee's attention. Cowley's book, which covers much the same ground from a different perspective, is more controversial.

Two provocative and readable studies of academic governance with special attention to the role of trustees are *Governance of Higher Education: Six Priority Problems* (Carnegie Commission on Higher Education, 1973) and *The Control of the Campus: A Report on the Governance of Higher Education* (Carnegie Foundation for the Advancement of Teaching, 1982).

Joseph Kauffman's *At the Pleasure of the Board* (1980) and *The Selection of College and University Presidents* (1974), although focused primarily on the president's role, contain shrewd and helpful comments on the relation between board and president.

In 1982, the Association of Governing Boards of Universities and Colleges (AGB) appointed a distinguished commission called Strengthening Presidential Leadership with Clark Kerr as chair. From extensive interviews, Kerr and his associate Marian L. Gade distilled three books, the third of which is *The Guardians: Boards of Trustees of American Colleges and Universities* (1989). Its subtitle is "What They Do and How Well They Do It."

In *Trusteeship in the Private College*, Miriam M. Wood (1985) provides case studies of the role of trustees in ten liberal arts colleges. Her critical conclusions should lead all trustees to reexamine their own performance.

The AGB has sponsored a number of useful publications on governance. J. L. Zwingle wrote three excellent pamphlets: *The Lay Governing Board* (1970), *Effective Trusteeship: Guidelines for Board Members* (1979) and *College Trustees: A Question of Legit-*

imacy (1974). *The Nature of Trusteeship: The Role and Responsibilities of College and University Boards* (Nason, 1982) examines in some detail the trustee responsibilities outlined in Chapter Six. *Working Effectively with Trustees* (Taylor, 1987) and *Making Trusteeship Work* (Ingram, 1988) both provide detailed analysis and helpful instructions to trustees.

Chapter Seven: Selecting the Chief Executive

The issues discussed in Chapter Seven are treated in greater detail in *Choosing a College President: Opportunities and Constraints* (McLaughlin and Riesman, 1990), a volume that contains chapter-length case studies of actual searches as well as many other illustrations drawn from college and university search experiences.

Several excellent manuals exist that can serve as guides to search procedures. *Presidential Search: A Guide to the Process of Selecting and Appointing College and University Presidents* (Nason and Axelrod, 1984) is a classic in this area. It was recently revised by Neff and Leondar (1992). *The Search Committee Handbook: A Guide to Recruiting Administrators* (Marchese and Lawrence, 1987) includes useful advice for presidential searches as well as searches at other administrative levels in higher education. Judith Block McLaughlin's chapter on the use of consultants in higher education searches, found in *The Art of Hiring in Higher Education* (Trachtenberg and Stein, 1992), addresses the possible advantages and potential hazards of employing professional assistance with the search. Although now over ten years old, *At the Pleasure of the Board* (Kauffman, 1980) is still one of the best studies of the college and university presidency and has an excellent section on the presidential search. Written for both the profit and nonprofit sectors, *Making a Leadership Change* (Gilmore, 1988) examines the search process in the context of the entire period of leadership transition.

Trustees and search committee members especially interested in issues of confidentiality and disclosure will find *The Costs and Benefits of Openness: Sunshine Laws and Higher Education* (Cleveland, 1985) interesting reading, although litigation continues in many states so some of the specifics he cites are somewhat dated.

"Plugging Search Committee Leaks" (McLaughlin, 1985) provides a discussion of measures that can be taken to avoid unwanted leaks of confidential information.

Chapter Eight: Supporting the
President and Assessing the Presidency

The relationship between the selection and appointment of the president and the assessment that follows is made clear in two books published by the AGB. *Presidential Search: A Guide to the Process of Selecting and Appointing College and University Presidents* (Neff and Leondar, 1992) is a revision of Nason and Axelrod's classic book (1984) on the subject. The second is *Presidential Assessment: A Guide to the Periodic Review of the Performance of Chief Executives* (1984), also a classic by Nason.

In 1984, the Commission on Strengthening Presidential Leadership, directed by Clark Kerr, published its report, *Presidents Make a Difference: Strengthening Leadership in Colleges and Universities*. This report suggests ways of supporting the presidency during a time of perceived leadership crisis.

Other studies by Clark Kerr and Marian Gade of governing boards and their relationship to the presidency suggest that presidential effectiveness depends very much on the nature of the board. Chapter Nine of *The Guardians: Boards of Trustees of American Colleges and Universities* (Kerr and Gade, 1989), "The Evaluation of Performance," cites twelve major problem areas related to board/president relations.

A comprehensive overview of different presidencies in different institutions can be found in *The Many Lives of Academic Presidents* (Kerr and Gade, 1986). This book stresses the relevance of context and setting to assessment. Chapter Fifteen, "Policies and Tactics of Trustees and Presidents," is especially useful in setting forth practical suggestions that bear on the evaluation of presidents. Kerr and Gade are experts on presidential leadership and board relationships. These studies, published by the AGB are recommended reading for every trustee of our nation's colleges and universities.

Chapter Nine: Ensuring Sound
Financial and Plant Management

For a much broader discussion of the trustee's role in overseeing the financial affairs of a college or university, the reader is directed to *Financial Responsibilities of Governing Boards* (Association of Governing Boards of Universities and Colleges, 1989a), which is based on an extensive study undertaken by the AGB. For those interested in a view from the administration angle, the small volume *Financial Management of Colleges and Universities* (Hyatt and Santiago, 1986) is easy reading in its question-and-answer format and gives an appreciation of the apparatus and practice of internal financial controls.

The most timely and important subject of the erosion of the capital base of institutions is covered with insight and good humor in the first broad exposition of the problem, *Hang Gliding or Looking for an Updraft* (Jenny, 1981), which is still completely current in its analysis. The concept of the plant reserve and some procedural applications are also covered in the book. Plant management, including central attention to the deferred major maintenance debacle, is well presented in *Crumbling Academe: Solving the Capital Renewal and Replacement Dilemma* (Kaiser, 1984) and again in *The Decaying American Campus* (Johnson and Rush, 1989). Both books tie the replacement problem into a discussion of good plant management practice with persuasive pointers about trustee responsibility.

Chapter Ten: Setting Investment
Policy and Monitoring Performance

Investing with the Best (Rosenberg, 1986) provides very useful insight into the criteria to be used when selecting investment advisers. It is written for investors by an investment adviser who understands the needs of both parties and seeks to help them find success.

Investing for Total Return (Heerwagen, 1988) provides a useful description of the total return concept that has become so widely accepted among successful current investors. The book also explains how the concept can be adopted to enhance performance at reasonable levels of risk.

Improving Endowment Management (Academy for Educational Development, 1985) is an excellent document that presents the findings of a comprehensive study of twenty-three institutions of higher education that focused on how those institutions manage their endowments. It identifies the many factors that result in success so that the reader may consider the adoption of such practices and policies.

Investment Policy (Ellis, 1985) offers the reader a basic understanding of institutional investing, a means of formulating specific policies to reach long-term objectives, and a way for institutions to manage their investment managers in order to attain their objectives.

Chapter Eleven: Clarifying the Fund-Raising Role

Most of the statistical material used in this chapter comes from a major study of current fund-raising practices and results undertaken by the AGB and reported, including statistical tables, in *Fund-Raising Leadership: A Guide for College and University Boards* (Association of Governing Boards of Universities and Colleges, 1989b). For those interested in even more statistics, the annual publications *Voluntary Support of Education* (Council for Aid to Education, 1990) and *Giving USA* (American Association of Fund-Raising Counsel, 1990) should more than suffice.

The "bible" of higher education fund raisers and one of the first books to treat the subject is Harold J. Seymour's *Designs for Fund-Raising*, first published in 1966; the most recent edition was issued in 1988. The *Handbook for Educational Fund-Raising* (Pray, 1981) remains a pertinent collection of papers by experienced professional fund raisers. Barbara Brittingham and Thomas Pezzullo are to be commended for *The Campus Green: Fund-Raising in Higher Education* (1990), which gives an excellent and concise summary of higher education fund raising today and a good long list of other reference publications. Simply to understand some of the miracles, pratfalls, and general joys of fund raising, *Born to Raise* (Panas, 1988) will mellow one's outlook and prepare one for the adventure of fund raising for one's own institution.

Chapter Twelve: Communicating with
Campus and External Constituencies

Although communication as an explicit trustee responsibility has not been ignored in the literature of trusteeship, it has usually been discussed as an ancillary matter under a variety of headings. This is the case, for example, with articles in *Handbook of College and University Trusteeship* (Ingram, 1980), such as Millett's "Working with Faculty and Students" and Nason's "Responsibilities of the Governing Board." *The Nature of Trusteeship* (Nason, 1982) also includes relevant material.

    In "Charting the Territory of NonProfit Boards," Chait and Taylor (1989) give trustees valuable counsel on the responsibilities they have in their relationships with constituents. Kauffman (1983) and Nelson (1985) offer help in the same area.

    AGB Reports has published a number of articles that discuss various aspects of communication. Among the most helpful are "How to Talk to Faculty and Students" (McGrath, 1977); "The Faculty Problem . . . Handle with Care" (Boyd, 1976); "How Strategic PR Can Pay Off" (Gilley and Ackerman, 1988). See also "When Boards Become Part of the Campus Community" (Taylor, 1989).

    "Academic Reputations: Hard to Come By, Easy to Lose" (National Center for Postsecondary Governance and Finance, 1990) includes an interesting checklist of "do's and don'ts" for handling campus issues that become public.

Chapter Thirteen: Responding to
Political, Social, and Ethical Issues

For a recent discussion of some current ethical issues in higher education, see *Ethics in Higher Education* (May, 1991). *The Effective Board of Trustees* (Chait, Holland, and Taylor, 1991) and *Governing Tomorrow's Campus* (Schuster, Miller, and others, 1989) both provide useful guidance for trustees seeking to improve their performance. Jerry Gaff (1991) explores curricular issues in *New Life for the College Curriculum,* and Richardson and Skinner (1991) tackle the difficult issue of equity and excellence in *Achieving Quality and Diversity.* Other useful volumes include *Shaping*

Higher Education's Future (Levine and Associates, 1989), *Today's Myths and Tomorrow's Realities* (Millard, 1991), *Culture and Ideology in Higher Education* (Tierney, 1991) *The Racial Crisis in American Higher Education* (Altbach and Lomotey, 1991), *Scholarship Reconsidered* (Boyer, 1990), and *The Prospect for Faculty in the Arts and Sciences* (Bowen and Sosa, 1989).

Chapter Fourteen: Setting Tenure and Personnel Policies

The AGB has published several useful volumes intended expressly for trustees. *Trustee Responsibility for Academic Affairs* (Chait, Mortimer, Taylor, and Wood, 1985) addresses in detail the roles and responsibilities of the academic affairs committee of the board with respect to promotion and tenure as well as academic programs and budgets, and faculty evaluation. *Strategic Decision Making* (Frances, Huxel, Meyerson, and Park, 1987) suggests key questions trustees should ask and critical indicators trustees should monitor in the academic area and related realms. A companion volume, *Strategic Analysis* (Taylor, Meyerson, Morrell, and Park, 1991) provides comparative data on faculty tenure, demographics, compensation, support, and development, and orients trustees to the ways to use such statistics.

The history of academic tenure has been eloquently recounted in *Faculty Tenure* (American Association of University Professors, 1973), a volume that also includes nearly fifty recommendations on policy and practice. *Beyond Traditional Tenure* (Chait and Ford, 1982) surveys and evaluates the alternatives and modifications to conventional tenure practices and elaborates on the suggestions outlined in Chapter Fourteen of this book to improve the administration of tenure systems.

On topics closely related to promotion and tenure, we have identified one or two resources as a place for trustees to start. *American Professors* (Bowen and Schuster, 1986) offers a readable and comprehensive overview of the faculty and work conditions in academe. *Affirmative Rhetoric, Negative Action: African American and Hispanic Faculty at Predominantly White Institutions* (Washington and Harvey, 1989) provides an introduction to the issue of hiring minority faculty members and offers policy recommendations and conclusions. *Changing Practices in Faculty Evaluation* (Seldin, 1984) and *Determining Faculty Effectiveness* (Centra, 1979) offer practical and clearheaded suggestions on how to develop faculty evaluation systems. Licata (1986) focuses specifically on the evaluation of tenured faculty. *Enhancing Faculty Careers* (Schuster, Wheeler, and Associates, 1990) and *Faculty Vitality and Institutional Productivity* (Clark and Lewis, 1985) delineate strategies to foster the faculty's professional development. Although it is concerned with the corporate sector, *Managing Human Assets* (Beer and others, 1984) provides excellent and relevant treatments of compensation, incentive structures, and the difficulties inherent in merit pay systems. *Pay for Performance* (National Research Council, 1991) covers the same topics with a particular focus on government employees. Chronister and Kepple (1987) describe early retirement programs and incentives. To understand the consequences and implications of faculty discrimination litigation, consult Chapter Eight of *Academics in Court* (LaNoue and Lee, 1987).

Chapter Fifteen: Defining, Assessing, and Nurturing Quality

A highly readable source on excellence in American life and education is John Gardner's book *Excellence: Can We Be Equal and Excellent Too?*, first published in 1961 and released again in a revised version in 1984. An informing companion volume that describes different models of excellence in collegiate life is Alexander Astin's 1985 book, *Achieving Educational Excellence.*

    The Evidence for Quality (Bogue and Saunders, 1992) furnishes a description and evaluation of current approaches to the definition and demonstration of quality in collegiate life. Lewis Mayhew, Patrick Ford, and Dean Hubbard (1990) present both a philosophical and historical examination of factors related to quality in colleges and universities in *The Quest for Quality*. Daniel Seymour's 1992 release *On Q: Causing Quality in Higher Education* is a treatment of how total quality management can and should be applied to higher education.

    On a related theme, board members who are curious about how college affects students will find Ernest Pascarella and Patrick

Terenzini's 1991 title of interest. This volume furnishes an informing and sometimes surprising treatment of the variables related to
college impact, a treatment that also has much to say about quality.
A digest that can be mastered in less time is carried in the Spring
1992 issue of the journal *Planning for Higher Education* and is
titled "Designing Colleges for Greater Learning" (Pascarella and
Terenzini, 1992).

In addition to W. Edwards Deming's 1986 book on strategic
quality management titled *Out of the Crisis,* readers will find *The
Deming Management Method* (Walton, 1986) an easy-to-read treatment of Deming's major ideas.

Finally, for the board member interested in more specific
approaches to the assessment of quality, *Assessing Student Learn
ing and Development* (Erwin, 1991) is commended as an informing
and easy-to-follow resource.

Chapter Sixteen: Selecting,
Orienting, and Developing Trustees

AGB provides a variety of resources for trustees, including "Fundamentals of Trusteeship," a trustee orientation and development
program consisting of a videotape, audiotape, and user's guide.
AGB publishes a bimonthly magazine, *Trusteeship,* that contains
articles and information directly relevant to trustee concerns. The
AGB Trustee Information Center is a clearinghouse of information
on trusteeship and higher education, accessible to members by
phone, fax, or mail. The Board Mentor Program provides experienced peer facilitators who can offer individualized assistance to
boards and presidents. AGB also offers many seminars and an annual conference. Finally, AGB publishes an annual list of publications for trustees and senior executives, available free upon request.

Four AGB publications especially useful to new trustees are:
Nominating Committee (Gale, 1986) from the Standing Committee
Series, *Trustee Responsibilities* (Pocket Publication no. 1) by Nason
(1989), *A Guide for New Trustees* (Pocket Publication no. 2) by
Axelrod (1989), and *Trustee Orientation and Development Programs* (Pocket Publication no. 3) by Ingram (1989b). John Nason's
classic, *The Nature of Trusteeship* (1982), should be read by all

trustees. *The Guardians* (Kerr and Gade, 1989) draws upon interviews with presidents, board chairs, and heads of faculty organizations to describe what makes boards effective.

AGB's *Recommendations for Improving Trustee Selection in Private Colleges and Universities* (Association of Governing Boards of Universities and Colleges, 1980), a report by a national commission, will be of interest to those concerned about the quality of private higher education governance.

Other relevant publications include *The Cheswick Process: Seven Steps to a More Effective Board* (Savage, 1982), a practical and thorough description of the board development process and particularly the steps involved in arranging a successful board retreat. *The Effective Board of Trustees* (Chait, Holland, and Taylor, 1991) describes the development and testing of a model of board effectiveness and contains specific suggestions for improving board performance.

Chapter Seventeen: Organizing and Staffing the Board

For staff development programs, *Working Effectively with Trustees: Building Cooperative Campus Leadership* (Taylor, 1987) is a useful monograph. It offers creative ideas on how to strengthen staff and board communication and cooperation. For more information about the responsibilities of the board or university secretary, see *The Role of the Board Secretary* (Perlman, 1989) and Smotony (1986, 1993) and Smotony and Summer (1979).

The AGB offers a series of pamphlets on each of nine traditional board standing committees, including the executive committee, which are also included in a single volume, *Making Trusteeship Work* (Ingram, 1988). Each version includes a suggested statement of responsibilities for the committee, the makeup of its membership, and its agenda.

Chapter Eighteen: Making Board and Committee Meetings Work

The Strategy of Meetings (Kieffer, 1988) is as provocative as it is useful in its advocacy of preparing for meetings by deciding in advance what you want to take away from them. His chapter on the same topic in the public sector version of this book is worthwhile reading because Kieffer (1993) writes as an experienced trustee who happens also to be an attorney.

Although unfortunately out of print, *Behind the Boardroom Door* (Mueller, 1984) is worth the search. For anyone who finds human behavior in meetings mystifying, this book is for you: it reveals the author's insightful experience on some thirty corporate boards as former chairman of Arthur D. Little. It is as humorous as it is helpful.

For those readers who like order in meetings and are convinced that they need to understand at least the most useful of General Henry M. Robert's rules, see O'Connell's helpful advice in *The Board Member's Book* (1985).

Chapter Nineteen: Understanding Chief
Executive and Board Chair Responsibilities

Recommendations on strengthening the board's relationship with the president and the presidency in general are included in the AGB's Commission on Strengthening Presidential Leadership (1984) report, *Presidents Make a Difference*. The report was the result of a three-year study and an extensive series of interviews with presidents and trustees. The commission looked at causes of the apparent declining tenure and growing dissatisfaction of presidents, and ways to correct these problems. The report urges governing boards to give more careful attention to their responsibilities and cautions that "unnecessary burdens" not be placed on presidents.

Fisher's controversial book *The Board and the President* (1991) offers a disputable view of college and university governance. Among its assertions is that boards have placed too many limits on the president's ability to lead and are the cause of the generally poor condition of the college and university presidency. According to Fisher, the policies and practices of most governing boards are antithetical to effective presidential leadership in that, typically, poorly conducted searches select the wrong kinds of leaders.

For a more specific treatment of board chair–president relations, see Pocock (1989a). Pocock notes the basic elements of a successful relationship and makes a number of suggestions. Three situations are examined: (1) when the board chair has the lead, ensuring that the president is in tune with the board's policies and that these are supportive of the president's work; (2) when the president has the lead, informing and advising the board, and serving as a communications link between it and institutional constituencies; and (3) joint responsibilities, where the responsibilities intermingle, such as in planning, resource allocation, and evaluation.

Chapter Twenty: Assessing Board Performance

Because sound board assessment begins with an understanding of board goals and responsibilities, Nason's classic *The Nature of Trusteeship* (1982) is a fine place to begin exploring the role and authority of governing boards. A useful companion piece to Nason, Houle's more recent *Governing Boards* (1989), considers board operations, structure, and relationships. Chait, Holland, and Taylor have developed in *The Effective Board of Trustees* (1991) a model of board effectiveness and specific suggestions for improving board performance that provide guidance in understanding what it means to be a competent board and how boards can enhance their capabilities.

There is little empirical literature relating specifically to college and university boards that describes the usefulness and limitations of assessment processes. The more general, but still very useful, organizational behavior literature that treats the subject includes Alderfer (1986), Lawler (1973), and Zander (1982). A thorough but technical treatment of self-assessment research and theory is found in Ashford (1989).

The Cheswick Process: Seven Steps to a More Effective Board (Savage, 1982) is a very practical and thorough description of the board development process and particularly of the steps involved in arranging a successful board retreat. AGB, whose Board Mentor Program has conducted scores of retreats, offers materials that describe the retreat process. AGB also offers several versions of its "Self-Study Criteria," which are useful for assessing board performance in a wide variety of institutional settings.

References

Academy for Educational Development. *Improving Endowment Management.* Washington, D.C.: Association of Governing Boards of Universities and Colleges, 1985.

AGB Notes, 1971, *2*(1), 1.

Alderfer, C. "The Invisible Director on Corporate Boards." *Harvard Business Review,* 1986, *64*(6), 38–52.

Alsalam, N. (ed.). *The Condition of Education, 1990.* Vol. 1: *Postsecondary Education.* Washington, D.C.: U.S. Government Printing Office, 1990a.

Alsalam, N. (ed.) *The Condition of Education, 1990.* Vol. II: *Postsecondary Education.* Washington, D.C.: U.S. Government Printing Office, 1990b.

Altbach, P. G., and Lomotey, K. *The Racial Crisis in American Higher Education.* Albany: State University of New York Press, 1991.

Alton, B. T. "Why Presidents Quit." *AGB Reports,* 1982, *24*, 47–53.

American Association of Fund-Raising Counsel. *Giving USA: 1989 Annual Report.* New York: American Association of Fund-Raising Counsel, 1990.

American Association of University Professors. *Statement on Gov-*

ernment of Colleges and Universities. Washington, D.C.: American Association of University Professors, 1966.

American Association of University Professors. *Policy Documents and Reports.* Washington, D.C.: American Association of University Professors, 1984.

American Association of University Professors and Association of American Colleges Commission on Academic Tenure. *Faculty Tenure: A Report and Recommendations.* San Francisco: Jossey-Bass, 1973.

American Council on Education. *Higher Education Today: Facts in Brief.* Washington, D.C.: American Council on Education, 1989.

Anderson, C. *Composition of Governing Boards, 1985: A Survey of College and University Governing Boards.* Washington, D.C.: Association of Governing Boards of Universities and Colleges, 1985.

Anderson, R. E. *Finance and Effectiveness: A Study of College Environments.* Princeton, N.J.: Educational Testing Service, 1983.

Anderson, R. E., and Meyerson, J. W. *Productivity and Higher Education.* Princeton, N.J.: Peterson's Guides, 1991.

Ashford, S. "Self-Assessments in Organizations." *Research in Organizational Behavior,* 1989, *11,* 133–174.

Assembly on University Goals and Governance. *A First Report.* Cambridge, Mass.: American Academy of Arts and Sciences, 1971.

Association of Governing Boards of Universities and Colleges. *Recommendations for Improving Trustee Selection in Private Colleges and Universities.* Washington, D.C.: Association of Governing Boards of Universities and Colleges, 1980.

Association of Governing Boards of Universities and Colleges. *Composition of Governing Boards, 1985.* Washington, D.C: Association of Governing Boards of Universities and Colleges, 1986.

Association of Governing Boards of Universities and Colleges. *Results of a National Survey of Board Characteristics, Policies, and Practices.* Washington, D.C.: Association of Governing Boards of Universities and Colleges, 1988.

Association of Governing Boards of Universities and Colleges. *Financial Responsibilities of Governing Boards.* (2nd ed.) Washington, D.C.: Association of Governing Boards of Universities and Colleges, 1989a.

Association of Governing Boards of Universities and Colleges. *Fund-Raising Leadership: A Guide for College and University Boards*. Washington, D.C.: Association of Governing Boards of Universities and Colleges, 1989b.

Association of Governing Boards of Universities and Colleges. *The Commitment of Trusteeship*. Washington, D.C.: Association of Governing Boards of Universities and Colleges, 1990.

Association of Governing Boards of Universities and Colleges. *Trustees and Troubled Times in Higher Education*. Washington, D.C.: Association of Governing Boards of Universities and Colleges, 1992.

Association of Physical Plant Administrators of Colleges and Universities. *The Decaying American Campus*. Washington, D.C.: Association of Physical Plant Administrators of Colleges and Universities, 1989.

Astin, A. *Four Critical Years: Effects of College on Beliefs, Attitudes, and Knowledge*. San Francisco: Jossey-Bass, 1977.

Astin, A. *Achieving Educational Excellence: A Critical Assessment of Priorities and Practices in Higher Education*. San Francisco: Jossey-Bass, 1985.

Astin, A. *What Matters in College: Four Critical Years Revisited*. San Francisco: Jossey-Bass, 1992.

Atelsek, F., and Gomberg, I. *Composition of College and University Governing Boards*. Higher Education Panel Report, no. 35. Washington, D.C.: American Council on Education, 1977.

Axelrod, N. *A Guide for New Trustees*. AGB Pocket Publication, no. 2. Washington, D.C.: Association of Governing Boards of Universities and Colleges, 1989.

Barber, C. A. *What to Do When OSHA Comes Calling*. Washington, D.C.: National Association of College and University Attorneys, 1991.

Baumol, W. "Electronics, the Cost Disease, and the Operation of Libraries." *Journal of the American Society for Information Sciences*, 1983, *34*(3), 181–191.

Beale, J. R. "Delivery of Legal Service to Institutions of Higher

Education." *Journal of College and University Law*, 1974, *2*(1), 5–12.

Beer, M., Eisenstat, R. A., and Spector, B. "Why Change Programs Don't Produce Change." *Harvard Business Review*, 1990, *68*, 158–166.

Beer, M., and others. *Managing Human Assets: The Groundbreaking Harvard Business School Program.* New York: Free Press, 1984.

Bennett, B. *Risky Business: Risk Management, Loss Prevention, and Insurance Procurement for Colleges and Universities.* Washington, D.C.: National Association of College and University Attorneys, 1990.

Bennis, W., and Nanus, B. *Leaders: Strategies for Taking Charge.* New York: HarperCollins, 1985.

Birnbaum, R. *How Academic Leadership Works: Understanding Success and Failure in the College Presidency.* San Francisco: Jossey-Bass, 1992.

Blackwell, J. "Faculty Issues: The Impact on Minorities." *The Review of Higher Education*, 1988, *11*(4), 417–434.

Bogue, E. G., and Saunders, R. L. *The Evidence for Quality: Strengthening the Tests of Academic and Administrative Effectiveness.* San Francisco: Jossey-Bass, 1992.

Bowen, H. R. *Investment in Learning: The Individual and Social Value of American Higher Education.* San Francisco: Jossey-Bass, 1977.

Bowen, H. R. *The Costs of Higher Education. How Much Do Colleges and Universities Spend Per Student and How Much Should They Spend?* San Francisco: Jossey-Bass, 1980.

Bowen, H. R. "What Determines the Costs of Higher Education." In L. Leslie and R. E. Anderson (eds.), *ASHE Reader on Finance in Higher Education.* San Francisco: Jossey-Bass, 1988.

Bowen, H., and Schuster, J. *American Professors: A National Resource Imperiled.* New York: Oxford University Press, 1986.

Bowen, W., and Sosa, J. *The Prospect for Faculty in the Arts and Sciences.* Princeton, N.J.: Princeton University Press, 1989.

Boyd, W. "The Faculty Problem . . . Handle with Care." *AGB Reports*, 1976, *18*(5), 37–42.

Boyer, E. *College: The Undergraduate Experience in America.* New York: HarperCollins, 1987.

Boyer, E. *Scholarship Reconsidered.* Princeton, N.J.: Carnegie Foundation for the Advancement of Teaching, 1990.

Breneman, D. W. "Are We Losing Our Liberal Arts Colleges?" *College Board Review,* 1990, *29,* 5–21.

Brittingham, B. E., and Pezzullo, T. R. *The Campus Green: Fund Raising in Higher Education.* Washington, D.C.: Association for the Study of Higher Education-ERIC Higher Education Reports, George Washington University, 1990.

Brown, S. *Increasing Minority Faculty: An Elusive Goal.* Princeton, N.J.: Educational Testing Service, 1988.

Bryson, M. *Strategic Management in Public and Nonprofit Organizations.* New York: Praeger, 1989.

Burling, P. *Crime on Campus: Analyzing and Managing the Increasing Risk of Institutional Liability.* Washington, D.C.: National Association of College and University Attorneys, 1990.

Carlzon, J. *Moments of Truth.* New York: HarperCollins, 1987.

Carnegie Commission on Higher Education. *Governance of Higher Education: Six Priority Problems.* New York: McGraw-Hill, 1973.

Carnegie Council on Policy Studies in Higher Education. *Making Affirmative Action Work in Higher Education: An Analysis of Institutional and Federal Policies with Recommendations.* San Francisco: Jossey-Bass, 1975.

Carnegie Foundation for the Advancement of Teaching. *The Control of the Campus: A Report on the Governance of Higher Education.* Princeton, N.J.: Carnegie Foundation for the Advancement of Teaching, 1982.

Carnegie Foundation for the Advancement of Teaching. *Classification of Institutions of Higher Education.* New York: Carnegie Foundation for the Advancement of Teaching, 1987.

Carnegie Foundation for the Advancement of Teaching. *The Condition of the Professoriate: Attitudes and Trends, 1989.* Princeton, N.J.: Carnegie Foundation for the Advancement of Teaching, 1989.

Carrier, S. C., and Davis-Van Atta, D. *Maintaining America's Scien-*

tific Productivity: The Necessity of the Liberal Arts Colleges. Oberlin, Ohio: Oberlin College Press, 1986.

Carver, J. *Boards That Make a Difference: A New Design for Leadership in Nonprofit and Public Organizations.* San Francisco: Jossey-Bass, 1990.

Centra, J. *Determining Faculty Effectiveness: Assessing Teaching, Research, and Service for Personnel Decisions and Improvement.* San Francisco: Jossey-Bass, 1979.

Chait, R. P., and Ford, A. *Beyond Traditional Tenure: A Guide to Sound Policies and Practices.* San Francisco: Jossey-Bass, 1982.

Chait, R. P., Holland, T. P., and Taylor, B. E. *The Effective Board of Trustees.* New York: American Council on Education/Macmillan, 1991.

Chait, R. P., Mortimer, K. P., Taylor, B. E., and Wood, M. M. *Trustee Responsibility for Academic Affairs.* Washington, D.C.: Association of Governing Boards of Universities and Colleges, 1985.

Chait, R. P., and Taylor, B. E. "Evaluating Boards of Trustees: Theory and Practice." Paper presented at the Association for the Study of Higher Education, Baltimore, Md., 1987.

Chait, R. P., and Taylor, B. E. "Charting the Territory of Nonprofit Boards." *Harvard Business Review*, 1989, *67*(1), 44–54.

Chronister, J., and Kepple, T., Jr. *Incentive Early Retirement Programs for Faculty.* Washington, D.C.: The Association for the Study of Higher Education, 1987.

Clark, S., and Lewis, C. (eds.). *Faculty Vitality and Institutional Productivity.* New York: Teachers College Press, 1985.

Cleveland, H. *The Costs and Benefits of Openness: Sunshine Laws and Higher Education.* Washington, D.C.: Association of Governing Boards of Universities and Colleges, 1985.

Commission on Strengthening Presidential Leadership. (C. Kerr, director.) *Presidents Make a Difference: Strengthening Leadership in Colleges and Universities.* Washington, D.C.: Association of Governing Boards of Universities and Colleges, 1984.

Corson, J. J. *The Governance of Colleges and Universities.* New York: McGraw-Hill, 1960, 1975.

Council for Aid to Education. *Voluntary Support of Education,*

1972 Annual Survey. New York: Council for Aid to Education, 1972.

Council for Aid to Education. *Voluntary Support of Education.* New York: Council for Aid to Education, 1990.

Council for Aid to Education. *Voluntary Support of Education, 1990 Annual Survey.* New York: Council for Aid to Education, 1991.

Cowley, W. H. *Presidents, Professors, and Trustees: The Evolution of American Academic Government.* San Francisco. Jossey-Bass, 1980.

Crosby, P. *Quality Without Tears.* New York: McGraw-Hill, 1984.

Daane, R. K. "The Role of University Counsel." *Journal of College and University Law,* 1985, *12*(3), 399–414.

Deming, W. E. *Out of the Crisis.* Cambridge, Mass.: MIT Press, 1986.

Drucker, P. F. "What Business Can Learn from Nonprofits." *Harvard Business Review,* 1989, *67*(4), 88–93.

Drucker, P. F. *Managing the Non-Profit Organization.* New York: HarperCollins, 1990.

Dutile, F. N. "Higher Education and the Courts: 1989 in Review." *Journal of College and University Law,* 1990, *17*(2), 149–242.

Education Commission of the States Task Force on State Policy and Independent Higher Education. *The Preservation of Excellence in American Higher Education: The Essential Role of Private Colleges and Universities.* Denver, Colo.: Education Commission of the States, 1990.

El-Khawas, E. *Campus Trends, 1990.* Washington, D.C.: American Council on Education, 1990.

Ellis, C. D. *Investment Policy.* Homewood, Ill.: Business One Irwin, 1985.

Enhancing Quality in an Era of Resource Constraints. Report of the Task Force on Costs in Higher Education. Ann Arbor: University of Michigan Press, 1990.

Erwin, T. D. *Assessing Student Learning and Development: A Guide to the Principles, Goals, and Methods of Determining College Outcomes.* San Francisco: Jossey-Bass, 1991.

Fisher, J. L. "Trustees and the Media." *AGB Reports,* 1980, *22*(4), 26–28.

Fisher, J. L. "Presidential Assessment: A Better Way." *AGB Reports*, 1986, *28*(5), 16–21.

Fisher, J. L. *The Board and the President.* New York: American Council on Education/Macmillan, 1991.

Fisher, J. L., and Quehl, G. "Presidential Assessment: Obstacles to Leadership." *Change*, 1984, *16*, 5–7.

"Fourteen Percent of CEOs Leave Annually." *AGB Reports*, 1992, *34*(6), 2.

Frances, C. "Key Economic Indicators for Higher Education." In K. H. Hanson and J. W. Meyerson (eds.), *Higher Education in a Changing Economy.* New York: American Council on Education/Macmillan, 1990.

Frances, C., Huxel, G., Meyerson, J., and Park, D. *Strategic Decision Making: Key Questions and Indicators for Trustees.* Washington, D.C.: Association of Governing Boards of Universities and Colleges, 1987.

Furniss, T. "The 1976 AAUP Retrenchment Policy." *Educational Record*, 1976, *57*(3), 133–139.

Furniss, T. "Status of AAUP Policy." *Educational Record*, 1978, *59*(1), 7–29.

Gaff, J. G. *New Life for the College Curriculum: Assessing Achievements and Furthering Progress in the Reform of General Education.* San Francisco: Jossey-Bass, 1991.

Galbraith, J. K. *The New Industrial State.* Boston: Houghton Mifflin, 1967.

Gale, R. *Nominating Committee.* Washington, D.C.: The Association of Governing Boards of Universities and Colleges, 1986.

Gardner, J. *Excellence: Can We Be Equal and Excellent Too?* (Rev. ed.) New York: W.W.Norton, 1984.

Gardner, J. *On Leadership.* New York: Free Press, 1990.

Garvin, D. *Managing Quality.* New York: Free Press, 1988.

Gibran, K. *Sand and Foam.* New York: Knopf, 1973.

Gilley, J. W., and Ackerman, H. "How Strategic PR Can Pay Off." *AGB Reports*, 1988, *30*(3), 9–11.

Gilmore, T. N. *Making a Leadership Change: How Organizations and Leaders Can Handle Leadership Transitions Successfully.* San Francisco: Jossey-Bass, 1988.

Greenleaf, R. K. *Trustees as Servants*. Indianapolis, Ind.: Robert K. Greenleaf Center, 1974.

Guaspari, J. *I Know It When I See It: A Modern Fable About Quality*. New York: AMACOM, 1985.

Hadden, E. M., and Blaire, A. F. *Nonprofit Organizations: Rights and Liabilities for Members, Directors, and Officers*. Wilmette, Ill.: Callaghan, 1987.

Hamel, G., and Prahalad, C. K. "Strategic Intent." *Harvard Business Review*, 1989, *67*, 63–76.

Hanson, K. H., and Meyerson, J. W. (eds.). *Higher Education in a Changing Economy*. New York: American Council on Education/Macmillan, 1990.

Hartnett, R. *College and University Trustees: Their Backgrounds, Roles, and Educational Attitudes*. Princeton, N.J.: Educational Testing Service, 1969.

Heerwagen, P. D. *Investing for Total Return*. Chicago: Probus, 1988.

Helms, L. B. "Patterns of Litigation in Postsecondary Education: A Case Law Study." *Journal of College and University Law*, 1987, *14*(1), 99–119.

Helms, L. B. "Litigation Patterns: Higher Education and the Courts in 1988." *Education Law Reporter*, 1990, *57*, 1–11.

Hodgkinson, H. *Demographic Perspectives on Higher Education*. Washington, D.C.: Association of Governing Boards of Universities and Colleges, 1990.

Houle, C. O. *Governing Boards: Their Nature and Nurture*. San Francisco: Jossey-Bass, 1989.

"How Aggressively Should Colleges Lobby Governors and Legislators for Money in the Midst of Recession?" *Chronicle of Higher Education*, Feb. 19, 1992, p. 23.

Hyatt, J. A., and Santiago, A. A. *Financial Management of Colleges and Universities*. Washington, D.C.: National Association of College and University Business Officers, 1986.

Hyer, P. "Affirmative Action for Women Faculty." *Journal of Higher Education*, 1985, *56*(3), 282–299.

Ingram, R. T. "Organizing the Board." In R. T. Ingram and Associates, *Handbook of College and University Trusteeship: A Practical Guide for Trustees, Chief Executives, and Other Lead-*

ers Responsible for Developing Effective Boards. San Francisco: Jossey-Bass, 1980b.

Ingram, R. T. *Executive Committee.* Washington, D.C.: Association of Governing Boards of Universities and Colleges, 1985.

Ingram, R. T. *Making Trusteeship Work.* Washington, D.C.: Association of Governing Boards of Universities and Colleges, 1988.

Ingram, R. T. *Making Advisory Committees and Boards Work.* Washington, D.C.: Association of Governing Boards of Universities and Colleges, 1989a.

Ingram, R. T. *Trustee Orientation and Development Programs.* AGB Pocket Publication, no. 3. Washington, D.C.: Association of Governing Boards of Universities and Colleges, 1989b.

Ingram, R. T., and Associates. *Handbook of College and University Trusteeship: A Practical Guide for Trustees, Chief Executives, and Other Leaders Responsible for Developing Effective Boards.* San Francisco: Jossey-Bass, 1980a.

Jenny, H. H. *Hang Gliding or Looking for an Updraft.* Wooster, Ohio: The College of Wooster Press, 1981.

Johnson, S. L., and Rush, S. C. *The Decaying American Campus.* Washington, D.C.: Association of Physical Plant Administrators of Colleges and Universities, 1989.

Kaiser, H. H. *Crumbling Academe: Solving the Capital Renewal and Replacement Dilemma.* Washington, D.C.: Association of Governing Boards of Universities and Colleges, 1984.

Kaplin, W. A. *The Law of Higher Education: Legal Implications of Administrative Decision Making.* San Francisco: Jossey-Bass, 1978.

Kaplin, W. A. *The Law of Higher Education, 1980.* San Francisco: Jossey-Bass, 1980.

Kaplin, W. A. *The Law of Higher Education: A Comprehensive Guide to Legal Implications of Administrative Decision Making.* (2nd ed.) San Francisco: Jossey-Bass, 1985a.

Kaplin, W. A. "Law on the Campus 1960–1985: Years of Growth and Challenge." *Journal of College and University Law,* 1985b, *12*(3), 269–299.

Kaplin, W. A., and Lee, B. *The Law of Higher Education, 1985–1990 Update.* Washington, D.C.: National Association of College and University Attorneys, 1990.

Kauffman, J. *The Selection of College and University Presidents.* Washington, D.C.: Association of American Colleges, 1974.

Kauffman, J. F. "Presidential Assessment and Development." In C. F. Fisher (ed.), *Developing and Evaluating Administrative Leadership.* New Directions for Higher Education, no. 22. San Francisco: Jossey-Bass, 1978.

Kauffman, J. F. *At the Pleasure of the Board.* Washington, D.C.: American Council on Education, 1980.

Kauffman, J. F. "The Conflict Between Policy and Administration." *AGB Reports,* 1983, *25*(6), 19–20.

Keller, G. *Academic Strategy: The Management Revolution in American Higher Education.* Baltimore, Md.: The Johns Hopkins University Press, 1983.

Kerr, C. *Presidents Make a Difference.* A Report of the Commission on Strengthening Presidential Leadership. Washington, D.C.: Association of Governing Boards of Universities and Colleges, 1984.

Kerr, C., and Gade, M. *The Many Lives of Academic Presidents: Time, Place, and Character.* Washington, D.C.: Association of Governing Boards of Universities and Colleges, 1986.

Kerr, C., and Gade, M. *The Guardians: Boards of Trustees of American Colleges and Universities.* Washington, D.C.: Association of Governing Boards of Universities and Colleges, 1989.

Kieffer, G. *The Strategy of Meetings.* New York: Simon & Schuster, 1988.

Kieffer, G. D. "Making Board Meetings Work." In R. T. Ingram and Associates, *Governing Public Colleges and Universities: A Handbook for Trustees, Chief Executives, and Other Campus Leaders.* San Francisco: Jossey-Bass, 1993.

Koteen, J. *Strategic Management in Public and Nonprofit Organizations.* New York: Praeger, 1989.

Kramer, M. "The Costs of Higher Education: Who Pays and Who Should Pay?" In *An Agenda for the Year 2000: Thirtieth Anniversary Colloquia Proceedings.* New York: The College Board, 1985.

Kramer, R. M. "Ideology, Status, and Power in Board-Executive Relationships." *Social Work,* 1965, *10*, 107–114.

Kurtz, D. L. *Board Liability: Guide for Nonprofit Directors.* Mt. Kisco, N.Y.: Moyer Bell Ltd., 1988.

LaNoue, G., and Lee, B. *Academics in Court: The Consequences of Faculty Discrimination Litigation.* Ann Arbor: University of Michigan Press, 1987.

"The Lattice and the Ratchet." *Policy Perspectives,* 1990, *2*(4), 1–8.

Lawler, E. *Motivation in Work Organizations.* Pacific Grove, Calif.: Brooks/Cole, 1973.

Lawler, E. E. *Strategic Pay: Aligning Organizational Strategies and Pay Systems.* San Francisco: Jossey-Bass, 1990.

Levin, H. "Raising Productivity in Higher Education." *Policy Perspectives,* 1989, *2*(1), 3–4.

Levine, A., and Associates. *Shaping Higher Education's Future: Demographic Realities and Opportunities, 1990–2000.* San Francisco: Jossey-Bass, 1989.

Licata, C. *Post-Tenure Faculty Evaluation: Threat or Opportunity?* Washington, D.C.: Association for the Study of Higher Education, 1986.

Lindsey, L. "The University and the Re-Emergence of Economic Individualism." In K. H. Hanson and J. W. Meyerson (eds.), *Higher Education in a Changing Economy.* New York: American Council on Education/Macmillan, 1990.

McGrath, C. P. "How to Talk to Faculty and Students." *AGB Reports,* 1977, *19*(2), 25–28.

McLaughlin, J. B. "Plugging Search Committee Leaks." *AGB Reports,* 1985, *27*(3), 24–30.

McLaughlin, J. B., and Riesman, D. *Choosing a College President: Opportunities and Constraints.* Princeton, N.J.: Carnegie Foundation for the Advancement of Teaching, 1990.

McMullan, S. H. Letter to Sanford H. Levine from General Counsel and Director of Risk Management, United Educators Insurance Risk Retention Group, Inc., July 1, 1991.

Marchese, T. J., and Lawrence, J. F. *The Search Committee Handbook: A Guide to Recruiting Administrators.* Washington, D.C.: American Association of Higher Education, 1987.

Marks, L. R. "Directors' Liability: What You Don't Know Can Hurt You." *Symphony Magazine,* 1987, *38*(5), 18–21, 60–61.

Mason, H. L. *College and University Government*. New Orleans, La.: Tulane University Press, 1972.

Massey, W. F. "Improving Academic Productivity." *Capital Ideas*, 1991, *6* (entire issue 2).

May, W. W. *Ethics in Higher Education*. New York: American Council on Education/Macmillan, 1991.

Mayhew, L. B., Ford, P. J., and Hubbard, D. L. *The Quest for Quality: The Challenge for Undergraduate Education in the 1990s*. San Francisco: Jossey-Bass, 1990.

Millard, R. M. *Today's Myths and Tomorrow's Realities: Overcoming Obstacles to Academic Leadership in the Twenty-First Century*. San Francisco: Jossey-Bass, 1991.

Millett, J. D. *The Academic Community: An Essay on Organization*. New York: McGraw-Hill, 1962.

Millett, J. D. "Interim Report on the Minnesota Community College System, Technical Report No. 1: Report on Enrollment and Costs, Minnesota Community College System." Unpublished paper, Minnesota Higher Education Coordinating Board, 1980a.

Millett, J. D. "Working with Faculty and Students." In R. T. Ingram and Associates, *Handbook of College and University Trusteeship: A Practical Guide for Trustees, Chief Executives, and Other Leaders Responsible for Developing Effective Governing Boards*. San Francisco: Jossey-Bass, 1980b.

Mintzberg, H. "Crafting Strategy." *Harvard Business Review*, 1987, *65*(4), 66-75.

Moots, P. R. "A Fresh Look at Your Bylaws." *AGB Reports*, 1991, *33*(3), 24-28.

Mueller, R. K. *Behind the Boardroom Door*. New York: Crown, 1984.

Munitz, B. "Reviewing Presidential Leadership." In R. T. Ingram and Associates, *Handbook of College and University Trusteeship: A Practical Guide for Trustees, Chief Executives, and Other Leaders Responsible for Developing Effective Governing Boards*. San Francisco: Jossey-Bass, 1980.

Nason, J. W. "Responsibilities of the Governing Board." In R. T. Ingram and Associates, *Handbook of College and University Trusteeship: A Practical Guide for Trustees, Chief Executives,*

and Other Leaders Responsible for Developing Effective Govern-
ing Boards. San Francisco: Jossey-Bass, 1980.

Nason, J. W. *The Nature of Trusteeship: The Role and Responsi-*
bilities of College and University Boards. Washington, D.C.: Association of Governing Boards of Universities and Colleges,
1982.

Nason, J. W. *Presidential Assessment: A Guide to the Periodic Re-*
view of the Performance of Chief Executives. Washington, D.C.:
Association of Governing Boards of Universities and Colleges,
1984.

Nason, J. W. *Trustee Responsibilities.* AGB Pocket Publication,
no. 1. Washington, D.C.: Association of Governing Boards of
Universities and Colleges, 1989.

Nason, J. W., and Axelrod, N. R. *Presidential Search: A Guide to*
the Process of Selecting and Appointing College and University
Presidents. (Rev. ed.) Washington, D.C.: Association of Governing Boards of Universities and Colleges, 1984.

National Association of College and University Attorneys. "Delivery of Legal Services to Higher Education Institutions: A Survey." *College Law Digest,* 1984, *15,* 7–33.

National Association of College and University Business Officers.
"Legal Services." In *College and University Business Adminis-*
tration. (4th ed.) Washington, D.C.: National Association of College and University Business Officers, 1982.

National Association of College and University Business Officers.
1992 Endowment Study. Washington, D.C.: National Association of College and University Business Officers, 1992.

National Center for Education Statistics. *Early Estimates, National*
Estimates of Higher Education: School Year 1988–89. CS/89-315,
Dec. 1988.

National Center for Education Statistics. *Digest of Education Sta-*
tistics, 1989. Washington, D.C.: U.S. Department of Education,
National Center for Education Statistics, 1989a.

National Center for Education Statistics. *Projections of Education*
Statistics to 1997–98. Washington, D.C.: U.S. Department of Education, Office of Educational Research and Improvement, 1989b.

National Center for Education Statistics. *Digest of Education Sta-*

tistics, 1990. Washington, D.C.: U.S. Department of Education, National Center for Education Statistics, 1990.

National Center for Postsecondary Governance and Finance. "Academic Reputations: Hard to Come By, Easy to Lose." *Centerpiece*, 1990, *5*(2), 1, 4.

National Institute of Independent Colleges and Universities. *Independent Colleges and Universities: A National Profile*. Washington, D.C.: National Institute of Independent Colleges and Universities, 1992.

National Research Council. *Pay for Performance: Evaluating Performance Appraisal and Merit Pay*. Washington, D.C.: National Academy Press, 1991.

Nearing, S. "Who's Who Among College Trustees." *School and Society*, 1917, *6*(141), 297-299.

Neff, C., and Leondar, B. *Presidential Search: A Guide to the Process of Selecting and Appointing College and University Presidents*. (Rev. ed.) Washington, D.C.: Association of Governing Boards of Universities and Colleges, 1992.

Nelson, C. "Improve Your Meetings Four Ways." *AGB Reports*, 1979, *21*(5), 26-29.

Nelson, C. *Distinguishing Between Policy and Administration*. Washington, D.C.: Association of Governing Boards of Universities and Colleges, 1985.

Ness, F. W. "Jim Fisher's Better Way Isn't." *AGB Reports*, 1986, *27*(6), 9-11.

Nevison, C. "Effects of Tenure and Retirement Policies on the College Faculty." *Journal of Higher Education*, 1980, *51*(2), 150-166.

Nordhaus, W. "Evaluating the Risks for Specific Institutions." In R. E. Anderson and J. W. Meyerson (eds.), *Financial Planning Under Economic Uncertainty*. New Directions for Higher Education, no. 69. San Francisco: Jossey-Bass, 1990.

O'Connell, B. *The Board Member's Book*. Washington, D.C.: The Foundation Center, 1985.

Paltridge, J. G. "Studying Board Effectiveness." In R. T. Ingram and Associates, *Handbook of College and University Trusteeship: A Practical Guide for Trustees, Chief Executives, and Other Leaders Responsible for Developing Effective Governing Boards*. San Francisco: Jossey-Bass, 1980.

Panas, J. *Born to Raise*. Chicago: Pluribus Press, 1988.

Pascarella, E. T., and Terenzini, P. T. *How College Affects Students: Findings and Insights from Twenty Years of Research*. San Francisco: Jossey-Bass, 1991.

Pascarella, E. T., and Terenzini, P. T. "Designing Colleges for Greater Learning," *Planning for Higher Education*, 1992, *20*, 1–5.

Peat, Marwick, Main & Company. *Directors' and Officers' Liability: A Crisis in the Making*. Montvale, N.J.: Peat, Marwick, Main & Company, 1987.

Perlman, D. H. *The Role of the Board Secretary*. AGB Pocket Publication, no. 13. Washington, D.C.: Association of Governing Boards of Universities and Colleges, 1989.

Peters, T., and Austin, N. *A Passion for Excellence*. New York: Random House, 1985.

Pocock, J. W. *The Board Chair–President Relationship*. AGB Pocket Publication, no. 4. Washington, D.C.: Association of Governing Boards of Universities and Colleges, 1989a.

Pocock, J. W. *Fund-Raising Leadership: A Guide for College and University Boards*. Washington, D.C.: Association of Governing Boards of Universities and Colleges, 1989b.

Porter, M. E. *Competitive Advantage*. New York: Free Press, 1985.

Porth, W. C. "Personal Liability of Trustees of Educational Institutions." *Journal of College and University Law*, 1975, *2*(2), 143–156.

Pray, F. C. *Handbook for Educational Fund Raising: A Guide to Successful Principles and Practices for Colleges, Universities, and Schools*. San Francisco: Jossey-Bass, 1981.

Project Kaleidoscope. *What Works: Building Natural Science Communities*. 2 vols. Washington, D.C.: Project Kaleidoscope, 1992.

Richardson, R. C., Jr., and Skinner, E. F. *Achieving Quality and Diversity*. New York: American Council on Education/Macmillan, 1991.

Riesman, D. "The Personal Side of the Presidency." *AGB Reports*, 1982, *24*(6), 35–39.

Riesman, D. "Epilogue: Refractions and Reflections." In J. Clodius and D. S. Magrath (eds.), *The President's Spouse*. National Association of State Universities and Land Grant Colleges, 1984.

Robert, H. M. *Robert's Rules of Order*. New York: Morrow, 1971.

Rosenberg, C. N., Jr. *Investing with the Best.* New York: Wiley, 1986.

Rudolph, F. *The American College and University.* New York: Knopf, 1965.

Rudolph, F. *The American College and University: A History.* Athens: The University of Georgia Press, 1990.

Savage, T. *The Cheswick Process: Seven Steps to a More Effective Board.* Belmont, Mass.: The Cheswick Center, 1982.

Schapiro, M. O., McPherson, M. S., and O'Malley, M. P. *Expenditure Patterns and Trends in U.S. Higher Education: How Do the "Elite" Colleges and Universities Compare with the Rest of Education?* Cambridge, Mass.: Consortium on Financing Higher Education, 1990.

Schein, E. H. *Process Consultation: Lessons for Managers and Consultants.* Reading, Mass.: Addison-Wesley, 1987.

Schmidtlein, F., and Milton, T. "College and University Planning: Perspectives from a Nationwide Survey." *Planning for Higher Education,* 1988-89, *17*(3), 1-19.

Schuster, J. H., Miller, L., and others. *Governing Tomorrow's Campus.* New York: American Council on Education/Macmillan, 1989.

Schuster, J. H., Wheeler, D. W., and Associates. *Enhancing Faculty Careers: Strategies for Development and Renewal.* San Francisco: Jossey-Bass, 1990.

Seldin, P. *Changing Practices in Faculty Evaluation: A Critical Assessment and Recommendations for Improvement.* San Francisco: Jossey-Bass, 1984.

Select Committee on Children, Youth, and Families. *U.S. Children and Their Families: Current Conditions and Recent Trends, 1989.* Washington, D.C.: U.S. Government Printing Office, 1989.

Senge, P. *The Fifth Discipline.* New York: Doubleday, 1990.

Seymour, D. *On Q: Causing Quality in Higher Education.* New York: American Council on Education/Macmillan, 1992.

Seymour, H. J. *Designs for Fund-Raising.* (2nd ed.) Rockville, Md.: Educational Fund-Raising Institute, 1988.

Shaw, K. A. "Presidential Assessment: Good Intentions Gone Wrong." *AGB Reports,* 1985, *27*(5), 20-23.

Singsen, M. P. "Charity Is No Defense: The Impact of the Insurance

Crises on Nonprofit Organizations and an Examination of Alternative Insurance Mechanisms." *University of San Francisco Law Review,* 1988, *22,* 599–634.

Smotony, B. "A Secretary Is Not Necessarily a Rose." *AGB Reports,* 1986, *28*(6), 33–36.

Smotony, B. "The Role of the Board Staff Secretary." In R. T. Ingram and Associates, *Governing Public Colleges and Universities: A Handbook for Trustees, Chief Executives, and Other Campus Leaders.* San Francisco: Jossey-Bass, 1993.

Smotony, B., and Summer, B. "What Do Board Secretaries Do?" *AGB Reports,* 1979, *21*(2), 33–36.

The Standard & Poor's Executive/College Survey, 1990. New York: Standard & Poor's Corporation, 1990.

Steeples, D. W. (ed.). *Successful Strategic Planning: Case Studies.* New Directions for Higher Education, no. 64. San Francisco: Jossey-Bass, 1988.

Stone, B., and North, C. *Risk Management and Insurance for Nonprofit Managers.* Madison, Wis.: Society for Non-profit Organizations, 1989.

Taylor, B. E. *Working Effectively with Trustees: Building Cooperative Campus Leadership.* Association for the Study of Higher Education-ERIC Research Report, no. 2. Washington, D.C.: Association for the Study of Higher Education, 1987.

Taylor, B. E. "Results of a National Survey of Board Characteristics, Policies, and Practices." In R. T. Ingram (ed.), *Making Trusteeship Work.* Washington, D.C.: Association of Governing Boards of Universities and Colleges, 1988.

Taylor, B. E. "When Boards Become Part of the Campus Community." *Educational Record,* 1989, *70*(3/4), 13–16.

Taylor, B. E., Meyerson, J. W., Morrell, L. R., and Park, D., Jr. *Strategic Analysis: Using Comparative Data to Understand Your Institution.* Washington, D.C.: Association of Governing Boards of Universities and Colleges, 1991.

Tierney, W. G. *Culture and Ideology in Higher Education.* New York: Praeger, 1991.

Trachtenberg, S. J., and Stein, R. H. *The Art of Hiring in Higher Education.* New York: Prometheus Books, 1992.

Tremper, C., and Babcock, G. *The Nonprofit Board's Role in Risk*

Management: More Than Buying Insurance. Washington, D.C.: National Center for Nonprofit Boards, 1990.

Ulich, R. *Three Thousand Years of Educational Wisdom.* Cambridge, Mass.: Harvard University Press, 1959.

U.S. Department of Education. *The Finance of Higher Education Institutions.* Washington, D.C.: U.S. Department of Education, 1990.

United Way of America. *Risk Management: A Guide for Nonprofits.* Alexandria, Va.: United Way of America, 1988.

Walton, M. *The Deming Management Method.* New York: Perigree, 1986.

Washington, V., and Harvey, W. *Affirmative Rhetoric, Negative Action: African American and Hispanic Faculty at Predominantly White Institutions.* Washington, D.C.: Association for the Study of Higher Education, 1989.

Weeks, K. M. *Trustees and Preventive Law.* AGB Pocket Publication, no. 10. Washington, D.C.: Association of Governing Boards of Universities and Colleges, 1980.

Wood, M. M. *Trusteeship in the Private College.* Baltimore, Md.: The Johns Hopkins University Press, 1985.

Zander, A. *Making Groups Effective.* San Francisco: Jossey-Bass, 1982.

Zirkel, P. A. "Higher Education Litigation: An Overview." *Education Law Reporter,* 1989, *56,* 705–708.

Zwingle, J. L. *The Lay Governing Board.* Washington, D.C.: Association of Governing Boards of Universities and Colleges, 1970.

Zwingle, J. L. *College Trustees: A Question of Legitimacy.* Washington, D.C.: American Association for Higher Education, 1974.

Zwingle, J. L. *Effective Trusteeship: Guidelines for Board Members.* Washington, D.C.: Association of Governing Boards of Universities and Colleges, 1979.

Index